Praise for *Lo*

Even two decades after their death, privileged enough to have known them. They were the best of our generation. This book will help people understand why.

—**Peter Beinart, author of** *The Crisis of Zionism*

The presentation of Matt's and Sara's writings in this book is a profound act of love. We miss their voices so much, but in their writings we can hear their laughter again and feel their love for Judaism. Our Sages tell us that the words of the righteous are their memorial. With the help of their writings, so beautifully edited by Rabbi Bernstein, Matt and Sara will be with us always.

—**Rabbi David Hoffman, PhD, Vice Chancellor and Chief Advancement Officer, The Jewish Theological Seminary**

I did not have the privilege of knowing Matthew Eisenfeld or Sara Duker. However, after reading the essays in this book I feel I know them and understand the tremendous loss that the Jewish people and all humanity suffered after they were so brutally killed in the terrorist action in Jerusalem. Their words are their legacy, their teachings are their path to eternity, and their memories are treasured not only by those who knew them and loved them, but now also by those who can read their words. This book allows us to appreciate their lives and their legacy. May their memories be for a blessing.

—**Rabbi Vernon Kurtz, Rabbi, North Suburban Synagogue Beth El, Highland Park, Illinois; President, The American Zionist Movement**

My heart alternated between love of these two bright souls, and sorrow at what they might have become.

—**Rabbi Jay Michaelson, co-editor,** *Az Yashir Moshe: A Book of Songs and Blessings*

This collection of writings is a gift—as much to those who knew Matt and Sara, as to those who will now get to meet them through their words. To read their musings and self-reflections, and behold their compassion for others, is to understand how a single person—and certainly two—can change the world.

—**Oshrat Carmiel,** *Bloomberg News*

Love Finer than Wine is a powerful testament that the brilliance, passion, and love of Matt's and Sara's souls will live on within all of us and that no evil will ever extinguish the light of our people.

—**Rabbi Sherre Hirsch, author of** *Thresholds*

Healing from violent trauma is a complicated process. There is the necessity to immerse oneself in the terror of the trauma *and* in the possibility of change and hope. *Love Finer Than Wine* provides us the opportunity to find hope and healing in the narrative of traumatic terror. Possibility in the present can evolve from the memory of the past.

—**Mary Jo Barrett, Author of** *Treating Complex Trauma:*
A Relational Blueprint for Collaboration and Change

What a fitting tribute to two wonderful young people, devoted to each other, to Torah, to Israel, and to the Jewish people. Even with the passage of time, those who knew Matt and Sara remember them with great warmth and affection.

—**Rabbi Kenneth E. Berger, Rabbi Emeritus,**
Congregation Beth Sholom, Teaneck, New Jersey

Through Matt's and Sara's varied writings, we gain insight into the hearts and souls of two precious people whose warmth, sensitivity, and intellectual depth are felt in every sentence. Both Matt and Sara acknowledged the world around them and yet never lost sight of the world as it could be and perhaps even should be. It is our great sorrow to live in this world without them, although this book allows their voices and their struggles still to be heard. May their memories always be for a blessing.

—**Rabbi Joel Pitkowsky, Rabbi,**
Congregation Beth Sholom, Teaneck, New Jersey

Twenty years ago, a cruel act of terror robbed the world of two future leaders and unique souls, Matthew Eisenfeld and Sara Duker. Here we see in their own words the deep Jewish commitment, intense focus, humanity, passion for life and love that graced their days. Rabbi Edward Bernstein has provided us the gift of seeing life through Matt's and Sara's eyes. Tinged with the poignant sadness of loss, we are also inspired by the lives of meaning they embraced.

—**Rabbi James Rosen, Rabbi, Beth El Temple,**
West Hartford, Connecticut

Rarely do I depart the cemetery of my congregation without visiting the grave of Matt and Sara. Even in the passing of 20 years, I feel overwhelming heartbreak recalling Matt and Sara. They are *never ever ever* to be forgotten.

—**Rabbi Stanley Kessler, Rabbi Emeritus,**
Beth El Temple, West Hartford, Connecticut

Love Finer Than Wine

Love Finer Than Wine

The Writings of Matthew Eisenfeld and Sara Duker

Edited by

EDWARD C. BERNSTEIN

With a Foreword by MIKE KELLY
author of *The Bus on Jaffa Road*

Love Finer Than Wine:
The Writings of Matthew Eisenfeld and Sara Duker

Copyright © 2016. Edward C. Bernstein

This book was made possible by generous grants from Dr. Leonard and Vicki Eisenfeld and the Sara Duker Tikkun Olam Fund.

ISBN-13: 978-1518738173
ISBN-10: 1518738176

Dedicated in memory of Matt and Sara,
who are with me always.

יהי זכרם ברוך
May their memory be for a blessing.

Contents

Foreword: A Memorial Book for Matt and Sara
Mike Kelly   xi

Preface and Acknowledgments
Rabbi Edward C. Bernstein   xv

Meet Matt and Sara

Matt's Journal   4

Sara Duker's Mission Statement, Fall 1995   27

Letter from Sara Duker to Friends
from the Tahoe-Baikal Institute   33

Matt's Essays for Admission to JTS Rabbinical School,
Submitted December, 1993   38

Matt's Application for the Institute
for Traditional Judaism   46

Biblical Scholarship

Why Was Yitzhak Bound?
Matthew Eisenfeld   55

Catching a Thief: Exodus 22:1–2a
Matthew Eisenfeld   58

God as Defender of Widows and Orphans
Matthew Eisenfeld   66

Samuel and the Evolution of the Prophet-Judge
Matthew Eisenfeld   75

Reflections on "Innovation Under the Sun"
Dr. Raymond Scheindlin   80

Innovation Under the Sun: Three Approaches to Sefer Kohelet
Matthew Eisenfeld   82

Thoughts on the Death of Matt and Sara
Dr. Bezalel Porten   117

Reflections on the Song of Songs
Matthew Eisenfeld   118

Rabbinic Scholarship

"V'nitz'ak: And We Cried Out."
Rabbi Matthew Berkowitz   127

Matt Eisenfeld's Notes on *'Arvei Pesahim*, the 10th Chapter
of Talmud, Massekhet Pesahim
Edited by Aryeh Bernstein   129

Sara and Elisha Ben Avuyah: Who Is the "Other"?
Celia Deutsch, N.D.S.   169

"Elisha Looked and Cut at the Shoots": Making the Myths
of the Other in Ancient Rabbinic Texts
Sara Duker   173

Philosophy

Reflection
Rabbi Shai Held   219

The Phenomenology of the Prophet: Experience and Response
Matthew Eisenfeld   222

Additional Essays

Food for Thought on Shabbat and Festivals
Matthew Eisenfeld   255

Reflections on Israel
Sara Duker   258

From Irkutsk to Jerusalem
Sara Duker   261

Every Yid a Prince: An Interview with Rabbi Shlomo Carlebach
Matthew Eisenfeld   266

Leaps of Faith: Uncertainty's Role in Religion
Matthew Eisenfeld   271

Hannah's Prayer
Matthew Eisenfeld   276

The Essence of the Shofar
Matthew Eisenfeld   286

A Reflection on the Marriage of Two Friends
Matthew Eisenfeld   294

Reflection
Dr. Tal Weinberger   298

Application for Dorot Fellowship in Israel
Sara Duker   301

Remembering Matt and Sara

Bombings in Israel: Victims; 2 Students Found Faith, Love and Death
John Sullivan   307

From *Jewish Advocate*   311

Eulogy for Matt Eisenfeld and Sara Duker:
Moshe Melekh ben Yehudah U'Zehavah
Sarah Rachel bat Ben Zion V'Ora
Rabbi William Lebeau   312

Reflection on the First Anniversary of the Death of Matt and Sara
Amy Eisenfeld   316

Sisterly Love
Tamara Duker Freuman   319

An Israeli Family Member Recalls Sara and Matt
Dr. Rivkah Duker Fishman   321

Were Matt and Sara Planning to Marry?
Rabbi Michael and Tracie Bernstein   324

"Friends of Matt and Sara"
Elli Sacks   326

Two Shining Lights
Rabbi David Lerner   328

Stop This Day and Night
Dr. Devorah Schoenfeld   331

Appendix   335

Foreword: A Memorial Book for Matt and Sara

MIKE KELLY

A PHOTOGRAPH SITS on a shelf above my desk. It shows a young man and a young woman on a balcony in Jerusalem. They are both smiling and are about to leave for an evening get-together with friends. He wears a crisp white shirt and dark pants; she, a rose-colored blouse, a floral print skirt, a black jacket. His left arm gently caresses her shoulder. Her right hand rests casually on his knee. It is late in the day and golden sunlight glistens off their hair.

This is one of the last photographs of Matthew Eisenfeld and Sara Duker, taken only weeks before they were killed along with two dozen others in the terrorist bus bombing of February 25, 1996, on Jerusalem's Jaffa Road. This photo—these smiling faces—greet me each morning when I take a seat at the desk in my home office where I do most of my writing.

In the midst of my research and writing of *The Bus on Jaffa Road,* which chronicles the efforts by the families of Matt and Sara to find the truth behind the murders of their children, I made a copy of this photograph and placed it in a frame above my desk. I could have chosen other photos. But this portrait seemed to capture the intimate vibrancy and infectious hopefulness of this remarkable couple—and it was that vibrancy and hope that I wanted to remember as I wrote about them.

Writing about terrorism is an inherently bleak journey. To do it honestly and completely, a writer must walk into the dark corners of the human soul and examine true evil—to look that evil in the eye, to study the words that attempt

Mike Kelly is the author of *The Bus on Jaffa Road: A Story of Middle East Terrorism and the Search for Justice* (Guilford, CT: Lyons Press, 2014).

to justify mass murder of innocents and to ask the basic questions that often become lost amid the jargon of international diplomacy.

In my journey, I returned to the intersection on Jaffa Road where a bomb, packed with nails, screws, and ball bearings, shredded the Number 18 bus and its passengers on that quiet Sunday in February. I talked to the Israeli police detectives who combed through the blackened, smoky rubble in search of clues, to the ambulance drivers who still weep as they recall picking up the wounded, to the doctors who tried to repair and restore so many broken bodies, to the pathologists who identified the dead, to the counter-terror agents who tried to find the bombers, to the political figures in Israel and in the United States who attempted to explain what all this meant, to the families who continue to battle the waves of grief that flooded into their lives so suddenly, so permanently.

My journey also took me to the Gaza strip where this bombing was planned, to Ramallah and East Jerusalem where some of the Hamas operatives hid, and, eventually, to a small community on a hillside near Hebron. Here, I found the father of the nineteen-year-old Palestinian man who was recruited to be the suicide bomber on the Number 18 bus—the bomber who took a seat across the aisle from where Matt and Sara had settled on that Sunday morning, setting forth on their own journey to what they hoped would be a weekend break at the Petra archeological ruins in Jordan. In what became a sad and somewhat tortured conversation with this father, I learned the true legacy of the hope and vibrancy of that photo of Matt and Sara that sits on the shelf above my desk back home in New Jersey.

This revelation came as I asked the father how people in his hometown remembered his son. The father had already told me that he would forever feel ashamed that his son murdered so many innocent people and conceded that he would have tried to stop his son if only he knew beforehand of the plot to blow up the Number 18 bus. But when I asked about his son's memory, the father paused, looked downward and shook his head. No one speaks about his son anymore, he said, or tries to preserve his memory. "Things like that," he added, "go into oblivion."

It was a painful admission by this father. No one cared enough about his son to remember him—and the father understood why. His son, after all, was a mass murderer.

But the more I pondered the father's words, the more my thoughts returned to Matt and Sara.

Matt and Sara have hardly faded into oblivion. If anything, their memory is very much alive two decades after they died. They continue to live in the form of scholarships in their name, in annual memorial services organized by their colleagues, in prayer groups in America and Israel and in the habit (and delight) among their friends of naming children after them.

I noticed this desire by so many to maintain a connection to Matt and Sara midway through my research for my book. And that realization became a turning point for me.

By necessity, I had to immerse myself in the politics and history of Middle East terrorism. I studied how bomb plots are organized and financed, how suicide bombers are recruited, how bombs are assembled. I even confronted the ringleader of the Jaffa Road bombing, Hassan Salameh, looking into his eyes on a Sunday morning in an Israeli prison and discovering he was still trapped in a twisted theology in which he claimed that God wanted him to murder innocent people.

But when I turned my eyes toward Matt and Sara and explored their lives, my research took on a new richness. Yes, my journey to examine a single act of terrorism and its aftermath certainly had its dark corners—corners that I could not avoid. But as part of that journey I also was privileged to encounter two remarkable people who continue to touch others all these years after they died on Jaffa Road.

Through the generosity of their parents and friends, I was able to walk into the sacred ground of their journals and diaries—including many of the pages that appear in this book. I read their academic papers and their letters and e-mails in which they mused about marriage and raising families and juggling careers and their spiritual paths toward a deeper understanding of Judaism.

And then, each morning as I began my work, I made a point of studying the photo on my desk—that final portrait of two young people who wanted to embrace life and each other in a way that was so fundamentally genuine that it still offers inspiration for many.

In the gentle smiles and welcoming eyes of Matt and Sara, you can still see the faith, hope, and love they cradled for themselves and those around them. In the sunlight that bathes them, you can still see a future they dreamed for—together.

That last photo captures only a brief moment of their lives. But Matt and Sara are not frozen in time.

They still live.

November 10, 2015

Preface and Acknowledgments

EDWARD C. BERNSTEIN

The last time I saw Matt Eisenfeld was Thursday morning, February 22, 1996. We were studying in Jerusalem for our rabbinical school year in Israel. I had finished my morning *davening* (prayers), eaten a light breakfast, and was ready to spend the day at the Hebrew University library to research a final paper for one of my courses. A little after eight o'clock, Matt came over. He was having problems with his laptop and asked me earlier that week if he could use my computer to type a paper for a course on the Song of Songs he had taken at the Schechter Institute in Jerusalem. While technically on a mid-winter vacation from classes, most students in our class were bogged down with final papers from the previous semester and were using the recess to work on them. Matt was particularly zealous in finishing his work from the first semester because he and his girlfriend, Sara Duker, were planning a long-awaited trip to Jordan and he did not want too much work hanging over him at that time.

Earlier that week I ran into Sara on the street. I was on my way to the Fuchsberg Center for Conservative Judaism to attend a class; she had just attended morning services there. An environmentalist ahead of her time, Sara was on her way to a demonstration protesting the construction of a new national highway that threatened damage to vital ecosystems in northern and central Israel. We conversed about this rally for several minutes on the median of Agron Street at its intersection with King George Street in Jerusalem. That's my last memory of Sara.

When Matt came over that Thursday, he shared a bag of fresh croissants that he had picked up at a bakery on his way to our apartment. For a few minutes, we schmoozed and caught each other up on the details of our personal lives. He then started working, and I left for the library. When I returned home, Matt had already gone for the day. Three days later he and Sara were gone forever.

For several weeks, Matt and Sara had been talking about traveling to Jordan. The day finally came, February 25, 1996. At around dawn, they boarded a

Number 18 bus, one of Jerusalem's busiest lines. They were on their way to the Central Bus Station to catch a bus to Petra, Jordan. At approximately 6:45 A.M., as the Number 18 was winding its way down Jaffa Road near the Central Bus Station, a Hamas terrorist detonated a bomb that killed twenty-six people and wounded forty-eight. Matt and Sara were among the dead. My roommate, Rabbi Eli Garfinkel, and I heard the explosion from our apartment near the Mahane Yehuda market on Jaffa Road, about a half-mile from the scene. It was a somber day in Israel. Everyone felt the shock, and all were anxious to hear news of any loved ones. Even with the pall over Jerusalem that day, it never dawned on me that I knew any of the victims until about 4:00 P.M. Rabbi Aaron Singer, a student advisor at the Schechter Institute, called with the news of my friends. I can't even begin to describe the shock I felt at that moment or for weeks and months thereafter.

The deaths of Matt and Sara were devastating for their family and friends. It was also a loss for the Jewish people and for humanity. Both were inspiring young adults, passionate about their Jewish observance with magnetic yet humble personalities. Matt graduated from Yale University and was destined for a brilliant career in the rabbinate. Sara graduated from Barnard College and was pursuing a career in environmental science. I often think of what might have been had they lived and achieved their full potential. There is no doubt that they would have made significant contributions to the Jewish communal landscape and the betterment of the world. Alas, we will never know for sure what they would have achieved.

And yet, there is much that Matt and Sara left behind that merits reexamination. An entire generation has passed since Matt and Sara were taken from us before their time. The purpose of this book is to reintroduce us to Matt and Sara in their own words. For two people who died so young—Matt, 25, and Sara, 23—the creative output that they left behind is extraordinary. This book is a collection of many of Matt's and Sara's significant writings that address life's most vital matters including faith, love, and self-identity.

The origins of this book date back to early 1997. One year after Matt's and Sara's deaths, the Jewish Theological Seminary dedicated its Beit Midrash in their memory. In conjunction with that ceremony marking their first *yahrzeit* (anniversary of death), I compiled a scrapbook of many of Matt's and Sara's writings that their parents graciously shared with me. At the time, I made four copies of this scrapbook: one for each of the families and two copies that are displayed in the Seminary Beit Midrash. This compilation was titled "The Matthew Eisenfeld and Sara Duker Beit Midrash Memorial Volume."

An original copy of the Memorial Volume housed in the Jewish Theological Seminary Beit Midrash

As I was compiling the material for the scrapbook, the Eisenfelds sent a number of documents, including key selections from Matt's copious journal. Vicki wrote in an attached personal note in January 1997, "[Matt's writing] really shows him struggling with heart, mind and soul—and always wanting to study and learn more about Torah, man, God." She indicated that Matt wrote much more than what she and her husband Lenny shared at the time. Arline Duker, Sara's mother, also shared significant selections of Sara's work for the scrapbook, though Sara left behind a lot more material than eventually could be included.

A number of factors converged that influenced selection of content for the Beit Midrash Volume, including focus on Matt's and Sara's Jewish spiritual yearnings; limited time in compiling the volume in time for the *yahrzeit* commemoration; limitations on space in housing the material; the emotional wherewithal of all parties in perusing Matt's and Sara's writings when the shock of their loss was still quite raw. While I don't think the families and I ever articulated an editorial policy for the 1997 volume, I believe we understood implicitly that, since the volume would be on display in the JTS Beit Midrash, the scope of the writings would mainly be limited to Jewish themes and Judaic scholarship. The selections represented windows into the depth of Matt's and Sara's personalities and included handwritten journal entries, essays, sermons, and scholarly papers.

Due to the Beit Midrash Volume's focus on Judaica, the majority of writings come from Matt, who was engaged in graduate-level Judaic studies at the time of his death. The collection draws heavily on many of his essays for the coursework in which he was engaged. It is especially remarkable that Sara, a young scientist, left behind so much Judaically oriented writing that was not the focus of her graduate studies.

Over the years, every time I visited the Seminary I would sit in the Beit Midrash and leaf through the scrapbook. The thought of publishing the collection was ever-present in my mind, but the pressures of life interfered. I was ordained in 1999 and entered the pulpit. I served congregations in New Rochelle, New York; Beachwood, Ohio; and Boynton Beach, Florida, my present pulpit. Over the years, I kept in touch with Lenny and Vicki and Arline. I saw them at anniversary commemorations and corresponded via e-mail. In 2000, I was honored when the Eisenfelds and Dukers invited me to testify in United States District Court in Washington, D.C., in the families' pathbreaking lawsuit against the Republic of Iran. In the mid-1990s, American victims of terror attacks carried out by countries on the U.S. State Department's list of state sponsors of terror, such as Iran, won the right to sue those countries in Federal Court and receive compensation from any of that country's assets held in the United States.

Less than a year before Matt's and Sara's deaths, on April 10, 1995, Alisa Flatow was killed in a Hamas-sponsored suicide bus bombing. Like Sara, Alisa was a graduate of the Frisch School in Paramus, New Jersey. Alisa's parents, Stephen and Rosalyn Flatow, successfully tested the new federal law in court. After Matt's and Sara's deaths, Stephen Flatow became a close advisor of the Eisenfelds and Dukers and guided them as they pursued their lawsuit. Iran was found liable in the deaths of Matt and Sara. During the trial, I testified along with several friends about Matt's and Sara's integrity, moral character, and the profound loss felt from their deaths. This testimony was a factor in Judge Royce Lamberth's historic judgment in favor of the families.

Time passed. I had moved to South Florida in 2011. In early 2013, I visited with Vicki and Lenny at an art show in West Palm Beach where Vicki was exhibiting her work. Lenny told me about Mike Kelly, a columnist for *The Bergen*

Record, who was writing a book about the 1996 bus bombing and its aftermath. Soon after, Kelly interviewed me.

Kelly's book, *The Bus on Jaffa Road: A Story of Middle East Terrorism and the Search for Justice,* was published in October 2014. Kelly reports on the pivotal role the bus bombing of February 25, 1996, played in Middle East politics, international diplomacy, and the attempts by American victims of terror to hold its sponsors accountable. In the process, Kelly devotes much attention to Matt and Sara and the meaning of their deaths. Kelly was clearly taken by the strength of their personalities even though he had never met them. In the course of his extensive reporting, he had consulted the Beit Midrash Volume that I compiled as a means to understand Matt and Sara through their own words.

In November 2014, I attended a ceremony at JTS in which the Seminary dedicated a new location of the Beit Midrash on the Seminary campus. Kelly was the evening's featured speaker. Once again, I leafed through the volume and considered its publication. Only this time, it occurred to me that the twentieth anniversary was not too far off and that this milestone would be an appropriate occasion for publication.

Finally, in March 2015, Kelly spoke at my synagogue in Boynton Beach about *The Bus on Jaffa Road.* Later that evening in a private conversation, I asked him what he thought about publication of the Beit Midrash Volume for the twentieth anniversary. He said, "Go for it." Kelly provided key advice on how to go about it, and I realized at that moment the urgency of publication.

Too often after terror attacks or natural disasters, we focus only on the statistics and lose sight of the lives lost and the hopes and dreams that are shattered. I was very moved by *The Bus on Jaffa Road,* not only because of Kelly's extensive reporting on the geopolitical ramifications of the bus bombing, but also because of his human portraits of Matt and Sara. He poignantly illustrates the profound influence Matt and Sara had on everyone around them. Matt and Sara are not with us physically, but their spirits remain present because, if nothing else, their own words continue to speak to us.

This book is not a comprehensive biography of Matt and Sara, nor is it an exhaustive anthology of everything they ever wrote. Rather, it is a collection of snapshots of Matt and Sara as young adults in their early twenties who were wrestling with critical issues in profound ways. Through their writings, along with reflections of key friends and relatives, I hope this book will provide a composite image of their personalities, painted mostly by their own brushstrokes.

To help set some context for this book, I do wish to share some of my own recollections of Matt and Sara and the impact they had on my life; Matt and Sara modeled friendship, kindness, and striving for the best of Jewish values.

Matt and Sara were idealists who put words and lofty goals into action. Sara's quotation in her high school yearbook is: "Keep both feet firmly planted in the clouds." This speaks volumes about both her personality and Matt's. One story illustrating their abundant kindness was when they befriended Ann, a homeless African American woman in Morningside Heights who often stood on Broadway outside the Jewish Thelogical Seminary. She was fairly artistic and enterprising and sold bookmarks that she made from scraps of cardboard or fabric. Most passersby, if they chose to engage Ann at all, would stop to buy a bookmark for fifty cents, perhaps out of pity, and continue on their way. Matt and Sara's moral imagination prompted them to do more. They taught Ann to knit *kippot*, which she could in turn sell to JTS students. Matt proudly wore one of these *kippot*. The story of Ann is almost mythical, but it is true and is the quintessential example of Matt's and Sara's abundant kindness.

I first met Matt in June 1991. The Jewish Theological Seminary held a one-month "mini-mester" in which college students could earn credit taking intensive Judaica courses every day, five days a week, for a month. I was already enrolled in the Seminary's List College, and Matt was visiting from Yale. We studied together in a course exploring Rashi's commentary on Torah taught by visiting professor Dr. Robert Goldenberg. Matt and I became fast friends, and I was taken by his fierce thirst for Jewish knowledge and his overall passion for life. Matt had studied Chinese and Eastern religions, and I was amazed that he could go into Chinatown on the Lower East Side and speak Mandarin to people on the street. Despite enjoying getting to know each other, we went our separate ways after completing the course and did not stay in touch.

Matt and I became reacquainted in the fall of 1993, in Israel. I arrived in Efrat to spend the year at Yeshivat HaMivtar for an immersion year in classical Jewish text study prior to entering JTS Rabbinical School the following year. I was thrilled to walk into the Beit Midrash on my first day to find Matt. I did not know anyone else, and it was refreshing to see a familiar face. We renewed our friendship and were roommates in the latter half of the year.

Our year at HaMivtar was a year of growth—and growing pains—for both of us. We each had grown up within Conservative Judaism, and we both intended to enroll in the Conservative Movement's JTS Rabbinical School in fall 1994. Yet there was a tantalizing energy of the Orthodox environment in Efrat, imbued with the spirit of its charismatic Chief Rabbi Shlomo Riskin. The yeshiva, led by

Rabbi Chaim Brovender, provided an atmosphere that was nurturing and all-encompassing. Within this environment, Matt was inspired by the intensive instruction and caring guidance of Talmud teacher Rabbi Menachem Schrader. On February 3, 1996, three weeks before his death, Matt celebrated his twenty-fifth birthday by making a *siyyum* (completion) of Tractate Qiddushin. Matt began his studies of this tractate with Rabbi Schrader and had continued studying it on his own through the following two years. Matt was very moved that Rabbi Schrader attended this *siyyum*, which in turn underscored the warm feelings Matt had for his yeshiva studies. Reflecting on his Talmud study at HaMivtar, Matt writes in his journal in December 1993, "I'm here pursuing a love that will never end, unlike any other love in the world."

Several pieces of Matt's writing in this book reflect his quest to find a spiritual home within the Jewish community. While he was moved by the spiritual energy of HaMivtar and other Orthodox environments, Matt was uncomfortable by the more limited role of women in Jewish ritual and leadership within the Orthodox community. On the other hand, within Conservative Judaism, Matt struggled with the large gap in observance between the clergy and laity. He questioned whether the Conservative Movement was as committed to *halakha* (Jewish Law) as its most elite members claimed.

Matt's spiritual struggle did not begin at HaMivtar. Prior to HaMivtar, Matt applied to JTS Rabbinical School but was turned down. In the application process, Matt was openly critical of the Conservative Movement, and the admissions committee felt he needed more time to consider whether JTS was the institution where he wanted to study. While at HaMivtar, Matt reapplied to JTS and was offered admission for fall 1994. The essays he submitted in this successful application are included in this book.

Matt's entry to JTS Rabbinical School did not mean that he had resolved all of his struggles. He and I shared an apartment that year and often talked late at night about our shared questions. Matt went so far as to submit an application to the Institute for Traditional Judaism, a small rabbinical school in Teaneck, New Jersey, affiliated with the Union for Traditional Judaism. These institutions were founded in the mid-1980s mainly by a traditionalist flank within the Conservative Movement and were viewed by many as a reaction to the 1983 JTS faculty vote in favor of ordaining women as rabbis. Rabbi David Weiss-Halivni, a preeminent Talmud scholar, left the JTS faculty for Columbia and also served as rector of ITJ. Matt's essays from his application are included in this book as well.

Despite his struggles, Matt never left JTS. The second year of the JTS program was a year spent in Israel at the Schechter Institute, and Matt wanted to return to Israel for this experience. Despite Matt's ideological questions, he felt at home at JTS and enjoyed the intellectual stimulation and camaraderie of a large and talented class. Matt was invited to participate in a new accelerated track for students who entered Rabbinical School with advanced skills in Talmud study. The high caliber of study exceeded his expectations. He became a well-respected leader of our class. I believe that, had he lived, Matt would have returned to JTS in the fall of 1996 and that he would have completed his rabbinical studies. Matt felt at home socially, ideologically, and intellectually. And, there was Sara.

I met Sara in fall 1991, when she began her undergraduate studies at Barnard College. I recall attending Conservative services for Columbia-Barnard students where Sara was an active participant from the moment she arrived on campus. Sara also attended services at JTS, and we were in overlapping social circles. I remember she wore a *tallit* (prayer shawl) during services. At a time when it was still relatively unusual for women who were not training to be clergy to adopt the practice, Sara stood out, but in her own understated, soft-spoken way.

Sara and Matt started dating during our year at HaMivtar. Sara was spending her junior year of college at Machon Pardes, a nondenominational yeshiva in Jerusalem. Pardes is generally geared toward post-college students, and it was unusual for an undergraduate to study for a full year there. Sara had already set her sights on a career in environmental science, and she knew that a long road lay ahead in order to advance in the field. At the same time, Sara wanted to further ground herself in the tradition of Jewish textual study. For Sara, the year of *Torah lishmah* (Torah study for its own sake) at Pardes may have been her last opportunity for such an immersive study.

Matt's and Sara's affection for each other was immediately apparent. They clearly had much in common: deep commitment to Jewish observance, passion for study of Jewish texts and a zest for life. At the same time, they complemented each other well.

Matt and Sara came from different Jewish backgrounds. Sara grew up in Teaneck, New Jersey, home to a large and diverse Jewish community. She attended Jewish day schools and graduated from the Frisch School, an Orthodox yeshiva in Paramus, New Jersey. At the same time, Sara's family attended Congregation Beth Shalom, an active Conservative congregation where men and women participate equally in all aspects of a traditional service. Sara's Jewish identity was rooted in a rigorous traditional Jewish education while pushing the boundaries of traditional gender roles in Jewish ritual. Sara's father, Ben-Zion Duker, died of brain cancer in 1984, when Sara was eleven years old. Ben-Zion had had a profound influence on Sara's Jewish identity to that point. Father and daughter often studied Hebrew together and walked to synagogue. In his absence, the enveloping support of her communities was even more important.

While Sara grew up in an intense Jewish environment and received an elite Jewish education, Matt grew up in several different Jewish communities, as his father, Dr. Leonard Eisenfeld, advanced in his field of pediatric medicine. Matt spent his early years in Pittsburgh during his father's residency, then moved to Alabama, where his father served in a fellowship. The family also lived in New Orleans and then settled in West Hartford, Connecticut, when Matt was twelve. Having spent much of his childhood in the South, Matt retained a hint of an endearing Southern drawl. Matt had diverse interests and captained three high school teams: wrestling, cross-country, and track. Matt's Jewish identity was influenced by all of American Jewry's major religious streams. As he describes in his JTS Rabbinical School admissions essays (contained in this book), he attended Camp Henry S. Jacobs, a Jewish overnight camp in Mississippi sponsored by the Reform Movement, where communal singing left a lasting impression. Matt also describes his formative experience in United Synagogue Youth, the Conservative Movement's youth organization. He served as the Connecticut region's *Ruah* Chair, overseeing communal songs and cheers at regional events. In selections from his journal contained in this book, Matt describes important encounters with Orthodox Judaism both at Yale and during a summer of study in Israel at Machon Pardes in 1992.

While Sara spent much of her childhood synthesizing Orthodox and Conservative Jewish practice, Matt came to this process a bit later in life. As his writings reveal, Matt was enamored by the energy, vitality, and commitment to Jewish learning that he encountered within Orthodox practices. At the same time, Matt was drawn to Conservative Judaism's more progressive approach to *halakha* (Jewish law), particularly regarding women's participation in ritual and communal leadership. At a time in his life when he could have made a spiritual home either in a Conservative or an Orthodox environment, I believe Sara helped him feel more grounded within the Conservative community. She was a living example, after all, that one could engage in a traditional education, live a traditionally observant lifestyle, *and* embrace equality for women in Jewish ritual life. Sara dared Matt to dream that he could inspire the masses to embrace the ideals of Conservative Judaism.

While I can speculate on how they might have fared had they lived, of course, we will never know for certain. Matt and Sara are forever frozen in time as a young couple in their twenties exuding abundant energy and idealism. The writings they left behind represent their unfinished symphony, but it is music nonetheless. I hope that in reading Matt's and Sara's words we might be inspired to continue their quest to seek a life well lived.

* * * * *

In this book, I have attempted to make the writings of Matt and Sara as accessible as possible to the average reader. I provide occasional annotation where additional context is required, particularly in Matt's journal entries. Where needed, I offer translations and transliterations of Hebrew phrases and texts so that non-Hebrew readers may access the context. In addition, several other key figures in the lives of Matt and Sara have contributed to this book in ways that shed light either on the context of a particular piece of writing or a particular aspect of the lives of Matt or Sara or both.

Rabbi William Lebeau served as Dean of the JTS Rabbinical School for most of the 1990s. He admitted Matt to the Rabbinical School, and they had deep admiration for each other. Rabbi Lebeau also had a close relationship with Sara through her Barnard years and continuing during her courtship with Matt.

Rabbi Lebeau was a rock of support to the entire Seminary community in both New York and Jerusalem, even as he was deeply bereaved himself. Rabbi Lebeau's moving eulogy delivered at the Schechter Institute memorial service on March 3, 1996, is reprinted in this book.

Also included in this book is a transcription of Matt's handwritten notes on Tractate Pesahim. These notes were found in Matt's backpack recovered from the bombing. Matt recorded his reflections of the tractate's tenth chapter, the chapter that outlines the Passover seder rituals that we recognize today. Matt spoke frequently of his desire to write a commentary to the Passover Haggadah to make the seder more accessible to lay readers. During the year in Israel, Matt had begun to annotate the chapter in order to develop his commentary. My brother Aryeh Bernstein transcribed and annotated Matt's notes. I am pleased to include this work of original scholarship in this book.

In the aftermath of Matt's and Sara's deaths, many news media outlets reported that they were engaged to be married. In truth, they had never announced their engagement. It was clear that they were very much in love, and most people close to them assumed they would eventually get married, probably after returning to the United States. Indeed, the decision of the Eisenfeld and Duker families to bury Matt and Sara side by side in West Hartford acknowledged that the pair would eventually marry. Rabbi Michael and Tracie Bernstein and Rabbi David Lerner in their reflections offer essential insight on Matt's and Sara's thoughts on marriage shortly before their death.

Matt and Sara had several friends who had established independent friendships with each prior to their courtship. Dr. Tal Brudnoy Weinberger was a friend of Sara at the Frisch School and Matt at Yale. Included in this book is a *D'var Torah* Matt wrote in honor of the marriage of Tal and her husband, Josh Weinberger. In response, Tal contributes to this book a letter to her dear friends.

Elli Sacks also knew Matt and Sara independently, then together. In recent years, he has leveraged the power of social media to create a "Friends of Matt and Sara Facebook Group." He contributes an essay here on the international online community of hundreds of people who are connected for the sake of remembering Matt and Sara.

Dr. Devorah Schoenfeld dreamed big dreams with both Sara and Matt about a Jewish world that transcended traditional denominational norms. In her reflection, she recalls her spiritual quest with Matt and Sara in seeking a more pluralistic Jewish world. She notes that recent trends, such as the ordination of women as Orthodox rabbis, help to realize dreams that they shared twenty years ago.

Much of the written material in this book is in the form of academic papers that Matt and Sara submitted to professors at Barnard, Yale, JTS, and the Schechter Institute. These works reflect the seriousness with which they approached scholarship and the depth of their Judaic knowledge.

In this book, Dr. Celia Deutsch of Barnard introduces Sara's senior thesis "Elisha Looked and Cut at the Shoots: Making the Myths of the Other in Ancient Rabbinic Texts." While Sara majored in environmental science, she was in the Centennial Scholars' Program, which provided a small group of outstanding students the opportunity for independent research outside their chosen area of concentration. Dr. Deutsch supervised Sara in this thesis and offers her own reflections on the thesis.

Matt wrote a senior thesis at Yale titled "The Phenomenology of the Prophet: Experience and Response. A Comparison of the Religious Philosophies of Martin Buber and Abraham Joshua Heschel," submitted to visiting professor Dr. Eliezer Schweid. The Eisenfeld family graciously made this essay available for this book. Rabbi Shai Held, a close friend of Matt's from Rabbinical

School, introduces this essay. He draws upon his own scholarship of Buber and Heschel and relates their teachings to Matt's exceptional kindness and concern for the other.

In the spring semester of 1995, Matt undertook an independent study with JTS Professor Raymond Scheindlin. The result was his paper "Innovation Under the Sun: Three Approaches to *Sefer Kohelet.*" As an introduction to this essay, Dr. Scheindlin contributes remarks he gave at the *Shloshim* commemoration in which he speculates on what may have drawn Matt, an upbeat young man, to the fatalistic wisdom of *Kohelet* (Ecclesiastes).

The last academic paper that Matt wrote was his take-home final exam on the biblical love poetry of *Shir Ha-Shirim* (The Song of Songs). Matt wrote this exam on my computer on February 22, and submitted it to his teacher, Professor Bezalel Porten, before leaving with Sara on their ill-fated bus trip to Jordan. Dr. Porten reread this paper twenty years later and offers his reflections. Among other verses, Matt analyzes Song of Songs 1:2 : "Oh, give me of the kisses of your mouth, For your love is more delightful than wine." The title of this book, *Love Finer Than Wine*, was inspired by the poignancy of this verse, the deep love that Matt and Sara had for each other, and the coincidence that Matt's last paper was on *Shir Ha-Shirim.*

A generation has passed since Matt's and Sara's deaths, and their spirits continue to reverberate with us. With the publication of *Love Finer Than Wine*, my hope is to help ensure that Matt's and Sara's legacy continues to beat in our hearts as readers encounter them in their own words. For those who knew them, their reflections on life and contemporary Judaism will bring them back into conversation as if they are sitting with us once again. For readers who did not meet them or who perhaps were not even alive at the time of their death, I invite you to meet this remarkable, optimistic couple whose writings open for us a window to their zest for life, their commitment to Judaism and Torah and their love of each other. It was love finer than wine. יהי זכרם ברוך, may their memory be for a blessing.

TRANSLITERATION

Matt and Sara employed different transliteration systems rendering Hebrew into English characters. These systems were neither consistent with each other, nor always consistent within their own respective writings. In general, the system employed here is based on the "general purpose" transliteration of Hebrew from the *Society of Biblical Literature Handbook of Style*. Exceptions include proper names that have common English spellings, such as R. Akiva, as opposed to R. ʿAqibʾa. Other exceptions have been made with some words that end with the letter *he*. While technically it is correct to end such words with "*h*," I have in certain instances opted not to for aesthetic reasons. Examples include *halakha, teshuva,* and *hevruta.* I hope such cases do not cause undue confusion.

א	*aleph*	ʾ or nothing
ב	*bet*	*b, v*
ג	*gimel*	*g*
ד	*dalet*	*d*
ה	*he*	*h*
ו	*waw*	*v*
ז	*zayin*	*z*
ח	*ḥet*	*ḥ*
ט	*tet*	*t*
י	*yod*	*y*
כ ך	*kaph*	*k, kh*
ל	*lamed*	*l*
מ ם	*mem*	*m*
נ ן	*nun*	*n*
ס	*samek*	*s*
ע	*ayin*	ʿ or nothing
פ ף	*pe*	*p*
צ ץ	*tsade*	*ts*
ק	*qoph*	*q*
ר	*resh*	*r*
שׂ	*sin*	*s*
שׁ	*shin*	*sh*
ת	*tav*	*t*

ACKNOWLEDGMENTS

This publication would not have been possible without the help of many people. I am constantly inspired by Dr. Leonard and Vicki Eisenfeld and Arline Duker. In the aftermath of Matt's and Sara's deaths, they have shown courage, faith, and a determination to affirm life. I am grateful to them for entrusting me with many of Matt's and Sara's writings nearly twenty years ago when I compiled the original JTS Beit Midrash Memorial Volume. I am humbled and honored that they have again entrusted me to help bring Matt's and Sara's writings to a larger audience through this book. They provided critical financing and, just as important, historical perspective. They provided most of the source materials and helped decipher handwritten documents. I am blessed to count Lenny, Vicki, and Arline, along with their children Amy Eisenfeld Genser, Tamara Duker Freuman, and Ariella Duker, and Arline's husband, Bill Werther, among my friends. I am especially grateful to Amy for consulting on the cover design and for contributing her speech at the 1997 *yahrzeit* commemoration. I am equally grateful to Tamara for her moving tribute incorporated in this book.

Words are inadequate for me to express my profound gratitude to Mike Kelly for his help and encouragement at every stage of development for this book, including and especially the powerful foreword that he contributed.

The original JTS Beit Midrash Volume and this book exist as a result of Matt's Jewish Theological Seminary Rabbinical School studies and Sara's long-time association with JTS and the Conservative Movement. Their writings express a yearning for religious meaning within a context of critical thinking, intellectual honesty, and the use of modern interpretive tools from the academy that help reveal the meaning of sacred religious texts. Just as Matt and Sara were shaped by the academic and social milieu of JTS, so was I. My Jewish identity and my rabbinate were similarly shaped by JTS.

In 1997, Dr. Ismar Schorsch, then JTS Chancellor, and Rabbi William Lebeau, then Rabbinical School Dean, enacted their vision to create a Beit Midrash at JTS in memory of Matt and Sara. As this vision became a reality, I compiled the original Memorial Volume that continues to be housed in the Beit Midrash. Over the last year, JTS continued to support my efforts to publish this book. Dr. Arnold Eisen, the current Chancellor, is leading a vibrant institution that would make Matt and Sara proud, and I appreciate his friendship and support. Special thanks to Rabbi Daniel Nevins, the Pearl Resnick Dean of JTS Rabbinical School; Martin Oppenheimer, JTS Counsel; and Rabbi Mordecai Schwartz, Director of the Matthew Eisenfeld and Sara Duker Beit Midrash, for their early support. During my work on this book I am grateful to have borrowed one of the original volumes.

Our Rabbinical School class spent the 1995–1996 academic year at the Schechter Institute of Jerusalem. It was a tumultuous year. The assassination of

Prime Minister Yitzhak Rabin on November 4, 1995, a traumatic moment in Israel, shocked us greatly. Then, just months later our friends were killed in the midst of horrific terror that shook the nation. At every step, the faculty and staff of the Schechter Institute were rocks of support, including Rabbi Benjamin Segal, then President; Rabbi David Golinkin, immediate past President; and Rabbi Shlomo Tucker, now retired as Rabbinical School Dean. Rabbi Segal, an expert on the Song of Songs, was particularly helpful when I was editing Matt's paper on the Song of Songs for this book.

I will always be grateful to the JTS Rabbinical School class of 1999. Most of us studied in Israel in 1995–1996 along with several students who graduated shortly before or after us. Through our collective trauma we forged lasting bonds. This outstanding group of Jewish leaders influenced Matt and Sara and was deeply influenced by them. This book would not exist without this dynamic relationship.

In the earliest stages of this book I consulted classmate Rabbi Shai Held, an inspiring rabbi and loyal friend of Matt and Sara. I knew I wanted to focus on Matt's and Sara's writings, but I also knew the book needed to provide readers with appropriate context and perspective. Shai suggested the basic format that I ultimately followed: a biographical introduction preceding the main texts that would be supplemented by contributions from key people in Matt's and Sara's lives. I am grateful to Shai for this advice that I believe provided the right balance of focus and depth.

Rabbi Menachem Creditor, a prolific and erudite colleague, opened my eyes to the world of self-publishing and provided valuable advice for plotting the course of this project.

I wish to thank others who enriched this edition and the story of Matt and Sara through the essays and artwork that they contributed: Amy Eisenfeld Genser, Tamara Duker Freuman, Rabbi William Lebeau, Dr. Celia Deutch, Dr. Rivka Duker Fishman, Rabbi Matthew Berkowitz, Dr. Devorah Schoenfeld, Elli Sacks, Dr. Tal Brudnoy Weinberger, Rabbi Michael and Tracie Bernstein, Rabbi David Lerner, Dr. Raymond Scheindlin and Dr. Bezalel Porten.

Rabbi James Ponet, the Howard M. Holtzmann Jewish Chaplain at Yale (Emeritus), provided critical background information on various issues Matt raises in his journal from his Yale years.

Rabbi David Levin-Kruss, Pardes Institute Director of Special Programs, verified key bits of information relating to Matt's study at Pardes in summer 1992 and Sara's study at Pardes in 1993–1994.

In his journal, Matt cites David DaSenda as an inspiration for some of his thinking on mysticism. I thank him for verifying his connection with Matt and reflecting on their friendship.

At the outset, I sought editorial assistance. Rabbis David Dalin and Fred Greenspahn, colleagues in South Florida, directed me to Maurya Horgan, a distinguished editor of biblical scholarship. Maurya helped systematize the transliteration of Hebrew throughout the book. My appreciation for her wisdom, acumen, and organizational skills grew at every stage of the project. Little did I know how large a task publication would be for a newcomer. To streamline the process, Maurya offered the services of her husband, Paul Kobelski, an experienced book designer and pre-press production specialist, who has been invaluable in the technical end of this book's production. Of course, any errors that appear are my responsibility alone.

I am grateful to the members of Temple Torat Emet in Boynton Beach, Florida, for supporting me in my rabbinate and for their interest in the story of Matt and Sara. My service to this community reminds me daily of my mission to serve and strengthen the Jewish people, a mission for which Matt and Sara were passionate.

I also wish to thank Geoff Menkowitz and Camp Ramah Darom for inviting me to serve as Rabbi-In-Residence. The serene ambience of Ramah was ideal as I worked on this project in its early stages. It happens that I worked on the final stages of production while attending Ramah Darom's Winter Family Camp. Both Matt and Sara loved the Ramah movement, so Ramah's role in this project is fitting.

Shortly after receiving word about the death of Matt and Sara, I had to make two phone calls to Chicago—to my parents, Roberta and Charles Bernstein, and to my grandmother, Adele Bernstein. I told them there was a bombing in Jerusalem, that I was okay but two of my best friends were killed. Those were hard phone calls to make and, for them, just as difficult to receive. As shocked and horrified as they all were, they were also incredibly supportive. A few weeks later I was in Chicago for Passover. In the wake of the trauma, I contemplated not going back to Israel for the remainder of the school year. However, my parents and grandmother encouraged me to finish my studies as planned. I am grateful for that. I am also grateful that they provided me with a strong Jewish foundation that inspired me to pursue my advanced Jewish studies, which brought Matt and Sara into my life.

Just as my parents and grandmother are my teachers for life's most enduring values, Sheila and Jerry Reback, my in-laws, are also my teachers, and I am blessed to have them in my life.

I'm privileged that Aryeh Bernstein is not only my brother but also my friend, confidant, and teacher. Aryeh studied in Israel and at JTS and grew close to Matt and Sara. We all shared many Shabbat meals in multiple settings. In 1997, Aryeh helped me collate the four original copies of the Memorial Volume. As Aryeh continued his undergraduate studies at JTS and Columbia, he was the founding editor of *Iggrot Ha'Ari: Columbia University Student Journal of Jewish Scholarship*, the first issue of which included Sara Duker's essay "Elisha Looked and Cut at the Shoots." This earlier publication eased the editing process of this essay for this book. Aryeh's transcription and annotation of Matt's notebook on Tractate Pesahim, Chapter 10, is an original, sensitive, and creative work of scholarship that enriches this book immensely. I also turned to Aryeh on many occasions with questions ranging from biblical scholarship to the identity of individuals mentioned in Matt's journal, and he always responded promptly with the relevant information.

My wife, Ariella Reback, is my rock, my love, and my best friend. I remember shortly after we started dating eighteen years ago, I showed her the Memorial Volume in the JTS Beit Midrash. She seemed to forge an instant connection with Matt and Sara. I thank her for her patience as I carried out this project over the past year and for her steadfast support. She is also an amazing editor. Ariella and I are blessed with three children, Samuel, Noam, and Esther, and Noam helped with some of the conversion of scanned documents from PDF to Word. My children are a key impetus to this book so that the next generation will know Matt and Sara. It is my most fervent prayer that they will grow up in a world that will not know of the violence that took Matt and Sara from this world. *'Oseh shalom bimromav hu ya'ase shalom aleinu v'al kol Yisrael v'al kol yoshvei teiveil v'imru amen.* May the One who makes peace in the heavens make peace for the entire people of Israel and for all of humanity, and let us say Amen.

February 2016

Part One

Meet Matt and Sara

The Following is a statement of my educational goals for the year. This year is to be spent studying at the Bet Midrash in Jerusalem with my class in Rabbinical School Year 2.

Underlying and influencing my education is the need to constantly re-examine the values I believe to be morally appropriate. This continual self-examination should lead me to involve myself in causes that serve others as I have a stake in the world around me and can be useful. This ultimate goal of becoming more and more useful should direct my energies while I study.

As a student this year, I should strive to create resources for myself. I should seek out individuals from whom I can learn, both from teaching and example. I should keep an open mind so as to easily identify such people. Furthermore, I should explore new ways to solve problems and answer questions with which I am faced.

As I search for resources, I should also be a resource to others. Being a resource involves my careful, attentive listening to others. I should speak politely and respectfully, and I should ask questions to ensure my understanding of what I am told.

Because much of my time will be spent in class or in front of open books, I should set practical goals as well. I should strive to learn something new from each of my classroom teachers and look for ways to incorporate the new methodologies I am taught.

Photo of two pages from Matt's journal listing his educational goals for the year (see p. 25)

I should make sure that my study partners understand everything I understand, in order that we build mutual trust, become friends, and share knowledge. I should begin each class with a good enough understanding of the subject to ask an intelligent question.

Among my more concrete goals are personal projects, begun outside of class. I am to finish Tractate Kiddushin before my birthday on the Jewish calendar, 11 Shevat. I should discipline myself to write about Parshat HaShavua at least once per month. Furthermore, I will begin work on a Pesach Haggadah to be used at family Sedarim. This Haggadah should clarify some of the symbols with which we interact as we perform the Mitzvot related to the evening, and should generate discussion.

Finally, and perhaps most important, I will decide which school I should attend for the completion of my rabbinic studies. I will make this decision based on my ability to fulfill the goals I have mentioned and the prospect of future improvement.

Nov. 18, 1995
כ"ה חשון תשנ"ו

Matt's Journal

Editor's note: The excerpts from Matt's journal that follow were selected by Matt's parents, Dr. Leonard and Vicki Eisenfeld for inclusion in the JTS Beit Midrash Memorial Volume in 1997. They span from April 1992 to November 1995 and generally reflect his wrestling with matters of Jewish spirituality. These entries were written in long-hand form. The following is my transcription. The headings in bold at the beginning of each entry are my addition. The explanatory footnotes and other occasional notes within the body of the text are mine as well. Matt frequently writes Hebrew terms in Hebrew characters. To preserve the feel of reading Matt's handwriting, I have reproduced Hebrew words he writes in the original Hebrew and added transliteration and translation in parentheses. As with other documents in this volume, I have made occasional corrections in spelling and grammar but have otherwise let the text stand as is. The final entry here, Matt's Statement of Goals, November 18, 1995, was posted on the wall above his bed and was referred to frequently in many eulogies and commemorations in the years since.—ECB

Trials and tribulations in the Yale Kosher Kitchen

April 6, 1992

Today also was the end of my attempt to start an egalitarian *minyan* at the Kosher Kitchen. Rabbi [Michael] Whitman[1] did not reject us on halakhic grounds.[2] He took us seriously and considered the matter, but rejected our

---

[1] Rabbi Whitman is an Orthodox rabbi who served as director of Yale University's Young Israel House Kosher Kitchen from 1987 to 2001, as noted at http://www.adathcongregation.org/rabbiCV.html.

[2] Rabbi James Ponet, Howard M. Holtzmann Jewish Chaplain at Yale University, contextualized Matt's struggles expressed in this entry in the following personal correspondence: "There was no centralized Jewish location during Matt's years at Yale. The Orthodox students had a basement dining room provided them by the university which they named Young Israel House at Yale. Often they would conduct services there. But there were other scattered locales

proposal because it would have upset many of the kitchen's members. I don't need to explain why I felt justified in asking and feel Conservative Judaism is right. But there is not a Conservative community here. This was to be the first step of community building—get people to pray together in a critical location. All I can say is that I'm disappointed. I'm disappointed that when I turn to Jews for help, they fail to lend a hand. I was joking with people today about how Jews are Jews' worst enemy. You'd think that in the long run, all Jews of all stripes would benefit from the building of community. Yet we act unwisely.

The irony of it all is that when Jews in this country didn't always have synagogues, churches allowed us to use their spaces. When we ask other Jews for help, we turn ourselves away empty-handed. We shoot ourselves in the feet for our short-sightedness.

Musings on law, creation and the problem of evil

April 12, 1992

Consider the following possibilities:

1. On Law—According to Rabbi [Shalom] Carmy,[3] what is permitted halakhically is not always the "most ethical" thing to do. Secular law is not tied to morality, but religious law would seem to be the area wherein the two are combined. R. Carmi would say that I'm reading this too technically. He would argue that motives must be understood before a rabbi can feel comfortable with [the] exercise of *halakha*.

2. On Creation—If God is all-benevolent and God is omnipotent, then why does evil exist? Leibniz[4] states that this must be the best possible world for

---

on campus where students of different davening [praying] styles would gather, common rooms, seminar rooms, and the like. Matt was a happy eater at YIH, an active singer of *zemirot* [Jewish festive songs], there at the conception and inception of Yale's still extant a capella singing group, Magevet, that emerged from shabbos zemirot at YIH. So I guess he made an effort to consolidate his life by bringing the Egal[itarian service] to YIH, an early gesture towards centralization that was not realized on the Yale campus until 1995 when Joseph Slifka Center for Jewish life at Yale opened."

[3] Rabbi Carmy is Professor of Philosophy at Yeshiva University, who at that time visited the Kosher Kitchen at Yale as a scholar-in-residence on multiple occasions.

[4] Gottfried Wilhelm Leibniz (1646–1716) was a rationalist philosopher and mathematician who invented calculus (independent of Isaac Newton) and coined the term "theodicy" in the philosophical attempt to wrestle with the problem of evil in the world.

the above reasons. Professor [Louis] Dupré[5] attacks Leibniz on grounds that this would imply other possible worlds from which God must choose. That this choice exists means that there are other worlds possible that will never be instituted since God chooses this world. This is absurd because it would limit God's freedom and omnipotence. This is [the] way [Baruch] Spinoza would say that this is the only possible world.

Evil is still a mystery. Professor Dupré suggests that if moral evil is the result of human choice, then perhaps the reason for allowing such a choice is that somehow this choice is a higher good than any works we could perform. . . .

In Western religious terms, this is understood as loving God through our faith and deeds. Freely chosen love of God must be somehow of great value.

It would seem that this conclusion must be accepted because we would think that an all-good, omnipotent deity would, of necessity, wipe out all evil.

Physical evil? David Lev[6] falls back on the naturalized explanations that these events have nothing to do with people, though we're often on the wrong end—and consider what happens to animals. This is indeed a great mystery.

Encountering new worlds in Jerusalem

27 Sivan (June 28), 1992

After an unscheduled stop in Athens, we landed in Tel-Aviv, Ben-Gurion Airport. I am taking the adventurous route. I came without accommodations and have been searching for a place to stay. I had no plans for the first night, but was invited by the man next to whom I sat on the plane to stay at his house. He lives in Kiryat Arba on the West Bank, the oldest settlement (1968). I was hesitant because I was a bit frightened and felt like an imposer, but I remembered that to take in guests is one of the *mitsvot* (commandments) for which we reap some reward in this world, but the principal reward is earned in the world to come. When I remembered this, I felt better. He said that it was good to have guests, and so I felt all right about accepting and how could I, in true adventurous spirit, turn down an invitation to a settlement?

Michael is married to Molly, a very generous hostess. They have five children—five boys—and an extremely playful puppy. It was good to meet them,

---

[5] Louis Dupré served as the T. Lawrason Riggs Professor in Yale University's religious studies department from 1973 to 1998.

[6] Also referred to as David DaSenda (see note 12).

but I tried to stay out of their way. After all, it was Michael's first time home in about six months and he certainly deserved to spend time with his family without having to worry about me. I will remember to invite them to dinner.

אם אשכחך . . .

"If I forget thee, O Jerusalem . . ." (Psalm 137:5)

I arrived in Jerusalem early the next morning, my thoughts of course on the settlements issue. I guess it really upsets me that Jews and Arabs can't figure out how to live together peacefully. I wonder if this issue wouldn't just die if the rest of the world were to stop giving the PLO viability. Maybe the right of self-determination is not an inalienable right of people. Yet, if I were to hold this conviction, how could I justify a *Jewish* state? Perhaps I could say that this is certainly a consideration, one that the British partition plan clearly took into account, but not an inalienable right. If we continue to encourage national separation, are we bound to split the world into tiny pieces? Czechoslovakia is now on the chopping block and before that, Yugoslavia. Why can't we all just respect and learn from one another? But then, this is a naive question. The Arabs have a hard time. But can I really believe that this is *because* of Jewish rule?

After looking for apartments—it looks like I'll be living in the Old City—I davened *minḥa,* at the Wall and gave some צדקה (*tsedaqah,* charity). I then made more phone calls and came back to the Wall for ערב שבת (*Erev Shabbat,* the Sabbath eve).

I ate dinner with a family in Meah Shearim. They didn't speak to me much, and I felt ambivalent about opening conversation. It didn't seem like the right thing to do. The food was excellent.

Today, I had no food. Oh well. I went to the Great Synagogue of Jerusalem, a huge Conservative[7] synagogue with an amazing choir. Yet, I didn't feel right there. Too big, not enough *kavana* (intention), and the choir was too much of a show. I mean, there was actually a conductor in front of the *'Aron* (Ark), conducting the choir. You see, they were so good that they took attention away from the תפילה (*tefillah,* prayer), and I desire a prayer experience, not a concert.

---

[7] The Great Synagogue is, of course, Orthodox. Even at this relatively early stage of Matt's spiritual search, he must have known the difference between Conservative and Orthodox. It's not clear if this reference is a simple error or if he was making a sociological observation that the frontal experience of services at the Great Synagogue mirrored formal services he had observed at large American Conservative synagogues.

Afterwards, I studied מסילת ישרים (*Mesillat Yesharim,* The Path of the Righteous)[8] with a guy named Johnny. He claimed to know very little and was bright-eyed about the prospect of embarking on Jewish study. I felt that it'd be better to study with a partner than alone—even if the partner feels he knows nothing. In this case, my understanding of העולם הבא (*Ha-ʿolam ha-baʾ,* the world to come) was improved dramatically. I shouldn't think about this as reward and punishment, rather as the culmination of our efforts to live the good life. Rabbi Tarfon compares העולם הבא (*Ha-ʿolam ha-baʾ*) to a worker's wages. The worker needs food and so he works to be paid. He is paid according to the time of his labor or for piece-work, or whatever system is used. Similarly, the Jew desires דבקות (*devequt,* attachment) with ה׳ (*Hashem,* God). The only place where this can be accomplished is העולם הבא (*Ha-ʿolam ha-baʾ*), and this is our purpose. The service of ה׳ (*Hashem*), only in this world, brings us to cleave to ה׳ (*Hashem*). Performance of מצות (*mitsvot,* commandments) enhances us more and more, until we're there. It is for ה׳'s (*Hashem's*) sake that we labor and, for the same reason, we succeed.

After a short nap, I went to a Torah study session in a small Sephardic synagogue nearby. I don't know whether it was a rabbi who was expounding or just a learned member of the congregation. In either case, he was learned. And animated. The discussion was entirely in Hebrew, and I understood little, but we studied Mishnah Berurah, ירושלמי (*Yerushalmi,* the Jerusalem Talmud), and he expounded Korah. The Korah I understood—a little, [but] why do we remember the evil? Because perhaps Korah and his congregation never died. If the earth had a mouth, he said, we'd hear them saying, "Moses and Aaron are right, and we are false." When the Messiah comes, the earth will reopen and Korah will emerge, this time a צדיק (*tsadiq,* a righteous person). A controversy not for heaven—Korah and his congregation, not Korah and Moses. Because Korah was hypocritical. His claim was that all the congregation was holy and that therefore one family should not exalt itself. Yet, here he wants to do something. He wants to be a leader. Korah's wife apparently knew this and argued with him about this.

Then we davened *minḥa*. They ate a snack afterwards. It was an intense snack. All kinds of fruit and cakes. They would each make a blessing over what they ate. If one had a piece of watermelon and a cake we'd make two blessings. All of them would say their blessings out loud at different times, and people who heard would respond, "Amen!"

---

[8] *Mesillat Yesharim* is a classic guide to character development by Rabb Moshe Chaim Luzzatto (1707–1746), published around 1738.

Then I took another nap before *Maariv*. I arrived a bit early to hear another man expounding Korah. He was discussing the house full of ספרי תורה (*sifrei Torah*, scrolls of the Torah), which Korah asked if it required a מזוזה (*mezzuzah*). Yes, but Korah's סברא (*sevara*, rationale) was wrong. The Mezzuzah [is] not to sanctify the house, but to remind the Jew to be observant outside as well as inside—ובלכתך בדרך (*u-velekhtekha vaderekh*, when you walk along the way). Like the other, this man was animated, pounding the table and waving his arms.

During *Maariv*, the שליח ציבור (*shliah tsibbur*, communal prayer leader) collapsed. An older man. He looked dead, but he was apparently okay. They called an ambulance for him, but we were all frightened. I wonder, though, if to die during prayer would be such a terrible thing. But he was okay, תודה לאל (*todah l'El*, Thank God).

We ended שבת (*Shabbat*), each person with בסמים (*besamim*, spices) provided by the congregation.

"It is an important commandment that one be happy always."

3 Tammuz (July 4, 1992)[9]

I'm living in the Old City with Raiza Leah and Tania Suskind. The former is a collector of short stories and on a different spiritual plane than the rest of us, while Tania paints and plays violin. Tania had not planned to move back in, so this surprise blocked my attempt to room with another student. These women believe that I will actually benefit from not living in a "student" apartment. Life is full of surprises, they say, and that we're not in control shouldn't bother us too much. It's just the way things are. Well, I did come to Jerusalem for surprises. I see no reason to complain, though, because so what? I will still experience Jerusalem, but it will be at my pace more as an individual than as a member of some kind of student clan.

There is a little placard on my wall which reads:

מצוה גדולה להיות בשמחה תמיד
רבי נחמן מברצלב[10]—

---

[9] This was a Saturday. Even though Matt might not have yet been fully Sabbath observant at this point, it is doubtful he would have engaged in writing, traditionally prohibited on the Sabbath, while a guest in an Orthodox home in the Old City of Jerusalem. It is likely that he wrote this after Shabbat. On the Jewish calendar it would already be 4 Tammuz.

[10] *Mitsvah gedolah lehiyot besimhah* (Rabbi Nachman of Breslov [1772–1810]).

I'm still trying to unravel all the meanings of the wonderful saying, "It is an important commandment that one be happy always."

So, I will honor the ground upon which I stand. Rather than flee in disgust, I will dig for the gems to be found.

Struggling to balance Orthodox and Conservative Judaism

5 Tammuz (July 6, 1992)

Raiza Leah (one of the women with whom I am living in the Old City) seems to have a different sense of reality than the rest of us. She criticizes religious movements that deviate from the traditional sources as somehow lacking in wisdom and understanding. As a result, these religions or practices go no deeper than a surface level of spirituality. Those that are real are rare, but are able to affect the environment around them.

American Jewry then is the quintessential example of Jewry that has lost its reality. Americans, presumably, are more interested in the moment or security than in desiring seriously things of real import. I wonder whether this is true.

To begin, I wonder if this "search for reality" is not something restricted to the upper classes of society who have time and energy to devote to these questions. It may be that this is not the case, because if it was, then presumably many Americans would involve themselves in this type of pursuit. The fact is, we don't.

I bought a טלית קטן (*tallit qatan*)[11] yesterday. It seemed like the right thing to do, seeing as I cannot understand law until I do it. A conversation with Tal Brudnoy moved me to really consider, again, these questions of reality and falsehood in regard to Judaism. Why do I feel happy only among the Orthodox, for example? I find their philosophies unpalatable. Can I really believe that the תורה, (Torah), with all that's in it comes from 'ה (*Hashem,* God), along with the Oral Law as well? I have rejected this theory as untenable. Yet, when I look at Conservative Judaism, whose assumptions I accept, even though the movement itself

---

[11] A small *tallit*, an undershirt with the *tsitsit*, fringes, attached to each of the four corners. It's the norm for traditionally observant males to wear such a garment. Many North American Jewish students from non-Orthodox backgrounds who go to Israel seeking deeper engagement with Jewish practice experiment with wearing *tsitsit* and *kippot*, skullcaps, at all times. [Note: Matt's Hebrew was not yet fluent, and in his handwriting, *tallit* is misspelled as תלית.]

flounders amid these assumptions, I am routinely displeased by what I see. It is almost as if Conservative Judaism possesses an empirical truth and yet misses the boat while the Orthodox lie—but are correct. It reminds me of a statement of David DaSenda (when he was still David Lev).[12] Moshe DeLeon claimed to have received the Zohar through Shimon Bar Yochai, but he wrote in the wrong Aramaic. So, is the Zohar false? No, says my teacher. DeLeon lied, but sometimes one must lie in order to approach the truth.

In this sense, truth takes on a whole different meaning, one that I have not yet begun to probe, one that confounds our use of language even more so than our original problem—that is, our speech about 'ה.

One more implication of what I say. If I am here correct, then perhaps it could follow that many people, from many different places, at many different times have been able to grasp this truth. It could not be confined to Judaism alone.

Action versus passivity

16 Tammuz (July 31, 1992)

This whole discussion of action and passivity has intrigued me as of late. The rabbis see activity as associated with male symbolism and passivity as associated with the female realm. I'm not sure why they chose activity to be associated with male and vice-versa, but it seems that those two are inseparable and the association of gender clues us in to the intimacy of the concept in all aspects of human life. Spinoza states that emotions inadequately understood are passive, as they cause us to *react* rather than to *act*. Since, according to his reasoning, a person would act only in order to bring about a good result or to achieve a projected better state of affairs, passivity is to be avoided. I doubt Spinoza would have made the same connection of passivity and female as did the rabbis. This would lend one to connect femininity with evil, and I do not believe this to be the case.

Lao Tze says that non-action is the ultimate action. How can this be true? Perhaps, one could say, we act until we are satisfied with our environment, at which point we stop acting? This would be a gross misrepresentation of Lao Tze. He meant simply to emphasize the power of passivity, which implies allowing oneself to be carried by the current of events. The need always to be an actor

---

[12] David DaSenda is a psychologist in Los Angeles and a lecturer on Jewish theology and mysticism. He and Matt met while both were on staff at Camp Ramah in the Berkshires. Matt expressed interest in David's expertise in Spanish Kabbalah, and they regularly corresponded with each other during Matt's years at Yale and JTS.

blinds us to other ideas and experiences that we need in our spiritual formation as well as in our mental health, period. I feel that, after these three weeks of not being in complete control, I've experienced a great deal that merits consideration. This line of thought also sheds light on the idea of שבת (*Shabbat*). It's no accident that we welcome "The Shabbat Queen," or the female, passive force of creation. The Friday night *Kiddush*[13] is also significantly superior to the Saturday afternoon *Kiddush*. On Shabbat, we let the passive forces of creation do their work. We, who are along for the ride, experience a higher level of soul on שבת (*Shabbat*), where our main duty is to rest and receive rather than to act.

I thought about the dichotomy today while contemplating the difference between the energy directed toward being a host and being a guest. On the surface, we would say that hosting is active whereas being a guest is passive. Yet, this is not always true. When one is involved in the continual formation of community, both hosting and being a guest are active roles. One's activity is unquestionable. The active guest, though, is active because the energy is directed toward carving a niche and developing relations between people. Guests are passive when they "borrow" a community. For example, tonight I will be the guest of a Hasidic family. This is an act of passivity because after the dinner, I will leave and most likely not see them again.

A passive host acts only in accordance with social norms. In this sense, a host feels compelled to act rather than desiring to act. The initiative, in other words, comes from outside the host, and this is what makes the host passive.

There's more to be said on this subject. For now, let it be said that, while we desire to be the molders of our environment and in control of our lives, sometimes the best alternative is to simply let things happen. This is one of the foremost lessons of שבת (*Shabbat*).

Reflections on Israel, the Diaspora and the meaning of communal fast days

יח תמוז (*18 Tammuz, August 1, 1992*)

Today we will observe the fast of the יז [17th of Tammuz]. Strange, but we fast on יח (18th). We commemorate the day the Romans broke through

---

[13] The traditional blessing over wine acknowledging the sanctity of the Sabbath.

Jerusalem's outer walls. After that, it was only a matter of time and human lives [lost] before they sacked the Temple.

The scrolls are burning, but the letters remain . . .[14]

Connected to this day, we see Israel fighting desperately for survival against and indestructible foe. 'ה (*Hashem*) has allowed the people to suffer, hiding 'ה's (*Hashem's*) face from us. Without the connection, Israel suffers immeasurably. The Romans break through. The end is assured, but still, Israel will not give up. If we were [not] to go down, we would be forced down. Even when 'ה's (*Hashem's*) face is hidden from us, we will not abandon 'ה as an act of volition. And so we fought, and we prayed, and we hoped. . . .

. . .[A]nd now, almost two thousand years later, another people occupies [the] Temple Mount. It is as if 'ה (*Hashem*) has taken another lover. We had so hoped it wouldn't happen, but it did. Right up to the end, we refused to believe it would. And so now we come to the ruins of what is left. Faithfully, we remember, we hope, we continue.

In reality, though, 'ה (*Hashem*) has not taken another lover, at least not to our exclusion. We can serve 'ה wherever we are and 'ה loves us all the same. But we are far from the perfection we could have.

Turning to other thoughts . . .

What does it really mean to stand up for one's principles? Does a person put an ideal before other people? My parents tell me to stand for that which I believe, and not to regard the opposition, at least not to give in to them. But what if one ideal conflicts with another? And how do we decide what is right?

I have an ideal to serve the Jewish people, to have a family, and to not open myself to regrets about what might have been. And here I am, in Eretz Yisrael (the Land of Israel), sweating about circumstance. I want to be among a vibrant Jewish community. That seems to point me here. I want to be a rabbi, be near my parents, and that points me homeward.

Is it better for me to shoot for the stars in גלות (*Galut*, Diaspora) or to live a less ambitious life here? What can I really call greatness?

---

[14] A reference to the tannaitic sage R. Haninah ben Teradyon. He was executed in the midst of the Hadrianic persecutions (132–135 C.E.). While he was being burned alive wrapped in a Torah scroll, his students asked him, "What do you see?" He replied, "I see parchment burning while the letter of the Law soars upward" (Sifre Deuteronomy 307).

I guess my foremost problem is the idea of the explicit/implicit command. If I *feel* commanded to do something, be it written or otherwise, I must react to this command. Either I obey or disobey—and disobedience is always punished one way or another. I am told it is a divine command to settle Eretz Yisrael. I feel this command. I am also commanded to honor my parents. I interpret this to mean to stay near them and be for them a source of joy. But maybe that command means that I should take it upon myself to live a life in accordance with my principles; again, to make them proud. But principles are in themselves empty without application. The pain that this application can cause mars the principle. Perhaps pragmatism requires that we therefore drop the principle? It seems that to live a life always looking toward an unattainable [goal] is a cause for great pain, but it is perhaps the pain that keeps us struggling as we search for a way to implement our ideas.

So, given what I have said, greatness is in the end a subjective measure. Without the personal impact, commands become chains. If I want to serve 'ה (*Hashem*) and the Jewish people, it is up to me to decide how best to do this. When this decision is made, I will achieve greatness by acting in consistency with that which I feel compelled to choose. The struggle will not end, because it is not a struggle from which I am meaning to emerge. Success is measured by my ability to continue struggling.

The value of choice

כ"א תמוז *(August 4, 1992)*

Perhaps 'ה (*Hashem*) created evil in order to allow for choice. Why choice? Presumably, choice is a greater good than compulsion. Why so? Choice allows for love. Love is a good whose existence outweighs the negativity in the world. This is a first principle.

Memory of transcendence

13 Av (August 12, 1992)

Rabbi Gedaliah[15] today spoke of memory of transcendance. This world is not alone. Life is a process in which we can experience 'ה at every moment.

---

[15] According to Rabbi David Levin-Kruss, a faculty member of Machon Pardes, the reference here likely refers to Rabbi Gedaliah Fleer. An expert in Jewish mysticism and Hasidic thought,

Anything less degenerates to goal orientation. I asked him if this was a luxury for people who had time, but this, he said, was the whole point. To develop a consciousness in which the day-to-day process is significant in some way sanctifies (he didn't use this language) every moment. To love life is to love the process.

One can never really "repent," only "return"—תשובה (*teshuva*). One can only repent when one understands the extent of damage done. This is generally impossible.

Religious people, beware, lest you use your religion as legitimization of behavior just as bad. I asked the question about luxury, and one of the students made a comment that that *was* the lesson. Of course, and I didn't understand, which was why I was asking! But the lesson I learned at that moment is that it hurts when one student does that to another—shows off his superiority of understanding. How many times have I done the exact same thing? How much damage have I done to the self-confidence of others? It was a powerful lesson tonight.

The Energy of Jerusalem

22 Av (August 21, 1992)

In the *Shmoneh Esrei*, we pray for Jerusalem to be rebuilt. This is because Jerusalem is a symbol aside from a mere physical location. Jerusalem is the ideal Jewish community, as Israel is the ideal nation. These are our archetypes. As a physical location, there is an energy to Jerusalem quite unlike anything else in the world. We see Jerusalem as the place where 'ה (*Hashem*) chose to allow 'ה's (*Hashem's*) presence to dwell. Yes.

But the reality today is that while Jerusalem is more or less physically rebuilt, it is not spiritually complete yet. The חרדים (*Haredim*, fervently Orthodox) would say that it will not be completed until we actually rebuild the Third Temple, something I choose to see in a more symbolic vein.

Do not forget this energy. Any Jewish community can partake of Jerusalem from anywhere in the world. Every Jewish community should strive to be

---

particularly the thought of Reb Nahman of Breslov, Rabbi Fleer has served as an occasional visiting teacher at Pardes. If this is true, that Matt refers to Rabbi Fleer, it suggests that Matt's reference to Reb Nahman in his August 23, 1992, entry was hardly accidental but was influenced by the teachings he had encountered over the previous several days. See also www.rebgedaliahfleer.com.

Jerusalem. Yes, this is an impossible task, but only the impossible tasks are worth pursuing.

"Religion welcomes the challenge of bringing damaged souls closer to perfection."

24 Av (August 23, 1992)

Rabbi Nachman teaches to always judge others on the scale of merit. And so now, on the eve of my departure from Eretz Yisrael, I will attempt to judge American Jewry on the scale of merit.

Most American Jews are not really interested in Judaism, but use the synagogue for social purposes. It becomes a ceremonial hall. Yet when it comes to serious Jewish endeavors, they shrink away. Why?

American Jews have grown up to treasure ideals of freedom, democracy, religious tolerance, and equality. We tend to believe that anything counter to these ideals is either archaic or wrong or both. If a system is not performing the way it should, then it is obviously the fault of the system and not the people.

Religion as a whole has not perfected the world when American Jews see the problems of Israel. Add this to the weak-eyed glances that organized religion receives in the West, they shrink away. To be part of a seemingly imperfect system is unpalatable for the majority of American Jews. Instead of understanding that Judaism demands human perfection from imperfect human beings and is a constant struggle against יצר הרע (*yetser ha-ra'*, evil inclination), they simply reject Judaism, as it is more convenient not to immerse oneself in the struggle. The only problem with this "valid" reality is that we lose our souls in the process.

It is possible to separate religion from its practitioners because, unlike a political philosophy that concerns itself only with people, religion points to [an] enlightened state of consciousness difficult to attain. Religion welcomes the challenge of bringing damaged souls closer to perfection.

Return to the United States after study in Israel

August 24, 1992

Tonight, on the כ"ו אב (26th of Av), I, משה מלך בן יהודה וזהבה (*Moshe Melekh ben Yehuda v' Zehava*), return to the United States.

יהי רצון מלפנ[י]ך יהוה ואלוהי אבותינו

[May it be Your will, Adonai, God of our ancestors]

That You always guide me in the right path.
That You bring understanding between the members of my family and me.
That You provide me with great teachers.
That You provide me.

"[A]s far as learning goes, I'm still only a lion's tail."

[Editor's note: The next two sentences are undated, but are likely within a day or two prior to the following entry that is dated 10 Elul, or September 8, 1992. This brief entry seems to suggest Matt's consideration to apply to Rabbinical School, which he did for first time later that fall.]

The Conservative Movement has not taken responsibility for learning—the question I must now answer is whether or not I want to take responsibility for my part within this attempt at genuine faith and intellectual honesty to encourage more learning.

But as far as learning goes, I'm still only a lion's tail.

The purpose of Yeshivot

10 Elul (September 8, 1992)

I feel I understand better why ישיבות (*yeshivot,* traditional centers of Torah study) are the way they are. Most of Jewish society does not take the time to sit and learn as part of the daily regimen, and so special institutions need to be created for this purpose. But the problem is that since ישיבות (*yeshivot*) strive so hard to accomplish this goal of uninterrupted study, they discourage participation with the distracting outside world. People criticize ישיבות (*yeshivot*) for representing the highest values yet not producing people who always exemplify these high values or present themselves well. And then there's the defensiveness that we who study develop—the fear that we must push everything else aside to learn. The discussion just isn't valued so much by the outside world.

Ideally, life should be lived with Torah as an integral part of every day. Since we do not act as such, we've needed to create these special institutions to replace years of our lives with an imposed rigor. We can't do it ourselves, and so we seclude ourselves.

"The Jewish struggle is not to overcome oneself but to be oneself."

7 Kislev (December 2, 1992)

The Jewish experience does not consist of sitting and lamenting about the sad condition of the world, even though the world may very well be in a sad condition. It does not consist of "wise men" who torture themselves to ask the right questions, though this is something that men who are called wise often do. It does not consist of rabbis, teachers, or preachers speaking publicly relating Torah lessons to our daily lives every day constantly. Nor are Jewish life and Jewish reality a mechanical performance of *mitsvot*. Jewish struggle at its best is never alone, although each individual must struggle alone. No, Jewish reality begins with the formation of a community in which Torah discussions are interesting and meaningful, where *minyanim*[16] and group *mitsvot* are not a joke, though we may indeed make light of their importance.

So no rabbi who delivers sermons will succeed in creating Jewish reality, even though Jewish realities cannot be without teachers.

The Jewish struggle is not to overcome oneself but to be oneself, in the truest possible sense of who one is. Do not forget this.

The problem with a "moment of silence"

10 Tevet 5753 (January 3, 1992)

We had a Shabbat dinner that I organized Friday night. It went well, but Sue asked for a moment of silence to think about those less fortunate than ourselves. Though at the time I could not explain why the moment made me uneasy, and I felt it to be inappropriate, I now understand.

Moments of silence do very little, if anything at all. In my opinion, a more appropriate action in this context of thinking about the less fortunate, would be to initiate a discussion about what we can do.

---

[16] A *minyan* is a quorum of ten people for Jewish communal prayer. *Minyanim* is the plural. The usage here refers more generally to services.

Finding the path to God

28 Tevet (January 21, 1993)

It occurs to me that the most superior form of religious understanding would be never to mention or invoke You, God. You should be like the Taoist emperor who acts behind the scene, putting all into place yet never emerging as the actor. The emperor provides and loves, yet remains unseen. You should be like the general honored by Sun Tzu, who responsibly eliminates the need for conflict. He is great, yet remains unsung. God, if the best way to serve You is to put Man and Woman whom You love before You, then we should be able to speak to men and women about men and women. Our actions should be justified and honored not because we mention you in their defense but because we instinctively know them to be great. And yet, all these paths lead back to You. This is Your path. O, teach us to walk.

"Why do we need to be taught to speak/call to God?"

10 Shevat (February 1, 1993)

In Parashat בשלח (*Beshalaḥ*) it is written:[17]

> י וּפַרְעֹה הִקְרִיב וַיִּשְׂאוּ בְנֵי־יִשְׂרָאֵל אֶת־עֵינֵיהֶם וְהִנֵּה מִצְרַיִם ׀ נֹסֵעַ אַחֲרֵיהֶם וַיִּירְאוּ מְאֹד וַיִּצְעֲקוּ בְנֵי־יִשְׂרָאֵל אֶל־יְהוָה: יא וַיֹּאמְרוּ אֶל־מֹשֶׁה הֲמִבְּלִי אֵין־קְבָרִים בְּמִצְרַיִם לְקַחְתָּנוּ לָמוּת בַּמִּדְבָּר מַה־זֹּאת עָשִׂיתָ לָּנוּ לְהוֹצִיאָנוּ מִמִּצְרָיִם: יב הֲלֹא־זֶה הַדָּבָר אֲשֶׁר דִּבַּרְנוּ אֵלֶיךָ בְמִצְרַיִם לֵאמֹר חֲדַל מִמֶּנּוּ וְנַעַבְדָה אֶת־מִצְרָיִם כִּי טוֹב לָנוּ עֲבֹד אֶת־מִצְרַיִם מִמֻּתֵנוּ בַּמִּדְבָּר:

I find these פסוקים (*pesuqim*, verses) precious. Israel at a time of dire stress calls to 'ה (*Hashem*). Seeing as that they don't know how, they complain to

---

[17] Exodus 14:10–12: (10) And when Pharaoh drew near, the people of Israel lifted up their eyes, and, behold, the Egyptians marched after them; and they were very afraid; and the people of Israel cried out to the Lord. (11) And they said to Moses, "Because there were no graves in Egypt, have you taken us away to die in the wilderness? Why have you dealt thus with us, to carry us forth out of Egypt? (12) Is not this the word that we did tell you in Egypt, saying, 'Let us alone, that we may serve the Egyptians?' For it had been better for us to serve the Egyptians, than that we should die in the wilderness" (Hebrew from Davka Torah Texts for Pages).

Moses; their cry is a cry of despair from fear. At this point, the people have not yet learned how to call to ה׳ (*Hashem*). They need a leader to teach them.

Why do we need to be taught to speak/call to God?

The purpose of Torah study

[Editor's note: the following entry is undated but likely comes from December 1993 while Matt was at Yeshivat HaMivtar and immersed in the study of Tractate Qiddushin.]

I then began to think about how my moods are connected to success and failure to understand a text. Most of my energy goes to Torah study now—anything else that I do, I feel a need to justify in some way as connected to learning. . . . I then realized that Jews who live by Torah do other things only in order that they may fulfill the מצוות (*mitsvot*), in turn making learning better. One does not learn מסכת קידושין (Massekhet/Tractate Qiddushin) in order to be married, but one takes a wife in order to מקיים (*meqayem,* fulfill) the lessons of קידושין (Qiddushin)! We now have an answer to the חז״ל (*Hazal*, sages of the Talmud) puzzle that learning takes precedence over actions because it leads to actions. The answer is that learning leads to better actions, to the fulfillment of מצוות (*mitsvot*) with כוונה (*kavana,* intention) to serve ה׳ (*Hashem*) as opposed to actions that we happen to know are מצוות (*mitsvot*). So too with actions that are not מצוות (*mitsvot*)—they can also be done בשם שמים (*beshem shamayim,* in the name of heaven), in order to facilitate learning or encourage the performance of other מצוות (*mitsvot*).

So why, then, do we study *halakhot* (laws) of תלמוד תורה (*Talmud Torah,* study of Torah)? Whenever we study a topic within Torah, for example, פאה (Pe'ah),[18] we learn how to connect with הקב״ה (*HaQadosh Barukh Hu,* the Holy One Blessed Be He) regarding the lessons of that topic. We can then act in order to perform מצוות and other actions facilitating the מצוות. This is also why we study character traits and listen to מוסר (*musar,* ethical teachings), in order to mold ourselves into watchful beings who want to do things that will bring us close to ה׳ (*Hashem*). So, what is Talmud Torah itself? This is the intellectual endeavor to uncover ה׳'s (*Hashem's*) desires vis-à-vis all aspects of life. So, when

---

[18] This tractate of the Talmud concerns the commandment to leave the corners of a field ungleaned for the poor to come and glean, derived from Leviticus 19:9 and 23:22.

we learn about the laws governing this process of inquiry, we are really learning about ourselves—about how we conduct this inquiry and how we learn about 'ה's desires and how to build this relationship as we continue.

As all actions can be directed toward מצוות (*mitsvot*), can all kinds of learning be devoted to Torah as well? If the רמב"ם (Rambam[19]) writes about פרד"ס (*Pardes*[20]), then we should think so because one must study logic, math, [and] physics before metaphysics.

Text study requires patience

יז כסלו (*17 Kislev 5754/December 1, 1993*)

On nights like tonight when פשט (*peshat*, plain meaning of a text) is so elusive, I have to remember that it's better to be frustrated because חיי עולם (*ḥayyei 'olam*/the eternal life) is elusive than to worry about חיי שעה (*ḥayyei sha'ah*, life of the moment). I didn't really understand R. Nahman's statement of when a man learns something that he doesn't understand, 'ה (*Hashem*) takes great pleasure in his effort. When a man cannot understand a סוגיא (*sugya*, passage of Talmud) or the like, he feels awful because he realizes that 'ה (*Hashem*) did not grant sin the ability to understand at that moment. Is it a mild form of הסתר פנים (*hester panim*, hiding of [God's] face)? Not really, just a withholding of grace which reminds man of his continued reliance on הקב"ה (*HaQadosh Barukh Hu*/ the Holy Blessed One) at all times. A man should miss this lack of communication and cry out to 'ה (*Hashem*), who will in His compassion reopen the dialogue and show us how to read the סוגיא (*sugya*) correctly.

Reflections on sleep

יח כסלו (*18 Kislev 5754/December 2, 1993*)

I'd like to play with an image a bit: "Behind Sleep." What is behind sleep? Or what would be behind sleep? And what could I mean by "behind." First, I need to consider what sleep is:

---

[19] Rabbi Moses b. Maimon (Maimonides) (1135–1204).

[20] Derived from Greek, *Pardes* means "orchard" and is also a Talmudic reference to the word's English cognate "paradise." See Sara Duker's thesis "Elisha Looked and Cut at the Shoots," and her extensive analysis of the Talmudic legend of the four rabbis who ventured into *Pardes* and were affected in different ways by this quest (e.g., Babylonian Talmud, Hagigah 14b).

When I say sleep, I think of inactivity, peace, rest, dreams, night, the necessity that the body exempt itself from activity every so often, passivity, loss of freedom of thought.

The Rambam writes[21] that Torah scholars should deny sleep to their eyes in order to learn. The Shulhan Arukh[22] *poskins*[23] that sleep is forbidden during the day unless for some purpose other than הנאה (*hana'ah*, pleasure). The משנה (*Mishnah*) in 8 פרק (chapter 8, Mishnah 5) of Sanhedrin informs us that sleep of the righteous is bad for them and the world, whereas for the wicked, good for them and the world.

So what is "behind" sleep would be "behind" what I've mentioned above. For example, [a] behind dream could be the motivations for the images produced while we dream, the experience that influences thought. While this would be a fascinating world to explore, since sleep is viewed with such "distaste" and since it represents a period of inactivity/passivity, it can also be a potentially dangerous world. At this point, I see a confrontation with Truth [that] comes about because I learn the reasons for my thoughts—or at least insofar as I am capable of knowing. Because I am not capable of knowing and understanding, I'm passive and need to receive in order to do anything.

Why is Truth potentially destructive? Is it because knowing Truth could involve loss of freedom to make a real choice between attractive alternatives? And who says that my alternatives need to be attractive anyway?

Another matter about sleep. Dan Jacoby[24] said that thinking is often one of the least honest ways of communicating with oneself. Perhaps more honest ways of communicating then are by dreams and daydreams, as Rabbi [David] Walk[25] suggested in his דבר תורה (*d'var Torah*, sermonette) two weeks ago, פ' ויצא (*Parashat Vayetze*).

---

[21] Laws of Torah Study 3:13.

[22] Rabbi Yosef Karo's seminal code of Jewish law, published in 1565; the law under discussion is from *Orah Hayyim*, 4:16

[23] An example of "Yeshivish," transforming a concept from its original Hebrew into an English transitive verb. A *pesak* is a rabbinic ruling. In this case, "to *poskin*" means to issue a rabbinic ruling.

[24] Identity unconfirmed at press time; possibly a fellow student.

[25] A faculty member at the time at Yeshivat HaMivtar.

24 Kislev [5754] (December 8, 1993)

I'm here pursuing a love that will never end, unlike any other love in the world.[26]

15 Tevet (December 29, 1993)

When we learn the *halakhot* (laws) of תלמוד תורה (*Talmud Torah*, study of Torah), we're really learning about ourselves and what we should value.

I was walking back to my room last night at 1:00 A.M. feeling bad that I didn't understand a ר"ן (RaN, R. Nissim b. Reuven, 1320–1376, Gerona) after hours upon hours of study. This learning is the central focus of my activity now and to fail to understand something is horribly frustrating. However, I started feeling better when I remembered Rabbi [David] Ebner's[27] שיחה (*siḥah*, formal discussion) in which he discussed ענוה ,יראה ,אימה (*'eimah, yirah, 'anavah*/fear, awe, humility). The main point of rejoicing in trembling is to recognize our needs by means of which we bind ourselves to 'ה (*Hashem*). The key for learning our needs and areas in which our needs are manifest is to learn Torah.

The Assassination of Prime Minister Yitzhak Rabin

(Monday, November 6, 1995)

The night before last, יצחק רבין (Yitzhak Rabin) was killed by a Jewish assassin who believed himself to be serving the Jewish people. Rabin had been a general who had fought in Israel's wars and died as a man who worked tirelessly for peace. His accomplishments, among others, are a peace treaty with Jordan and the formation of an autonomous Palestinian state in which Yasser Arafat, a former enemy, became an ally.[28] I admired Yitzhak Rabin and had confidence in

---

[26] Presumably "here" is the yeshiva environment and the "love" is the study of Torah. It's interesting to note that this is probably slightly before he started dating Sara, though they certainly already knew each other.

[27] Rabbi Ebner was on the faculty of Yeshivat HaMivtar at the time. He now serves as Rosh Yeshiva and Mashgiach Ruchani (chief spiritual advisor) at Yeshivat Eretz HaTzvi in Jerusalem.

[28] In a bitter irony, Mike Kelly reports that Arafat had advance knowledge of the Hamas bus bombing of February 25, 1996, that killed Matt and Sara (*The Bus on Jaffa Road*, 24–25).

the Israeli government because of him. I feel like the country is in disarray at this point because nobody can really fill his shoes.

What sickens me even more is that a lot of Israelis don't seem to understand the significance of what has happened. People say things like, "another victim in the peace process. It hurts that we've lost a Jew to a Jew, but really is he any more significant than any other terror victim? One shouldn't mourn too much."

Or worse: "Rabin should not be allowed burial in a Jewish cemetery because he was a traitor." They just don't understand—the Prime Minister has been killed. Will this country ever be the same again?

In the בית מדרש (*Beit Midrash*)[29] yesterday, the school tried to conduct classes as usual, but we students voted otherwise with our feet. We said תהילים (*Tehillim,* Psalms), sang dirges, cried, and listened to a הספד (*Hesped,* eulogy). I am subdued, sleepy, and feel lousy. My nose keeps running and I've got a canker sore at the place where my tongue connects to the bottom of my mouth. I'm bothered by cigarette smoke and the fumes from the candles that are lit in the crowds that gather to walk quietly and cry. Today I will try to walk in the לוויה (*levayah,* funeral procession) and watch the funeral speakers on TV. I want to hear the nations of the world speak and pay tribute to יצחק רבין (Yitzhak Rabin). I want Israelis to understand whom they've lost.

יצחק רבין יהי זכרו ברוך

[Yitzhak Rabin, *yehi zikhro varukh,* may his memory be for a blessing.]

Creating a new yeshiva

Tues[day], Nov[ember] 7, [1995]

Devorah [Schoenfeld][30] just called to tell me about their yeshiva that she and others would begin in Israel next year. This could be my opportunity to become one of the founders and builders of a new openness and passion. Do I dare to dream this dream? To be a shaper of a new yeshiva and to eventually take the רבנות (*Rabbanut*) exams?[31] I could be in Israel, marry Sara, learn Torah, and work to build a vision of good purpose. Rather than read poems, I could live a

---

[29] This refers specifically to Schechter Institute in Jerusalem, where Matt was studying for the year.

[30] See Reflection by Dr. Devorah Schoenfeld on p. 331.

[31] For certification as rabbi by Israel's state-sponsored Orthodox chief rabbinate.

poem. Do I dare? I feel now as if God has heard my prayers to help me stop my rage and to build sturdy structures—words of truth, acceptable words written in good form.

Statement of educational goals

The following is a statement of my educational goals for the year. This year is to be spent studying at the Beit Midrash in Jerusalem with my class in Rabbinical School, Year 2.

Underlying and influencing my education is the need to constantly reexamine the values I believe to be morally appropriate. This continual self-examination should lead me to involve myself in causes that serve others, as I have a stake in the world around me and can be useful. This ultimate goal of becoming more useful should direct my energies while I study.

As a student this year, I should strive to create resources for myself. I should seek out individuals from whom I can learn, both from teaching and example. I should keep an open mind so as to easily identify such people. Furthermore, I should explore new ways to solve problems and answer questions with which I am faced.

As I search for resources, I should also be a resource to others. Being a resource involves my careful, attentive listening to others. I should speak politely and respectfully, and I should ask questions to ensure my understanding of what I am told.

Because much of my time will be spent in class in front of open books, I should set practical goals as well. I should strive to learn something new from each of my classroom teachers and look for ways to incorporate the new methodologies I am taught. I should make sure that my study partners understand everything I understand in order that we build mutual trust, become friends, and share knowledge. I should begin each class with a good enough understanding of the subject to ask an intelligent question.

Among my more concrete goals are personal projects begun outside of class. I am to finish Tractate Qiddushin before my birthday on the Jewish calendar, 11 Shevat.[32] I should discipline myself to write about *Parashat Ha-Shavua* at least once per month. Furthermore, I will begin work on a *Pesach* Haggadah to

---

[32] That corresponded to Thursday, February 1, 1996. His birthday on the secular calendar is February 5. On Saturday night, February 3, Matt hosted a celebration at his apartment with

be used at family *sedarim*. This Haggadah should clarify some of the symbols with which we interact as we perform the *mitsvot* related to the evening and should generate discussion.

Finally, and perhaps most important, I will decide which school I should attend for the completion of my rabbinic studies. I will make this decision based on my ability to fulfill the goals I have mentioned and the prospect of future improvement.

(Signed) Matt Eisenfeld
Nov. 18, 1995[33]
כ"ה חשון התשנ"ו (25 Heshvan 5756)

---

many of his classmates and teachers present, during which he made a *siyyum*, completion, of Tractate Qiddushin.

[33] In the Hebrew date that follows, 25 Heshvan, 5756, Matt broke from convention in writing a 'ה' indicating 5000 years. Generally, the Hebrew year is written without the marker of thousands of years, as it is understood. The Hebrew year in which this statement was written, 5756, would normally be written תשנ"ו, literally equal to 756. It is not clear why Matt chose to depart from this convention here, as it does not appear elsewhere.

Sara Duker's Mission Statement, Fall 1995

A Mission Statement

I believe:

- That there is a God (or at least try to believe, because this[1] is something beyond my human capacity to understand), and because of this God and forces God put into motion, we have a world, nature, humanity, diversity infinite levels of complexity—all these things we can see and cannot, can imagine and cannot.
- That I am present on this earth and alive, human.
- That I ought to be as alive as possible.

I recognize that I am not here of my own accord, and therefore am responsible to those whose infinite kindnesses sustain me and have kept me well cared for, being:

1. God (for the infinite variety of food, shelter, comforts that are on this earth and[2] available to me).

2. My family, especially my mother, who has devoted herself, time, caring, love, resources, self to ensuring I grow up healthy, well prepared for life, happy.

3. Other members of my circle of support, right now, Matt, in particular.

I know I only live once, and therefore must live well.

I believe that living well means both happiness and personal satisfaction, maintaining and improving the world, and productivity, helping others live in

---

These excerpts of Sara's journal were selected by Arline Duker for the original 1997 memorial volume. This selection contains a mission statement that parallels Matt's list of goals. It is possible that Matt's and Sara's propensity for writing mission statements was influenced by the book *The Seven Habits of Highly Effective People,* by Steven Covey (New York: Simon & Schuster, 1989), a book recommended by Rabbi William Lebeau to Matt, who then recommended it to Sara.

[1] Original text reads "there."

[2] Original text has "+," instead of "and."

vital productive ways. I define productivity as related to creativity, vision, achieving good relationships, knowledge, understanding.

Not *Things*[3]

Most of all, I must not do damage to the world around me which supports me, nor to others whose LIFE is as important as my own.

I believe that I must treat LIFE as sacred, and that my actions should reflect this.[4]

I believe life is well lived with active learning, a broad understanding, a constant need to continue learning, wonder and appreciation, BALANCED with appropriate action.

I believe I must fight against impulses such as materialism, superficiality, selfishness, indifference.

To these ends, I have been offered religious teachings of Judaism the way my ancestors have chosen to understand God and the amazingness/fleetingness of LIFE and the cruelty that often befalls [people who are perceived as "different" in some way, or who challenge the status quo].[5]

I know that a person cannot understand all meanings without deep thought directed at narratives and rituals and laws. I believe that the laws are meant to be a support and a challenge in areas of life where we are prone to trouble, to help us focus on God and the LIFE which matters.

I believe other people have ways of understanding God that are also good and worth learning from. I do not claim to be able to know all of whatever truth exists.

I do not know why evil exits, but I know I must do nothing to promote it.

Therefore:

I treat all of LIFE with respect.

---

[3] The purpose of this heading is not clear; in the margin nearby, she writes, "being joyous, not having 'pleasures.'"

[4] Marginal note: "b/c it is so amazing and strange and strong and fleeting."

[5] The text in brackets is suggested by Arline Duker. The original handwritten page from this journal excerpt ends with "befalls." The next page was not available at the time of publication of this edition. Arline suggests, "The notion of being the 'other' and being shunned or treated with disrespect was something important to Sara. She herself experienced some of the cruelty in middle school—and her scholars' project was on Elisha ben Avuyah—the 'Other'" (see pp. 173–209 below).

God:

I try to understand what God wants of me as a living being and as a Jew, and be reliable to do it.

I do nothing thoughtlessly.

I will not throw away my precious gifts of time and talent.[6]

I support a community that believes in my God.

I protect the environment.

My Family:

I treat my relatives with respect, even when I find them difficult.

I support my mother—physically, emotionally, financially, no matter what. Same for my sisters, grandpa, and aunt if they need me.

I make an effort to build relationships with them, calling, writing, getting together.

My Friends:

I treat with respect, forethought, love and generosity. I try to understand them as they want to be understood. I try to take an interest in the issues which concern them. I share my own thoughts and favorite activities with them.

Work:

My work is creative and not destructive. It engages all facets (or as many as possible) of my self.

[*Last line on page not legible*]

I do not rest on belief alone, but my actions reflect what I believe and understand.

I work hard.

I am reliable and cooperative with those who work with me.

Study:

I am interested in many subjects.

I read professionally related work *and* work of the heart.

He who does not increase his knowledge decreases it.[7]

---

[6] From margin.

[7] Added in margin.

My goals for this year

1) To improve my educational and career prospects
   and outlook + ideas.

2) To combine knowledge with action. To live as I ought
   to now, not later.

3) To live with TIME as my most valuable resource

4) To learn to live better with relationships

5) To maintain skills I have + develop new ones

6) To grow + with me grow my outlook and ideas
   on the world and on Judaism. Not to stop
   understanding

7) (Not to go in the hole financially,
   to be able to visit distant friends/travel)

Therefore

. Take useful courses.
. work hard in the lab
. get involved in activities related to but not
  exactly what I do in the lab.

. Volunteer for environmental organization.
  (covers 1 + 2)

(. Don't play solitaire, shop for things unneeded
   go places or do things I don't want to)

Attend at
least one
cultural event
per week.   . Spend time with Tammy Fishman, Matt Dowiak
               . Write home + to friends regularly
               . Consider my friends needs + act on them
               . LISTEN.

Find a
hevruta +
a class.   . Read Hebrew newspapers, books, speak Hebrew
               . Read one Russian paper per week. Talk about
attend   it with Airam and Peter
faithfully
               . Read a lot of other things
               . Write a diary, series - at least one thing per week

Photo of a page from Sara's journal listing her goals
for the year (see p. 31)

I pitch in a helping hand in my community.

I reflect on what I do.

I enjoy the outdoors (hiking) singing, dancing, art (others' creativity) food, laughing, reading, religion, other people, quiet, writing, resting, sex

And if too long a time passes without enjoying these, there is something wrong

My goals for the year

1. To improve my educational and career prospects and outlook and ideas.
2. To combine knowledge with action. To live as I ought to *now*, not later.
3. To live with TIME as my most valuable resource.
4. To learn to live better with relationships.
5. To maintain skills I have and develop new ones.
6. To grow and with me grow my outlook and ideas on the world and on Judaism; not to stop understanding (and not to go in the hole financially; to be able to visit distant friends/travel)

Therefore

- Take useful courses
- Work hard in the lab
- Get involved in activities related to but not exactly what I do in the lab
- Volunteer for environmental organization (covers 1 and 2)
- (Don't play solitaire, shop for things unneeded, go places or do things I don't want to do)
- Attend at least one weekday *minyan* per week[8]
- Spend time with Tammy, Fishmans, Matt, Devorah
- Write home to friends regularly
- Consider my friends' needs and act on them
- LISTEN
- Find a *ḥevruta* and/or a class, attend faithfully[9]
- Read Hebrew newspapers, books, speak Hebrew
- Read one Russian paper per week. Talk about it with Aaron (?) and Peter
- Read a lot of other things
- Write in diary, stories—at least one thing per week

---

[8] Added in margin.
[9] Added in margin.

Sara leading a group in the Maariv evening service overlooking Jerusalem, circa 1993–1994. Photograph provided by Arline Duker.

Letter from Sara Duker to Friends from the Tahoe-Baikal Institute

IF I EVER GET AROUND to sending this letter to you, my apologies right now for it not being addressed to you or handwritten personally. I hope you are well, wherever and whenever it is you receive this.

First of all, hello from Jerusalem, where life almost always seems to border on the surreal. It's been sort of an uneasy reunion with the city I claim to love. I'll also tell you that I am homeless at the moment, homeless long term (I'll explain. I'm not living out of a box in the park), which is why I'm writing at all.

I came here with high expectations of this beautiful city, of learning Russian at the end of this summer to ride off into the sunset (or sunrise, as we fly). Somehow, it was very disconcerting to find that in no space here, have I found much natural ground to step in. There is green around the stone courtyards here, but very little pure green space. Traffic can easily crowd the narrow streets, and Israeli drivers are not known for patience.

Meanwhile, this week has been the holiday of Sukkot, a celebration of the end of the harvest, the completion of the cycle of Torah readings, a holiday of dwelling in temporary shelters called *sukkot* (singular *sukkah*). These shelters may not be too tall or too short, must have at least 2 1/2 walls, no more than one against a permanent structure. The roof must be made of or derived from

In the summer of 1995, Sara traveled to Russia to attend the Tahoe-Baikal Institute, a program in which contingents of Americans and Russians work cooperatively to save Lake Tahoe and Lake Baikal from ecological destruction (see http://www.tahoebaikal.org/about/history). This letter from the fall of 1995 was transcribed from a handwritten letter that Sara sent from Jerusalem to the fellows in the program with whom she studied. This letter encapsulates many of Sara's passions: concern for the environment, devotion to Jewish tradition, and a longing for a more pluralistic Judaism.

branches thick enough to cover, not thick enough to obscure the stars at night. Essentially, one is supposed to pretend to be homeless for a week and perform as many normal life functions as possible in this *sukkah*. The idea is to recognize the fleetingness of human achievements even as we celebrate them. *Sukkot* can be found on courtyards, balconies and roofs of Jerusalem apartments.

Part of the time I've been here, I've been learning with my best friend on this side of the Atlantic, Devorah [Schoenfeld], and her new roommate from New York, Avigayl [Young]. I helped them build a *sukkah* on the roof of their building in an area of town called Nahlaot. From her roof we can look out onto a neighborhood full of people of recently eastern origin. Two synagogues are across the street serving Jewish communities from Persia and Kurdistan, respectively, and they wake their congregants at 5:00 every morning with cries of "*Tefillah!*" ("Prayer!"). The streets, named after famous rivers mentioned in the Bible, used to be slum-like until some recent renewal projects have put my friends in a place with pretty cobblestone streets, newly planted trees, and better garbage removal.

Back to the *sukkah*: we made it from pre-fab metal frames and made three walls from old linens--a huge stained white-knit blanket is one side; a second is a highly ugly blue- and brown-patterned sheet and a pink tablecloth with holes burned into it; the third is a plastic-coated fake-lace tablecloth with green gingham card tablecloths hid underneath. The roof is a thin bamboo mat. It's unfurnished, save for the old furry bathmats and left-behind rug that soften the roof-floor.

I have spent four nights sleeping there where it is still warmer than Russia at night.[1] (The weather here in October is gorgeous--steamy warm sun, cloudless skies by day, cool and breezy at night. Rain should come soon, as the rain prayer in Israel is said tomorrow.) With my trusty sleeping bag, I have been faithfully homeless for the week. Still, bright light dims the stars, traffic from the nearby thoroughfare continues till very late, with the sound reaching the roof, and a huge, ugly Holiday Inn blocks an otherwise good skyline.

I wander between the apartment in Nahlaot and one in Rehavia, a wealthy area within walking distance of everything you might need, where the streets are named after the most prolific of the medieval rabbis. (The residents of this apartment do not have a *sukkah*.) This walk of about 20 minutes that I generally do at least once or twice a day goes along a sort of highway for much of it. I pass by

---

[1] Perhaps she means to say here that it's warmer at night in Jerusalem than in Russia during the day.

a park, where part of its expanse has been ploughed through to make a bypass to a more distant part of the city. (Nobody goes there anyway, claims Devorah, in complaint about the disaster wreaked on her beloved neighborhood.) It looks like they are replanting green and parkland on top of the underpass, but a permanent hole is there, and a permanent hole in the sanctity of the city parks.

Closer to Rehavia there is a new development called Wolfson Towers. They are mostly just ugly and don't ruin the skyline of the whole city--just the people who live behind them. What I mean by skyline is the unobtrusiveness of the buildings. A Jerusalem building code prohibits the construction of buildings taller than the Tower of David in the Old City, limiting the average apartment buildings to 3–5 stories. Exceptions are made, though, mostly for very large hotels and condos. More exceptions than ever have been made recently.

This is the reason I feel disaffected and wandering, and wanting to go back and live in the wilderness of Djerginsky Zapovednik. Then, I remind myself that Jerusalem never pretended to be lush countryside--it is the city, the capital.

More than physical surroundings make a home. It's not just this land that makes this place "home" but the fact that it is filled with other Jews. Avigayl and I went to the Western Wall--the last remainder of the ancient Temple—one morning during the holiday to hear the priestly blessing. Hundreds of men, claiming descent from the priests of old (we Jews don't lie about these things) spread their hands and say to the thousands gathered in crowds over the whole plaza at the Wall--"May God bless you and keep you. May God shine His [sic] light upon you and show you favor. May God turn his face to you and grant you peace." For this day, I am one of the pilgrims for the festival, even as I remind myself that many of my experiences in this place have been painful. Here, where men and women are strictly separated, I have been unable to hear the reading from the Torah on the holiday of the giving of the Torah (Shavuot). I have had nasty words thrown my way as part of a women's prayer group that dares to sing out loud. Overlooking this place, overzealous Jewish missionaries see a young woman who does not *look* like a traditionally religious person and try to bring her into their outreach seminars for undereducated Jews, trying to read her diary as she writes. It's the most political and religious of places. Had I not come here, I might have forgotten the differences between me and the others.

I think of this disorientation of return to this country around festive celebrations of the holiday and the city's 3,000th anniversary. Traditional songs about the city now have political connotations. Right-wing nationalism may hijack a celebration with a lot of songs about Jerusalem, the whole; about rebuilding the Temple; about the Messiah. One has to prove oneself apolitical--at one concert we went to sponsored by the city the group sang one song that could be construed as nationalist, then nonchalantly followed it with a song about peace, for balance.

Any of you who may have known me a year or two ago will know about my old trademark green hat and how traumatic it was to lose it in the bowels of the Port Authority. Perhaps some homeless person picked it up and is using it to stay warm, my mother suggested. All for the best, I now agree, as green hats are now the trademark of the "Women in Green"--women who oppose the [Oslo] peace accords.

One of the residents of this apartment in Rehavia, Shai, the American son of Israelis, claims discomfort with wearing his *kippah* in public, lest he be mistaken for a "religious Zionist." Why such a fuss over symbols? The rhetoric and violence are strident. Demonstrations everywhere. Politicians accuse each other of everything. Graffiti call Prime Minister Rabin a traitor. Benjamin Netanyahu, opposition leader, calls [Rabin's] plan to return some of the West Bank to the Palestinians an un-Jewish act. "Rabin is distant from Jewish values," says the man of three marriages and ever more extramarital affairs.

[My opinion on the matter is underinformed, admittedly, but here it is: I'm not celebrating giving back parts of this ancient homeland. Maybe it's never been done in Jewish history. But I don't think we've ever in history been interested in being oppressors either, a situation in which both sides lose lives in the end. I support the peace process plan because it is a plan, an attempt to work out such a sticky problem of two peoples' coexistence. The other side merely has nasty rhetoric--no plan-- and it is agitating to listen to it.]

On another issue, every year before the High Holidays, some rabbis issue a "DIRE WARNING" to the people of Israel about the dangers of getting hooked into a Conservative or Reform synagogue, where the evil ones masquerade as real Jews. Posters of this sort are plastered on various billboards of the city. Once upon a time, these hurt. Now I find them funny and will hang one on my wall. How amazing it is to be a dangerous heretic. Until I hear the story of a young man, engaged in conversation by a Jewish Brother at the Wall over the unusual *tallit* (prayer shawl) he wore. Questions of background and hometown led to the revelation that his father was a Conservative rabbi. "We have nothing to talk about then," remarked the once friendly Brothers.

"Why is this?" I ask, that Siberians, strangers in religion and background could treat a Jew like family, and my fellow Jews could treat me like a "stranger"?

The temptations arise to jump ship and spend my life as a nomad, in the beautiful places only, leaving once it gets ugly. This, though, is the theory that leads us to the carelessness with our environments--be they social or physical.

If a person knows that he/she is to live in a place permanently, using a local river for drinking water, what is the likelihood that they would consciously pollute it? And if you buy a house, then you repair it and decorate it well. Unpermanent houses are more easily abused. I often think if people learned to see small places as an unleavable home, they would soon realize that earth is an unleavable home as well, so we'd better take care of it. The message I'd like to pass along to my fellow "homeless" Americans is that homes don't just magically become ones. We have to invest in them and make them ours, accept that they are not perfect and decide it matters to us to make them more perfect. I hope after a year, and probably some more insults or nasty surprises, that Jerusalem will more fully be the home it was supposed to be.

Matt's Essays for Admission to JTS Rabbinical School, Submitted December, 1993

ESSAY 1: WHY I WANT TO BECOME A RABBI

For an hour, my partner and I sat in *hevruta'*, enveloped in our attempt to understand the seventh *'aliyah* of *Parshat Ki Tavo* (Deuteronomy 26:1–29:8). After the long list of curses, Moses says, "You have seen all the wonders that God did before your eyes in the land of Egypt unto Pharaoh, and unto all his servants, and to all his land; the great trials you have seen. . . . Yet God has not given you a heart to know, and eyes to see, and ears to hear, until this day." Recalling that most of the generation that had left Egypt died in the wilderness, we know that the vast majority of Israelites had not, in fact, witnessed the plagues or crossed the Red Sea. Moses continues, reminding our ancestors that their clothes and shoes had not worn, and that they had been victorious in warfare—achievements that could not be understood without faith in God. We noted that the reminder about clothes precedes the reminder about military victories,

---

Matt initially applied to JTS Rabbinical School during his senior year at Yale and visited the Seminary for his admissions interview in February 1993. Due to a harsh tone that he expressed toward the Conservative Movement, he was denied admission at that time but was encouraged to reapply after reflecting more deeply on Conservative Judaism and his relationship to the Conservative Movement. He reapplied the following fall from Israel and was offered admission for the fall of 1994. He wrote and submitted these admissions essays while attending Yeshivat Hamivtar, an Orthodox yeshiva in Efrat, Israel, during the 1993–1994 academic year. During that year, he immersed himself in Talmudic study and continued to wrestle with his place in the Jewish world, as one can detect from this essay. His yeshiva immersion that year was in an all-male environment. He notes advantages to that arrangement yet also expresses preference for egalitarianism between men and women in Jewish life. Over the next two years, he continued his quest to bridge what he saw as the best of two worlds: the spiritual fervor of an Orthodox community and egalitarianism and greater intellectual freedom within the Conservative community.

38

suggesting that to perceive holiness in common experience leads one to perceive holiness in the rarer moments. After forty years of wandering, when this new generation had proved itself faithful and therefore worthy to enter Eretz Yisrael, God grants the people the ability to recognize and appreciate the less obvious instances of holiness.

My partner and I concluded that we too should learn to appreciate the smaller gifts in searching for holiness in the world rather than those that are grandiose. Furthermore, we came to understand that in our mutual endeavor to learn what the text offered, we too had participated in one of these moments of holy encounter. Having spent the last hour learning Torah together was as important and as meaningful as the lesson itself. We learned that to feel close to God, one need not have danced with Miriam at the Red Sea or remember the smell of the smoke at Sinai, but rather to appreciate the sublimity of ordinary living.

I believe that coming to this recognition is what begins to make a person religious. The world is a place of beauty and wonder that strangely requires learning and labor in order to be appreciated. It is through Torah study that we Jews explore the means by which to sanctify life, learning how to strive for moral perfection. Through study and action, we sculpt reality towards our ideal. Perhaps the reason why Torah study so successfully creates friendships is because in studying, the partners actually participate in the labor of recognition while struggling together to discover new ways in which to sanctify everyday existence. This process requires that partners reveal their concerns, fears, and assumptions about how the world is and should be.

Like the memory of a particularly inspiring session of Talmud Torah, my best memories are all connected to Judaism. Whether I remember moments such as the song sessions as a camper in the UAHC's[1] summer camp in Mississippi, Henry S. Jacobs Camp, or a late night studying with a college classmate for a Hebrew exam, participating in USY[2], or even debates about revelation with my Orthodox friends, these moments are the most precious to me. It is at these moments when I am most aware that I stand before God, conscious of God's watchful eye. I experience myself as held in God's hand, carefully examined and commanded to live in God's presence. I continue to seek these moments.

---

[1] Union of American Hebrew Congregations, the former name of Reform Judaism's main organization. It is now known as URJ, Union for Reform Judaism.

[2] United Synagogue Youth, the youth organization of Conservative Judaism's United Synagogue of Conservative Judaism (formerly United Synagogue of America).

The question as to why I want to become a rabbi remains partially unanswered because it is difficult to describe what I mean when I say that I must live with the awareness that I stand in God's presence. Were I applying to medical school, I could name something concrete such as a desire to heal people as my motivation. Similarly, I could name a love for justice as a reason to attend law school, or good wages and benefits as a reason to become a warehouseman. When choosing to become a rabbi , I cannot point to any concrete motivation such as "a desire to serve the Jewish people" because any such motivation is only a means by which we strengthen our relationship with God. This relationship by its very nature is shrouded in uncertainty because God cannot be known as another human being, and because I ultimately remain ignorant of my purpose. In these essays, I have tried to share moments as well as ideas because these are the reasons why I want to be a rabbi. I believe that by devoting myself to the task of studying and teaching Torah, I can best do my part to help us remember Sinai's smoke.

ESSAY 2: THOUGHTS ON A PARTICULAR RABBINIC CAREER

A Jew can fill day and night learning and performing *mitsvot*. The surefire test of whether or not one has understood the lessons, however, is the ability to communicate that new understanding. Teaching is important, then, not because educated individuals thereby influence students to adopt a particular worldview, but because the teachers are forced to clarify and present their thoughts so that they are comprehensible. The reward of good teaching is good dialogue, as students grade their teachers by asking questions and by happily participating in class. Accordingly, good teachers should be good listeners in order to continue the dialogue. The best teachers are those who are able to interact with diverse groups of people, and for this reason, I would like to become either a pulpit rabbi or teach in a day school or yeshiva.

I believe that pulpit rabbis should be among the best of teachers because they encounter the most diverse groups of individuals. Though Conservative congregations may often contain people of similar economic class, we differ as to age, education, and sex. Furthermore, not only is the audience diverse, but the mode by which the rabbi teaches also varies. For example, American rabbis are expected to visit hospital patients, officiate at weddings and funerals, work with youth groups, and raise funds. Pulpit rabbis are forced to be flexible and must understand that all of the different situations they encounter are opportunities to teach. The congregation is always testing their knowledge.

I think that I would be a good pulpit rabbi because I have had some good role models of leaders, such as Rabbi Stanley Kessler and Rabbi James Rosen at my home synagogue, Beth El in West Hartford, and role models of good congregations, such as the Egalitarian *minyan* at Yale. Rabbi Kessler, for example, is influential in his outspokenness for social justice, while with Rabbi Rosen, the synagogue is growing and new faces have entered the dialogue. The *minyan* at Yale has helped me to learn the crucial skill of listening because every week we would discuss the Torah portion; often, the people's real statements and questions were different than their words. I yearn to continue to be active in this kind of dialogue and to form the long-term relationships that good pulpit rabbis are privileged to develop. It would be exciting to live in a community and to be involved in the decisions the community makes, as we undergraduates were at Yale.

I fear, however, that the pulpit rabbi may not be my wisest decision because pastoral duties will take time away from my great love, Talmud Torah. Both rabbis Kessler and Rosen rise at 5:00 A.M. to learn because the early morning is the only time that belongs completely to them. Though I love people and want to be involved with them, congregants can also become intrusive and a congregation can easily, even though unintentionally, deprive a rabbi of a private life. Furthermore, though involvement with a community is appealing, there will be occasions when the community will decide matters contrary to my wishes. The grandiose vision of the superb teacher whose students of all ages eagerly await the dialogue is unfortunately not always a picture of reality.

Perhaps I would be more effective as a day school teacher or yeshiva rabbi who teaches college-aged students. In these environments, students come expecting a lesson and are often more willing to involve themselves in the dialogue. For a teacher, communication would be less difficult, and I would be challenged so as not to waste the students' time with poor preparation. The yeshiva rabbi is challenged by older, yet impressionable students These students ask textual questions at a higher level than the rest of the community and require teachers who devote themselves to learning full time. In this type of environment, I could attach myself to Talmud Torah and attract others as students and companions.

School teachers, however, are frustrated because they do not continue to interact with the same students year after year. Furthermore, school teachers also must concern themselves with discipline. Teaching the seventh grade at the Yale

Hillel Children's School for three years, I learned that the dialogue extends beyond the classroom to include a student's family, a variable that differs for every student and always influences the teaching. A good teacher, however, should understand how to involve the parents in the dialogue as well.

I look forward to testing myself through learning and teaching, doing my share to increase the dialogue concerning our spiritual health. I have mentioned that I would be interested in teaching college-aged students in a Conservative yeshiva. At this moment, however, I know of no such yeshiva, and the movement would have to build one first. This is a subject for the next essay.

Essay 3: My Dream Rabbinate

It is true that the Conservative Movement has day schools, youth groups, and summer camps, but outside of the Seminary's summer programs, I know of no other yeshiva-type experience where young adults can devote themselves to Torah study full time. Here at Yeshivat Ha-Mivtar, I have met many Jews who grew up Conservative and are committed in their love for Torah but have left the movement for Orthodoxy because they fail to find learned communities. The problem of building these learned communities seems to be one of the greatest problems presently confronting the Conservative Movement, and a solution would need somehow to involve college or post-college youth in learning. I would like for us to improve our commitment to learning by creating new opportunities to learn. We can create these opportunities by building yeshivot.

In recent years, my Jewish education has included the Seminary's summer program, a summer at Pardes, _hevruta'_ work at Yeshiva Gedola (Chabad) in New Haven, and currently, Yeshivat Ha-Mivtar. The differences among these institutions seem to be in either style or topics studied. Both Pardes and Ha-Mivtar, for example, are similar in subject, but while Pardes is co-ed, Ha-Mivtar is all-male. The Seminary's summer program differs from Chabad in subject matter; Lubavitchers study the Tanya every day. A Conservative yeshiva would stress textual study: Gemara, _Humash_, _halakha_, and Jewish thought. This yeshiva would differ from Orthodox yeshivot in that teaching _halakha_ would involve learning Conservative and Masorti responsa as well as _Mishnah Brurah_. Jewish thought might differ in that we might read Buber or Rabbi Heschel as well as the Rambam. I doubt, however, that there would be a place for historical criticism in the Conservative yeshiva because I would want students to focus on building the textual skills necessary to learn from the sages of the past.

I would begin this process by building one yeshiva with the hope of eventually building more. Because the largest Conservative population is in the United States, I would want to locate this first yeshiva in the States. The early years will be difficult because it is unlikely that American Jews will commit themselves to extended time in a new program without a reputation in Israel. If the program is in the States, however, people may choose to come for a summer or a semester, allowing the institution to gain notoriety. Perhaps the yeshiva could be in a place like Vermont, away from the distractions of city but in an environment suitable for hikes, boating trips, and other such *tiyulim* (educational field trips or hikes) in order to keep the students energized. My experience has led me to believe that we need extended time to sit and learn without interruption, and so we need to create an intense environment where students will come to understand the seriousness of undertaking Torah study.

This issue of distraction forces us to consider the issue of coeducation. While I am committed to the idea of egalitarianism and would not build a yeshiva where anybody would be excluded, I am also committed to minimizing all impediments to each individual student's progress. I must admit that I am undecided as to how the yeshiva is to be integrated. Would men and women learn together and subject themselves to sexual tension, or would men and women remain separate except for *tefillah*, meals, and Shabbat. Certainly, the age and maturity level of the students is a factor in this decision, but sexual tension is not a difficulty to be considered lightly.

Building a yeshiva will not solve the problem of building a knowledgeable, committed Conservative community, but it will catch some of the youth at a critical moment and be an important step. Other projects include classes for adults or even families. Conservative Judaism need not define itself in opposition to Orthodoxy and Reform, because we have our own assumptions and philosophy, but we need the yeshivot in order to build a stronger grassroots level of knowledge. Hopefully, this first yeshiva will succeed so that others may be built in the States, in Israel, and around the world. If Chabad can do it, so can we.

Essay 4: A Personal Theology

I understand faith as the dialectic between belief and doubt which leads one to develop a relationship with God and the Jewish people. Rabbi Heschel names Man's greatness as the ability to wrestle with ultimately unanswerable questions such as, Does God exist? or Does God care about creation? or Do I have a purpose? As Jews, we answer together in the affirmative and then try to live as we choose. We Jews have asked these questions in every generation for thousands of years. If we have humility today, then we will listen and allow ourselves to be guided by the voices of the past.

However, I find myself with reason to doubt tradition at times and believe my doubt to be legitimate. I do not believe the traditionalist ideas of revelation, for example, but understand revelation as the divinely guided process by which we Jews choose the Torah as our text and continue to understand that text in every generation. How the Torah was compiled is an issue for historical analysis, yet once a text is adopted as authoritative, the community is met with practical consequences; our tradition developed *halakha*. If we are to question our ideas about revelation, then we must also question our understanding of *halakha*.

If *halakha* is established upon the traditionalist model of revelation at Sinai, then we who question that assumption need to come to an understanding as to why the stories we tell are so central to a Jewish world outlook. In order to learn from the past, we must commit ourselves to studying *ta'amei ha-mitsvot*.[3] A question as to why we understand a law as we do is inadequately answered if all we can say is "God says so!" or "That's what's written in the Torah!" I would like for us to be able to discuss our answers from the human side of experience, which is all we are really sure to possess. When asking about *ta'amei ha-mitsvot* however, we should not be asking why we observe particular *halakhot* but rather, "What does this commandment come to teach us about the human condition as we Jews understand?" or "Why do we believe that this action furthers our relationship with God?" This process of asking needs to be accompanied by doing, because actions teach as well as studying. I believe that only the learning and the action together can bring us closer to God.

Besides the need to learn through action, I believe that Jews need to try to act together as a nation in attempt to further the developing relationship with God. Even if God did not hand the Torah to Moses at Sinai, the endeavor to use the Torah to systematize a way of life in which Jews work together to serve God is of extraordinary value because the system keeps us Jews working together. Were I, the individual, to rely on my own experience, I might reject any idea of a connection to God whatsoever. After all, we live in a world where evil, both moral and physical, exists alongside good. This is a world where most animals

---

[3] Literally, "reasons for the commandments." He refers here to the discipline of seeking rationale for specific commandments, particularly where reasons are neither self-evident nor explained in the Torah.

die of starvation, predation, exposure, or disease. Some people can say with confidence, "I love God because He created me." This may be true, but God also created tornadoes and diseases.

In spite of all reasons to doubt, our tradition has tried to set people on a course of living by which we may extract some meaning in acting according to what we understand as God's commandments. Though we do not experience a perfect world, we need not necessarily conclude that we are abandoned. The Torah commands us to love God, yet love does not seem possible if we have no other option. Our very doubts, therefore, are fundamental to the process of relationship. Because I believe that God favors our group attempt, I am trying to live a life committed to *halakha*. Over the last few years, I have adopted the *mitsvot* and tried to find opportunities to study Torah. In this way, I choose to identify as a Conservative Jew and to retain my place in the dialogue of divine service guided by *halakha*.

Matt's Application for the Institute for Traditional Judaism

ESSAY 1—ON BECOMING A RABBI

When asked why I want to be a rabbi, I stumble and stutter because I have no way of answering the question in a fashion that satisfies the asker. I could discuss my good youthful experiences at Henry S. Jacobs, a Reform summer camp in Utica, Mississippi, or describe the social opportunities of USY [United Synagogue Youth] and my combative attitude toward its leadership. Alternatively, I could reminisce about my high school study of Chinese and subsequent summer trip to China to study language and culture. I fell in love with China and Chinese culture, yet I understood clearly that I am not Chinese nor will I ever be. Not only am I not Chinese, but I have no desire to be Chinese—my own cultural heritage happens to be unbelievably rich in its own right.

I used to say that I wanted to be a rabbi because many of my best experiences were somehow connected to Judaism and what better way to continue the experiences than to involve myself in Jewish leadership? Admittedly, such a statement need not direct one to become a rabbi. I could work for Federation, or a community center, or any other Jewish organization. I need not even become a

---

Matt Eisenfeld's first year of Rabbinical School at JTS, 1994–1995, was a struggle. Matt felt torn between the Orthodox and Conservative Jewish worlds. During his first year at JTS in 1994–1995, he indicated his intent to remain at the Seminary at least long enough to spend the 1995–1996 year at the Beit Midrash in Jerusalem. Nevertheless, he submitted an application to the Institute of Traditional Judaism (ITJ) with the possibility of finishing his rabbinic training there. For those who knew Matt, it was apparent that over the course of the year in Israel he had made peace with JTS and egalitarianism and probably would have continued at JTS in the fall of 1996. Shortly before leaving for his year in Israel, Matt submitted his application to ITJ. These four essays that he left behind tell us much about his thoughts on theology, *halakha*, and his vision of serving as a rabbi.

Jewish professional, but could sculpt a lifestyle in which I include Torah study and community participation. When aware of this realization, I know that I am unable to answer the question of why I want to become a rabbi.

If I had wanted to involve myself in any other kind of work, I could identify key reasons why I personally would be motivated. Were I to be entering medical school, I could claim that I was doing so out of a desire to help other people to fight illness. Were I to be entering law school, I could claim that I was doing so out of a love for justice and a desire to do my part to ensure that people act justly. Were I to become a garbage man, I could claim that it is important to me to make sure that the streets are clean so as to prevent cities from stinking or being breeding grounds for infectious diseases. In almost any profession, I could label good reasons as to why I was motivated.

When asked why I want to be a rabbi, though, I usually fail to answer. Perhaps I find myself groping for words because, classically, "rabbi" is not really a profession, and I am a bit embarrassed to be studying for what is ostensibly a professional degree for something ideally not a profession! "Rabbi" is an honorable title that a community bestows upon on individual because that's what he is, rather than something generically created the way a lawyer can be created. This rosy picture, however, is an idealization and not the reality in which we American Jews live. Here, we train people to be rabbis, and that's what I want to do, but I still have difficulty in saying why. Were I to invoke Torah study, and the desire to bring Torah to others, I could say that I may do better as the private individual who learns with a *hevruta* (study partner), or a small study group where I would not be distracted by pastoral duties, or simply be written off by compartmentalized individuals who only hear the rabbi say "what he's supposed to say." Were I to invoke pastoral duties and service to individuals, perhaps I'd be more effective as a social worker or nurse. In short, I know of little that a rabbi does that cannot be fulfilled by others.

All this being said, however, I have an inner compulsion to work intimately with a congregation because I have a hunch that I would do well. I want to work incredibly hard and go to sleep with the assurance that I have not wasted the day because I have tried to do the kinds of work the Torah commands to the best of my ability. While studying in yeshiva, I used to go to sleep late, feeling terrible frustration in not understanding a Ran on a *sugya*, [1] yet also a sense of

---

[1] Rabbeinu Nissim of Gerona (1320–1376), known by the Hebrew acronym R"N, wrote extensive commentary on the Talmud that is often appended to the back of most standard printed

accomplishment because my frustration was based on a worthy cause. This kind of frustration was healthy, and I would live well to experience it and much more.

Essay 2—On *Halakha*

I like to think of *halakha* as our attempt to witness God's presence in the world. We say that we are the Chosen People and that we Jews have a special mission: to bring about the kingdom of God here on Earth. I cannot understand this idea unless it is to say that we believe our God-given law to be some step in the actualization of this goal, if not the entire realization in itself. To adhere to *halakha* is to allow God to act through us.

I believe this ideology to be represented in the story of Ruth, whose theme seems to be that "*ḥesed* preserves *'Am Yisra'el* in *Erets Yisra'el*."[2] The word *ḥesed* may be understood in different ways. In rabbinic literature, *ḥesed* seems to be about kindness, as in the term *gemilut ḥasadim*. In the Tanakh, however, according to Dr. Edward Greenstein, the word means "covenantal loyalty." In other words, God rewards or punishes Israel by making continued national existence easier or more difficult. This relationship runs *midah keneged midah* (measure for measure), as the quality of Israel's relationship to God is dependent on national desire to obey. Ruth captures this situation by the story of the restoration of the family of Elimelekh.

Ruth is set in the time when the judges judged, before Israel had a king. This was a time when Israel was put to the test by God, punished with warfare for idolatry and intermarriage, crimes that would erode national integrity. In Ruth, the land suffers famine, probably a punishment for these same crimes, as warned in the second paragraph of the *Shema*. Famine is a slow punishment, the effects of which can be mollified through intense cooperation. As a covenantal punishment, famine gives an errant people a chance to do *teshuvah* (literally, "return," often understood as "repentance"). The story is told on a national and individual level, as the labor to reestablish the seed of Elimelekh on his ancestral portion mirrors the labor of Israel to remain in the Land, retaining its special relationship with God.

In the book of Ruth, acts of *ḥesed* attributed to God are done by people.

---

editions of several of the Talmudic tractates. When Matt writes "a Ran on a *sugya*," he means a commentary by Rabbeinu Nissim on a particular passage of Talmud.

[2] Loving-kindness preserves the people of Israel in the Land of Israel.

Naomi claims that "the hand of God has gone against me," because she has lost what she had before, yet we the readers know that Ruth stands with her and will provide for her. Ruth herself cannot imagine her identity as anyone other than Ruth the Moabitess, as she asks Boaz why he cares for her, "when I am a foreigner?" Boaz recognizes her as an *eshet ḥayil* ("woman of valor"; see Proverbs 31:10–31) because of her deeds and returns her kindness through institutionalized practices such as *pe'ah,*[3] *leqet,*[4] *shikheḥah,*[5] and the redemption of property. In other words, Elimelekh's family may be restored because the main characters of the story act as they are supposed to act. We praise characters like Ruth, Boaz, and Naomi because they are models of *ḥesed* and allow God to act through their initiative. The book ends with a genealogy, as if to show us that the fulfillment of God's plans goes far beyond the individual. The witnessing of God's presence is a task that takes generations to fulfill.

I believe that *halakha* is our attempt to define our own role in the continually unfolding story. Whether a *mitsvah* be technically classified as *ben adam le-makom* (between people and God) or *ben adam le-ḥavero* (between human beings) is of little importance, because all *mitsvot* pertain to both God and humankind. Wearing *tsitsit*, for example, may remind me of my membership in the Jewish community and guide me to act responsibly, while giving *tsedaqah* (money for the needy) may allow me to acknowledge God as king because I fulfill a command to help my fellow human beings. So what role does *halakha* play in my personal lifestyle? *Halakha* is the guiding force in my lifestyle, and I must continually struggle to live up to the standard ordained for me.

ESSAY 3—ON BOOKS READ RECENTLY

I must admit a measure of embarrassment at this question, because I have read very few books lately. The reason why my reading of the past two years is lacking is because I have devoted almost all of my time to Torah study. When I have had spare time and absolutely needed a break, I have read short stories, poetry, and essays. The authors I've read are W. Sommerset Maugham, Gabriel García Márquez, and William Faulkner. Though I've read a number of poems by Yeats, Whitman, and Dylan Thomas, I can't claim to have a favorite poet because

---

[3] The corners of the field to be left for the poor, from Leviticus 19:9, 23:22.

[4] Gleanings of field to be left for the poor, from Leviticus 19: 9, 23:22.

[5] Forgotten sheaves of grain that are to be left for the poor, from Deuteronomy 24:19.

I appreciate individual works and rarely compare one to another. While at Brovender's,[6] a few friends and I would gather for late night readings and allow our imaginations to soar, temporarily escaping from the confines of Efrat into a world of rhythm and color. Analysis was not a priority.

I am currently reading *The Seven Habits of Highly Effective People*, by Stephen R. Covey, at the suggestion of Rabbi Bill Lebeau, and have read through the first habit, Proactivity. The book seems to me a study in common sense, and I appreciate what it offers. Covey defines proactivity as the recognition of responsibility and the ability to act accordingly. Such recognition involves understanding of one's own assets and abilities, strengths and weaknesses. Once a person is equipped with this knowledge, he or she is empowered to recognize these traits in others and to interact in a productive manner. Covey notes that to develop this important recognition is no easy task and requires years of cultivation. He does not write in order to sell a quick-fix solution.

Aside from *The Seven Habits*, I would have to label Sefer Kohelet the most important book [that I've read] in recent memory.[7] Kohelet is important to me, and was the choice topic of a research essay I wrote this year, hopefully as a beginning of further research that the book deserves. The lesson I feel I learned from Kohelet is that the principle of reward and punishment is limited and should not serve as our main motivational force in serving God because we cannot explain the problem of *tsadiq ve-ra lo, rasha ve-tov lo*.[8] After studying Ibn Ezra, Ibn Ghiyyat, and the Ramban, the message I learn from this book is that our ultimate reward *and* punishment for whatever we do are that which we do.

Studying Kohelet was important to me not only because of its message but also for the experience of studying a book of the Tanakh in an involved, intense way. When I was at Brovender's, we analyzed <u>Humash</u> with Rashi and Ramban. Such study was an exercise in close reading and involved thought as to how the *parshan*[9] approached not only the text but the entire ideology of Judaism. At JTS, study of Tanakh was restricted to critical study, outside of a beginner's level class on Ibn Ezra's commentary to Bereshit taught by Dr. Scheindlin. While studying Kohelet, I realized that similar study on a systematic level is necessary

---

[6] Common reference to Yeshivat HaMivtar in Efrat, then led by Rabbi Chaim Brovender, along with Rabbi Shlomo Riskin. Matt studied there 1993–1994.

[7] See the essay in this collection "Innovation under the Sun: Three Approaches to Kohelet," a paper Matt submitted to Professor Raymond Scheindlin at the end of the fall semester, 1995.

[8] A righteous person to whom bad things occur, an evil person to whom good things occur.

[9] Classical commentator on biblical text.

and missing from most yeshiva curricula of which I know. Could it be that I could have some effect in this area? Eventually, I would like to teach *shiurim*[10] not only in *Shas*[11] and *poseqim*,[12] but also Tanakh.

ESSAY 4—ON THE IDEAL JEWISH COMMUNITY

In my mind, the ideal Jewish community conforms to *halakha* under the guide of this generation's *poseqim* and dares to dream. The community must conform to *halakha* because this is the way a Jewish community grows and continues. We define ourselves in relationship to God and constantly try to know God through what we do. Without the guidance of our ancestors and current sages, then, we are no different from any other community in the world. Having established our uniqueness in the world as those who observe the Torah, we need to "take a step backwards" and recognize that we are far from God and have not accomplished the goals of the Torah. Every year we go through Tisha B'Av and Yom Kippur; the former reminds us of our failure, and the latter celebrates our continued effort. If we want to improve ourselves, we must learn from our mistakes and take cues from others.

Learning from others means that we Jews need to study the religions of other peoples with respect, both textually and through dialogue. Through this kind of study, we are enabled to compare different approaches to various problems in life. We enlist others in the process of Tiqun Olam and sharpen our own understanding of ourselves and the wisdom of our own worldview. Furthermore, with advanced knowledge and greater consciousness, we can learn to dream better and more realistic dreams.

I understand "dreaming" as a way in which a community sets goals for itself. The members of a synagogue may meet, for example, and discuss the problem of homelessness. They may decide that the mission of the synagogue over the next few months is to learn about this problem and establish itself as a community resource to help homeless people. Alternatively, the synagogue may decide that it wants to improve the quality of its *tefillah* (prayer) and allocate its resources in that direction. Furthermore, the people who convene to discuss these problems need not be from a synagogue. It could be a Jewish Community Center, or

---

[10] Courses in classical Jewish texts.

[11] The Hebrew acronym SH"S stands for *Shishah Sedarim*, the six orders of the Talmud.

[12] Rabbinic experts in adjudication of *halakha*.

Old Age Home, or Youth Group, or even a family. The important issue is that we Jews understand ourselves as having a stake in what our community does, and we take responsibility for achieving goals greater than our own immediate needs.

As we dream and become more and more aware of problems that require our attention, it is important to remain loyal to *halakha* lest we lose our identity or abandon our attempt to locate God in the world. As one of my friends from Brovender's once said, "We need to develop our awareness and desire to act according to what is *mutar al pi halakha* [permitted, according to Jewish law]. So many people forget and focus exclusively on what is forbidden." We cannot forget that, while acting within the bounds of Jewish law, we can do much good for ourselves, and for the world. After all, we would be unable to see ourselves as a *mamlekhet kohanim ve-goy qadosh*[13] if we believed otherwise.

---

[13] A kingdom of priests and a holy nation (Exodus 19:6).

Part Two
Biblical Scholarship

Why Was Yitzhak Bound?

MATTHEW EISENFELD

UNCERTAINTY AS TO HOW God's promises are to be fulfilled motivates Avraham and Sarah to act in extraordinary ways. Although God promises Avraham that he will father a son who will be his heir in Bereshit 15:4, the covenantal narrative is silent concerning Sarah's role. The story that follows is filled with tragic moments, as Avraham and Sarah accustom themselves to living a life dependent on miracles.

Sarah's awareness of her infertility leads her to recommend to her husband that he take to wife her Egyptian maidservant (16:2). Avraham will sire the child, fulfilling the promise, and Sarah will raise the child of her maidservant. Natural human desire intervenes, however, and Hagar, the maidservant, learns to despise her mistress (16:4). Sarah afflicts Hagar, who flees to the wilderness, only to be returned to the family through divine intervention. She gives birth to Yishmael, yet he is not the child whom God had intended to be Avraham's heir.

In chapter 17, God appears to Avraham once again, announcing this time that Sarah will give birth. Avraham's reaction is laughter—how could such an old couple become parents (17:17)? Avraham is reassured and receives the command to circumcise himself and all males in his house. Though he obeys the command, he seems to harbor a measure of incredulity, and we see in the next chapter that Sarah is unaware of this new promise. For whatever reason, Avraham has neglected to inform her.

Upon hearing that she will give birth after all these years, Sarah reacts as did her husband, with laughter. The reason is the same: how is such a wonderful thing possible? This time God becomes upset, inquires as to the reason for Sarah's disbelief and sends Avraham to rebuke her. When Sarah gives birth a year later (21:2), the happy parents can do nothing but rejoice. However, doubt

Originally published in *Dikhtiv*, December 1995.

colors even this celebration, as Sarah's jubilant declarations of triumph (21:6–7) involve recognition that God has done something unbelievable. Avraham throws a great party on the day Yitzhak is weaned, but on that same day Sarah reacts strongly and forcefully to the sight of Yishmael's playing.

A key word throughout this story is the word *tsehoq,* as it signals this dialectical theme of disbelief and recognition of miracles. *Tsehoq* is the initial reaction of both parents to the news that Sarah will give birth. That Avraham could sire a son through Hagar was understandable, but Sarah? Yitzhak is named accordingly: he is the son of miraculous birth and is walking testimony to God's loyalty and ability to fulfill promises. In 21:9, however, Sarah sees Yishmael *metsaheq* and can no longer tolerate the boy.

The traditional commentators debate the meaning of what Yishmael actually does here. Rashi, motivated by a desire to clear Avraham and Sarah of any wrongdoing, comments that Yishmael is guilty of either murder, idolatry, or a sexual crime, as he says that the word *tsehoq* is an expression for any of these and cites verses to his support. Ramban disagrees with Rashi, noting that the next verse tells us explicitly why Sarah is concerned: he "will not inherit with my son" (v.10). According to Ramban, Yishmael makes fun of Yitzhak on the day he is weaned because he expects to inherit as his father's firstborn son, born in the natural way to a young woman, even though she may not be the woman of the house. The jealousy Yishmael must have felt was unbearable, notes the Ramban, and for this reason Sarah demands his expulsion, lest greater problems arise in the future.

Ibn Ezra offers yet another view, that Yishmael is innocent and merely playing as any boy would play. Sarah then sees him and understands that her son will have to share his inheritance with the son of a woman whom she hates. Perhaps there exists another possibility, inspired by Ibn Ezra. Yishmael is indeed playing as any boy would play, but the choice of the word *metsaheq* is a wordplay on Yitzhak's name. Sarah sees Yishmael taking on the role she wants for her son, perhaps even standing in his place Although Yitzhak is born through a miracle and Yishmael through the laws of nature, she is reminded of her own lingering doubt. Is it possible that this son of a maidservant will stand in the way of her son? God gave her a son, but will he become the man he is destined to be if Yishmael remains in the house? Sarah decides she must take matters into her own hands and demands the expulsion of Hagar and Yishmael.

Avraham is troubled but is reassured by God that Sarah's demand must be met because it is through Yitzhak that the promise will be fulfilled. This "reassurance" must have been crippling to Avraham's conception of himself and his role in life. He had been given a promise and had acted to bring the promise to fruition. His action, however, was not of God's plan as communicated. Yishmael, too, is to become a great nation, for he is of Avraham's seed; however, he will not bear the covenant like Yitzhak. The role he is to play begins to develop as he is saved from death in a miraculous way, but Yishmael effectively leaves the story at this point.

In light of this experience comes the test of the *Akedah* [the binding of Isaac]. Now that the natural threat of Hagar and Yishmael is removed, God plays into Avraham's fears and asks for Yitzhak. As Yitzhak had been given miraculously, God asks for his return by Avraham's hand, that same hand that had acted so decisively in the pursuit of the fulfillment of the promises. On the mountain, a divine messenger tells Avraham that God now knows that Avraham fears God, as if to say that Avraham has finally put all his scheming aside because he has learned to trust. For Sarah, who was not commanded in the *Akedah*, what happens between her husband and son may match her actions measure for measure. As she demanded the banishment of Hagar and Yishmael, resulting in the boy's near death, she too must undergo a similar experience.

The *Akedah* serves as a final teacher to Avraham and Sarah. They were given a special mission, which required their confident participation. For no fault other than human limitation on imagination, they were unable to act as required. God promised them good, and so they acted to bring about this good. Generally, we have a rule that one should not rely on miracles, but here they are promised miracles. In response, God tests Avraham in such a way that he is unable to "improve" or hasten the task given. Avraham seems to have finally learned the lesson toward the end of his life when he sends his servant to find a wife for Yitzhak. When the servant starts to ask logistical questions, Avraham confidently assures him that God will provide.

Catching a Thief: Exodus 22:1–2a

MATTHEW EISENFELD

AFTER PRESENTING A SERIES of laws concerning compensation for damages, the Torah turns to the question of theft in Exodus 21:37–22:3.[1] Theft follows damages, as both concepts involve a loss of property and require restitution; but, as thieves present additional danger to society, the restitution demanded from them is more severe. The Torah requires multiple payment from a thief, as outlined in 21:37 and 22:3. If the thief has stolen an ox or a sheep and slaughtered or sold the animal, he pays fivefold for the ox and fourfold for the sheep. If the animal remains in the thief's possession, then he pays double the value of the animal. These verses prescribing the amount of compensation bracket two verses, 22:1–2, that concern the case of a thief caught in the act. Here, the homeowner is exposed to a dangerous situation, which may prompt his immediate action, and the Torah anticipates his response. The verses read as follows:

> [1]If the thief is found digging into the house and is struck dead, there is no bloodguilt on his account. [2]If the sun has risen upon him, there is bloodguilt on his account. He will make restitution, and if unable, then he will be sold on account of his theft. (my translation)

While 21:37 and 22:3 seem to complement each other, the two middle verses seem to read as an interruption. The RSV [Revised Standard Version] even changes their order, placing verses 1 and 2 after verse 3. Brevard S. Childs suggests that these verses are an interpolation into an older law, but he notes that this

---

Prof. Moshe Greenberg (1928–2010), a preeminent Bible scholar, taught a course on Exodus at the Schechter Institute in Jerusalem in the fall semester, 1995–1996. The course was taught in Hebrew and was open only to Israeli students and students from abroad who had placed in the highest level of Hebrew instruction for non-native Israelis. Since Matt had done so, he was able to enroll in Greenberg's course. Matt submitted this essay to Prof. Greenberg on December 18, 1995.

[1] In the *Biblia Hebraica Stuttgartensia*, this is 22:1–4.

insertion is probably very old as well, writing, "the verses focus attention on the more important problem relating to theft, namely, the loss of life through a resultant act of violence."[2] Umberto Cassuto, on the other hand, maintains that this section always read as written, as he posits that legal sections of the Torah were written to give ethical direction on judicial subjects.[3] The inclusion of these two cases in the law of compensation thereby instructs us as to the values that the Torah wishes to teach in its formulation of these guidelines, namely, that even though a thief is a criminal, society must be concerned for his life as well.

Before discussing the question of the thief who breaks into the house, it is fitting to consider the bracketing verses. Martin Noth explains that the reason a thief pays so much more than the value of what he stole is that theft is more serious than a case of negligence or accidental damage. Theft involves an "evil intent," which cannot go unpunished,[4] and so his restitution to the homeowner, be it double, quadruple, or quintuple, includes in some sense his debt to society. A similar phenomenon appears in Hammurabi's Code, where a thief makes restitution in multiples of the damage. In the Code, however, the thief who cannot pay is put to death.[5] In 22:2b, however, the Torah specifies that the thief who cannot pay is sold as a slave. While one might originally connect this second part of the verse to the case of the break-in, it reads better as a consequence of the thief's inability to pay.[6] The Torah thus opposes Hammurabi's Code concerning restitution. If the thief has a debt to pay to society, let him pay financially, and not with his life.

Exodus 22:1 and 2a present the complementary cases of the thief who breaks into the house at night and the thief who robs by day. The language of the Torah is peculiar, chosen perhaps, as Cassuto would argue, to express its concern for human life. Terms such as *mahteret, damim,* and *zarhah ha-shemesh 'alayv* require explanation, as they describe contrasting situations and the responses legitimated therein. In general, a thief is not sentenced to capital punishment but is held responsible and is required to make amends. The situation in which

---

[2] Brevard S. Childs, *The Book of Exodus: A Critical, Theological Commentary* (Old Testament Library; Philadelphia: Westminster, 1974), 474.

[3] Umberto Cassuto, *A Commentary on the Book of Exodus* (trans. Israel Abrahams; Jerusalem: Magnes Press, Hebrew University, 1967), 282.

[4] Martin Noth, *Exodus: A Commentary* (trans. John S. Bowden; Old Testament Library; Philadelphia: Westminster, 1962), 183.

[5] Code of Hammurabi, 8 and 22, trans. Theophile J. Meek in J. B. Pritchard, ed., *Ancient Near Eastern Texts Relating to the Old Testament* (2nd ed., corr. and enl.; Princeton, NJ: Princeton University Press, 1955), 166, 167.

[6] This view finds support from Ibn Ezra, Ramban, and the NJPS translation.

the Torah allows him to be killed, however, occurs without the benefit of a court. In this case, the individual is permitted to act as a vigilante. The contrasting cases of the two verses are *'im ba-mahteret . . . 'ayn lo damim* (verse 1) and *'im zarhah ha-shemesh 'alayv . . . damim lo* (verse 2a). The word *mahteret* appears only one other time in the Tanakh, in Jeremiah 2:34, where the prophet accuses his audience of wearing garments covered with the blood of the innocent poor who were killed without justification. When he says, *lo' ba-mahteret metsa'tim,* "You did not find them breaking in," he assumes prior understanding of the case. Accordingly, this verse cannot be used to define exactly what this thief does. All the *mefarshim* agree, however, that the verse describes a case where the thief is digging, tunneling his way into the house with the intention to steal. It is also apparent that this action takes place at night, as Ibn Ezra and Shadal refer to the next verse as a proof-text. They and Rabbenu Hannanel cite Job 24:16, *hatar ba-hoshekh batim,* "In the dark they break into houses," as a further indication that this attempted theft occurs at night.[7]

The primary proof-text to understand 22:1 is verse 2a, as *zerihat ha-shemesh* is an expression for sunrise. Other verses that support this understanding include Judges 9:33, 2 Kings 3:22, and 2 Samuel 23:4. Each one of these verses uses the expression in juxtaposition with the word *boqer,* "morning." However, the expression found at the beginning of 22:2 is out of the ordinary, as it reads *'im zarhah ha-shemesh 'alayv,* "if the sun rise upon him." This last word, *'alayv,* becomes the impetus from which Rabbi Ishmael learns a leniency; he interprets the phrase figuratively,[8] as it is impossible that the sun could rise only on this thief. According to a *peshat* reading, however, the expression can stand, as a similar linguistic expression is found in Bereshit 32:32, *Va-yizrah lo ha-shemesh ka-'asher 'avar 'et penu'el,* "and the sun rose as he passed Penuel . . . ." After Jacob has wrestled all night, the sun rises as he returns to camp. While there is a difference between *lo* and *'alayv,* Rabbi Ishmael's question could be asked here as well, as the sun certainly did not rise only for Jacob. In either case, the Torah is talking about an event, namely, sunrise. Perhaps the Torah uses the word *'alayv* as it uses *lo,* or perhaps the Torah uses *'alayv* to describe why the thief is caught. For example, Shadal teaches that, in verse 2, the sun rises while the thief is digging. If this reading is acceptable, then one could say that, if this thief, who started digging at night and was caught because the sun rose before he was finished, is not killed,

---

[7] Ibn Ezra cites this verse in his Short Commentary only.

[8] Mekhilta. "Is it possible that the sun could rise only upon him?" The leniency is that one more case is excluded from the law of *mahteret.* This is to be discussed below.

then all the more so, any thief who breaks in during the day may not be killed. The Torah merely teaches the most extreme leniency.

The opposition of these two cases determines the extent to which the life of this thief is protected. If the thief breaks in at night, *'ayn lo damim*, and the meaning of this pronouncement is debated by the *mefarshim*. While some hold that this thief is "not alive,"[9] others interpret the statement to mean that no restitution is to be exacted from the homeowner, and they read the words to say, "there is no bloodguilt on his account."[10] The first reading is metaphorical and in line with an image that later Jewish law wishes to convey. The *derash* on these words, then, is to read them literally.[11] Shadal argues for this literal reading as he claims that the word *lo* can describe only the thief, and he cites Deuteronomy 22:26, the words *'ayn la-na'ara het' mavet,* "the girl has committed no mortal sin." As the *lamed* describes the girl, who has no sin, so too this thief has no "life," but is a walking dead man.

This reading, however, is forced, as other uses of the word in the Torah refer to a form of justice, and not the legal status of the thief. This technical status of one already dead is introduced in later Jewish law and will be examined below.

The second interpretation, that no vengeance is taken against the killer of the thief, is more in consonance with other uses of the term *damim*. Ibn Ezra refers the term to the homeowner, writing that "there is no bloodshed on his account." In other words, the homeowner is not to be killed for his actions. His proof texts are 2 Samuel 16:8, Leviticus 20:9, and Leviticus 17:14. In all these cases, the word *dam* or *damim* describes someone deserving of capital punishment. Here, too, the word refers to a legal category specific to the incidence of a killing, as used in Deuteronomy 19:10, *ve-lo' yishafekh dam naqi be-qerev 'artsekha . . . ve-hayah 'alekha damim,* "do not shed innocent blood in your land . . . that you incur bloodguilt." If this second reading is accepted, then the Torah seems to be writing shorthand, for what might be *'ayn la-mukah ta'anat damim 'al ba'al ha-bayit,* "The injured party has no claim of bloodshed on the homeowner."

As mentioned above, bloodguilt is a legal status. The Torah legislates in Genesis 9:6 that anyone who kills another is to have his own blood shed. The chiastic structure of this verse seems to suggest that the killer's blood should be shed by

---

[9] Such as Rash, Shadal, and Benno Jacob. Their reasoning is to be explained below.

[10] Such as Ibn Ezra, Rav Saadya Gaon, and Cassuto.

[11] The idea that a *derash* can be a literal reading comes from Dr. Edward Greenstein, "Medieval Commentators," in *Back to the Sources* (ed. Barry Holtz; New York: Summit Books, 1984), 219.

the victim himself,[12] but as this is impossible, the Torah assigns this responsibility to the next of kin who becomes the "blood avenger."[13] As specified in Numbers 35:33–34, blood can only be expiated by blood because murder is an affront to God and pollutes the land in which God dwells. The accidental killer, however, may flee to safety in a Levitical city of refuge (35:11), where he must live until the death of the Kohen Gadol. For the Torah to state here, *'ayn lo damim,* is to say that even though this killing is not accidental, the killer is exempted from these aforementioned laws and need not flee to a Levitical refuge city.

The Torah exempts the killer from bloodguilt in Exodus 22:1 because the killing is an act of self-defense. Even so, such a killing is not recommended, as the Torah employs the passive form of the verb "to strike," *ve-hukah.* The homeowner is not commanded to kill such a thief, but if he happens to do so, he bears no guilt. Cited earlier, Childs explains that the laws of compensation for theft focus attention on the violence, either inherent or actual, involved in an act of theft. If so, the reading of the rabbis of the Gemara, Sanhedrin 72a, is acceptable. They assume that because people defend their property, the thief who breaks in at night is prepared to kill the homeowner, and therefore must be stopped in any way possible.

This case differs from verse 2a, however, where the homeowner is not permitted to kill and is held responsible if he does. According to Targum Onkelos, which translates *'im zarḥah ha-shemesh 'alayv* as *'im 'eyna desahadaya' nefalat 'alohi,* "if the eye of testimony falls upon him," the difference between day and night is witnesses, and the possibility to call for help. Since in the case of the night burglar, the homeowner must stand alone against a thief, he is permitted to kill. During the day, however, when help is available and the homeowner can produce witnesses to bring the thief to court, he is a murderer if he kills. In reality, one can imagine circumstances during the day in which no help is available, or at night when help is available. Accordingly, Cassuto suggests that the Torah merely teaches the general case, but that other circumstances exist in which either law is applicable.[14]

Like the laws of compensation, this law stands in stark contrast to the laws of Hammurabi's Code. In law 21, the Code stipulates, "If a seignior made a breach in a house, they shall put him to death in front of that breach and wall him in." Since the Code views theft as a grave moral offense, the thief is punished severely. The Torah, on the other hand, seeks to protect the thief, allowing him to be killed only in an act of self-defense. At the moment when the possibility of

---

[12] Class lecture, Moshe Greenberg, October 22, 1995.

[13] The existence of a blood avenger is assumed in Numbers 35:12 and Deuteronomy 19:6.

[14] Cassuto, *Commentary on the Book of Exodus,* 282.

society exacting compensation by means of a court, the thief, who is no longer a safety threat, may not be killed. Later Jewish law expanded the discussion of this burglar and, in the rabbis' sometimes metaphoric reading of the text, brought the laws of the Torah to their logical resolution.

The rabbis adopted two metaphorical readings that influence each other. These are readings of the words *damim* and *'im zarḥah ha-shemesh 'alayv*. The second term, as explained above, is ambiguous, as the sun seems to rise on one individual. The idiomatic language prompts the Gemara's question, "Is it that the sun rises on him alone? Rather, just as sun represents peace in the world, so too this case, if it is known that he would act peaceably, then this one is guilty."[15] In other words, if it is clear to the homeowner that the thief will not kill, then the homeowner is not permitted to kill him. The example the Gemara provides is that of a father robbing a son. Alternatively, one could read the *derasha* to say that one may kill only when it is clear that one's life is endangered. The effect of such a reading is to limit further the cases in which a night burglar may be killed, as the rabbis seek to limit the cases where an individual acts as a vigilante.

Understanding this metaphor is an aid to understanding the reading of *'ayn lo damim,* to say that this thief is considered to be already dead. According to Benno Jacob, this reading is a legal fiction created by the Torah in order to avoid the aversion to killing another human being. One may be killed only in the case of great need. To the individual, night burglary is one such case, and to society, one guilty of a capital crime is another case.[16] Mishna Sanhedrin supports Jacob's reading, as it positions the laws concerning this tunneling night burglar between the stubborn and rebellious child and criminals who are permitted to be killed in order to save their victims.[17] A rebellious child is a special case of the Torah in which, according to the rabbis, a boy is put to death *'al shem sofo,* "on account

---

[15] The Gemara's statement, in Sanhedrin 72a, is taken from Mekhilta, where Rabbi Ishmael includes this verse with two other legal verses that he reads as metaphor. The other two are Exodus 21:19 and Deuteronomy 22:17. In Exodus 21:19, the man walking on his staff has regained sufficient health to walk in public. In Deuteronomy, the man who falsely accuses his wife is punished if the matter is "as clear to the judges as cloth."

[16] Benno Jacob, *The Second Book of the Bible: Exodus* (Hoboken, NJ: , Ktav, 1992), 681.

[17] Mishna Sanhedrin, chapter 8. An alternative reading of the latter case would be that it is the criminals themselves who are saved by being killed. They are "saved" in that they are prevented from committing a terrible sin, just as the death of the stubborn, rebellious son is judged according to his end. I have chosen to present the other reading, as I believe the cases of "pursuer" and "on account of the end" to be slightly different. The burglar is put between these two cases because he shares characteristics of both. See the Gemara's discussion, Sanhedrin 72 a-b.

of his end." Though he has not yet committed a capital crime, that he will eventually do so motivates the Torah to stringency.[18] The laws of the pursuing criminal, *din rodef*, involve persons who are involved in a violent action against other people. One may kill a *rodef* to spare the other damage. The tunneling night thief is compared to both cases. On one hand, the thief has not yet committed a capital crime and is judged *'al shem sofo*. On the other hand, since the assumption is that this thief is prepared to kill, he is considered a *rodef*. His status makes him a convenient literary bridge for the Mishna between two similar concepts.

The great innovation of this perspective is that the killing of this thief must somehow be justified, and it is in this understanding that Jacob's point is suggestive. Normally, people are considered of equal value,[19] and, if so, then why should this thief be killed? Unlike in Hammurabi's Code, this thief is not killed because of the act of breaking and entering, or even that of stealing. Rather, the rabbis rule that this thief, because of his end, is considered to be a *rodef*, and therefore it is permissible to kill him. Even though at the moment of his digging, his intention is only to move from the outside to the inside, because of his imputed preparedness to kill, he is compared to one whom a court has sentenced to death. Such a person is considered to be a walking dead man, who, if killed illegitimately, according to Jewish law, is not avenged. Because of the danger this man presents, the Gemara allows for anyone, not only the homeowner, to kill this thief (Sanhedrin 72b). On the other hand, as he is judged *'al shem sofo*, the rabbis look for reasons to overturn the normal assumption that this man is a killer. If they can, then they have saved his life.

As the rabbis read the Torah through metaphor, they have not departed radically from *peshat*. The oral tradition accompanies the written, and the laws are not updated but are more clearly defined. Cassuto had mentioned that circumstances different from the cases listed would call for applications of the laws in Exodus 22:1 and 2a, and so the rabbis merely seek to determine the limits of such cases. A father who robs his son may not be killed, as he is not assumed to be prepared to murder, but perhaps the owner of a house far from the city may kill even during the day. Because the thief is killed out of self-defense, permission to kill him must cease as soon as the homeowner is out of danger. The key motivation for metaphorical reading is the saving of life. As the Torah seeks to protect the lives of both the homeowner and the thief, so the rabbis follow in stride.

---

[18] Deuteronomy 21:18–21. According to the rabbis, the case involves a boy addicted to meat and wine. A modern comparison might be a teenage drug addict.

[19] Sanhedrin 74a: "Who says your blood is redder than his?"

BIBLIOGRAPHY

Childs, Brevard S. *The Book of Exodus: A Critical, Theological Commentary*. Old Testament Library. Philadelphia: Westminster, 1974. Page 474.

Cassuto, Umberto. *A Commentary on the Book of Exodus*. Translated by Israel Abrahams. Jerusalem: Magnes Press, Hebrew University, 1967. Pages 281–83.

Jacob, Benno. *The Second Book of the Bible: Exodus*. Hoboken, NJ: Ktav, 1992. Pages 645, 680–81.

Luzzatto, S. D. (Shadal). *Commentary to the Pentateuch*. Edited by P. Schlesinger. Tel Aviv: Dvir, 1965.

Noth, Martin. *Exodus: A Commentary*. Translated by John S. Bowden. Old Testament Library. Philadelphia: Westminster, 1962. Page 183.

Greenberg, Moshe. "Bloodguilt." In *The Interpreter's Dictionary of the Bible*, edited by George A. Buttrick, 1:449. 4 vols. New York: Abingdon, 1962.

Greenstein, Edward. "Medieval Commentators." In *Back to the Sources*, edited by Barry Holtz. New York: Summit Books, 1984. Pages 219–20.

Talmud Tractate Sanhedrin Chapter 8.

Traditional Torah commentators as found in *Torat Hayyim*. Jerusalem: Mosad HaRav Kook, 1988.

God as Defender of Widows and Orphans

MATTHEW EISENFELD

ALTHOUGH THE LAWS OF THE TORAH legislate to all Israelites and non-idolatrous sojourners among them, ancient Israelite thought imputes an ultimate righteousness to God, which involves special concern for those at the bottom of the social ladder. Accordingly, God is the protector of weak individuals, including the resident alien, the widow, the fatherless child, and the poor. The status of the resident alien and the poor is understandable. Aliens are subject to marginalization by virtue of not being Israelite, while the poor are desperate to acquire basic necessities. It is not immediately clear, however, why widows and orphans are included in this list, especially when the verses in the Book of the Covenant speaking of them in Exodus 22:21–23 read as follows:

> 21 You shall not harm any widow or orphan. 22 If you do mistreat one, and if he cries out to me, then I will surely hear his cry. 23 And My anger will blaze forth, and I will kill you with the sword, and your wives will be widows and your children will be orphans. (my translation)

Not only are widows and orphans given special protection, but they are avenged in a spectacular fashion. God hears the cry of the widow or orphan as surely as the cry of the impoverished debtor whose one garment has been taken as a pledge (Exodus 22:26), yet a severe punishment, extending even beyond the crime is established here. This punishment is not measure for measure. Furthermore, this passage is unique in the Book of the Covenant, in that it alone implicates the entire group.[1] Finally, the responsibility of exacting punishment is not

Presented to Professor Moshe Greenberg, January 28, 1996.

[1] Although verse 20 addresses the audience in the plural, "Because you were aliens in the land

consigned to society, but is taken by God, who will punish through the agency of foreigners.

A first interpretive step is to examine the particular case of the widow and orphan. The commentators offer two distinct but complementary reasons as to why they are included in this list. According to some, the reason the widow and orphan are included is because they are "of lowly spirit."[2] Because they are particularly sad, they are more sensitive to wrongdoing and easily hurt. Others adopt a more economic approach to the issue and state that the problem of widows and orphans is that they lack legal representation, a function performed by adult males.[3] Both positions have integrity and merit further consideration.

That a widow or orphan is "of lowly spirit" finds support in other verses that describe them. The book of Lamentations begins comparing desolate Jerusalem to a widow who sits alone (1:1). Job praises himself as one who "gladdened the heart of the widow" (Job 29:13 NJPS), as he asserts his innocence and injustice of his suffering. Not only did he do nothing to harm her, but he went out of his way to make her happier. He makes a similar claim in 31:16–17, adding that he was a father to the fatherless. Finally, when Naomi and Ruth arrive in Bethlehem, Naomi rebukes the women who surround them, "'Do not call me Naomi,' she replied. 'Call me Mara, for Shaddai has made my lot very bitter. I went away full, and the Lord has brought me back empty. How can you call me Naomi when the Lord has dealt harshly with me, when Shaddai has brought misfortune upon me!'" (Ruth 1:20–21).

The economic approach also finds support from biblical verses. The curses toward the end of the book of Deuteronomy highlight the widow's and orphan's precarious social position, including them with the alien, as 27:19 reads, "Cursed be he who subverts the rights of the stranger, the fatherless and the widow. And the people shall say, Amen." Isaiah decries the lack of legal protection afforded

---

of Egypt," this statement lends additional meaning to the prohibition of oppressing aliens and does not involve group punishment.

[2] Ramban and Dat Mikra, as explained by Amos Hakham, *Hamishah Humshe Torah 'im Perush Rashi ve-'im Da'at Miqra: Sefer Shemot,* vol. 2 (Jerusalem: Mosad Ha-Rav Kook, 1991).

[3] See Umberto Cassuto, *A Commentary on the Book of Exodus* (trans. Israel Abrahams; Jerusalem: Magnes Press, Hebrew University, 1967); Brevard S. Childs, *The Book of Exodus: A Critical, Theological Commentary* (Old Testament Library; Philadelphia: Westminster, 1974); S. R. Driver, *The Book of Exodus: In the Revised Version, with Introduction and Notes* (Cambridge Bible for Schools and Colleges; Cambridge: Cambridge University Press, 1911); Martin Noth, *Exodus: A Commentary* (trans. John S. Bowden; Old Testament Library; Philadelphia: Westminster, 1962); and Dale Patrick, *Old Testament Law* (Atlanta: John Knox, 1985).

them in 1:23, saying, "Your rulers are rogues and cronies of thieves, every one avid for presents and greedy for gifts; they do not judge the case of the orphan, and the widow's cause never reaches them." Similarly, Jeremiah rebukes the king of Judah for his failure to fulfill his responsibility to guarantee justice, saying, "Do what is just and right; rescue from the defrauder him who is robbed; do not wrong the stranger, the fatherless, and the widow" (22:3).

That injustice is so easily committed against widows and orphans is a function of the organization of a patriarchal Israelite society based on tribal loyalty. According to Hanokh Raviv, "the clan was the basic unit of traditional Israelite society,"[4] in which individuals were empowered based on their connection to a family descended from fathers. As a woman's tribal allegiance could change, a widow could find herself abandoned after her husband's death. The tribe supported her because her husband was a member, but after his death, she becomes dependent on extended family and the community.[5] That society is structured in such a fashion is seen in the genealogies and censuses taken throughout the Tanakh. For example, when the Torah reveals the pedigree of Moses and Aaron, it lists the clans from which they come, beginning, "These are the heads of the clans of the sons of Reuben, firstborn of Israel. Hanokh and Falu, Hetsron and Karmi, these are the families of Reuben" (Exodus 6:14; see also Number 26:5–65). Related to the laws of pedigree are the laws of inheritance, which apply in most circumstances to men alone. When the daughters of Zelophehad inherit their father's portion, the elders of the family of Gilead complain to Moses that the clan will lose territory when the women marry (Numbers 36:1), and so they devise a compromise solution, that the women will marry within their clan. Under normal circumstances, land would be bequeathed from father to son, thus remaining in the tribe.

The biblical understanding of God as the protector of the weak reflects ancient Israel's conception of righteousness, most clearly articulated by the prophets.[6] According to Norman Snaith, "There is a deep-seated and fundamental bias at the root of their ethical teaching,"[7] and this bias is in favor of those whom society most easily oppresses. This bias to which Snaith is sensitive opposes

---

[4] Hanokh Raviv, *Ha-Hevrah Be-Mamlekhut Yisra'el ve-Yehudah, Sifriyat Ha'Intsayklopediyah Ha-Miqra'it* (Jerusalem: Mosad Bi'alik, 1993).

[5] Patrick, *Old Testament Law*, 86.

[6] See, for example, Isaiah 1:17; Ezekiel 22:7; Jeremiah 49:11; Malachi 3:5; and others.

[7] Norman H. Snaith, *The Distinctive Ideas of the Old Testament* (New York: Schocken Books, 1964), 68.

an explicit command not to "favor the poor or show deference to the rich" (Leviticus 19:15), and Rashi's explanation of our particular verse says, "this is the law for any person, but the verse addresses the common case." Much of the prophetic teaching, however, does direct itself to the plight of commonly oppressed individuals, most likely because society could measure its own moral success in relation to how they fare.

According to Abraham Joshua Heschel, where societal justice is concerned, God is at stake. In Heschel's words, "People act as they please, doing what they will, abusing the weak, not realizing that they are fighting God, affronting the divine, or that oppression of man is a humiliation of God,"[8] because a society that functions well reinforces faith in Israel's God. Accordingly, God takes a special interest in the weak, not only because they are the measure of whether or not the justice system really works but because their welfare reflects God's own power and effectiveness. Heschel cites Proverbs 14:31, "He who withholds what is due to the poor affronts his Maker; He who shows pity for the needy honors Him," to show that God attaches himself to the downtrodden.[9] In fact, in many verses God personally assumes the role of protector of widows and orphans.

God's provisioning for the weak is multifaceted. For example, God is "the father of orphans, the champion of widows" (Psalm 68:6), "gives courage to the orphan and widow" (Psalm 146:9), and "upholds the cause of the fatherless and the widow" (Deuteronomy 10:18). While our passage addresses the question of oppression, the laws of the Torah command Israelites to provide basic necessities. Deuteronomy 24:19–21 enumerates agricultural laws concerning gleanings of the field, adding in each verse that "it shall go to the stranger, the fatherless, and the widow." In the seven-year cycle of tithing, years 3 and 6 are dedicated to the Levite, alien, widow, and orphan (Deuteronomy 14:29). Furthermore, the widow and orphan are to be fed and included with the community in national festivities (16: 11, 14). Their maintenance and welfare are a religious obligation.

God's role as defender of widows and orphans is articulated clearly and forcefully in our passage, Exodus 22: 21–23. According to Amos Hakham, verse 21 itself employs three grammatical peculiarities that serve as strengthening devices, including the word *kol*, the precedence of subject to verb, and the final *nun* of the word *te'anun*. The first word of the verse, *kol*, seems superfluous, as the law could have been taught without its usage. Ramban is also sensitive to this

---

[8] Abraham Joshua Heschel, *The Prophets* (Philadelphia: Jewish Publication Society, 1962), 198.

[9] Ibid. He also cites 17:5, which reads, "He who mocks the poor insults his Maker."

word but reads it to include "even the rich" widows and orphans. His reading
supports his contention that the primary reason these individuals are given special protection is because they are sad. Hakham's statement that the precedence
of subject to verb strengthens the law is consistent with other apodictic statements of this code, such as the preceding verses 17–20. The final word of this
verse could have been written te'anu. The final nun, then, gives the verse a poetic
flourish that emphasizes that this law requires special attention. As the punishment for this crime is national in character, the law requires highlighting.
Hakham writes that the concept of 'inuyi includes any kind of degradation, and
that "it is forbidden to anger them, belittle them, cause them pain, exploit them,
or cause them to lose money." Another way to understand the verse is to read the
word "choice" as reflective of Israel's experience in Egypt (Exodus 1:11). This
reading more readily connects verse 21 with the preceding verse and arouses the
sympathy of those who have been made to suffer themselves.

Verse 22 contains two primary difficulties, namely, the unfinished conditional clause that begins the verse, and a threefold doubling of words.[10] That this
opening is an unfinished conditional is subject to disagreement among the commentators. According to Rashi, this condition is a terse statement that remains
unfulfilled. Perhaps it remains open as an ideological statement of shock. Hizkuni is more direct, stating that the condition is open because the punishment
is unspecified when the oppressed remains silent. This is also the approach taken
by Ramban and Benno Jacob, though they disagree that this is an unfulfilled
condition. Rather, the victim is heard if and only if he or she cries out to God.
That God reacts to the cry of the oppressed is also reflective of national experience, as it was God's hearing of Israel's cries under Egyptian oppression that
motivates God's first speech to Moses (Exodus 2:23–25). According to Umberto
Cassuto, the opening of this verse is an expression of an oath that God utters, as
if to say, "if you oppress them, so help me I will hear them when they cry out to
me!" Cassuto's explanation complements that of the Ramban, as their common
ground is the understanding that God's help is conditional upon the calling out
of the oppressed, and that it is their initiative that awakens God's anger. Such an
interpretation also accounts for the doubling of the words 'ane te'ane . . . tsa'oq
yits'aq, and shamoa' eshm'a. All of these words are emphatic and promise God's

---

[10] A third difficulty is the interpretation of the word 'oto. The commentators struggle to
establish who the subject of this word is. Who is actually calling to God? I have chosen not to
address this question, but in my opinion, 'oto is the singular form of whatever group calls out to
God, much like the words shor or seh in 21:37.

attention if the abused person calls. On a sociological level, we could understand this cry as the publicizing of the societal problem—that this is in fact a society in which widows and orphans are abused. Such a society is unacceptable, insulting to the honor of God, and calls for divine vengeance.

When the oppressed person calls out to God, God's anger blazes. The words *ve-ḥara 'api* are anthropomorphic, not only because anger is attributed to God but because the expression is visual. Literally, the words mean, "My nostrils will flare," as happens to some people who become angry. This anthropomorphism is compounded with the phrase, *ve-haragti 'etkhem be-ḥarev*, "and I will kill you with the sword," depicting an executioner standing over the offender ready to behead him, and is significant, as it directly identifies God as prepared to avenge the widow and orphan. In the words of Ramban, "You oppress them because they have no savior from your hand, but they are aided more so than any person. Other people bother after their savior to protect them, and after helpers to avenge them, and maybe they will be effective and save them, but maybe not. But this one, with his cry alone is saved by God."

In actual terms, punishment by the sword is usually understood to mean punishment by the hand of a foreign enemy (Rashi, Benno Jacob). As a result of the men's death in battle, their wives are left widows and their children orphans, establishing what Dale Patrick calls, "poetic justice." This justice is poetic because it is not actual but much more severe than the crime. Why should oppression be punished so strictly? Furthermore, this law sounds much like the laws of Hammurabi's Code, according to which a builder's son is executed if the building he built collapses on the son of a seignior.[11]

A compelling answer is offered by Shadal, who argues that this section, including verse 20, pulls at one's heartstrings in order to inculcate a merciful personality. Shadal argues that the laws concerning the alien, as well as the laws of the widow and orphan, are articulated in such a way as to connect to one's own experience. Israel remembers what it was like to live as aliens in Egypt, and so individuals should refrain from abusing the alien because they understand the evil they commit. The same people are commanded not to oppress widows and orphans—they should picture their own wives as widows and children as orphans to comprehend the evil that they do. Like Rashi, Shadal argues that these laws do not apply to these particular groups alone, but to all people, as the intention

---

[11] Law #230. Translated by Theophile J. Meek in James B. Pritchard, ed., *Ancient Near Eastern Texts Relating to the Old Testament* (3rd ed.; Princeton, NJ: Princeton University Press, 1969).

of the Torah is to teach moral behavior through involving individuals personally in the results of acts they commit. Further strengthening of this approach derives from the fact that it is a foreign enemy that becomes the "rod of God's anger." As the widow, orphan, and alien are people without representation in society, so too the families of the oppressors are made into people without representation.

As stated above, Hizkuni noted that this section, verses 21–23, is the only section of the Book of the Covenant whose punishment is phrased in the plural. Given many of the ideas mentioned above, it is possible to posit some reasons for this. Ibn Ezra attempts to solve this problem by linking the individual who harms a widow or orphan to the ones who witness and remain silent. Under such circumstances, all of society is guilty and deserving of punishment. Another approach is that of Shadal, to claim that the Torah wants to teach sensitivity and so uses an example in which the individual imagines his own wife and children taken advantage of by strangers—but, in actuality, the law is the same for all persons. Perhaps most compelling, though, is the approach of Heschel and Snaith, who claim that the treatment of the weak is the measuring rod of societal justice and is exemplary of the fulfillment of God's will. In the words of Snaith,

> Inasmuch, therefore, as it is God's concern to establish *tsedeq* (righteousness) in the land, He must perforce pay particular attention to the case of the poor and outcast, the widow and the orphan. . . . It is incidental that *tsedeq* stands for justice. It is incidental because *tsedeq* actually stands for the establishment of God's will in the land, and secondarily for justice, because that in part is God's will.[12]

As Heschel phrases this conviction, Abraham was chosen not because he knew how to build pyramids, altars, and temples but "in order that he may charge his children and his household after him to keep the way of the Lord, by doing righteousness and justice (Genesis 18:18–19)."[13] In other words, protection of the weak is and must always be a societal concern if the society is to identify itself as reflective of the will of God.

Finally, the three verses, Exodus 11:21–23, come close to chiastic structure. The section begins, *kol 'almanah ve-yatom lo te'anun*, with the subject preceding the verb. The chiasmus is then interrupted by verse 22, whose threefold doubling calls special attention to this law. The turning point of this case is the cry of the

---

[12] Snaith, *Exodus*, 69–70.
[13] Heschel, *Prophets*, 210.

oppressed, which awakens God's anger. Verse 23 then continues, *ve-ḥara 'api ve-haragti 'etkhem be-ḥarev*. These words parallel *lo te'anun* from verse 21. Then, the conclusion, *ve-hayu nesheykhem 'almanot u-veneykhem yetomim*, parallels the beginning of this section. Just as you oppressed people who seemed to have no protector, I will punish you personally and no man will protect you from Me. Just as your society failed to protect the rights of the weak, so your society will be destroyed and will be ruled by strangers. Under their captivity, your wives and children will be subject to the same treatment that you allowed to the members of your society. The structure highlights the societal nature of the crime and identifies God as the personal defender of the weak. As God cares enough to take note of even the most marginal persons, so too the Israelite should be trained likewise.

BIBLIOGRAPHY

Cassuto, Umberto. *A Commentary on the Book of Exodus*. Translated by Israel Abrahams. Jerusalem: Magnes Press, Hebrew University, 1967.

Childs, Brevard. *The Book of Exodus: A Critical, Theological Commentary*. Old Testament Library. Philadelphia: Westminster, 1974. Page 478.

Driver, S. R. *The Book of Exodus: In the Revised Version, with Introduction and Notes*. Cambridge Bible for Schools and Colleges. Cambridge: Cambridge University Press, 1911.

Hakham, Amos. *Ḥamishah Ḥumshe Torah 'im Perush Rashi ve-'im Da'at Miqra: Sefer Shemot*, vol. 2 (Jerusalem: Mosad Ha-Rav Kook, 1991).

Heschel, Abraham Joshua. *The Prophets*. Philadelphia: Jewish Publication Society of America, 1974. Pages 198, 210.

Jacob, Benno. *The Second Book of the Bible: Exodus*. Hoboken, NJ: Ktav, 1992. Pages 704, 705.

Kaufmann, Yehezkel. *The Religion of Israel*. Translated by Moshe Greenberg. New York: Schocken Books, 1972. Pages 321, 322.

Luzzatto, S. D. (Shadal). *Commentary to the Pentateuch*. Edited by P. Schlesinger. Tel Aviv: Dvir, 1965.

Noth, Martin. *Exodus: A Commentary*. Translated by John S. Bowden. Old Testament Library. Philadelphia: Westminster, 1962. Page 186.

Patrick, Dale. *Old Testament Law*. Atlanta: John Knox, 1985. Pages 85–86.

Snaith, Norman H. *Distinctive Ideas of the Old Testament*. New York: Schocken Books, 1964. Pages 68–70.

Raviv, Hanokh. *Ha-Ḥevrah Be-Mamlekhut Yisra'el ve-Yehudah, Sifriyat Ha-'Intsiklopediyah Ha-Miqra'it.* Jerusalem: Mosad Bi'alik, 1993. Pages 43–60.
Traditional Torah commentators as found in *Torat Ḥayyim.* Jerusalem: Mosad HaRav Kook, 1988.

Samuel and the Evolution of the Prophet-Judge

MATTHEW EISENFELD

IF BY THE TERM "TRAGEDY" we understand that a story's hero possesses some flaw that brings about his or her downfall, then we cannot call Samuel the "tragic figure of the book which bears his name." Although Samuel's role is diminished from that of prophet-priest-political leader to that of prophet over the course of the narrative, Samuel does not lose the respect Israel shows him, nor does he lose God's favor. Samuel's problem is that his kind of leadership represents the Old Order, or what Yehezkel Kaufmann calls "prophetic theocracy," which is showcased in the book of Judges.[1] Previously, Israel lived on a precarious cycle of apostasy–servitude–repentance–salvation, relying on God to save her from her enemies' hands, only to degenerate further in succeeding generations. Now, the people come to the prophet and demand a king, who will "judge us, like all the nations" (1 Samuel 8:5). The people want a visible symbol of their unity, around whom they can rally in times of crisis. This move stands as a rejection of the model of Judges because the people no longer wish to rely on their righteousness alone to save them from their enemies. In opposing the people's desire to change their national orientation from a kingdom of God fostered by repentance to a kingdom of Man strengthened by a military, Samuel reveals his pathos, which is actually the pathos of a God whose ideal desire has failed. Instead of living a life of repentance, the people will instead turn to "vain things" (1 Samuel 12:21). However, the model of divine leadership strengthened by the

---

This paper was originally a midterm essay that Matt submitted to Prof. Edward Greenstein in spring 1995.

[1] Yehezkel Kaufmann, *The Religion of Israel* (trans. Moshe Greenberg; New York: Schocken Books, 1972), 262.

people's righteousness does not completely depart from Israel, as the king will still be subject to God's supervision.

Samuel represents the Old Order in that his leadership is based on prophecy granted because of an outcry. In the book of Judges, God raises a judge when Israel "cries to the Lord," as exemplified by the stories of Othniel (Judges 3:9) and Deborah (Judges 4:3).[2] In Samuel's story, however, the initial outcry comes not from Israel but from Hannah, the prophet's mother, and from the beginning, it appears as if the prophetic theocracy is about to be reinaugurated. The barren Hannah, who takes the initiative to pray for "a man child" whom she will give "to the Lord all the days of his life, and no razor shall come upon his head" (1 Samuel 1:11), parallels the barren wife of Manoah (Judges 13). Significantly, Hannah is active where her predecessor is passive; whereas Samson is like a hint to Israel, a judge who is apparently created in order that Israel might be inspired, Samuel is born through his mother's inspiration. The story of his birth reads like a reversal of Israel's current trend toward degeneracy. The people had degenerated to the point where God had needed to create judges from the womb. Now, a lone individual initiates a change.

Samuel's first speech to Israel reflects the prophetic theocratic ideology of the book of Judges, as he promises deliverance from the Philistines conditional upon Israel's covenantal loyalty (1 Samuel 7:3). This ascendancy to power reads much like a story from Judges.[3] The Ark of the Covenant has been returned and remains in Qiryat-ye'arim, "and all the house of Israel sighed after the Lord" (1 Samuel 7:2) Samuel delivers his speech and gathers Israel together at Mizpa, where the Philistines attack. The people charge their leader saying, "Cease not to cry to the Lord our God for us, that he will save us out of the hand of the Philistines!" (1 Samuel 7:8). After Samuel offers a sacrifice, God thunders upon the Philistines and they are defeated. Samuel marks the location with a stone, which he names Even-ha'ezer, to commemorate God's saving Israel, harking back to stories such as Samson's naming of Ramat-lehi and En-haqqore (Judges 15:17, 19).[4] The chapter closes with a remark that "Samuel judged Israel all the days of

---

[2] So too Ehud, Gideon, and the others.

[3] James Ackerman notes a difference—that "Israel needs no charismatic warrior leader when they are in a right relationship with God" ("Who Can Stand before YHWH, This Holy God? A Reading of I Samuel 1–15," *Prooftexts* 11 [1991]: 8–9). This comment strengthens my argument because it reveals a Samuel who is even more successful than the judges during their term of office; however, if Israel is true to form, then there will be a corresponding hard fall.

[4] Ramat-lehi is named for the jawbone with which Samson killed a thousand Philistines and En-haqqore is named for the well that sprang from a rock at his request.

his life" (1 Samuel 7:15) and then goes on to describe Samuel's circuitous travel in order to fulfill his job. Samuel's term of office is marked by vigorous leadership along this model of how things go well when Israel turns to God.

The next chapter informs us that Israel is in danger of completing her historical cycle—that as she rose turning to God, she will backslide and lose divine favor. Having anticipated the question of succession, Samuel has appointed his sons to judge after him, much as his master, Eli, had done. Like Eli, however, Samuel's sons "walked not in his ways, but turned aside after unjust gain, and took bribes, and perverted justice" (1 Samuel 8:3). Not only did Samuel reinvigorate the glory of God's leadership, but he has also planted the seeds of Israel's downfall in appointing new leaders who would lose divine favor. Yet, as Joel Rosenberg notes, monarchy as a solution is a somewhat ironic request.[5] If the elders who approach Samuel fear the results of bad succession, what guarantee do they have that a king's sons will rule in justice?

The reasons for Samuel's negative reaction to Israel's request for monarchy seem unclear. James Ackerman suggests that the prophet reacts to the words "Give us a king to judge us" rather than, "like all the nations" (1 Samuel 8:6) because he is personally offended at the prospect of being replaced[6] and requires consolation from God. Yet Ackerman also reads Samuel's sending the people home after God has agreed to give Israel a king as a refusal to fulfill the divine command. If Samuel has been instructed not to be offended, he should fulfill his charge. Rather, aside from taking offense, Samuel understands the extent to which a king will abuse the power bestowed upon him, and he goes into great detail to warn the people about the results of this choice. Furthermore, God's statement that the people have rejected Him implies that they understand the monarchy as an answer to prophetic theocracy, because reliance upon divine support is too difficult.

Chapter 12 contributes to further understanding of Samuel's opposition when he warns the people not to turn from following God, "for then you should go after vain things, which cannot profit nor deliver; for they are vain" (v. 21). Although God has agreed to change the current form of government, Samuel warns the people against putting too much trust in this ruler of flesh and blood. When the people had made their original request, they had asked for a king, "that we may also be like all the nations; and that our king may judge us, and go

---

[5] Joel Rosenberg, "1 and 2 Samuel," in *The Literary Guide to the Bible* (ed. Robert Alter and Frank Kermode; Cambridge, MA: Belknap Press of Harvard University Press, 1987), 126.

[6] Ackerman, "Who Can Stand," 10.

out before us, and fight our battles" (1 Samuel 8:20). Even though God will grant a king, the people now risk losing their focus as to how to live as God's people. Israel is Israel not because of strength but because of covenantal devotion to God, which is now at risk when the people voluntarily introduce a new leader to whom they must devote themselves.

Israel manages to develop a monarchy, however, that retains facets of the prophetic theocracy—enough that, as Yehezkel Kaufmann comments, no prophetic opposition is shown to the monarchy after chapter 12.[7] From the beginning of the next chapter to the end of the Tanakh, the monarchy represents the grace of God in preserving the Israelite people.[8] Under kings, Israel prospers, managing to retain political independence and national distinctiveness. In the formation of this new system of national government, Samuel is far from a passive participant, but actively involves himself in the workings of the early monarchy. To be sure, he acts under God's commands, but in this regard, his role is no different from the old role that he played.

Ackerman notes that God sets out to make Israel's monarchy different from those of other nations in giving the new king the title *nagid*.[9] Explaining the implications of this term, Ackerman writes, "Through accommodating to their request YHWH keeps control of the situation. Israel has its leader; but both leader and people will still be subject to YHWH in a covenant relationship."[10] Samuel acts as God's mouth in explaining exactly how this new leadership is to function. In chapter 10, he "told the people the rules of the kingdom, and wrote it in a book, and laid it up before the Lord" (v. 25). This kingdom is to function according to God's laws, and not according to a king's whim. In chapter 12, Samuel warns the people one last time about the danger they have incurred in choosing monarchy over the old theocracy, but he assures them that things will continue to go well for Israel as long as the people continue to fear God. In other words, though the institution of leadership has changed, Israel is promised that her welfare still depends on gaining or losing divine favor. As for his own part, Samuel assures the people that he will not cease to pray for their welfare (1 Samuel 12:23). Thus, the monarchy is established as a new institution that will strengthen the nation who will continue to follow God. As Kaufmann writes, "Henceforth, the apostle (prophet) was no longer sent to 'judge' and deliver, but

---

[7] Kaufmann, *Religion of Israel,* 263.
[8] Ibid., 265.
[9] Ackerman, "Who Can Stand," 11.
[10] Ibid., 11–12.

to anoint YHWH's elect, to rebuke him, or oppose him. Thus the ancient prophetic theocracy came to an end."[11] From this moment on, Samuel adopts a role in which he rebukes Saul, announces the end of his reign, and anoints David to rule in his place.

For all of his activity and effort to support and build Israel, Samuel is not a tragic figure. The one way in which one could view him as tragic is that the king with whom he is most involved fails. Samuel will cry the whole night through for Saul, probably beseeching God to relent and forgive the errant king but to no avail. Instead, he is instructed to anoint David, who will eventually merit an everlasting covenant for his dynasty. Yet, although Samuel is forced to inform Saul of his imminent downfall, he personally will not live to see Saul's final demise and it is his ghost that will speak to the doomed Saul on the eve of his death. Eventually, the kings will commit all the trespasses against which Samuel warned in chapter 8, yet they will also come to symbolize Israel's national strength and protect the people's independence, thus benefiting the people more than the previously perceived benefits of prophetic theocracy.

---

[11] Kaufmann, *Religion of Israel,* 262.

Reflections on "Innovation Under the Sun"

DR. RAYMOND SCHEINDLIN

MATT TOOK MY COURSE on Abraham Ibn Ezra's Bible commentary in the fall term of 1994. Toward the end of the term he asked whether I would be willing to supervise an independent study; he told me that Kohelet was a long-term project of his and he wanted me to help him with medieval commentators. We decided that he would study the commentaries of Abraham Ibn Ezra and Isaac Ibn Ghiyyat and write a paper; eventually he added Ramban to the source material as well. We met regularly to go over passages in the commentaries and sometimes just to chat about the book and about life. It was clear that he had studied the book a good bit on his own, and it was his intention to continue to study the book from every angle. He had made it one of the focal points of his studies of Judaica in general, and he expected to go on to deal with it in other ways in the years ahead. I don't know what he did with Kohelet in Israel before his death.

Nor do I know exactly why he was so focused on the book. He was a young man with promise, energy, and, as I later learned, love; he seemed to be an optimist. Kohelet is a gloomy work, a book famous for its pessimism, even cynicism. Nor does it easily allow itself to be assimilated into the outlook of rabbinic Judaism of which Matt was such a committed devotee.

I dealt with the shock of his death by putting my energies into speculating on that very question, reading and rereading the book to try to determine what it might have been that spurred and sustained his interest in it, that made him

Excerpts from reflections on Matt's "Innovation Under the Sun," by Dr. Raymond P. Scheindlin, Professor of Medieval Hebrew Literature and Director of Shalom Spiegel Institute of Medieval Hebrew Poetry at the Jewish Theological Seminary; delivered at the JTS Shloshim ceremony in memory of Matt and Sara, March 29, 1996.

imagine it as an intellectual companion for the long term. Of course, on one level, it may simply have been that he enjoyed the sheer intellectual and spiritual challenge of resisting the book's seductive gloom. Or maybe he was determined somehow to redeem the book, to ponder it until he had come up with the interpretation that would save it—and its readers—from destructive potential. Or perhaps the book presented some attraction to him that I cannot fathom because I did not know him well enough. Perhaps he himself did not know why the book fascinated him; perhaps he studied it with such determination in order to find out.

Innovation Under the Sun:
Three Approaches to Sefer Kohelet

MATTHEW EISENFELD

INTRODUCTION

THIS PAPER IS AN INVESTIGATION of the methodologies of three of the great Bible commentators (*mefarshim*) of Sefarad, Rabbis Yitshak ben Yehudah Ibn Ghiyyat (1038–1089), Abraham Ibn Ezra (1089–1164), and Moses ben Nahman, or Nahmanides (Ramban, 1194–1270), and of how they understand *Sefer Kohelet* (the book of Ecclesiastes). I will attempt to determine what metho odology each employs, and how these differing methodologies produce content. Due to the vast amount of material they write about *Sefer Kohelet,* I will confine this examination to sections I believe pivotal for understanding the differences between these commentators and their overall understanding of the message of Kohelet. I will begin as they begin, examining the questions they present in their introductions and then move to particular passages in their works. In Ibn Ezra and Ibn Ghiyyat, this examination takes the form of a close reading of Kohelet 2:12–26, and I will evaluate the three lessons the Ramban believes the book to teach. The Ramban did not write a line-by-line commentary as did Ibn Ezra and Ibn Ghiyyat, but a *derashah,* or sermon, in which he explains individual verses and then attempts to explain the purpose of the book as a whole. His *Derashah al Divre Kohelet* addresses many of the issues raised by the other two commenta-tors and is worthy of comparison despite the radical difference in form.

In the spring 1995 semester, Matt completed an independent study with Professor Raymond Scheindlin on the Book of Kohelet (Ecclesiastes). It is not clear why Matt was so taken with Kohelet, but he was considering further study of Kohelet as the focus of future graduate studies in Bible. The paper that follows was to be the beginning of further research into this complex book of the Bible.

I chose to study Kohelet because it is a book with which I have been fascinated for the past three years. Kohelet is a difficult book, complicated in its own right and even more mysterious when viewed in the context of the rest of the Tanakh, where it appears as an ideological outsider. I became curious as to how this book is read in the rabbinic tradition and wanted to begin a program of study that would raise new and better questions as the study progressed. This paper represents the beginning of my inquiry.

The study led me to ask the question of how a *parshan* reads a text and why. By the time the medieval *mefarshim* began their individual endeavors to explain the books of the Tanakh they were operating within a tradition that had long written about the books to which they now sought to introduce innovative understandings. Existing side by side in these communities were the concepts of the *peshat* and *derash* of the text. *Peshat* can be understood as the meaning the author intended,[1] but such a definition often cannot be attained. Another way, then, to understand *peshat* is as the contextual meaning of a passage.[2] *Derash,* on the other hand, is an exegetical method that uses the words of the text as a starting point to teach lessons not bound by the context of the passage. While these definitions may seem straightforward, the boundary marking where *peshat* ends and *derash* begins was often obscured, as these communities were raised with the *midrashim* of the classical rabbis. Sometimes the community had become so attached to a *midrash* that this teaching became accepted as the *peshat.* Adding to the confusion, some *midrashim* actually claim to represent the true contextual meaning of a verse that would remain inaccessible were the lesson not taught! The problem was so ingrained in the medieval world that *mefarshim* such as R. Abraham Ibn Ezra of Sefarad and R. Shemuel ben Meir (Rashbam [1085?–1174?]) of Ashkenaz saw need to write almost exclusively about *peshat* and to announce to the rest of the Jewish world that this was what they, and sometimes only they, would do. *Derash* had become the standard approach through which Jews understood their texts, and these *mefarshim* sought to broaden their understanding by searching for a different level of meaning.

The three *mefarshim* introduced in this paper can be characterized according to their use (or ignoring) of *midrash.* Ibn Ghiyyat, for example, may be the most conservative of the three commentators. Even when confronted with the

---

[1] I heard this definition from Baruch Feldstern in a class at Machon Pardes in Jerusalem in the summer of 1992.

[2] Edward L. Greenstein, "Medieval Bible Commentaries," in *Back to the Sources: Reading the Classic Jewish Texts,* ed. Barry Holtz (New York: Summit Books, 1964), 220.

philosophy and science of his day, he seeks to explain Kohelet along with the rabbis. His explanation takes on a philosophical flavor backed by grammatical analysis, sometimes changing what appears to be the simple meaning of a *midrash*. To Ibn Ghiyyat, it was inconceivable that the rabbis should represent a system of thought less sophisticated than the philosophy he had studied. *Midrash* must therefore be at least in accordance with the best of philosophy.

Ibn Ezra, as mentioned above, was primarily a *peshat* commentator seeking to explain Scripture in an objective fashion. *Midrash*, by its acontextual nature, was incapable of serving this function. Nevertheless, when faced with the numerous difficulties of Kohelet, Ibn Ezra relies on philosophy to save his objective commentary. In his approach, philosophy replaces *midrash* because philosophy, like grammar, is an objective science.

The Ramban may be the most critical and innovative of the three in his use of *midrash*. For him, *derash* need not be seen as a contextual method of exegesis, but as an intercontextual approach to study. As a book of the Tanakh, Kohelet must fit somehow into the Tanakh's ideological scheme and share ideas found in other books. The Ramban will accept and reject the rabbis' *derashot* based on his ability to defend them.[3]

PART 1: COMPARISON OF INTRODUCTIONS

In addressing the question of how a *parshan* reads a text and why, it is most helpful to read what the author of a commentary himself writes about his work. Medieval Sefardi *mefarshim* wrote introductions to their commentaries,[4] which read as statements of purpose and sometimes tell us what criteria inform the investigation of the book they read. Because Kohelet is a book of the Tanakh, the *mefarshim* all confront the question as to what it comes to teach, and what makes this problematic book part of the "Holy" Scripture. They are not alone in this endeavor, as the rabbis of the Talmud asked many of the same questions. Mishnah 3:5 of Tractate Yadaim presents a controversy as to whether or not Kohelet "defiles the hands," indicating whether such a book falls within the

---

[3] See *Vikuah ha-Ramban* in *Kitve Ramban,* vol. 1, ed. C. Chavel (Jerusalem: Mosad Harav Kook, 1963), 306. The Ramban notes that a Jew need not believe all *midrashim*.

[4] Uriel Simon, lecture, "Ibn Ezra and Rashbam: Different Approaches to *Peshat*," April 2, 1995, at the Jewish Theological Seminary. Dr. Simon noted that the writing of introductions was customary in Sefarad, whereas Ashkenazi writers such as Rashi or Rashbam generally began with the first verse of a text.

canon of sacred texts.[5] A discussion found in Shabbat 30b announces that "the sages sought to suppress *Sefer Kohelet* because its words contradict one another." Connected to this fundamental question are issues of authorship; while the sages agree that King Solomon is the writer of Kohelet, why is his identity important? Finally, all the commentators raise personal issues, whether arising from curiosity or necessitated from their style.

Ibn Ghiyyat[6]

Rabbi Yitshak ben Yehudah Ibn Ghiyyat was the chief rabbinic authority of Lucena, where he served as *Rosh Yeshiva*. He became famous as a Talmudist and wrote compendia of Jewish law that preserve otherwise lost quotations from the *geonim* and customs particular to Sephardi Jewry.[7] Like other educated Sefardi Jews, Ibn Ghiyyat was trained in philosophy and poetry, and he became a literary giant as well as a Talmudist and *parshan*.[8] Ibn Ghiyyat indicates to the reader what he believes *Sefer Kohelet* teaches by the very title he chooses for his commentary, *Sefer Ha-Prishut*, "the Book of Asceticism," or "Separation."

Ibn Ghiyyat believes Kohelet to be a book that seeks to explain certain attitudes necessary for proper fulfillment of the precepts of the Torah. He writes that Kohelet addresses every academic field in existence, that in it one finds issues of science, theology, philosophy, geometry, and so on. In fact, because of its intricacies, Kohelet may demand commentary more than any other book of the Tanakh! Like other books of the Prophets and Writings, however, Kohelet is opaque to the student for lack of explanation. Ibn Ghiyyat's mission as a *parshan*, then, is to clarify the words and ideas presented in order that valuable lessons not be lost.

---

[5] The issue at stake concerns a rabbinic pronouncement that books of the Tanakh "rendered the hands ritually impure," requiring washing after their handling, or, more important for the real issue, forbidding the *kohanim* (priests) from storing their tithes in proximity to the books (and thus attracting mice).

[6] Unlike the other two *mefarshim* to be compared in this paper, Ibn Ghiyyat wrote in Arabic and was translated into modern Hebrew by R. Yosef Kafah in 1962, who mistakenly attributes his commentary to Rav Saadiah Gaon. The commentary is published in a collection called *Hamesh Megillot*. R. Kafah's is the translation from which I have worked (*Hamesh Megillot* [Jerusalem: Institute for the Preservation of Sacred Texts of Yemen, 1962, now available online at http://www.hebrewbooks.org/39855).

[7] See "Ibn Ghayyat (Ghiyyat)," *Encyclopedia Judaica* 8:1175–76.

[8] See Eliyahu Ashtor, *The Jews of Moslem Spain*, vol. 2 (trans. Aaron Klein and Jenny Machlowitz Klein; Philadelphia: Jewish Publication Society, 1979), 144–49.

Outlining his methodology, Ibn Ghiyyat writes that in order properly to understand an idea the reader must have a complete grasp of the meanings of the words chosen and their connotations in context. The *parshan* must pay careful attention to grammar throughout his commentary, and Ibn Ghiyyat relies heavily on verses from other books of the Tanakh to exemplify similar uses of a word. Furthermore, he defines eight propositions that he feels must inform the student throughout the reading of the commentary. These eight include (1) the author of Kohelet; (2) understanding the book's name; (3) the identity of the writer and the time; (4) Kohelet's place among the other books of the Tanakh; (5) whether the content of the book is from the author's own wisdom or from *ha-qodesh* (holy spirit); (6) whether the message of the book is novel or was known previously; (7) the principles upon which the book is written; (8) explanation concerning the scope of the message. Ibn Ghiyyat then continues to explain each proposition.

From the start, we see that Ibn Ghiyyat will remain true to the rabbinic tradition of interpretation, locating the writing and redaction of Kohelet as do his predecessors. Ibn Ghiyyat explains why he remains loyal to rabbinic *midrash* in the first five of his propositions. In his first proposition, Ibn Ghiyyat writes that everyone agrees that the author of Kohelet is King Solomon. His proof-texts for this conclusion are the first and twelfth verses of the book, the first of which identifies the writer as "Kohelet son of David, king in Jerusalem," while the other tells us that "I Kohelet was king of Israel in Jerusalem." Solomon was the only of David's sons to rule over all of Israel. The second proposition is that the name, "Kohelet" refers to one who gathers people together. This statement is helpful not only in explanation of the name of the book but also in understanding the importance of the attribution of the book to Solomon. Following the *midrash* (*Kohelet Rabbah* 1:1), Ibn Ghiyyat cites the verse, *'az yaqhel Shlomo,* "Then Solomon gathered" (1 Kings 8:1), which refers to Solomon's gathering the elders and tribal heads of Israel together to begin the dedication of the Temple. The dominant idea is that Solomon is one who brings people together to introduce them to holiness, whether it be to inaugurate the Temple or to teach wisdom. In both instances, Israel receives new instruction.

While the first two propositions identified Solomon as a teacher, the next three establish a precedent for interpretation. The third proposition is that Kohelet was copied down into the text we now have before us by "King Hezekiah and his men." This comment follows the Gemara that states in Bava Batra 15a, "Hezekiah and his men copied Isaiah, Proverbs, Shir Ha-Shirim and Kohelet."

This statement itself is based on a verse from the book of Proverbs that reads, "These are also Proverbs of Solomon, which the men of Hezekiah, king of Judah copied" (25:1). Identification with the position of the Gemara connects with other issues Ibn Ghiyyat raises, namely, the next two propositions. Kohelet is at the same level of *qedushah* (holiness) as other books within the Tanakh. As they were all written with *ha-qodesh* so too Kohelet was written with *ha-qodesh*. Ibn Ghiyyat understands *ha-qodesh* as a gift from God in which one acquires the ability to understand hidden wisdom and then make it accessible to the rest of the community. In other words, the prophet prophesies or sage expounds in order to teach. Therefore, just as the rabbis explained other books of the Tanakh as containing normative instruction, Ibn Ghiyyat is careful to treat Kohelet in the same fashion and writes to make Solomon's wisdom more accessible.

The next three propositions instruct the student as to how to understand the content of Solomon's message. Ibn Ghiyyat's sixth proposition is that, though the instruction that Kohelet teaches is not new, the way of *prishut*, or separation from worldly pleasure, was never before taught as clearly, or with such emphasis. Here, Ibn Ghiyyat quotes a statement found in Yevamot 21a: "Ulla said in the name of R. Eliezer. 'At first, the Torah resembled a box without handles, until Solomon came and affixed upon it handles.'" In Yevamot, this statement appears in discussion of the issue of *shniot*, or rabbinic additions to the Torah's list of sexual prohibitions. There, the Gemara emphasizes the seriousness of rabbinic injunctions designed to protect Torah law and exemplifies Solomon, who in Eruvin (21b) is said to have ordained the laws of *'eruvin*[9] and washing of hands before eating.[10] Just as Solomon championed rabbinic law to keep one far from trampling the law of the Torah itself, so too Solomon wrote Kohelet to inculcate the correct attitude with which one should live a life of *mitsvot,* thereby successfully grasping and holding the Torah. The correct degree of separation from the world protects one from overinvolvement in wordly affairs and keeps one far from sin.

Ibn Ghiyyat's seventh proposition is that every person must acquire *hokhmah* through which one will come to recognize the truth of God and the

---

[9] An *'eruv* is a legal convention in which two or more houses are joined together to create one large private dwelling. Such a convention is important, as it permits the act of carrying objects from one house to another on the Sabbath.

[10] This protects a member of the priesthood from defiling his tithes, which must be eaten in purity. Here, Solomon has made the act of hand washing obligatory for everybody, reducing the chances that the priest will actually defile his sacred food.

mitsvot. For this reason, *ḥokhmah* is a central concern to Kohelet. Most people's actions in this world, claims Kohelet, are motivated by jealousy (4:4), which is a concern limited to material gain. People are sunk in the pleasures of this world and must be saved from their own desire. Kohelet writes, then, not to disparage the world but to educate those who have lost themselves in endless pursuit of futility. Accordingly, Ibn Ghiyyat's eighth proposition is that the degree of *prishut* ordained by the Torah is limited, and that ultimately one should cultivate an independence from worldly goods, learning to abandon the search for fleeting things. Finally, as the *Pirke Avot* teach, an individual should be happy with one's lot.

Thus far, Ibn Ghiyyat has laid out his regimen for investigation of Kohelet and instructs us to keep the midrashic path in mind. Though he will never abandon *midrash*, he will introduce his own innovations. Kohelet's message may not have been unknown, but the book nevertheless emphasizes a perspective on the worthiness of a life of Torah and *mitsvot*, different from that of most other books. Though *ḥokhmah* will guide those who are endowed with it to better service of God, *ḥokhmah* need not necessarily be identified with the Torah itself. Ibn Ghiyyat defines *ḥokhmah* in his commentary to chapter 2 and will receive treatment in its place. In summary, Kohelet will serve as an instruction manual by which one comes to God utilizing the proper tools—one's brain and one's actions.

Ibn Ezra[11]

Rabbi Abraham ben Meir Ibn Ezra lived his life wandering from city to city after leaving the Iberian peninsula in 1140. Kohelet was the first book of the Tanakh to which he wrote a commentary, perhaps out of a sense of identification with the book. In his opening poem to his introduction, the poet places himself in the midst of Kohelet's drama, telling the story of his exile from his home in Sefarad to Rome, to where he has descended *be-nefesh nivhelet*, with a confounded soul. Perhaps, he may feel, if he can remind himself of the lessons taught in the *sefer,* he can again rise to a higher level of spiritual satisfaction. God, who gives *ḥokhmah,* will forgive his shame in his explanation of Kohelet.

As he begins his introduction, Ibn Ezra lays the philosophical foundation that buoys his explanation of Kohelet. He opens with a quotation from the book of Proverbs (15:24), "The way of life for the wise leads upwards in order that he

---

[11] In studying Ibn Ezra, I used the standard *Mikron Gedolot Devarim* (Jerusalem, 5732 [1971–72]), 487–575.

may depart from Sheol beneath." He reads this verse as describing the path of the *maskelet,*[12] or divine part of the soul, as his desire is to turn away from this world, which he identifies with the nether world (*Sheol matah*), and to climb back toward God from where it came. While a person lives, the soul is trapped inside a body that keeps it connected to the world and mixes it with its impurities, dragging it farther and farther away from God. Tellingly, Ibn Ezra compares the state of the soul's longing to return from earthly prison to a captive who wishes to return to his home and family. The soul is joined to the body for a specified amount of time, in which a person must cleanse himself of these impurities in order that the soul should be allowed to return after its separation from the body and not be effaced along with all other unworthy souls.

In order to fulfill the desire to rise, the individual must cultivate a supernal wisdom in order to distinguish between right and wrong. Ibn Ezra informs us that this supernal *hokhmah* makes its beneficiary clear-sighted, "that what is far becomes close before it, and that the night be like day." The second part of this statement paraphrases a verse from the book of Psalms (139:12), which, in describing God's wisdom, reads, "Darkness is not dark for You, night is as light as day; darkness and light are the same." Psalm 139 appropriately describes the desire that Ibn Ezra attributes to the *ruah maskelet* and clarifies the kind of wisdom to which one must aspire to avoid futility. One must try to cultivate not human wisdom but God's wisdom, which the psalmist describes as "too wonderful for me; it is high. I cannot attain it" (139:6). God has created the human being to act and think, yet God has also limited the individual.

Ibn Ezra echoes this thought, emphasizing the difficulty of cultivating God's wisdom in his poem *'Ahalai yikonu derakhai,*[13] where he writes, "Nothing is like you; what trope can I use / For you or your works, when they are everything?" (lines 6–7). Many stanzas of this poem parallel Psalm 139, expressing God's intimate knowledge of all that people do, see, know, and say. Accordingly,

---

[12] In his comment to 7:3, Ibn Ezra describes the three levels of soul within a human being. The first level is called the *ha-tsomekhet* or *nefesh*, which succeeds for a fixed time and then perishes. This level of the soul controls physical desire. The second level is called the *ha-benemah* or *rush* and controls the emotions, sensory perception, and the ability to move. The third and highest level is called the *rush ha-maskelet* or *neshamah* and controls the ability to speak and reason, especially to know the difference between truth and falsehood. While the other two parts of the soul perish with the body, the *maskelet* returns to the higher realms from where it came.

[13] Translated and explained by Raymond P. Scheindlin, *The Gazelle: Medieval Hebrew Poems on God, Israel, and the Soul* (Philadelphia: Jewish Publication Society, 1991), 218–25, poem #29. See Appendix 2 below.

there exist no media through which one may objectively contemplate God or God's attributes, as every subject of contemplation is a creation of God. As Raymond Sheindlin writes in his commentary to the poem, "the very idea of comparison becomes empty."[14] For Man to attain any knowledge of God requires God's grace, as the last strophe relates. Scheindlin explains the ending as a plea that God raise "those who are spiritually and intellectually developed enough to achieve knowledge of God."[15]

This last comment seems paradoxical. On the one hand, comparison is empty because there exists no objective media through which to contemplate God. On the other hand, there is such a person who is "spiritually and intellectually developed enough to achieve knowledge of God." This paradox however, is linked to a second question raised by Ibn Ezra's description of the soul's imprisonment: why does God condemn the *maskelet* to life on earth? The answer seems straightforward: the *maskelet* is exiled from the heights in order that it may learn from earthly experience to improve and purify itself. As the *maskelet* differs from the other levels of soul in that it distinguishes truth from falsehood, so this is the ability it must sharpen. In this way, the *maskelet* improves itself as it comes to resemble God. Living, however, is fraught with peril, for one can become entrapped in the falsehood represented by transitory pleasures and forget one's mission. Such straying destroys the *maskelet*.

To support this answer, Ibn Ezra must make a theological statement to "justify" why God would give us the chance to destroy ourselves: all acts of *God* are good and any evil that we perceive is our own fault. God's actions can be classified as completely good, mostly good, completely evil or mostly evil. God does not permit the second two opinions to exist, and the only reason why we perceive some events as merely "mostly good" is because of our inability to see clearly. Even though events may pain us, God will not eliminate them, "for it is not His way to wipe out much good for a little evil." The greater one's perception, the better enabled one is to recognize the good and properly serve God.

Perception differs among subjects due to their differing natures. Ibn Ezra illustrates his point comparing clothes laid to bleach in the sun to the launderer; they turn white while he is suntanned. As fabric is constructed differently from human skin, so too people's ability to perceive is conditioned by various factors, and it is in this description that Ibn Ezra resolves the paradox previously

---

[14] Scheindlin, *Gazelle,* 223.
[15] Ibid., 225.

mentioned. Though God's wisdom is ultimately unattainable, individuals are naturally able to partake of some measure of it, the magnitude of which differs from person to person. Thought-influencing factors that contribute to a person's perception include body, astrological configuration at birth, the location of sun and the person who receives its strength,[16] the country where one lives, the religion one practices, and the food and drink one consumes. Though ultimately any knowledge of God depends on God's grace, some people are simply better prepared to receive this grace than others. In fact, God is always showing grace to the created beings, many of whom are simply not trained to receive. Furthermore, all people are pure in their own sight, thus inhibiting their perception by conceit.

As an additional attempt to show grace to human beings, God aroused King Solomon with *ruaḥ ha-qodesh* to write *Sefer Kohelet* in order to teach the true *derekh yesharah*, as all human deeds are transient vainglorious struggling. One can never accomplish anything permanent but only effect temporary changes in the details of life, which continually change on their own. Only the fear of God is eternal, and to cultivate a genuine fear is the task with which we are charged, that we may be freed from conceit and allowed to perceive. It is the soul's key to return to its supernal realm. Ibn Ezra concludes his introduction writing that "a man cannot grasp the proper level of His fear until he ascends the ladder of *ḥokhmah* and builds and prepares himself with understanding." Noteworthy enough, this task of purification is to be accomplished not primarily through action but through thought.[17]

---

[16] The relationship between the coordination of the strength of the sun and location of individual standing on earth and one's ability to think philosophically was a geographical idea common to the Muslim world at its height. Ibn Ezra refers to this doctrine in his comment to 1:12 in order to explain the significance of Kohelet's statement that he was *melekh 'al Yisrael be-Yerushalayim*. He says that the world is divided into seven climatic zones, of which only three are suitable to support a culture that would produce philosophy. Jerusalem lies in the middle of the third zone and is thus most suitable for the exercise of philosophy.

For more information about the seven climatic zones and their influences on human civilization, see Ibn Khaldun, *The Muqadimmah* (trans. Franz Rosenthal, abridged and ed. N. J. Dawood; Bollingen Series; Princeton, NJ: Princeton University Press, 1969), 58–70.

[17] This thought may echo Bahya Ibn Pakuda, who in the Third Treatise of *Hovot al Ha-Levavot* writes that the Torah was given as a tool through which we might better our intellect, as the essential service of God is through the heart. See Bahya ben Joseph Ibn Pakuda, *Duties of the Heart* (trans. Jehuda Ibn Tibbon, with English translation by Rev. Moses Hyamson; 5 vols.; New York: Bloch, 1925–47), 2:37.

Ramban[18]

Rabbi Moses ben Nahman delivered his *Derashah al Divre Kohelet* in 1267 prior to leaving Sefarad. As with Ibn Ezra, Ramban's leaving his homeland is the occasion for reflection on the words of the book of Kohelet. Unlike his predecessor, however, Ramban leaves for Eretz Yisrael and argues that settling the land is one of the most important *mitsvot,* the fulfillment of which teaches one to love God. Unlike the other *mefarshim*, he identifies Solomon as the author of Kohelet, yet is profoundly disturbed by the possible interpretations of the *sefer* and seeks to locate Kohelet firmly within the midrashic tradition. As the title of his work suggests, the *derashah* does not confine itself to a strict, contextual understanding of the words of the *sefer* but flows freely into lessons taught by the rabbis. The Ramban feels he must employ *derashot,* as the language of grammar and context alone cannot convey the text's true meaning. Kohelet calls for intertextual analysis, lest the *peshat* be lost. If one can use *midrash* then one can make the true message of Kohelet accessible, thus making the *midrash* itself into *peshat*. When moving from grammatical/contextual explanation to midrashic, the Ramban must defend his method with intertextual reading and logic.

Ramban must defend the *midrashim* concerning the authorship of Kohelet from the beginning. That Solomon wrote Kohelet is insufficient information to make the book worthy of canonization. Not only is there a controversy from antiquity as to whether Kohelet was written with *ruaḥ ha-qodesh* (Mishnah Yadaim 3:5),[19] but an additional book ascribed to Solomon, known as the *Wisdom of Solomon* was not canonized. Ramban opens his discourse quoting from *Shir Ha-Shirim Rabbah* (1:10), which states that Solomon not only wrote Kohelet as an old man but Shir Ha-Shirim in his youth and Proverbs in his maturity. Such a statement includes Kohelet in the same group with other canonized books and is a necessary notation because Kohelet is problematic. Ramban states that, were the author of Kohelet unknown, the reader could claim that "a man who never earned two *prutot* in his life is disparaging all the wealth in the world!" but in Solomon's mouth, the words are meaningful. This *midrash* gains support in comparison with a statement by King Nebuchadnezzar in the book of Daniel, where the King says that "all the inhabitants of the earth are of no

---

[18] References taken from *Derashah al Divre Kohelet* in *Kitve Ramban,* vol. 1, ed. C. Chavel (Jerusalem: Mosad ha-Rav Kook, 1963).

[19] An opinion in *Megillah* 7a states that Kohelet was written not from *ruah ha-kodesh*, but from Solomon's own *ḥokhmah*.

account" (4:32). Because God made Nebuchadnezzar king over even the animals and birds (2:38), such a statement is meaningful and teaches important informag tion. In any case, the words of Kohelet are worth hearing, and, though subject to challenge, the speaker is one by whom it is appropriate to be advised.

The problematic nature of Kohelet is more strongly pronounced in the next paragraph, as Ramban states that to dismiss the created world as futility is a vicious insult to its Maker. A *ḥakham* should not come to such a conclusion, pronouncing all works under heaven meaningless. Furthermore, the traditionally understood limitation of the words *taḥat ha-shamayim*[20] in 1:13 to refer only to the world under the heavens is inadequate. The heavens, after all, are created in order to preserve the earth! If one is disparaged, so is the other. If Solomon is to disparage the created world, then he contradicts the Torah itself, where in the first chapter of Genesis, God praises the newly created world.

For a *ḥakham* to conclude that the world is a vain creation and that God, by implication, is a vain Creator, undermines the entire concept of Jewish religiosity. In another essay, "The 613 Mitzvot as They Are Derived from the Ten Commandments,"[21] the Ramban argues that the very first *mitsvah* impels one to "seek and to search and to look and to recognize his God and to know Him." Likewise, one is also impelled to love God. What point is there in knowing, and how is it possible to love one whose actions are meaningless? The text therefore requires *derash,* in order that we may understand the true message. The Ramban will read Kohelet as a work that teaches about the limitations of life when disconne nected from God.

To summarize the statements of purpose related above, we see that all three *mefarshim* understand Kohelet as teaching about the relationship of the individual to God. However, while Ibn Ghiyyat and Ibn Ezra view the book as a manual that teaches character traits necessary for proper service of God, Ramsban reads Kohelet as a description of a worldview that the enlightened should avoid. The contrast among these three approaches calls special attention to each, and if one understands their differences, each approach may be better appreciated. All three are concerned with the proper understanding of the words themselves and are determined that the book read smoothly. While Ibn Ghiyyat and Ramban employ *midrash,* they do so to teach different conclusions. Ibn Ezra may

---

[20] Many say that *taḥat ha-shamayim* and *taḥat ha-shemesh* are interchangeable. See Ibn Ezra, comment to 1:13.

[21] *Kitve Ramban,* 2:521.

agree with aspects of Ibn Ghiyyat and the Ramban's readings of the text, but his approach is entirely *peshat*-oriented.

The next section will compare these differing approaches in seeking to understand Kohelet's own initial conclusions to his search. These conclusions are found in chapter 2. The section to be compared is Kohelet's conclusions about *ḥokhmah* itself—verses 12–26.

KOHELET CHAPTER 2

The following is H. L. Ginsberg's translation of chapter 2 as found in the *Tanakh* published by the Jewish Publication Society.[22]

1 I said to myself, "Come, I will treat you to merriment. Taste mirth!" That too, I found, was futile.

2 Of revelry I said, "It's mad!" Of merriment, "What good is that?"

3 I ventured to tempt my flesh with wine, and to grasp folly, while letting my mind direct with wisdom, to the end that I might learn which of the two was better for men to practice in their few days of life under heaven. 4 I multiplied my possessions. I built myself houses and I planted vineyards. 5 I laid out gardens and groves, in which I planted every kind of fruit tree. 6 I constructed pools of water, enough to irrigate a forest shooting up with trees. 7 I bought male and female slaves, and I acquired stewards. I also acquired more cattle, both herds and flocks, than all who were before me in Jerusalem. 8 I further amassed silver and gold and treasures of kings and provinces; and I got myself male and female singers, as well as the luxuries of commoners—coffers and coffers of them. 9 Thus, I gained more wealth than anyone before me in Jerusalem. In addition, my wisdom remained with me: 10 I withheld from my eyes nothing they asked for, and denied myself no enjoyment; rather, I got enjoyment out of all my wealth. And that was all I got out of my wealth.

11 Then my thoughts turned to all the fortune my hands had built up, to the wealth I had acquired and won—and oh, it was all futile and pursuit of wind; there was no real value under the sun! 12 For what will the man be like who will succeed the one who is ruling over what was built up long ago?

My thoughts also turned to appraising wisdom and madness and folly.

13 I found that wisdom is superior to folly / As light is superior to darkness;

[22] *Tanakh: The Holy Scriptures. A New Translation of the Holy Scriptures according to the Traditional Hebrew Text* (Philadelphia: Jewish Publication Society, 1985). As translation itself is a commentary to the text, I wanted to use a translation that was written in accordance with none of the above three *mefarshim*.

14 A wise man has his eyes in his head, / Whereas a fool walks in darkness. But I also realized that the same fate awaits them both. 15 So I reflected: "The fate of the fool is also destined for me; to what advantage, then, have I been wise?" And I came to the conclusion that that too was futile, 16 because the wise man, just like the fool, is not remembered forever; for, as the succeeding days roll by, both are forgotten. Alas, the wise man dies, just like the fool!

17 And so I loathed life. For I was distressed by all that goes on under the sun, because everything is futile and pursuit of wind.

18 So, too, I loathed all the wealth that I was gaining under the sun. For I shall leave it to the man who will succeed me—19 and who knows whether he will be wise or foolish?—and he will control all the wealth that I gained by toil and wisdom under the sun. That too is futile. 20 And so I came to view with despair all the gains I had made under the sun. 21 For sometimes a person whose fortune was made with wisdom, knowledge, and skill must hand it on to be the portion of somebody who did not toil for it. That too is futile, and a grave evil. 22 For what does a man get for all the toiling and worrying he does under the sun? 23 All his days his thoughts are grief and heartache, and even at night his mind has no respite. That too is futile!

24 There is nothing worthwhile for a man but to eat and drink and afford himself enjoyment with his means. And even that, I noted, comes from God. 25 For who eats and who enjoys but myself? 26 To the man, namely, who pleases Him He has given the wisdom and shrewdness to enjoy himself; and to him who displeases, He has given the urge to gather and amass—only for handing on to one who is pleasing to God. That too is futile and pursuit of wind.

Ibn Ghiyyat

Encouraging his reader to cultivate a lifestyle of detachment from the pleasures of this world, Ibn Ghiyyat structures his comments on this chapter so that verses 12–26 read as an answer to the problem articulated in verses 4–11. He reads the first three verses as Kohelet's statement of purpose and the conclusion to which his experiment has brought him, namely, that revelry is not the key to a fulfilled life. He then goes on to describe his doings. Ibn Ghiyyat lumps verses 4–11 together, defining carefully each enjoyment Kohelet took for himself. At the end of this description, Ibn Ghiyyat first implores the reader not to think that Kohelet recorded his actions out of pride or exhibitionism, rather by way of instruction—that we might learn through his experience. The rest of the chapter reads as an explanation of why it is incumbent upon individuals to become as learned in all fields as possible.

The commentary to verses 12–16 begins with the statement, "After passing through description of the worthlessness of the enjoyments mentioned, which have no permanent goal, he [Kohelet] comes to explain the value of *hokhmah,* which is eternal and enduring, a good which is tied to a man. . . ." *Hokhmah* is knowledge of God gained through study and contemplation. The whole endeavor or philosophy, according to Ibn Ghiyyat is only to know God, and this is the topic to which Kohelet now turns. Ibn Ghiyyat reads the words, *'aḥarei ha-melekh* (translated above as "after the one who rules," as a statement of purpose—that all should come to follow God. The words *ki meh ha-'adam,* read as the informational question, "For what is man?" the answer to which is, "That he may come to follow the King." Realizing, perhaps, that such a reading seems forced, Ibn Ghiyyat lists three citations of other verses that are written similarly (Esther 6:3; Genesis 21:29–30; and Genesis 20:10–11). Even though the verses he cites are actually more disjointed, in that narration intercedes between the question and the answer, Ibn Ghiyyat could rely on the cantillation of this verse to show a similar break between question and response.

The words, *ki meh ha-'adam* read as a complete phrase chanted as a unit, followed by the words, *she-yavo 'aḥarei ha-melekh,* which in themselves are also a complete phrase.[23] Ibn Ghiyyat understands this "following" as comprehension, and so to follow the King is accomplished through an act of thought.

In order that one may come to follow God through thought, one must first involve oneself in Torah and *mitsvot,* thus following God through conduct. This study of Torah, however, is not an act done primarily for its own practical sake.

Rather, one studies Torah in order that one may come to understand God better, as an individual is obligated to imitate the character traits of God in action. R. Kafah notes that this statement alludes to a *baraita* in Sotah 14a, which reads:

> And Rabbi Hama said in the name of R. Hanina, "What is the meaning of 'Walk after God'? Is it possible for Man to follow after the Divine Presence? Is it not writtten, 'The Lord your God is a consuming fire'? Rather, to imitate God's traits: Just as God clothes the naked . . . so too you clothe the naked. Just as God visits the sick . . . so too you visit the sick. Just as God consoles

---

[23] The words *ki meh ha-'adam* are assigned the troop *munakh-munakh-revi'i,* which reads as a complete unit. The next words, *she-yavo' 'aḥarei ha-melekh* are assigned *pashta-munakh-zaqef qaton,* also a complete phrase.

mourners . . . so too you console mourners. Just as God buries the dead . . . so too you bury the dead."[24]

This Gemara is usually understood as a poetic description of one's responsibility to act with *hesed,* or kindness, as these particular *mitsvot* are considered among the most important and compared to imitating God. Ibn Ghiyyat focuses on the aspect of imitation, perhaps exclusively. Although the activities mentioned in the *baraita* are acts of kindness reflective of social responsibility, the reason why one should clothe the naked, console the mourner, or bury the dead is because this is the way God acts.

Rabbi Hanina might well have added, *"Just as God is the source of wisdom, so too you pursue wisdom,"* and when Ibn Ghiyyat obligates labor in intellectual endeavors, it is a further attempt to follow God's path. This *baraita* is not read according to its own contextual meaning but has been "broadened" to serve Ibn Ghiyyat's pen.

Ibn Ghiyyat continues to explain the advantage of *hokhmah* over *sikhlut* (foolishness), as Kohelet himself says, "Wisdom is superior to folly as light is superior to darkness. This means that the *hakham* is one who understands a matter quickly because his "eyes are in his head," while the fool walks in darkness. In other words, as soon as an issue is made known to a *hakham*, he will understand and know how to act, whereas the fool will stumble. Yet even this realization is not enough to calm Kohelet's fears that nothing is eternal—the *hakham* and the *ksil* (fool) are equal in that they will both die. Here he asks, "If I am equal in this event [death] then of what value is my learning so much?" However, this thought is short-lived, as the immediate answer, *ve-dibarti be-libi she-gam zeh havel,* ("And I said to myself that this also is futile . . ."), refers to the question. The idea that the *hakham* and the *ksil* could ever be alike is simply unpalatable.

A *hakham* differ from a *ksil* because his memory lives on, even years after death. The *ksil* is forgotten, "and this is the meaning of the statement that 'there is no memory of the wise with the foot.'" Even this statement, however, provides no more than momentary comfort, as Kohelet continues to say that eventually everything will be forgotten. Perhaps the *ksil* will be forgotten immediately, but in the days to come, so will everything else, including the *hakham*. Ultimately, wisdom is no more of a life-preserver than foolishness.

Verses 17–19 provide a second answer to the question of the value of wisdom. Kohelet declares that he hates life because all that he has acquired will be

---

[24] My translation. I have omitted the verses brought in as proof-texts.

left to another, whether he be wise or foolish. Ibn Ghiyyat explains that to Kohelet life is disgusting because people long for things that disappear. Any material thing acquired can be lost, and acquisition has little to do with wisdom or folly. Wisdom and matters of religion and fear of God differ in that they are retained by the one who acquires them and are not passed on to another. The suggestion of these verses, then, is that the advantage of *ḥokhmah* is that it, unlike all other acquisitions, is permanent and entirely personal.

Kohelet seems to be satisfied with this conclusion and commits himself to *prishut,* describing in verses 20–23 the situation of the continuously laboring man who is sunk in the morass of earthly desire. Ibn Ghiyyat writes concerning this man that "his days are troubled, and in his nights he has no pleasure, and he cannot sleep from his many worries and deeds." This man has no advantage of which to speak because he cannot even enjoy that for which he labors! Were he able to be sure that his successor would be a *ḥakham,* then perhaps such labor would be more easily endured, yet to Kohelet, it is clear that a *ksil* will inherit his labor. Ibn Ghiyyat does not explain this last point, and we can ask how it is that Kohelet knows that he will be succeeded by a *ksil*. Perhaps we may answer that Solomon knew his successor would be Rehoboam, a man under whom the kingdom of Israel would be lost. Solomon's enormous wealth is described in 1 Kings 10:14–29. For all this wealth to be left to a man like Rehoboam, who would not enjoy God's favor, is truly an evil thing not only to the concerned king of a united empire but also to Israel and Judah.[25]

Ending the chapter, the last three verses, 24–26, bring the experiment to a close. Kohelet notes that there is some pleasure in worldly goods, namely, to eat, drink, and be satisfied with one's labor. Ibn Ghiyyat adds that this is all that one achieves and reminds us that this pleasure is fleeting. Nevertheless, that which one does attain is given from the hand of God. Ibn Ghiyyat reads the last verse of the chapter as a statement of reward and punishment: he who is righteous will prosper in pursuit of wisdom, while the sinner will be "rewarded" with the desire to increase possessions without end and without rest. The righteous are given what they need in this world in order to continue their studies, and they are content with this allotment. The wicked, on the other hand, are infused with desire and will work endlessly without satisfaction. In the end, their wealth will be given to another.

---

[25] Rehoboam is depicted as a foolish king by the account of his coronation. He takes the advice of the young men to speak roughly to Israel over the counsel of the elders (1 Kings 12:5–17) and loses Israel. Furthermore, his own kingdom degenerates during his rule (14:22–24).

In this chapter, Ibn Ghiyyat combines philosophy with *midrash* in order to produce a cogent reading. The chapter contains difficult ideas that seem to contradict one another, sometimes one verse after another. As Ibn Ghiyyat assumes that Solomon is writing to teach about how to serve God properly, then these verses cannot read as a disparagement of *ḥokhmah*, which is the fundamental tool through which one reaches toward God. This idea found expression in Ibn Ghiyyat's use of the *baraita* from tractate Sotah. Therefore, verses that could potentially read as disparagement are understood in accordance with the main point. The words *ki meh ha-'adam she-yavo 'aḥarei ha-melekh,* for example, are understood as a teleological statement concerning humankind. People must learn to follow God. The words *ve-dibarti be-libi she-gam zeh ḥavel* at the end of verse 16 refer to the thought expressed in the verse, and not to the acquisition of *ḥokhmah* itself.

The technique of midrashic reading in order to understand the meaning of the words finds clearer expression in other passages. For example, Ibn Ghiyyat reads 9:7–10 as programmatic use of metaphor. These verses encourage one to eat and drink in happiness, to wear white[26] clothing and to anoint oneself with oil, to love a woman, and to do whatever one can with all of one's power. Ibn Ghiyyat first states that this advice determines general categories of action that enable one to increase *ma'asim tovim* (good works) and that they are the support and maintenance of one's body, the raising of children, and the betterment of one's actions. Next, he cites *Kohelet Rabbah* and understands the activities encouraged as referring to Torah. For example, verse 8, which reads, "at all times let your clothes be white, and let not the oil upon your head lack," speaks not about what a person wears but about repentance and good deeds. The *midrash* itself tells us why such a reading is necessary:

> "At all times let your clothes be white and let not the oil upon your head lack." R. Yohanan ben Zakai said: if the verse really speaks about white clothing, then how many white garments do the nations of the world possess? And if the verse really speaks about good oils, then how many good oils do the nations of the world possess? The verse only speaks about mitsvot and good deeds. (*Kohelet Rabbah* 9:5)

In other words, if the verse is to be understood as discussing actual clothing and oil, then the verse has nothing to teach. It seems not only hedonistic but

---

[26] H. L. Ginsberg translates "freshly washed."

encouraging of practices that should not be Jewish concerns. Since Ibn Ghiyyat understands Kohelet as a guide to living religiously, he must read the text on both levels. Though speaking of supporting the body, ultimately the message is to live a life of repentance. Thus, *derash* replaces *peshat* as the primary interpretation of the text.

Another telling passage in Ibn Ghiyyat is his reading of 9:11–12, where he states a general religious philosophy in accordance with Rav Saadiah Gaon. The verses read:

> 11 I have further observed under the sun that / The race is not won by the swift, nor the battle by the valiant; nor is bread won by the wise, nor wealth by the intelligent, nor favor by the learned. For the time of mischance comes to all. 12 And a man cannot even know his time. As fishes are enmeshed in a fatal net, and as birds are trapped in a snare, so men are caught at the time of calamity, when it comes upon them without warning.

Ibn Ghiyyat says that Kohelet teaches three important lessons in these verses: (1) that matters of this world are not distributed to those who are deserving; (2) that everything acquired is a gift of God (and this is the meaning of *ki 'et vafega' yiqreh 'et kulam*[27]); and (3) that no ability, such as speed, strength, or wisdom, can stave off death when each person's allotted time arrives.

Ibn Ghiyyat parallels Rav Saadiah Gaon in that neither of them connects material reward or punishment to the performance of *mitsvot*. Ibn Ghiyyat came close to making such a connection in his comment to 2:26, where he said that the wise receives what is necessary to continue study while in the fool is implanted material desire never to be requited. Such a statement, however, cannot be understood in terms of an explicit reward or punishment because of the very nature of what is given. The wise "profits" in that he is allowed to continue that which he does, just like the fool.

In treatise 4, chapter 4 of his book *Ha-'Emunot ve-De'ot*, R. Saadiah writes that "the Creator, magnified be His majesty, does not in any way interfere with the actions of men and that He does not exercise any force upon them either to obey or disobey Him.[28] R. Saadiah argues that, were God to interfere in any way,

---

[27] I leave this untranslated because Ibn Ghiyyat would disagree with Dr. Ginsberg. Instead of "mischance," Ibn Ghiyyat writes of times preordained for individuals. *'Et va-fega'* refers to good things as well as calamity.

[28] Saadiah Gaon, *The Book of Beliefs and Opinions,* trans. from Arabic and Hebrew by Samuel Rosenblatt (Yale Judaica Series 1; New Haven: Yale University Press, 1948), 188.

it would disrupt the entire concept of *mitsvot*, which assumes that God's commands are nonsensical unless the subject has every opportunity in this world to obey. Jews earn merit in this world by fulfilling *mitsvot* chosen freely, but this freedom involves complete noninterference from God even for one's benefit. Ibn Ghiyyat adopts this stance and insists that material wealth or lack thereof has nothing to do with one's service of God. All will be requited in the world to come, which is *'olam ha-gemul*. Here, on the other hand, one's level of wisdom and that of "reward" do not coincide.[29]

Even in this world, however, there is still some advantage to *ḥokhmah,* as Ibn Ghiyyat presented in chapter 2. The wise see dearly and understand the changing nature of the times and seasons. The *ḥakham,* then, is able to interpret each season as it arrives and to act accordingly. In this way, the wise are always provided with what they need to continue their study, while the fools who walk in darkness continually wallow in their unrequited desire.

Kohelet's ultimate lesson is now clear: in this world, one's ultimate reward or punishment for what one does is the very thing that one does. One may take Solomon's worldly instruction and cultivate a disattachment from material goods, become happy with one's lot, and improve one's wisdom. Hopefully, the result of such an undertaking would in fact be less desire for pleasure and greater appreciation for God's presence. Alternatively, one may also pursue personal gain, probably never to satisfaction. In either case, God allows for the individual's choice and strengthens the resolve to continue. In the world to come, God will hold each individual to account meting out reward and punishment appropriately. Here, however, we are given rein to act as we please.

Ibn Ezra

Though Ibn Ezra is known as a *peshat* commentator, his work is not without midrashic influence necessitated by his assumption that Solomon wrote Kohelet in order to educate the *ruaḥ maskelet.* Furthermore, Ibn Ezra is well aware of the difficulties concerning verses that seem to contradict one another and must turn to philosophy in order to create distinctions under which contradictory verses may be categorized. His long comment to 7:3 states the problem explicitly, quoting the Gemara of tractate Shabbat 30b, which reads, *Rav Yehuda the son of Rav*

---

[29] A question left lingering from such an explanation is this: How do Ibn Ghiyyat and Rav Saadiah Gaon understand the miracles of the Tanakh? The question of their understanding is unfortunately beyond the scope of this paper. However, this very question is the focus of Ramban.

Shmuel bar Shilet said in the name of Rav, "the sages requested to put away sefer Kohelet because its words contradict one another." Ibn Ezra remarks that, on the surface, Kohelet appears to be wrought with contradiction but that "not even the most insignificant of sages would write a book whose words contradicted one another." It is in this comment where he elaborates the differences between the various levels of soul, that which he calls *nefesh, ruaḥ,* and *neshamah.* He continues to name a long list of contradictory verses, all of which can be resolved by reference to some part of the soul to the exclusion of others.

Use of philosophy offered Ibn Ezra a way in which he could write a believable *peshat* commentary without resorting to use of the *midrash* to explain difficult or contradictory passages such as mentioned above. Ibn Ezra believed that a *peshat* commentary should not employ *derashot,* as there exist contradictory *derashot.* They often have inner meanings that are not clearly articulated to the reader, and they ignore grammar.[30] For similar reasons, poor grammar, and incomprehensibility, he campaigns vigorously in his comment to 5:1 against the *piyyutim* of R. Eliezer Kalir, labeling them unfit for use in prayer. *Derashot,* therefore, are incapable of stating the true meaning of a verse but come to teach other lessons. *Peshat,* on the other hand, searches for a clear, objective meaning to the text and requires scientific methodology. Ibn Ezra assumed that because the Tanakh speaks the truth, its texts had to teach lessons that could be found in modern philosophy. Thus, contradictory verses can be made to refer to different parts of the soul, and *Sefer Kohelet* itself becomes a work describing the *ruaḥ maskelet* and its desire to climb back toward God.

At first glance, Ibn Ezra seems to read chapter 2 in a manner completely opposite to the reading of Ibn Ghiyyat. Whereas Ibn Ghiyyat reads the chapter in praise of *ḥokhmah* after disparaging worldly pleasures, Ibn Ezra reads the chapter as disparaging even *ḥokhmah.* Like Ibn Ghiyyat, Ibn Ezra identifies each pleasure Kohelet sought in the first half of the chapter. At the end of his comment to verse 10, he comments on the words, *ve-zeh hayah ḥelqi mikol 'amali,* "and this was my portion in all of my works," to read, "My happiness with my work was the reward for my labor, and that alone was my portion." All of this labor was incapable of producing any satisfaction beyond the immediate satisfaction of having accomplished what he did. This realization led Kohelet to conclude that all of this labor was futile.

---

[30] Introduction to Commentary to the Torah.

Kohelet complains that even though he has made himself great through wisdom and pleasure, he still accounts for little. Ibn Ezra rejects Ibn Ghiyyat's reading of the words *ki meh ha-'adam she-yavo 'aharei ha-melekh*[31] and instead refers to Psalm 8, of which verse 5 reads, *Mah 'enosh ki tizkerenu uven 'adam ki tifkedenu*, "What is Man that you take note of him, or mortals that you visit them?" This Psalm accounts for verse 12 of our chapter both grammatically and thematically. Grammatically, the construction is similar, and the meaning is "of what value is man?" Thematically, the Psalm contrasts the lone man with the splendor of something greater than he. In the Psalm, humankind pales in comparison to rest of the works of God, and in Kohelet, the individual's achievements lose importance when juxtaposed with those of the king.

Kohelet then turns to evaluate the *hokhmah* he has acquired and at first notes that there is an advantage to *hokhmah*. Ibn Ezra alludes to his Introduction, noting that the way of *hokhmah* is to allow one to see things near and far in their proper place. The next verse continues this thought: the *hakham* is clear-sighted and can avoid trouble. However, Kohelet also knows that, as the *ksil* will die, so will he.

In verse 15, Kohelet expresses frustration that, since he will die like the fool, why did he bother to become so wise? The labor was futile, and so was the acquisition of this wisdom. Ibn Ezra mentions in 7:3 that the preceding verse is true, but here he comments, "In all that I busied myself with the matters of the world, that I labored and that I became wise under the sun—I said to myself that also this wisdom is futile!" From the addition of these words, "under the sun," one must ask whether Ibn Ezra qualifies the kind of wisdom about which he now speaks. In his comment to 1:3, Ibn Ezra urges the pursuit of wisdom, stating that "the soul of man is not under the sun."[32] Could it be that here Kohelet changes his mind, or will he need to find another "advantage" to *hokhmah*?

Kohelet continues his speech, noting that the sage is forgotten along with the fool in the days to come. Ibn Ezra notes that this is the great evil with which one must contend, and he does not try to relocate Kohelet's exclamation of "futility!" as Ibn Ghiyyat does. This realization leads Kohelet to hate life, for life is but continuous struggle to no avail. Ibn Ezra amplifies this idea by citing Psalm

---

[31] Ibn Ezra brings Ibn Ghiyyat's explanation in the name of *yesh 'omrim*, "some say . . . ."

[32] Nothing is new under the sun, but the soul of man, the *ruah maskelet*, is not beneath the sun because it comes from a divine source. Therefore, it is possible for the *ruah maskelet* to gain new insights and better itself.

90:10, which disparages the labor of living. He writes that we labor on earth for a specified amount of time, after which we are cut off from life, as if we fly away.

Furthermore, whatever one acquires through labor and wisdom will be left to another, who may not be wise. Kohelet complains about this reality through verses 19–21, and Ibn Ezra's comments are mostly grammatical, as he feels Kohelet needs no explanation. Verses 22–23 challenge the assumption that wealth is an advantage because the rich man never rests. Ibn Ezra comments on verse 23, saying that matters are never settled for this man. Because of his many thoughts concerning his property during the day, he has no release at night, when he is haunted by nightmares about his responsibilities.

Kohelet concludes, as already stated in verse 10, that the good of life is to eat and drink, and that this is all the satisfaction one receives from one's labor. Yet even this achievement is actually a gift of God and unrelated to the labor one performs. The chapter ends as Kohelet states that all is in God's hands, and it is God who will requite one's labor. Ibn Ezra says that God rewards some with *hokhmah* without causing them all the stress and labor undergone by most people, as what they are given is a reward for their righteousness. The righteous, furthermore, will be happy with their lot, whether great or small, as that is their portion from God. God ordains that the sinner, however, labor ceaselessly, so that in the end, the fruits of his toil may be given to one whom God favors.

Ibn Ezra reads chapter 2 as an ascension through all the various possibilities of "the good life." Kohelet has enjoyed wine, riches, comforts, music, women, and wisdom and concluded that the pursuit of all of these is futile. Whatever enjoyment one can achieve is temporary, consisting of the enjoyment while it lasts, or the process of labor itself, if that is possible for one to enjoy. Continuing his comments into the next chapter, Ibn Ezra develops the thought with which Kohelet ended the previous section. All is in God's hands and to all purposes are appointed seasons. From individual comments in chapter 3, we can understand better Ibn Ezra's understanding of the role and value of *hokhmah,* which was disparaged previously.

In his commentary to 3:1, Ibn Ezra explains that "everything under the sun has a time and destiny . . . because the times are fixed, and when the time arrives Adam moves to what He has prepared for him, and his movements are like the movements of a shadow, as the matter, 'Man walks about as a mere shadow. . . .'" The last quotation is from Psalm 39:7, which can be read as a summary of chapter 2. The full verse reads, "Man walks about as a mere shadow; mere futility is his hustle and bustle, amassing and not knowing who will gather in," declaring that whatever works are accomplished during one's lifetime cannot amount to much. Ibn Ezra continues this direction rephrasing Kohelet's question in verse 9, "What advantage is there to the actor in whatever he toils? as "What good is effort if all is dependent upon time and fate? What advantage is there to Man in all that he toils, when it is possible that the time will come when his labor will be destroyed and his wealth will depart, and he will be left empty-handed?" Finally, in verse 14, he states that "God acts so that no created being can add or detract, in order that humankind will fear God," that we are powerless to affect God's designs.

In view of this fatalism, it becomes easier to understand Ibn Ezra's reading of the role of *ḥokhmah* in chapter 2. No matter how wise one becomes, one is still incapable of deriving any additional pleasure from the material world. Therefore, when Kohelet waxed rich and became wise, he could not achieve any sense of permanence or sense of meaning different from what he had achieved previously. Arriving at this position, Ibn Ezra ultimately agrees with Ibn Ghiyyat, that, though wisdom may be important, its role is not to increase worldly pleasure in any sense. He still maintains, however, that it is good to be wise, as he writes in 7:3: "and (the verse) 'that there is an advantage to wisdom' is the truth,"[33] because through cultivation of wisdom, the *ruaḥ maskelet* learns to recognize the difference between truth and falsehood, enabling it to cling to God's presence. Finally, in 9:11, we learn why Kohelet has disparaged *ḥokhmah* in chapter 2. The verse describes the reality that the best do not always merit what they should, and among those mentioned are the wise, who lack food. Ibn Ezra explains this sad state of affairs. "Because mortals do not have the ability to do this (succeed by their own merit), and the proof is that the wise, the intelligent ones who understand work are without food." Wisdom may not help to amass food because only God distributes food. Material gain is beyond our control, and so the levels of *nefesh* and *ruaḥ* may go unsatisfied, but fear of God and learning to recognize the Presence remain within our grasp. The *neshamah* is always able to grow.

Nahmanides

Ramban reads chapter 2 as a pedagogical starting point. *Sefer Kohelet* was not written in order to disparage creation but to teach three important lessons. Ultimately, the Ramban will interpret Kohelet through *midrash,* and he does

---

[33] In his comment to 7:3, Ibn Ezra contextualizes many contradictory verses. This particular comment refers back to 2:13.

so because without rabbinic treatment the text is misleading. *Derash* is not the freewheeling endeavor that Ibn Ezra decries but actually an intertextual reading that involves other books of the Tanakh. As Ibn Ezra understands the derivation of *peshat* to involve objective reasoning, so too *derash* requires logic and justification.

The first lesson Kohelet teaches is that one should not turn "after the pleasures of the world because they are things that pass away and are lost quickly." Kohelet teaches this lesson in the first eleven verses of his second chapter. Though Ramban does not define each pleasure in detail, as did Ibn Ezra and Ibn Ghiyyat, the content of this teaching mirrors theirs.

The second lesson is that one should not disparage the world denouncing any part of creation as vanity. The Ramban says that Kohelet mentioned that, even though individuals live and die, and even though the details of life change constantly, the fundamental elements of creation continue to operate the system. This was the purpose of verses 4–7 in the first chapter, where Kohelet discusses the eternity of the earth, the sun, wind, and so on. The vanity that Kohelet laments is the ability of the individual. He cites 3:14, similar to Ibn Ezra, yet saying that God created a world from which a mortal may not add or detract in order that mortals come to fear God.

At this juncture, the Ramban makes a point that is key for understanding the second half of the *Derashah*. He writes:

> Know that Solomon does not mention the Ineffable Name in this book at all, but always uses the name *Elokim*. Thus, the attribute of Fear is the name *Elokim* as it is said, *veha-Elokim asah she-yiru milfanav* [3:14] and finishes in the end with *et Elokim yera* [12:13], but the book cf Proverbs is not such. . . . And the reason is that this book speaks of the world as it is conducted underneath the sun, and the way it is conducted is according to the attribute of Justice, which conducts every person. And the righteous in this book who follow Solomon's injunctions will be like Abraham, Isaac, and Jacob.[34]

God was not known to the patriarchs by the Ineffable Name, and Ramban understands this difference between them and Moses according to the degree of divine intercession that pervaded their lives. While the generation of the Exodus knew a God who performed wonders before their eyes, the affection shown to

---

[34] *Derashah*, 191. My translation and added verse references. The translation of the verse reads, "And God acts in order that Man fear Him."

the patriarchs is not as obviously pronounced. As the patriarchs did not know God by this Name, they were constantly protected by "hidden miracles."

Ramban explains further that "hidden miracles" are those that are every day realized in nature, materialized through divine intervention. Rewards and punishments take the form of these hidden miracles, such as the promise in Leviticus 26:4, which assures rain and produce to the Land of Israel in its proper time if the people obey the *mitsvot*. C. Chavel notes that these miracles are called "hidden" because "one can deny [them] and say that it was through nature."[35] In other words, the world has a natural order through which it operates, and God may choose to protect an individual through manipulation of common events, or withdraw protection to leave one prone to the same natural forces.

The issue of God's involvement, protecting individuals or leaving them to the "accidents of the natural world" finds expression in Professor David Berger's essay "Miracles and the Natural Order in Nahmanides."[36] Berger writes that, according to Nahmanides, "ordinary people are excluded from the regular operation of hidden miracles and are left, as in the *Commentary to Genesis*, to the customary natural order. . . . [P]eople left to accidents will be subjected to good or evil according to 'their way and their actions' in a purely naturalistic sense."[37] God allows the world to run its course, providing protection or punishment to the righteous or wicked respectively. Although God is involved with every action that occurs, the world conducts itself in a predetermined manner around which civilization organizes itself.

Ramban writes that, although the righteous spoken of in this book resemble the patriarchs, another level exists at which open miracles may be performed on behalf of an individual or group. This is the level of those who cling to the Ineffable Name. This group is represented by notables such as Moses and the generation of the Exodus. About them Ramban writes, "there will not occur any

---

[35] *Derashah*, 192.

[36] David Berger, "Miracles and the Natural Order in Nahmanides," in *Rabbi Moses Nahmanides (Ramban): Explorations in His Religious and Literary Virtuosity* (ed. Isadore Twersky; Texts and Studies, Harvard University Center for Jewish Studies 1; Cambridge, MA: Harvard University Press, 1983), 107–28.

[37] Ibid., 117. Berger is seeking to synthesize a comment from the *Commentary to Genesis* on Genesis 18:19 with the introduction to the *Commentary to Job*. The comment to 18:19 reads, "Know that miracles are performed for the good or ill only for the absolutely righteous (*tsadiqim gemurim*) or the absolutely wicked. Those in the middle have good or ill occur to them according to the customary order of the world "in accordance with their way and their actions" (Ezekiel 36:17).

accident to those who cleave to Him. Rather for them, the sea and the Jordan are split, and he brings down manna for them, and the likes . . . and, therefore, Solomon says in the book of Proverbs, *The fear of God adds days* (10:27)."[38] At this point, Ramban can reread the *midrash* on the words "and nothing is new under the sun" (1:3) to refer not to any comparison between God and Man, or the sky and the earth, but to a spiritual relationship cultivated between the individual and God. The newly interpreted *midrash* reads as follows:

> And the rule is that those who cleave to the Ineffable Name are not subject to the rule or the planets (fate/natural occurrences) at all. And this is what our sages mentioned concerning the issue of this book, "Under the sun there is no (advantage). Above the sun, there is."

Those who serve God from fear only, as this is the way their world has been ordained, will at best be protected by hidden miracles. For them, nothing is new under the sun. On the other hand, God's lovers witness open miracles.

In teaching the third lesson, Ramban states that Kohelet addresses what is perhaps the greatest religious problem ever, the question of *Tsadiq ve-ra' lo, rasha' be-tov lo,* "Why do the righteous suffer, while the wicked prosper?" As Ibn Ezra and Ibn Ghiyyat address the problem by removing the issue of reward and punishment from actualization in this life, to be granted in the afterworld, Ibn Ezra even stating in commentary to 7:3 that at least most righteous individuals prosper while most of the wicked suffer, Ramban follows in their footsteps. He derives the question "Why do the wicked prosper?" from 2:9, from the words, "and so I hated life because deeds were evil to me," and so on. The verse resembles the opening to Psalm 73, where the Psalmist struggles with the same question, asking about the suffering *tsadiq* explicitly. The Psalm describes the envy and frustration of a righteous man who witnesses the good fortune enjoyed by the wicked until the day he realizes that all will eventually be brought to judgment. He will receive his just reward, while the wicked whom he envies will be punished. Following the Psalm, Ramban concludes that this classic problem loses strength when one understands that there will be fair recompense in the next world.

Concluding discussion of this lesson, Ramban reinterprets the position of Rabbi Akiva in the *mishnah* in Tractate Yadaim (3:5), which presents the controversy as to whether or not *Sefer Kohelet* can be included within the sacred writings. The relevant section of the *mishnah* reads as follows:

---

[38] The verse reads with the Ineffable Name and not the name Elokim.

Rabbi Akiva said, "God forbid anyone should disagree and say that Shir ha-Shirim does not defile the hands because the whole world is not worthy of the day on which Shir ha-Shirim was written! For all of the writings are holy, and Shir ha-Shirim is "holy of holies." And if there is a disagreement, the disagreement concerns Kohelet.

Ramban interprets R. Akiva as saying that

[Kohelet] only speaks in the name Elokim, the attribute of Justice upon which the world is conducted. But the righteous of the Torah who serve from love are not governed by this book. Therefore, it is not sacred.

By definition, holiness must apply to everyone. Shir ha-Shirim describes the path of the ones who love God, presenting a model to which all can aspire. If Kohelet, on the other hand, cannot offer similar teaching, it cannot be considered sacred. The controversy is resolved favorably, however, saved by the *midrash,* which directs the careful student to the true meanings of the book.

*   *   *

While Ramban has already taught the lessons that (1) the identity of the person from whom one takes advice matters, (2) the three lessons mentioned above, and (3) that holiness must apply to everybody, he continues to expound, in order to instruct his audience in two especially important *mitsvot*. These *mitsvot* include *yishuv Eretz Yisrael,* settling the Land of Israel and the giving of *tsedaqah.*[39] One who lives in Eretz Yisrael, as well as the one who gives *tsedaqah* are included among God's lovers—righteous people who may rise to the level of miraculous existence and escape from the world of the natural order.

The act of residing in Eretz Yisrael places one among God's lovers and withdraws one from the natural order, as life in the Land is the "fundamental fulfillment of the *mitsvot*."[40] In other words, all *mitsvot* that one can do are truly effective only when observed as a resident of the Land. In exile, on the other hand, the Jew observes *mitsvot* "in order not to forget them upon return."[41] Because residence in the Land is the fundamental observance of the *mitsvot,* Eretz Yisrael presents a Jew with the best opportunity to cleave to the Ineffable Name. As Ibn Ezra states, Ramban writes that Eretz Yisrael "is the center of the

---

[39] *Tsedaqah* is often translated as "charity," though the English word does not carry the connotation of an obligatory act. I will retain the Hebrew.

[40] *Derashah,* 200.

[41] Sifre, *Parashat Ekev,* 43.

world, the inheritance of God, set aside to His Name, and not given to the angels, a guide, overseer, or ruler (Proverbs 6:7)." It is unlike the lands of foreign peoples, which "even though all belongs to the Honored Name, they are not wholly pure, because they are ruled by servants."

Just as *yishuv* Eretz Yisrael withdraws one from control of the natural order, so too does *tsedaqah*. The Ramban ends his *Derashah* presenting proof-texts on the importance of *tsedaqah* from the Torah, the Prophets, the Writings and from the Talmud, and finally closing with full citation of the *Mishneh Torah* of Maimonides, chapter 10 of *Hilkhot Matanot Ani'im* (Laws of Gifts to the Poor). Berger indirectly teaches about how *tsedaqah* withdraws one from control of the natural order in citation of a responsum, which he presents in order to illustrate the power of the natural order.[42] In the responsum, Ramban rules that, though one should not consult astrologers, it is permissible to believe an astrologer and that one should be attentive to their words, especially if their prediction is for ill. An astrologer, after all, is one who understands how to read the signs of the natural world well enough to predict the future. Since most individuals are subject to the musing of nature, one may believe an astrologer. His proof-text in this argument is Tractate Shabbat 156a-b, where the Gemara teaches a story about the daughter of R. Akiva. In the story, the daughter is informed that she will die on the day of her wedding but is saved through an act of *tsedaqah*.

R. Akiva concludes *tsedaqah tatsil mimavet* (Proverbs 10:2), *tsedaqah* saves one from death. His daughter was saved from her fate through an act that withdrew her from natural control.

The Ramban concludes his *Derashah* teaching lessons not found in Kohelet, but which he feels must be taught in light of the book. Solomon wrote about the world as it is conducted and adjures the reader to rise above a life of naturalistic living where one fears God by the name of *Elokim*. The world is not futile but is built especially to allow for such individual progress. It is given to the individual to try.

CONCLUSION

The writing of a commentary that seeks to explain the texts with which one's community is already familiar is indeed a gutsy endeavor. All three of the

---

[42] Berger, "Miracles and the Natural Order," 123. The reference is to *Teshuvot ha-Ramban B'Inyanei Emunot V'De'ot* in *Kitvei Ha-Ramban*, 1:379.

midrashim discussed in this paper struggle not only with *Sefer Kohelet* but with an entire heritage inherited from the past. Furthermore, the *mefarshim* live in a world different from that of their ancestors. They wrestle with their own ideas of how the world operates and compare their experience to that of Kohelet. They bring a new set of questions to the books they and their communities read and seek to become authoritative voices as to how the next generation should study.

These same forces, however, that humble the *parshan* also call him or her to action, because at stake is a set of fundamental religious questions. These questions can be phrased as "What can I, the individual Jew, do with the tradition handed down to me?" or "Is there room for my own creativity, or has all that is worth saying been said?" Others ask, "What contribution can I make to my community?" A *parshan* must write *because* other voices have spoken, and the new perspective that he or she sees should not be lost to the world. Each of the *mefarshim* in this paper developed his unique method to interact with the inheritance of the past.

As one who upholds the past, Ramban seeks to rework classical *midrash*. Ramban is known as the *parshan* who defends Rashi against Ibn Ezra[43] and those who seek to criticize traditional methodologies in the study of *ḥumash*, and as the *ri'shon* who defends Rabenu Yitshak al-Fasi against the Ravad and Ba'al Ha-Meor. In the *Derashah*, he remains true to form and defends the *midrash*. His reasoning seeks to show that *midrash* is an abbreviated form of complex textual analysis. The student sees only the outcome and not the reasoning behind the lesson, similar to the study of *mishnah* without Gemara. The rabbis of the past have provided the pithy statements, and he must develop their argument so that the student understands why the lesson must be true. If the method leads him to reject a *midrash,* he will usually stand another in its place.

That Ramban asserts his vigorous defense of *midrash* raises further questions about his textual assumptions. It is clear that he believes in a greater unity of the books of the Tanakh, as all are either written by God or through *ruaḥ ha-qodesh* and therefore may be read in light of one another. However, how far does this unity extend? Does there arrive a point at which one must recognize

---

[43] Whether or not Ibn Ezra actually knew of Rashi's commentary is still open to debate. However, Ramban juxtaposes the two commentaries as differing modes of interpretation to which he must respond. In his introduction to his *Perush 'al ha-Torah,* he says explicitly that he will defend Rashi and refute Ibn Ezra (even while loving him in secret).

differing messages from different books where one may no longer draw such conclusions?[44]

Ibn Ghiyyat may be asked the same question, yet although he also relies on similar texts to illustrate the meaning he advances, his commentary makes use of other tools, remaining philosophical and grammatical as well as midrashic. He was called "conservative" in the preface above, because when he cites the *midrash,* he feels little need to justify his interpretative choice. If the *midrash* teaches one lesson, it may be the primary lesson the student should know, or it may be one of many ideas the verse contains. We saw an example of a dual reading of 9:8 concerning the interpretation of "white clothes." Where Ibn Ghiyyat said that the verses encourage physical well-being, the *midrash* reads the verses as referring to Torah. Ibn Ghiyyat accepts both interpretations. Whereas Ramban would struggle to explain how the *midrash* fits context, which in the case of 9:8 may require a full citation, Ibn Ghiyyat simply lists the *midrash* among his other explanations of the verse.

At the other extreme, Ibn Ezra cannot accept *derash* as the authoritative voice of how to read text but must seek to establish the text as it was written with its peculiar nuance. The proof-texts he cites are usually of similar nuance, and the explanation must be able to stand the test of logic. It is on this point, however, where we may raise questions about his method. Ibn Ezra resorts to philosophy because he cannot avoid stepping outside of the text he explains, just as one cannot define the meaning of a word without using other words. While he believes philosophy to be the most objective, scientific tool at his disposal, his philosophical arguments are no longer invoked by most philosophers because Neoplatonism is no longer the philosophical language of academia. Accordingly, his commentary today does not evoke the same compelling power as it would have in his day. We see that philosophy, like *midrash*, cannot necessarily be the authoritative interpretation of a text because it is subjective to time and place.

The last question to ask concerns *Sefer Kohelet* itself: How do we read the book? Whose approach works best and why? Neither question can be answered with satisfaction, yet insights may still be gleaned from other areas. The student can interpret the text with the traditional rabbinic approach as a guide, understanding that *midrash* is often acontextual and may not convey the message of

---

[44] For example, is it really appropriate to compare Solomon, who was rich and can therefore disparage wealth, to Nebuchadnezzar, who was powerful and could disparage power? Are we to read the reports of their respective wealth and power literally in each book? It seems that Ramban would affirm such questions but must still explain why.

the book's author. One may respond by seeking to recontextualize the lesson, as did Ramban, or accept it as one of many possible lessons, as did Ibn Ghiyyat. Alternatively, one may blaze a new trail, as did Ibn Ezra, recognizing that what one believes to be an objective methodology may be discredited at a later date. Whatever the choice of the student, the decision reflects a religious consciousness that strives to locate itself in relation to the communities that read the text studied. According to all three of these *mefarshim*, Solomon wrote Kohelet in order to teach. The content of that lesson, however, is ours to find.

Appendix 1. Mishnah Yadaim 35

(My Translation)

A book which is erased from which remain eighty-five letters, such as the section, "When the Ark would travel" defiles the hands. A scroll upon which is written eighty-five letters, such as the section, "When the Ark would travel," defiles the hands. All sacred writings defile the hands. The Song of Songs and Ecclesiastes defile the hands. Rabbi Yehudah says: The Song of Songs defiles the hands, and there is disagreement concerning Ecclesiastes. Rabbi Yossi says: Ecclesiastes does not defile the hands, and concerning Song of Songs there is disagreement. Rabbi Shimon says: Ecclesiastes goes as one of the leniences of Bet Shamai and the stringencies of Bet Hillel. Says Rabbi Shimon ben Azai: I have received from seventy-two sages on the day when they installed Rabbi El'azar ben Azarya in the Academy, that the Song of Songs and Ecclesiastes defile the hands. Says Rabbi Akiva: God forbid! No Jew should disagree concerning the Song of Songs that it does not defile the hands, because the entire world is not worthy of the day Song of Songs was given to Israel, because if all the writings are holy, Song of Songs is Holy of Holies; and if they disagree, they can only disagree concerning Ecclesiastes. Says Rabbi Yohanan ben Yehoshu'a ben hamiv shel Rabbi Akiva: As the words of Ben Azai they disagreed and concluded.

Appendix 2: 'Aḥalai Yikonu Derakhai

(Translation by Dr. Raymond Scheindlin, *The Gazelle*, 218–25)

O for a clear way to keep Your commands!
For only in Your love do I find rest.

I am Your servant; guide me in Your ways.
    I have no care but to deserve Your grace;
    I only ask that I may see Your face.

Nothing is like You; what trope can I use
For You or Your works, when they are everything?
You made me: what else should I say to You?
    To You belong my thoughts and all my wealth.
    You made them not for me, but for Yourself.

Your grace is infinite; who would not praise?
For nothing else is; only Your works and You;
As those who deny Your name themselves attest.
    Whichever way I seek You, you are there.
    No bar between us—You are everywhere.

I turn from You, and, turning to You I turn.
No vision can I see except Your light;
No speech is in my ear except Your word.
    The secret sealed in me Your eye sees clear,
    Before I speak, my speech is in Your ear.

Send grace to save Your creature, evil's slave.
Put Your name in his mouth, in his heart Your home.
Pity him as he lifts his eyes toward Your throne.
    Stretch forth Your hand, and let it on Your folk alight.
    We live in darkness—lift Your face to give us light.

ACKNOWLEDGMENTS

I would like to thank Dr. Raymond Scheindlin for his patient assistance and guidance in helping me to research this material.

BIBLIOGRAPHY

Primary Sources

Kohelet

Derashah 'al Divre Kohelet, Vikuah ha-Ramban, Teshuvot Ha-Rambam be-Inyane Emunot ve-De'ot, in *Kitve Ha-Ramban,* vol. 1; and *Taryag*

Ha-Mitsvot Ha-Yotzim me-Aseret ha-Dibrot, in vol. 2. Translated by C. Chavel. 11th ed. Jerusalem: Mosad Harav Kook, 5751 [1990–91].

Ibn Ezra. Commentary to Sefer Kohelet in *Mikraot Gedolot Devarim,* 487–575. Jerusalem: Paer ha-Torah, 5732 [1971–72].

———. *Perush 'al ha-Torah.*

Ibn Ghiyyat. *Sefer Ha-Prishut: Commentary to Kohelet by Rav Saadiah Gaon* (actually by R. Yitshak ben Yehudah Ibn Ghiyyat). In *Hamesh Megillot,* 161–296. Translated by R. Yosef Kafah. Jerusalem: Institute for the Preservation of Sacred Texts of Yemen, Jerusalem, 1962. Now available online at http://www.hebrewbooks.org/39855, 1962.

Ramban. *Perush 'al ha-Torah.* Edited by C. Chavel. Jerusalem: Mossad HaRav Kook, 1959.

Tanakh: The Holy Scriptures. A New Translation of the Holy Scriptures according to the Traditional Hebrew Text. Philadelphia: Jewish Publication Society of America, 1985. [Ecclesiastes is translated by H. L. Ginsberg.]

Secondary Sources

Ashtor, Eliyahu. *The Jews of Moslem Spain,* 2:144–49. Translated by Aaron Klein and Jenny Machlowitz Klein. Philadelphia: Jewish Publication Society of America, 1979.

Bahya Ibn Pakuda. *Duties of the Heart.* Translation of *Hovot 'al ha-Levavot,* from Arabic by Jehuda Ibn Tibbon, with English translation by Rev. Moses Hyamson. 5 vols. New York: Bloch, 1925–47.

Berger, David. "Miracles and the Natural Order in Nahmanides." In *Rabbi Moses Nahmanides (Ramban): Explorations in His Religious and Literary Virtuosity,* edited by Isadore Twersky. Cambridge, MA: Harvard University Press, 1983.

Goldziher, Ignaz. *Introduction to Islamic Theology and Law.* Translated by Andras Hamori and Ruth Hamori. Princeton, NJ: Princeton University Press, 1981. Pp. 116–66.

Greenstein, Edward L. "Medieval Bible Commentaries." In *Back to the Sources: Reading the Classic Jewish Texts,* edited by Barry W. Holtz, 213–57. New York: Summit Books, 1984.

"Ibn Ghayyat (Ghiyyat)." *Encyclopedia Judaica,* 8:1175–76. Jerusalem: Keter, 1973.

Ibn Khaldun. *The Muqaddimah.* Translated by Franz Rosenthal. Abridged and edited by N. J. Dawood. Princeton, NJ: Princeton University Press, 1969. Pp. 56–70.

Isaac Israeli. Translation and commentary by A. Altman and S. M. Stern. Scripta Judaica 1. London: Oxford University Press, 1958. Pp. 185–95.

Saadiah Gaon, Rav. *The Book of Beliefs and Opinions.* Translation of *Ha Emunot ve-De'ot* from Arabic to Hebrew by Samuel Rosenblatt. Yale Judaica Series 1. New Haven: Yale University Press, 1948.

Scheindlin, Raymond P. *The Gazelle: Medieval Hebrew Poems on God, Israel, and the Soul.* Philadelphia: Jewish Publication Society, 5751 [1991]. Pp. 218–25, Poem #29

Septimus, Bernard. "Open Rebuke and Concealed Love: Nahmanides and the Andalusian Tradition." In *Rabbi Moses Nahmanides (Ramban): Explorations in His Religious and Literary Virtuosity,* edited by Isadore Twersky. Cambridge, MA: Harvard University Press, 1983.

Simon, Uriel. Lectures at the Jewish Theological Seminary of America: "Ibn Ezra andRashbam: Different Approaches to *Peshat,*" April 2, 1995; "Ibn Ezra's Commentary to Bereshit," April 3, 1995; and "Ibn Ezra as Bible Critic?" April 6, 1995.

Wolfson, Elliot R. "God, the Demiurge and the Intellect: On the usage of the word *Kol* in Abraham Ibn Ezra." *Revue des études juives* 149 (1990): 77–111.

Thoughts on the Death of Matt and Sara

DR. BEZALEL PORTEN

As Kiddush ushers in the Sabbath, so Havdalah ushers it out. It proclaims separation, between holy and profane, light and darkness, Israel and the nations. Separation was present at creation, when God first separated light from darkness, the waters above from the waters below. Song of Songs was a powerful love song, so powerful that the rabbis felt its bright light had to be shielded from the eyes of the beholder, filtered through the lens of homiletical interpretation. The text may have said one thing, but it meant another. An academic study of the book had to acknowledge both approaches, that of an erotic love tale between a lass and a lad, and that of a passionate relationship between God and Israel. My final exam required the student to choose any five verses from the book and explain them both as *peshat* and *derash* two separate entities. Matt succeeded eminently in doing justice to both approaches. In his choice of verses, we observe the sensuous ("may he kiss me with the kisses of his mouth"), the imploring ("arise my darling, my fair one, come away"), and the metaphorical ("like the Tower of David is your neck"). Of the latter image, he wrote, "Perhaps she carries herself in a secure, dignified fashion, much like a fortress stands unafraid of the surrounding countryside, rather all are in awe of it." One may imagine that, for Matt, these verses bore a personal meaning. Song of Songs concludes, "Let me be a seal upon your heart, Like the seal upon your hand. For love is fierce as death . . . a divine flame (שלהבתיה). . . . Vast floods cannot quench love." Neither the waters above nor the waters below. What remains is the sanctification for those whose rest is now eternal, unseparately entombed—יתגדל ויתקדש.

The author is Professor Emeritus in the Department of Jewish History at the Hebrew University of Jerusalem.

Reflections on the Song of Songs

MATTHEW EISENFELD

Song of Songs 1:2: *Yishaqeni mi-neshiqot pihu ki-tovim dodekha mi-yayin.*
That he would kiss me with the kisses of his mouth, for your love is better than wine.

Peshat. In this opening verse to the Song of Songs, we are introduced to ideas that will recur. The most glaring problem of the verse is the switch from speech in the third person to speech in the second, which leads us to question whether the woman who speaks of her lover is actually addressing anybody, or, as Ibn Ezra says, is simply gazing upon a passing shepherd and daydreaming. In his opinion, she switches to second person as thought of actually kissing her lover excites her and makes him seem more present. Benjamin Segal notes that the change of voice introduces the theme of proximity and distance.[1] If in fact she does address her lover in v. 2b, then perhaps also in v. 2a, yet under her breath, or even aloud in a teasing fashion, as if to say, "My lover would kiss me on the

---

Editor's reflection: During the fall semester 1995–1996, Matt took a course in the Song of Songs with Professor Bezalel Porten. At the end of the semester, the students were given a take-home exam that required analysis of a selection of biblical verses according to interpretations of both *peshat* (plain sense of a text) and *derash* (homiletic interpretations in classical rabbinic texts).

As noted in the Introduction, Matt was eager to complete all of his assignments because he and Sara were planning to leave on February 25 for a trip to Jordan during the last week of the inter-semester break. While many other students worked throughout the recess to complete papers and exams, Matt worked diligently to complete all of his work much earlier. Matt's laptop computer was broken, and he came to my apartment on February 22 and completed this assignment on my laptop. I believe this is the last document he wrote, or at least typed.

[1] Benjamin J. Segal, *The Song of Songs: A Woman in Love* (Jerusalem: Gefen, 2009). Rabbi Segal, then president of the Schechter Institute, made available to the students an early draft of his commentary on Song of Songs.

118

mouth if he were really my lover!" This understanding reads well with 1:8, where he seems to tease her.

The parallelism of mouth and wine is the first image of the Song. This first image is internal, as one needs to take something into one's body in order to taste, a sense even more intimate than touch. It is no surprise, then, that the first line of a love poem is so sensual. Kisses and love are compared to wine because wine is often understood as symbolic of all pleasure (e.g., Psalm 104:15). *Da'at Mikra*[2] adds that not only is wine sweet, but may make one drunk as well, a sensation shared by people in love (Song 5:1). The word *dodekha*, love, or love making, is in the plural, as it is an abstract noun.

Derash. The Targum understands King Solomon to bless God, who spoke to Israel, giving the Written and Oral Law to Moses, speaking face to face. The Targum could have stopped here, understanding the shift from third to second person (as does Rashi), as a distinction in the way one addresses God, sometimes in the third out of respect, and sometimes in the second from love. The Targum, however, seems to read against our punctuation *(dodayikh)* for the second half of the verse, saying that Israel is more beloved of God than the seventy nations (the numerical value of *yayin* is 70) and therefore received the Torah.

This verse finds use in Tractate Avodah Zarah as Rabbi Yehoshua's last attempt to get Rabbi Yishmael to stop asking him questions about why the rabbis forbade the cheese of non-Jews. Rav Dimi explains Rabbi Yishmael's reading of the word *dodayikh* to mean that Israel says that the sages and their decrees (or, God's lovers) are sweeter to Israel than the wine of Torah.[3]

---

[2] Aharon Mirsky, *Shir HaShirim* (Jerusalem: Mosad HaRav Kook, 1990).

[3] Mishnah Avodah Zarah 2:5: Rabbi Judah said: Rabbi Ishmael put this question to Rabbi Joshua as they were walking on the way, "Why have they forbidden the cheese of non-Jews?"

1) He replied, because they curdle it with the rennet of a nevelah (an animal that was not properly slaughtered)."

2) He (Rabbi Ishmael) said: "but is not the rennet of a burnt-offering more strictly forbidden than the rennet of a nevelah? [and yet] it was said that a priest who is not fastidious may suck it out raw."

1) (Though the Sages disagreed with this opinion, and they said that no benefit may be derived from it, although one who consumed it did not trespass [temple property]).

3) Rabbi Joshua responded: "The reason then is because they curdle it with the rennet from calves sacrificed to idols."

4) He (Rabbi Ishmael) said to him: "if that be so, why do they not extend the prohibition to any benefit derived from it?"

5) He (Rabbi Joshua) diverted him to another matter, saying: "Ishmael, how do you read— for your [masc.] love is more delightful than wine" or "your [fem.] love etc. (Song of Songs 1:2)"

Song of Songs 2:10: *'Anah dodi ve-'amar li qumi lakh ra'yati yafati u-lekhi lakh*
My beloved called to me, saying, "Arise my love, my beauty, and come with
me!"

Peshat. According to the *Interpreter's Bible*, this verse, along with the very
first verse, constitutes the only prose of the Song. If so, then what we see is a type
scene that the lover calls to his beloved to join him and she stalls (here, 5:2–5;
7:9–12). I follow Segal in translating *'anah* as "called," because the image is concrete and fits the lover's desire. This form of *'anah . . . 'amar* is found in Job 3:2,
where an embittered Job speaks for the first time to his friends and one can
imagine him calling out with passion as he curses the day of his birth. From the
words *qumi lakh* and further, what we hear is the report of the lover's speech.

The woman is likely lying in bed here as we find her in 5:2. Her beloved
invites her to join him, calling her by two names, *ra'yati* and *yafati,* and adding
the word *lakh* to the imperative verbs. *Da'at Mikra* explains the two names as a
poetic way of writing *ra'yati ha-yafah,* or "my beautiful one," but Segal explains
that these are two nearly synonymous terms. I have chosen to translate as above
because of the use of the word *lakh.* While one can argue that the form *qumi
lakh,* is simply a poeticism, *Da'at Mikra* senses that the meaning of his call for
her to rise is for her to join him, as in Jeremiah 2:2. I would like to add that the
poeticisms here add another dimension, as we see two *lakh's* sandwiching two
first-person possessives, calling attention to both ideas *of me* and *you.* The lover
emphasizes that he wants *her* to rise and come with him as she is *his* locked garden (4:12).

Derash. According to the Targum, God answers Israel, saying "Rise O Israel,
my beloved of old and beautiful in deeds, and go forth from Egyptian slavery!"
'Anah may be understood in the most literal sense here, as God answers Israel
when Israel cries out under oppression. It is the cry that arouses God to action
(Exodus 2:23–25) in Egypt, just as it is the cry of the widow or orphan that
arouses God to vengeance in Exodus 22:21–23. The twofold name by which
Israel is called is made to refer to two reasons why God loves Israel, because God
has loved Israel always, and because Israel performs *mitsvot.* As the rabbis read

---

1) He replied: "your [fem.] love is better . . ."

2) He said to him: this is not so, as it is proved by its fellow [-verse]: your ointments [masc.]
have a goodly fragrance … [therefore do the maidens love you] (Song of Songs 1:3)."
(As translated by Joshua Kulp, *Mishnah Yomit* at mishnahyomit.org/avodahzarah/
Avodah%20Zarah%202-5.doc)

the Song of Songs allegorically, many of the verses refer either to the Exodus from Egypt or to the giving of the Torah. The man loves the woman in Song of Songs because she is the "most beautiful of women." What makes Israel attractive to God are the *mitsvot* Israel fulfills, establishing God's will on earth.

> Song of Songs 2:14: *Yonati be-ḥagvei ha-selaʿ be-seter ha-madregah har'ini 'et mar'ayikh hashmi'ini 'et qolekh ki qolekh 'arev u-mar'ekh na'veh.*
> My dove in the clefts of the rock, hidden in the cliff, show me your face, let me hear your voice, for your voice is sweet and your face is comely.

Peshat. The lover calls his beloved, "my dove," adding to the names by which he calls her. "My dove" suggests that she is gentle and sweet. Marvin Pope,[4] Segal, and *Da'at Mikra* mention the dove's monogamous mating pattern, which, accompanied by the fact that she is hidden, suggests modesty. This idea fits well with 4:1, where her eyes are compared to "two doves behind the veil." In 5:2 and 6:9, the word *yonati* is paired with *tamati,* "my perfect one." As a dove is pleasant to look upon and sweet of voice, so is she, as she is perfect for him.

Doves live on cliffs among rocks, where they make their nests and hide from birds of prey. In this verse, the beloved is compared to a dove in hiding as she listens to her beloved from her room and does not join her lover. The words *be-seter ha-madregot* parallel *ḥagvei ha-selaʿ* as he emphasizes her reluctance to join him.

After inviting her with descriptions of the budding flowers and singing birds, he invites her to be like these singing birds and be seen and sing for him. Likewise, she invites him to be like the stag or young gazelle (2:17) to which she compared him (2:9). As he asks her to come out to him, he says that he wishes to see her face. I have translated *marayikh* as "face" following Michael V. Fox,[5] Support for this approach comes from the descriptions of Leah and Rachel in Genesis 29:17. Focus on the face and mouth is reminiscent of Song of Songs 1:2, where she focuses her attention on the lover's mouth.

Derash. An interesting observation about this method of interpretation is that when *derash* allegorizes, it seeks to connect images with concrete events rather than simply create a sensation (see Rashi on Genesis 49:3–28). Here Rashi follows the Targum, explaining that Israel was first compared to a dove by

---

[4] Marvin Pope, *Song of Songs: A New Translation with Introduction and Commentary* (Anchor Bible 7C; Garden City, NY: Doubleday, 1995).

[5] Michael V. Fox, *The Song of Songs and Ancient Egyptian Love Songs* (Madison: University of Wisconsin Press, 1985).

Pharaoh, who exclaimed that they were lost and enclosed in the desert (Exodus 14:3). He continues to say that at the moment when the Egyptian chariots approached, Israel resembled a trapped animal. As a dove who flees from a hawk tries to take refuge in the cleft of the rock and finds a snake there, so was Israel surrounded, with the sea in front, the Egyptian chariots behind them, and the open desert filled with scorpions on either side. True to form, the image corresponds to a textual reality of the past. If Israel is to be compared to a dove, then Israel must really have resembled a dove at some point.

When Israel called out to God, God split the sea in response. Thus, God now asks to hear Israel's voice again rising in prayer and see the worship of the Temple and performance of *mitsvot* because these are pleasing to God.

In Berakhot 24a, this verse is cited by Shmuel as the proof-text for the saying *Kol be-'ishah 'ervah,* "a woman's voice is like nudity."

> Song of Songs 4:4: *Ke-migdal David tsava'rekh banuyi le-talpiyot 'elef ha-magen taluyi 'alav kol shiltei ha-giborim.*
> Like the Tower of David is your neck, built in courses, a thousand shields are hung upon it, all the bucklers of warriors.

Peshat. This verse is included in a list where the lover describes his beloved. He praises her body from her eyes to her breasts, but only the neck is compared to an inanimate object. This description of neck like a tower is repeated in 7:5. In that same verse, he also compares her nose to a tower. She compares her breasts to towers in 8:10. The implication, then, is that her neck is long. Perhaps she carries herself in a secure, dignified fashion, much as a fortress stands unafraid of the surrounding countryside—all are in awe of it.

The main difficulty of this verse is the word *talpiyot*, as this usage is unique in the Tanakh. Some (for example, Ibn Ezra and the NJPS) associate the word with hanging swords, as a double-edged sword is called a *ḥerev pipiyot* and one can imagine a fortress from which weapons hang. Fox and Segal translate the word as "courses" or "rows," as the tower is built out of bricks. This appears more acceptable to me because *banuyi le-talpiyot* parallels *migdal David* and not the next two images about shields and bucklers (which are also types of shields). Either interpretation, though, makes note of the necklaces and other jewelry that hangs on the woman's neck, covering her throat like a shield. That shields might hang in a fortress for practical or decorative purposes is seen in 1 Kings 10:16–17, where Solomon hangs golden shields.

Derash. The Targum seizes upon the association with King David to praise Israel's Torah giants, in particular, the Head of the Academy. This comparison comes from the association of the *talpiyot* with the Temple and will be discussed below. The Targum understands the Head of the Academy as the representative of the Stone Chamber, or room in which the Sanhedrin met in the Temple, and praises him as meritorious and causing other institutions of Torah study to be built. The students thrive, and their learning protects Israel, as if they wield weapons. Rashi moves away from describing the neck as an actual person but retains the comparison to the Stone Chamber, from which Torah went out to Israel, the merit of which protects the nation.

The idea of comparing the neck to the Temple and then subsequent structures in its proximity comes from Moses' blessing of the tribe of Benjamin where he says, "Beloved of the Lord, he rests securely beside Him / Ever does He protect him, as He rests between his shoulders." As the Temple is built among the slopes of Benjamin's territory, God's dwelling place is like a neck. This image is found in other places in Midrash, as Rashi employs it to explain Genesis 45:14, where Joseph cries *'al tsava'rei Binyamin* and Benjamin cries *'al tsavarav.* Benjamin's neck is pluralized, as two Temples will be built on his land, both of which will be destroyed, while only the Sanctuary at Shiloh will be built on Joseph's territory. And why is the Temple called *talpiyot*? In Berakhot 30a, Rav Avin, and some say Rav Avina, says that the Temple is called *talpiyat* because it is the *tel she-kal piyot ponim bo,* "it is the hill to which all mouths turn."

Once *talpiyot* has been identified with a structure of the Temple, it is identified with the Stone Chamber and associated with Torah study because of the imagery of warfare. God compares his "Servant" to an arrow that has been kept in a quiver and must now be fired out to the world in Isaiah 49:2–6. In Qiddushin 30b, the Gemara reads Psalm 127:4–5, which describes a man's sons as arrows in a quiver, as a discussion of the nature of Torah study. At first, the teacher and student are enemies, but they do not move from their place until they understand and come to love one another.

> Song of Songs 4:5: *Shenei shadayikh ke-shenei 'ofarim te'omei tseviyah ha-ro'im ba-shoshanim.*
> Your two breasts are like two fawns, twins of a gazelle which graze among the lillies.

Peshat. The descriptions of this first narrative of the woman's perfect body end with her breasts as the lover is then aroused and digresses. The image is repeated in 7:5, but here the line about grazing is added. Fox notes that this is "the only tristich in this Praise Song." He writes that the function served by this addition is to show their [breasts'] delicacy; that they eat lilies, not only grass, and are fragrant connects literarily to him, who also grazes among lilies, and paints a pastoral image. As fawns graze with their mouths to the ground, her nipples resemble their noses.

According to *Da'at Mikra* (on 2:7), gazelles poetically represent pure love as they are pleasant to look upon and graceful in their movement. The image of the lover as a gazelle recurs in the Song (2:9, 17; 8:14) and also in Proverbs (5:19, in feminine form).

Derash. The Targum writes that the twin breasts are actually the future Messiahs, one from David and one from Joseph, who will resemble Moses and Aaron, who led Israel through the desert collecting merit upon leaving Egypt. This comparison is explained well by the Ritva in his commentary to the Haggadah.

As the Haggadah expounds from the Torah passage *'Arami 'oved 'avi*, "My father was a wandering Aramean" (Deuteronomy 26:5–9) it begins to explain the verse *va-yehi sham le-goy gadol' atsum ve-rav*, "And became there a great nation, mighty and numerous (Deuteronomy 26:5), it comes to the word *ve-rav* and quotes a verse from Ezekiel 16:7, in which the prophet metaphorically describes how God found and cared for Israel. The Ritva expounds this verse to say that Israel was "naked and bare," devoid of any *mitsvot* or merit through which the nation would deserve redemption. The Exodus can only be seen in a miraculous light. God redeems Israel then, because of a promise made to Abraham, Isaac, and Jacob, who themselves managed to be righteous under unnatural circumstances as he explains (for example, they all have siblings who depart from, or never followed, God's path). Because God made a promise to Abraham between the parts (Genesis 15) and specified an end of the exile, God fulfills the promise and brings Israel out at the right time. The Ritva explains Ezekiel's comparison of a maturing young woman to Israel, who, although unworthy, has reached the time when she is to be brought to intimacy with God. The two growing breasts, which are signs of puberty, correspond to Moses and Aaron, who have been born at the proper time.

Returning to the Targum, we can now say that the Messiahs will be born at the proper time as well. Not only will they teach Torah to Israel, but they will be born at the proper time, which God will determine.

Part Three
Rabbinic Scholarship

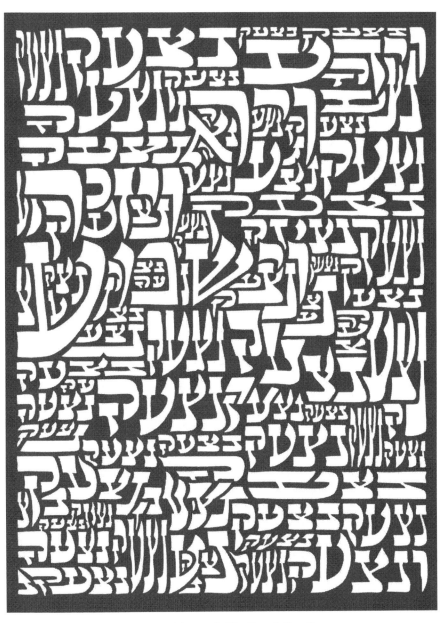

"V'nitz'ak: And We Cried Out."
Copyright 2006 Rabbi Matthew L Berkowitz, *The Lovell Haggadah*.

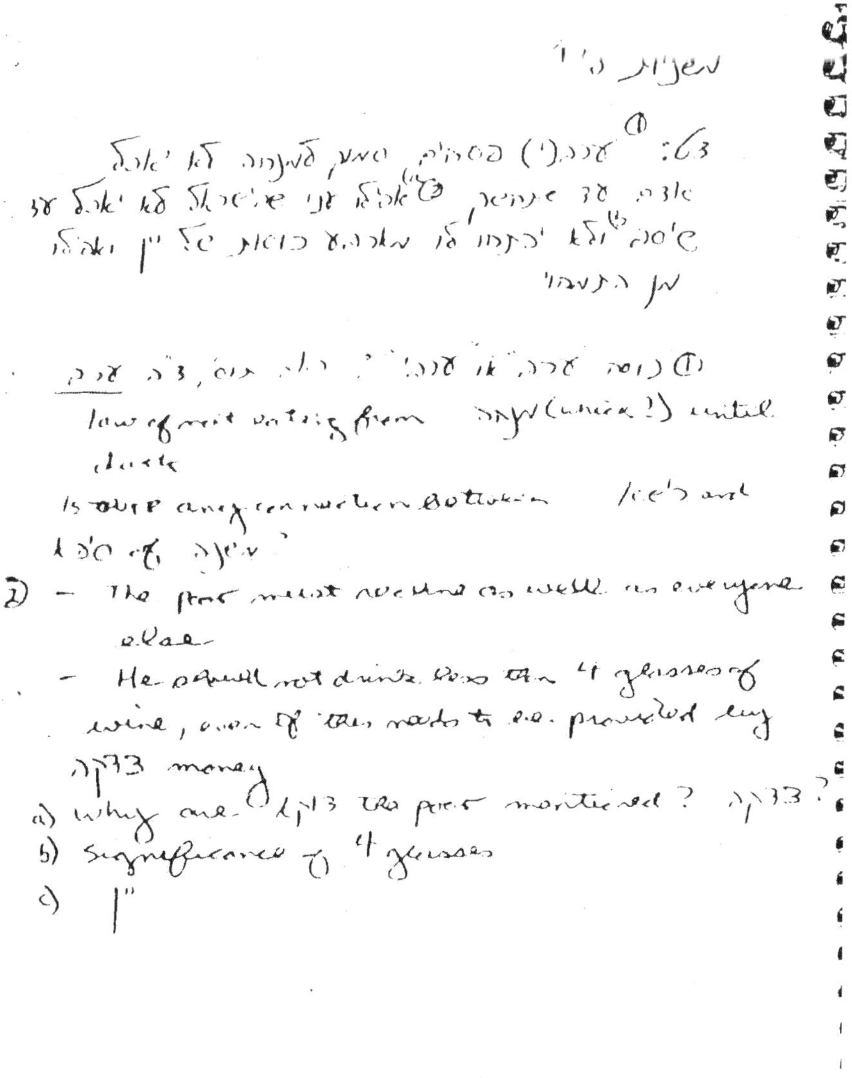

פסחים ק"ג

63: ארב(?) סומך, בשעת חתימה, ארבעה דברים... לא יאכל... [Hebrew handwriting, partially legible]

[Hebrew lines]

(1) ...

(1) ...
law of not eating from _____ (which?) until dusk

Is there any connection between _____ Iic's and ...?

2) — The ____ must recline as well as everyone else.

— He should not drink less than 4 glasses of wine, even if this leads to e.e. provided by צדקה money

a) why are צדקה the poor mentioned? צדקה?
b) Significance of 4 glasses
c) |"

Photo of First Page of Matt's Notebook on Tractate Pesaḥim

Matt Eisenfeld's Notes on 'Arvei Pesaḥim, the 10th Chapter of Talmud, Massekhet Pesaḥim

Editor's Introduction

In the months before his death, Matt Eisenfeld was studying the tenth chapter of *Massekhet Pesaḥim* of the Babylonian Talmud, which addresses the Passover seder. It was his intention to write a commentary on the Haggadah informed by this learning. This was quintessential Matt: striving to bring deep rabbinic learning to the most popular Jewish setting, the seder, where loved ones unfamiliar with Torah study could access it, and demonstrating the rigor and discipline to carry it out methodically over a sustained period of time.

Among the items found in his backpack at the scene of the bombing was his notebook with many pages of his notes on the chapter. The original memorial volume of 1997 included photocopies of these notes among Matt and Sara's writings. When my brother Ed discussed with me his plan to edit and publish the memorial volume for the 20th anniversary of Matt and Sara's passing, it was clear that these notes had to be included in the collection. Matt's budding Talmudic scholarship had to be demonstrated in the record, and not just described. Our hope was that the skeleton of Matt's intended Haggadah commentary could be constructed out of these notes, that Matt could be our teacher on this most central Jewish text. That particular hope will not be realized: most of the notes cover the first half of the chapter, which discusses laws of Kiddush and Havdalah and other, general, ritual matters; only toward the end do the notes touch on Talmudic passages about the seder. The notes, while thorough, are also fragmentary, mostly jotting down main lines and themes, and recording or summarizing key explanations of various commentaries. Very little synthesis, analysis, or personal reflection, can be found in these notes; he hadn't gotten there yet.

While we may not learn much about Pesach from these notes, we can learn something about Matt, as the notes do provide a glimpse into his learning process. A few observations.

1) His learning process prioritized covering foundation texts thoroughly. We first find notes on every mishnah in the chapter, and then on biblical passages about Pesach, before he begins reading the Gemara.

2) His commitment to thoroughness is also reflected in his methodical, chronological movement through the chapter. Inasmuch as his goal was to write a Haggadah commentary, he could have skipped the first half of the Gemara but instead chose to cover everything and to learn the material on the seder in its editorial context.

3) His learning began with questions, especially on the Mishnah, as he frontloaded that which he did not understand or which aroused his curiosity in a first read, guiding further learning toward addressing those questions.

4) He was rooted in the original, Hebrew and Aramaic terminology. Though he wrote the notes in English, he recorded all names and terms in Hebrew, never transliterating and rarely translating. For example, he will always write ברכה, not *berakhah,* or blessing. I suspect that this reflects two factors: (a) that he was steeped in the material and thinking about it on its own terms, such that it was easier and more seamless to write a term in the original than in his native tongue, even as that was the language of the notes; (b) his reaction to the heavy filtering of texts in the liberal Jewish world and his attraction to the direct contact and familiarity with texts and their language that he found in the yeshiva world. Throughout the notes, "yeshivish" vocal tics can be detected, which provide a truthful snapshot of Matt in his last years: even as his relationship with some of the values and practices of the yeshiva world remained critical and ambivalent, he remained steadfastly partial to its privileging of texts and his language shows that allegiance.

5) His learning consists almost entirely of noticing the questions and statements of the Gemara passages, and mining the *Rishonim* (medieval commentators) for their explanations. He consistently tracks Rashi,[1]

---

[1] R. Shlomo Yitzhaki, 1040–1105, Troyes.

the Rashbam,[2] Tosafot,[3] the Rif,[4] and the Ran,[5] and sometimes the
Rambam,[6] the Ba'al HaMaor,[7] Ravad,[8] the Ramban,[9] and the Rosh.[10]
His only ventures outside the *Rishonim* are a handful of references to
the *Tosefta Kifshuta* of Prof. Saul Lieberman[11] (whom he refers to by the
rabbinic honorific GR"Sh, for Gaon Rabbeinu Shaul), for his take on
questions that come up in the *Rishonim*. This focus shows the influence
of his teacher the previous year, Prof. Israel Francus, and continues the
style of learning that occupied Matt that year in his legendary *shiur*. The
notes indicate no engagement whatsoever with questions about the
composition of the Gemara, which were the focus of his learning with
Prof. Shamma Friedman concurrent with his learning of Pesaḥim.
Whether this indicates a preference or just that he first was learning the
Rishonim exhaustively and then planned a second run through for
source-critical study, or, simply, that this was a side project for which he
deemed compositional analysis irrelevant, is impossible to say.

The content of these notes may not be of interest to anyone not learning
this Talmudic chapter, and they will not be particularly useful to someone who
is; Matt never gets to the point of explaining a *sugya* or offering a *ḥiddush*. Their
primary utility is to provide a window into Matt as a learner, so I have tried to
leave his voice in the notes as unaltered as possible. Toward this end, I have
usually left his Hebrew terminology intact, but added a slash and an English

---

[2] R. Shmuel b. Meir, grandson of Rashi, 1085–1158, Troyes.

[3] Commentaries on outer margins of standard printed editions of the Talmud opposite
commentary of Rashi; comments include those of Rashi's sons-in-law and grandsons as well as
their contemporaries and students.

[4] R. Yitzhak Alfasi, 1013–1103, Fez.

[5] R. Nissim b. Reuven, 1320–1376, Gerona.

[6] R. Moshe b. Maimon (Maimonides), 1135–1204, born in Spain, spent much of his adult
life in Cairo.

[7] R. Zerachia b. Yitzhak HaLevi Gerondi, 1125–1186, Lunel.

[8] R. Abraham b. David, 1125–1198, Provence.

[9] R. Moshe b. Nachman (Nachmanides), 1194–1270, Catalonia.

[10] R. Asher b. Yehiel, ca. 1259–1327, Toledo. Born in western Germany, he was a key bridge
between the Ashkenazic community of North-Central Europe and the Sephardic community of
Spain and the Mediterranean rim.

[11] 1898–1983. Born in Belarus and an elite student at the great Lithuanian yeshiva of
Slobodka, he was a renowned professor of Talmud at the Jewish Theological Seminary in New
York.

translation. Though inelegant, I hope this will enable you to get a feel for how he wrote and thought while also translating terms that may be unfamiliar. I also provide English translations of all full textual passages that he records in his notes. Sometimes, I flesh out sentence fragments to help clarify the flow of his thinking; and where he writes sentences that gesture toward a fuller idea, I try to tighten the notes and stitch a paragraph. On a few occasions, I add footnotes explaining concepts or questioning Matt's presentation of an issue. To contrast my voice from Matt's, I use a sans serif font for his material. I hope that these notes can restore for us a glimmer of the vitality, seriousness, and passion with which Matt learned Torah, and may that glimmer inspire us, as Matt did in life, to add our own embers to it.

Aryeh Bernstein
Chicago
Kislev, 5776

PART I: THE MISHNAH: NOTES AND QUESTIONS

Mishnah 1, 99b:

(1)   ערב(י) פסחים סמוך למנחה לא יאכל אדם עד שתחשך.

(a2)   ואפלו עני שבישראל לא יאכל עד שיסב.

(b2)   ולא יפחתו לו מארבעה כוסות של יין, ואפלו מן התמחוי.

(**1**)   On the eve(s) of Pesachs, close to the afternoon offering, no one must eat until nightfall.

(**2a**)   And even a poor Israelite person must not eat unless he reclines.

(**2b**)   And they must give him no fewer than four cups of wine, even if from the charity plate.

(1) Three questions on this clause:

*Is the correct text "ערב" ("eve") or "ערבי" ("eves")?

See Tosafot 99b, s.v. ערב פסחים.

There, Tosafot notes the two different versions of the text and that the plural, ערבי, seems to make more sense, presumably, since פסחים is also plural, such that the clause means "every year on the eve of Pesach." Not able to dismiss the other textual variant, Tosafot suggests that if ערב פסחים is the correct text, it means either, "On the evening when Pesach sacrifices are offered" or "On the eve of First and Second Pesach," i.e., the holiday sacrifice itself, on the 14th of Nisan, and the makeup date a month later offered by the Torah (Bemidbar 9) to those who were unable to offer it on the proper date.

*The law prohibits eating from מנחה until dark; is that referring to מנחה גדולה (the early time for מנחה) or מנחה קטנה (the later time in the afternoon for the מנחה)?

*Is there any connection between the רישא and סיפא [the beginning and the end] of the mishna?

(2) Poor people must recline as well as everyone else and should not drink fewer than four glasses of wine, even if this needs to be provided by *tsedaqah* money.

  a. Why are *davka* the poor mentioned? *Tsedaqah?*

  b. What is the significance of four glasses?

  c. Why the special emphasis on wine?

Mishnah 2, 114a:

קי"ד.

מזגו לו כוס ראשון - בית שמאי אומרים: מברך על היום, ואחר כך מברך על היין.
ובית הלל אומרים: מברך על היין, ואחר כך מברך על היום.

They mix him a first cup: the House of Shammai say: He blesses for the day
and then blesses for the wine. But the House of Hillel say: He blesses for the
wine and then blesses for the day.

This mishna is a debate over the question of precedence to day over
wine or wine over day in the two *berakhot* of Kiddush.
—Why is this משנה repeated from *Massekhet Berakhot* (8:1)? Are there
   any changes?
—What ideas are in opposition concerning wine or day?
—Who is preparing this cup?

Mishnah 3, 114a:

הביאו לפניו, מטבל בחזרת עד שמגיע לפרפרת הפת.
הביאו לפניו מצה וחזרת וחרסת ושני תבשילין, אף על פי שאין חרסת מצוה.
רבי אליעזר ברבי צדוק אומר: מצוה.
ובמקדש היו מביאים לפניו גופו של פסח.

They brought before him; he would dip the lettuce until he reaches the
appetizer to the bread.
They brought before him matzah, lettuce, *ḥaroset*, and two cooked dishes,
although the *ḥaroset* is not a *mitsvah*.
Rabbi Eliezer, the son of Rabbi Tzadok says: It is a *mitsvah*.
And in the Temple they would bring before him the body of the Pesach
sacrifice.

Questions:
Following steps of the seder:
—What do they bring before him? Why is the mishna silent?
—What constitutes פרפרת הפת/the appetizer before the bread and why is it
   significant here?
—What is the symbolic value of *matzah*, *ḥazeret*/lettuce, *ḥaroset*, and the
   cooked dishes, or מצות בפני עצמן/matzot on their own? What is the reason
   for the order?

—About what issue is the מחלוקת/dispute about whether _ḥaroset_ is a mitsvah?

—What is the significance of the bringing of the Pesach sacrifice and when?

Mishnah 4, 116a:

קט"ז.

מזגו לו כוס שני, וכאן הבן שואל אביו. ואם אין דעת בבן, אביו מלמדו:
מה נשתנה הלילה הזה מכל הלילות,
שבכל הלילות אנו אוכלין חמץ ומצה, הלילה הזה כלו מצה.
שבכל הלילות אנו אוכלין שאר ירקות, הלילה הזה מרור.
שבכל הלילות אנו אוכלין בשר צלי שלוק ומבשל, הלילה הזה כלו צלי.
שבכל הלילות אנו מטבילין פעם אחת, הלילה הזה שתי פעמים.
ולפי דעתו של בן אביו מלמדו. מתחיל בגנות ומסים בשבח, ודורש מארמי אובד אבי
(דברים כו:ה), עד שיגמור כל הפרשה כולה.

They mix him a second cup, and here the son questions his father. And if the son lacks cognitive capacity, his father teaches him:

How different is this night from all nights!

For on all nights, we eat leavened bread or matzah; on this night, only matzah.

For on all nights, we eat all kinds of vegetables; on this night, bitter herbs.

For on all nights, we eat meat roasted, stewed or boiled; on this night, only roasted.

For on all nights, we dip one time; on this night, two times.

And according to the son's cognitive capacity, his father teaches him.

He begins with disgrace and concludes with praise, and expounds from "My father was a wandering Aramean" (Devarim 26:5) until he completes the whole passage.

Questions:

—Why is the son asking here?

—Is there a discernible uniting character to these questions?

—What is the significance of the style of storytelling?

—What relationship exists between ארמי אובד אבי ("My father was a wandering Aramean") and Pesach?

—For whom is the דרשה/expounding?

—Are the son's questions answered over the course of the seder and how?

—Are these *davka* the questions which should be asked or are they examples?

Mishnah 5-6, 116a-b:

קטז:-.

רבן גמליאל היה אומר: כל שלא אמר שלשה דברים אלו בפסח, לא יצא ידי חובתו, ואלו הן: פסח, מצה, ומרור. פסח - על שום שפסח המקום על בתי אבותינו במצרים. מצה - על שום שנגאלו אבותינו ממצרים. מרור - על שום שמררו המצרים את חיי אבותינו במצרים. בכל דור ודור חיב אדם לראות את עצמו כאלו הוא יצא ממצרים, שנאמר (שמות יג:ח) והגדת לבנך ביום ההוא לאמר, בעבור זה עשה ה' לי בצאתי ממצרים. לפיכך אנחנו חיבין להודות, להלל, לשבח, לפאר, לרומם, להדר, לברך, לעלה ולקלס למי שעשה לאבותינו ולנו את כל הנסים האלו, הוציאנו מעבדות לחרות, מיגון לשמחה, ומאבל ליום טוב, ומאפלה לאור גדול, ומשעבוד לגאלה. ונאמר לפניו הללויה.

עד היכן הוא אומר, בית שמאי אומרים: עד אם הבנים שמחה, ובית הלל אומרים: עד חלמיש למעינו מים. וחותם בגאלה. רבי טרפון אומר: אשר גאלנו וגאל את אבותינו ממצרים, ולא היה חותם. רבי עקיבא אומר: כן ה' אלהינו ואלהי אבותינו יגיענו למועדים ולרגלים אחרים הבאים לקראתנו לשלום, שמחים בבנין עירך וששים בעבודתך, ונאכל שם מן הזבחים ומן הפסחים כו', עד ברוך אתה ה' גאל ישראל.

Rabban Gamaliel would say: Whoever has not mentioned these three things on Pesach has not fulfilled his duty, and these are they: the Pesach sacrifice, matzah, and bitter herbs. The Pesach sacrifice—because the Omnipresent passed over the houses of our ancestors in Egypt. Matzah—because our ancestors were redeemed from Egypt. Bitter herbs because the Egyptians embittered the lives of our ancestors in Egypt.

In each and every generation a person must regard himself as though he personally had gone out of Egypt, as it is said: "And you shall tell your son in that day, saying: 'It is because of what YHWH did for me when I came forth out of Egypt'" (Shemot 13:8). Therefore, we are obligated to thank, praise, laud, glorify, exalt, honor, bless, extol, and adore the One Who performed all these miracles for our ancestors and us, for bringing us forth from bondage into freedom, from sorrow into joy, from mourning into festivity, from darkness into great light, and from servitude into redemption. So, let us say before Him, Hallelujah!

Up until which point should he recite? The House of Shammai says: Up to "as a happy mother of children" (Psalm 113:9). The House of Hillel says: Up to "flint into a water-spring" (Psalm 114:7).

And one concludes with the redemption.

Rabbi Tarfon says: "Who redeemed us and our ancestors from Egypt," and would not conclude.

Rabbi Akiva says: "So, YHWH our God and God of our ancestors, may we come to reach other seasons and festivals in peace, joyful in the rebuilding of Your city, and jubilant in Your service, where we will eat from the offerings and Pesach sacrifices etc." until "Blessed are you, YHWH, Who has Redeemed Israel."

Four parts:
1) Rabban Gamaliel
2) *Bekhol Dor Vador* ["In each and every generation . . ."]
3) Reason for obligation of praise
4) The specific נוסח/text of praise

Questions:

—Is R. Gamaliel's statement to be included in the story (and therefore go with previous mishnah)?

—Why does R. Gamaliel specify these three items ? What obligation is at stake?

—Why are פסוקים/biblical verses bracketed in the printed text of the Talmud?

—Are the reasons given for the discussion the reasons we have the three or are they the reasons for discussing the three?

   • Is בכל דור ודור ["In each and every generation . . ."] the essential statement and *mitsvah* of Pesach?

—On what prior statement does the mishnah say לפיכך ["Therefore . . ."]?

—Why does the mishnah wax poetic?

—Is there a difference between praises and אמירה [Recitation, the term used in the dispute between Beit Shammai and Beit Hillel about how much of Hallel one should recite at that point in the seder]?

—What is the significance of the מחלוקת/dispute? Is this a 4-way or two 2-way? Are these teleologies or ideas?

—Issues of חתימה/conclusion; what is the חתימה?

Mishnah 7, 117b:

קי"ז:

מזגו לו כוס שלישי, מברך על מזונו.

רביעי, גומר עליו את ההלל, ואומר עליו ברכת השיר.

בין הכוסות הללו אם רוצה לשתות, ישתה. בין שלישי לרביעי לא ישתה.

They mix him a third cup; he blesses over his food.

Fourth—he concludes the Hallel over it, and recites the song blessing over it.
Between these cups, if he wishes to drink, he may drink. Between the third
and the fourth, he may not drink.

—Each cup seems to have a separate function; is there a unifying
function?

—What is ברכת השיר/the song blessing and why does its cup have two
functions?

—Is the connection between the רישא/beginning and סיפא/end merely
thematic?

—Why is drinking prohibited and permitted at different times during the
seder?

Mishnah 8, 119b:

קיט:

אין מפטירין אחר הפסח אפיקומן.

No *afiqoman* may be added after the Pesach sacrifice.

Questions:

—What is אפיקומן?

—Why is the Pesach sacrifice the last food to be eaten?

Mishnah 8-9, 120a-b:

ק.-כ:

ישנו מקצתן - יאכלו, כולן - לא יאכלו.

רבי יוסי אומר: נתנמנמו - יאכלו. נרדמו - לא יאכלו.

הפסח אחר חצות מטמא את הידים. הפגול והנותר מטמאין את הידים.

If a few of them slept, they may eat. If all of them, they may not eat.

Rabbi Yosi says: if they nod off, they may eat. If they fall into deep sleep, they
may not eat.

The Pesach sacrifice after midnight renders the hands impure. *Piggul* [12] and
notar render the hands impure.

---

[12] *Piggul* and *notar* are terms used in VaYikra 7:17-18 and 19:5-7 for sacrificial meat beyond

Questions:

—What is the connection between sleep and eating the Pesach sacrifice?

—R. Yosi and the distinction between levels of sleep?

—What is the connection between רישא/beginning and סיפא/end?

—Is this טומאת ידים/impurity of hands actual טומאה/impurity or merely דרבנן/on rabbinic authority?

—What do we mean by טומאת ידים/impurity of hands?

Mishnah 9, 121a:

קכא.

ברך ברכת הפסח - פטר את של זבח, ברך את של זבח - לא פטר את של פסח, דברי רבי ישמעאל. רבי עקיבא אומר: לא זו פוטרת זו, ולא זו פוטרת זו.

If one blessed the blessing over the Pesach sacrifice, he has exempted for the one for another sacrifice. If he blessed the blessing over another sacrifice, he has not exempted for the one for the Pesach sacrifice; these are the words of Rabbi Yishmael. Rabbi Akiva says: Neither does this one exempt that, nor that one exempt this.

Questions:

—What is the significance of various ברכות/blessings and the reason for the מחלוקת/dispute?

—Why might one ברכה/blessing cover another?

—Why does the מסכת/tractate end with this mishnah?

PART II: SCRIPTURAL VERSES ABOUT PESACH

פסוקים על פסח

[Pesach in Egypt and preparation of the פסח מצרים והכנת הקרבן — שמות יב sacrifice]

---

their appointed time. The Rabbis define *piggul* as a sacrifice that becomes unfit due to the intention of the officiating priest, while preparing or offering it, to consume it after its permitted time (Mishnah Zevachim 2:3), while *notar* retains the plain, biblical meaning of a sacrifice that becomes unfit due to being left unconsumed until after the time limit for its consumption. The mishnah (Kereitot 1:1) lists consumption of *piggul* and *notar* as crimes punishable by *karet*—excision from the people.

ויקרא כג:ה   announcement of festivals

במדבר ט, כח:טז — פסח שני, מוספים   (sacrifices [Second Pesach, *Mussaf*])

דברים טז

מלכים ב כג

דברי הימים ב ל, לה

יהושע ה

עזרא ו

יחזקאל מה

מצות/Matzot

שופאים ו

שמואל א כח: כד

שמות יב   פסח מצרים א-נא

Shemot 12   Egyptian Pesach, verses 1–51

1) This is to be the beginning for the nation.
2) Communal membership expressed through circumcision and eating קרבן פסח/Pesach sacrifice.
3) Blood of Pesach to be put on doorposts, frame, and door so that God will "skip over" Jewish houses.
4) Sacrifice must be roasted and eaten in a group.
5) Must be eaten in a state of preparedness to leave.
6) This is the night upon which firstborn are killed.
7) This night is to be remembered, told to children.
8) Command to eat matzah precedes actual story of how the matzot were baked and why.
9) Children will ask questions.
10) Israelites were "given" the possessions of Egyptians.
11) An ערב רב/mixed multitude came out with Israel.
12) Reciprocity of ליל שמורים/night of vigil, God and Israel.

דברים טז   Restatement—Devarim 16

1) Matzah and Pesach connected: Problem with מצה seems to be an issue concerning קרבנות/sacrifices.
2) Matzah is called לחם עני/bread of poverty, "because you were taken out of Egypt in a hurry."
3) Purpose of matzah is to remember the day of leaving.

4) Pesach may be offered only in one place.
5) The word ובשלת/"and you shall boil" seems to contradict שמות יב/Shemot 12.
6) Issue of returning to tents.

יהושע ה   פסח לפני הכיבוש

Yehoshua 5   Pesach before the Conquest

1) *Benei Yisrael* are circumcised for the first time in forty years.
2) The מן/manna ceases after Israel celebrates the Pesach.
3) Yehoshua meets the שר-צבא-ה'/"Captain of YHWH's host", is commanded to take off his shoes.

מלכים ב כג:כא-כג   פסח יאשיהו

2 Kings 23:21–23   King Yoshiahu's Pesach

1) Takes place in midst of national reform.
2) Foreshadowed by promise of destruction.
3) No Pesach had been like this since time of שופטים/judges.

יחזקאל מה:יח-כה

Yehezkel 45:18–25

1) Additional rituals for ניסן/Nissan
2) Rosh Ḥodesh, repetition (?) of blood on doorposts of עזרה/'azarah and blood in four corners.
3) A קרבן חטאת/sin-offering of נשיא/Prince, a פר/bull on behalf of the nation.

עזרא ו:ט-כה   פסח קבוץ גליות

Ezra 6:9–25   Pesach of the Returning Exiles

1) Celebrated by people returning from exile who have just been purified.
2) Celebrated with שמחה/rejoicing because God makes them happy.
3) King of אשור/Assyria is helpful—הסב [because God inclined his heart].

דברי הימים ב לה:א-יט

2 Chronicles 35:1–19

1) The פסחים/Pesach sacrifices came out of the royal budget.
2) Not seen since days of Shmuel.

Part III: Notes on the Gemara

דתיח צטו:-קז.

Pages 99b-107a

There are three major issues in this section:

1) 99b-102b: interruption of a meal
   a. 99b-100a: identification of a dispute with regard to *Erev Pesach* and introduction of special concerns
   b. 100a-b: How to make a division [(a) and (b) can be combined]
   c. 100b-101a: אין קידוש אלא במקום סעודה ולהיפך/Kiddush is made only at the site of the meal, and vice versa
   d. 101a-102a: שינוי — דברים שטעונים/Change — required things

The last *baraita* of 102a begins the next *sugya*: Havdalah is introduced by way of Kiddush and the *sugya* will end by comparing the two.

2) Havdalah
   a. 102a-b: אין עושין מצות חבילות חבילות: הבדלה וקידוש חדא מילתא היא/ *Mitsvot* may not be done in bundles: Havdalah and Kiddush are one thing.
   b. 102b-105a: The order and language of the blessings
   c. 105a-106a: פרטי דינים בקידוש/Particular laws of Kiddush

3) Function of wine
   a. 106a: לימוד קידוש — קידושא רבה/Learning the source of Kiddush— The "Great Kiddush"
   b. 106a-107a: Until when for Havdalah and the issue of tasting
   c. 107a: What kind of wine?

These issues seem to be chosen for discussion because of the special relationship they have with the seder. If we say that everyone admits to the mishnah of refraining from eating because of matzah (like Rav Huna), then we know that the related issues will speak similarly. The Gemara bothers itself with issues of Kiddush and Havdalah as they may be the first things done in a seder and therefore require special attention here as the entire seder is meant to be symbolic.

On another level, we can learn about Kiddush and Havdalah from this juxtaposition with seder here. Just as the seder is the archetypal סעודת מצוה/mandatory meal, in which we are supposed to see ourselves as having come out of Egypt, so too every סעודת מצוה serves a function and is meant to point beyond the immediate eating and drinking. The position holding אין קידוש אלא במקום סעודה/Kiddush is made only at the place of the meal, for example, seeks to bring to life a verse from Yesh'ayahu 58:13, which reads:

אִם־תָּשִׁיב מִשַּׁבָּת רַגְלֶךָ עֲשׂוֹת חֲפָצֶךָ בְּיוֹם קָדְשִׁי וְקָרָאתָ לַשַּׁבָּת עֹנֶג לִקְדוֹשׁ יְהוָה מְכֻבָּד וְכִבַּדְתּוֹ מֵעֲשׂוֹת דְּרָכֶיךָ מִמְּצוֹא חֶפְצְךָ וְדַבֵּר דָּבָר.

If you turn your foot away from the shabbat, from doing your business on My holy day, and you call the shabbat a delight/'oneg, the holy of YHWH honored, and if you honor it, and not go about your ways, nor look to your affairs, nor speaking thereof.

We say, "in the place where you call Shabbat, there should be your 'oneg." The law of קידוש רבה/"The Great Kiddush" also exemplifies such an attempt to further sanctify Shabbat as its purpose seems to be to make a division between the סעודה/meal of Shabbat and any other סעודה.

Havdalah seems to serve two functions. The first is simply to divide Shabbat from the rest of the week, and we take the opportunity to make a ברכה/blessing on a God who divides. As the purpose of some *mitsvot* seems to be the recognition of God in the world, we take the opportunity to make ברכות/blessings, but say them only at certain times and events when particular aspects of God are recognizable. As a division, Havdalah functions as a bookend: Kiddush is on one side, Havdalah on the other. Both ברכות mention the holiness of Shabbat, both involve wine. This issue is highlighted by the last section of the Gemara, which discusses the use of wine and seeks to understand the issue by asking from Kiddush to Havdalah and vice versa.

צט:

99b
Superfluity?
Rav Huna — Perhaps R. Yosi admits that Pesach is a special case because there exists a חיוב/obligation to eat matzah.
Rav Pappa — Perhaps the difference is between סמוך למנחה/just before Minhah and מן המנחה ולמעלה/from Minhah and later.
Is סמוך למנחה/just before Minhah permitted? What is meant by סמוך/"just before"?

100a

הפסקה/Is the שבת ויום טוב/Shabbat and Holidays or on נחלוקת/dispute on the הפסקה/interruption?

This is a סוגיא/passage that tries to reconcile a mishnah with three ברייתות/baraitot or two ברייתות, one with two versions.

The Tosefta (Berakhot 5:1) reads: לא יאכל אדם בערב שבת מן המנחה/"A person may not eat on the eve of Shabbat from Minḥah time . . ." The Bavli adds the words וימים טובים/"and holidays."
The מעשה/narrative event, where R. Yehudah is present, shows that they began eating בהיתר/with permission and continued their meal.

Question as to what constitutes הפסקה/interruption:
Rishonim: עקירת השולחן וברכת המזון/Removing the table and saying grace after meals
GR"Sh Lieberman (*Tosefta Kifshuta, Berakhot*, p. 73): רק עקירת השולחן/Only removing the table

Rif (19b): מנחה ולמעלה — the explanation of this is 9 שעות ולמעלה/from the end of hour 9 and onward; the מנחה itself is 9.5.

הלכה כרבי יוסי מחבירו — בערב פסח אסור, דברי הכל משום חיובא דמצה — לשיטת רב הונא.
Halakha accords with R. Yosi over his colleagues: On the eve of Pesach, it is forbidden, according to everyone because of the obligation of matzah, according to the view of Rav Huna.

From the Rashbam:
99b, s.v., ולא יפחתו לו

ולא יפחתו לו — על גבאי הצדקה קאי.
- "And they should give him no fewer . . ." — this refers to the *tsedaqah* collector.
- The four cups represent four expressions of גאולה/redemption, as taught by the midrash in Bereshit Rabbah 88:5, referring to the four verbs in Bereshit 6:6-7.
- The reason for requiring hunger when eating matzah is the value of הדור מצוה/beautifying *mitsvot*.

- Re: the stipulation that one should have no fewer than four cups of wine even if it must come from the תמחוי/charity plate: the עני/poor person who has enough food for at least two סעודות/meals may not take from the תמחוי. But an עני must make every effort to afford four cups of wine. (On one hand, the עני must be included. On other hand, he must make every effort to include himself.)

99b, s.v., מתשעה שעות ולמעלה:

מתשעה שעות = סמוך למנחה שהיינו חצי שעה לפני

- "From 9 hours" = Just before Minḥah, which is a half hour beforehand.

Tosafot, 99b

S.v. לא: Rest of year, forbidden to eat סמוך למנחה/just before Minḥah.

S.v. עד: The significance of שתחשך/"until nightfall" is that there is a special *mitsvah* for the Pesach sacrifice, for matzah, and for maror at night, whereas סעודת שבת/the Shabbat meal can be eaten before dark.

S.v. ואפילו: Even the עני/poor person who hasn't eaten needs to wait.

S.v. לא יפחתו: How is one יוצא/fulfilled the *mitsvah* of four כוסות/cups? Through actual drinking or mere שמיעה/hearing?

S.v. רבי יוסי: What about סעודת מצוה/the mandatory meal for Shabbat? What about קדוש במקום סעודה/Kiddush at the site of the meal? Perhaps according to Rabbi Yosi, because Kiddush follows immediately after, the Kiddush goes on the meal and the meal goes on Shabbat.

Question: Why does Kiddush have to be במקום סעודה/at the site of the meal?

The Ran on the Rif (19a, in Rif pages):

S.v. לא יאכל אדם: The Ran explains that the חיובא/obligation of matzah not being until night is because אכילה גסה לא שמיה אכילה/excessive, crude eating is not called eating. This is similar to Yom Kippur (Shulḥan Arukh O"Ch 612:6).

S.v. מארבעה כוסות של יין: The drinking of four cups is also against התר־ עלה/poison, which God will in the future feed to עכו"ם/idolators, that God will destroy the evil enemies of Israel. This is a reason for saying שפוך חמתך/"Pour out Your wrath . . ." in the seder over the fourth cup.

S.v. דתניא מפסיקין לשבתות דברי ר' יהודה: Merely removing the table without saying ברכת המזון/grace after meals is not considered a הפסק/interruption from the meal; the interruption of a meal is called "removing the table" by the Gemara, because they ate on small tables. הפסקת אכילה נקרא[ת] עקירת השולחן] מפני שאכלו על שולחנות קטנות.

Rambam:
In Hilkhot Shabbat and Hilkhot Yom Tov, he highlights the issue of כבוד/ honor for Shabbat and Yom Tov, which is an additional concern. Accor**S** ding to this understanding, then, the *mitsvah* of eating matzah merits entering Pesach hungry as we match eating with eating. Eating with כבוד ועונג/honor and delight, on the other hand, according to R. Yosi, need not be matched.

ק. -: מפה

100a-b: Tablecloth:
The definition of מפסיקין/interruption for most *Rishonim* is clearing of the table and ברכת המזון/grace after meals.

The גר"ש Lieberman (*Tosefta Kifshuta, Berakhot*, p. 73) says it is simply clearing the table, even without ברכת המזון and says that the difference between R. Yehudah and Shemuel is removing of the table or of the covering.

Rashbam, 100a, s.v., ולא כרבי יוסי:
1) Shemuel's ruling to spread a tablecloth and make Kiddush, is like the practice on all Shabbatot of covering the challah;
2) שמואל מחמיר על עצמו/Shemuel is stringent with himself not to finish the meal, even though the core law follows R. Yosi.

Tosafot:
100a, s.v. אלא: Shemuel is holding שיטת חכמים/the position of the Sages, as found in the Yerushalmi.
100b, s.v. שאין: Today our tables are too long to bring out, so we cover with a napkin. The She'iltot (*Parashat Yitro* #54) adds that this is זכר למן/ in commemoration of the manna.

Rif (19b on Rif pages):
• With regard to הפסקה/interruption, he rules like Shemuel;
• No הפסקה for Havdalah; he simply rejects this;

- The הפסקה for Kiddush requires an additional המוציא/blessing over the bread;

Rambam (Hil. Shabbat 29:12) leaves out the need for an additional המוציא.

קק:-קא.   אותם בני אדם שקידשו בבית הכנסת

100b–101a: People who made Kiddush in the synagogue

Possibilities: one can fulfill either Kiddush or יין/wine, or both, or neither.
1) Why is there a חיוב/obligation for wine?
2) Why the מחלוקת/dispute on the principle אין קידוש אלא במקום סעודה/Kiddush is made only at the site of the meal?

Rashi
100b, s.v. ידי יין לא יצאו: If they will drink wine at home, they will have to make another ברכה/blessing since they changed places.

Rashbam:
100b, s.v. ידי יין לא יצאו: Changing places is היסח הדעת/diversion of attention.

101a, s.v. אף ידי קידוש לא יצא: This teaching that אין קודוש אלא במקום סעודה/Kiddush is made only at the site of the meal is a *derasha* from Yeshaya 58:

"וקראת לשבת עונג": במקום שאתה קורא לשבת, כלומר קרייה דקידוש, שם תהא עונג: זוכרהו על היין.

"And you call Shabbat a delight": In the place where you call it Shabbat, that is, the calling out of Kiddush, there shall be the delight: Remember it over wine.

Tosafot
100b, s.v. ידי קידוש יצאו: Usually, *halakha* is like Rav in איסורים/prohibitions and ritual law, and Rav holds that יש קידוש שלא במקום/Kiddush can be made elsewhere, and R. Yochanan holds like Rav, but later אמוראים/Talmudic rabbis hold like Shemuel.

היסח הדעת/Diversion of Attention

Moshe Benovitz:[13] According to the Yerushalmi, perhaps Rav is the מחמיר/stringent opinion because he requires you to go to a place where

---

[13] Moshe Benovitz is a Talmud professor at Machon Schechter in Jerusalem and was one of Matt's teachers the year he was killed.

they drink wine to hear Kiddush, even if you must leave your place of
סעודה/meal.

Rif, 21b in Rif pagination

This is a clear statement of how Shabbat is established on something:
The פסוק/verse from Yesh'ayahu 58: וקראת לשבת ענג, and one gets
enjoyment from eating and drinking; to Rashbam, this means that any
"eating" on Shabbat is called קבע because one derives ענג.[14]

In the words of the Rif:

איסתלק להו כל פירי מתורת עראי והוו להו בשבת כמאן דאזמנינהו למיכל מינייהו
בשבת בתורת קבע.

All produce is removed for them from the status of casual and on Shabbat,
becomes for them like that which was summoned to eat on Shabbat with a
status of appointed

Rif (21b) holds that *halakha* follows רבנן דבי רב אשי/the Rabbis of Rav
Ashi's house.

Ran (21b in Rif pagination, s.v. רבנן) adds: Only on Havdalah.

Rif's understanding of Kiddush is like Ma'aser—issue of עונג.

Ba'al HaMaor, 21b in Rif pagination:

1) Kiddush and Havdalah and Ma'aser only takes effect at dark, not בין
   השמשות/dusk, as we see from the מחלוקת/dispute between R. Eliezer
   and R. Yehoshua on Beitza 35a.

2) Points out that Rif accepts רבנן דבי רב אשי and not Shmuel from
   100a-b as he said there.

Milhemet Hashem, 21b in Rif pagination.

• Agrees with Ba'al HaMaor!!!
• Rif explains Gemara the reverse way of how we find it.
• Shabbat establishes self at dark.

Ra'avad, 21b in Rif pagination.

Rif explains based on גירסא/textual variant of Geonim, which reads פוק חזי
אי כזה יומא/go out and see if it still looks like day, implying בין השמשות/dusk,
and one should hold like the Rif, who is מחמיר/strict.

---

[14] I am not sure to which comment of the Rashbam Matt refers here.

Ran, 21b in Rif pagination, s.v. פוק
Defends Rif with mishnayot. חשכה ודאי לאו דוקא/Being dark is, of course, not stated as a particular requirement.

Rosh, 10:12-13

Brings the Ba'al Ha-'Ittur, who says that the ספק/uncertainty of Shabbat with regard to בין השמשות/dusk is what causes one to stop and make a הפסק/interruption, but rejects it. It does not stand to reason that the Gemara's many fine distinctions apply דוקא/specifically on בין השמשות and no other time.

There is a *minhag* of leaving בתי מדרש/study houses because Moshe Rabbeinu died בין השמשות of מוצ״ש/dusk at the end of Shabbat, but this couldn't be: a midrash teaches that he wrote thirteen Torah scrolls on the day, so it could not have been Shabbat.

Rambam, Hilkhot Shabbat 29:12
Appears to go like Ba'al HaMaor

קא.-: שיטת רבי יוחנן

101a-b: Rabbi Yochanan's Position:

א״ר חנין בר אביי א״ר פדת אמר ר' יוחנן אחד שינוי יין ואחד שינוי מקום א״צ לברך.
Said Rabbi Chanin bar Abaye, said Rabbi Pedat, said Rabbi Yochanan: Whether for a change of wine or for a change in place, one need not make a blessing.

Rashbam:

101a, s.v. אחד שינוי יין: "A change in wine" refers to a wine of different taste, from a new barrel, but according to Rav Yosef bar Ada in the name of R. Yochanan on Berakhot 59b, one still needs to say הטוב והמטיב/the blessing, "Praised are You . . . Who is good and makes good."

On 101b, Rav Chisda teaches:

שנוי מקום צריך לברך לא אמרן אלא בדברים שאין טעונין ברכה לאחריהן במקומן אבל
דברים הטעונין ברכה לאחריהן במקומן, אין צריך לברך.
We taught that a change in place requires a new blessing only with regard to items that do not require a blessing after their consumption in their place, but for items that do require a blessing afterward in their place, one does not need a new blessing for a change in place.

Rashi:

101b, s.v. אבל דברים הטעונים and s.v. בדברים שאין טעונים ברכה לאחריהם כו' בו: For things that don't require post-כו' בו/blessing, such as water and fruit, standing is considered ending of the meal, and new sitting is the start of another, but things that require a ברכה do not have this הפסקה, and so the new sitting is a continuation of the first. S.v. לקביעיה קמא הדר: It is with conscious focus on the first meal that the person is eating now, to conclude that meal. על דעת סעודה הראשונה הוא אוכל עכשיו לסיים סעודתו.

Rashbam:

101b, s.v. בדברים שאין טעונים ברכה לאחריהן במקומן: The blessing בורא נפשות is a general ברכה as it is nonspecific. (But what about meat?) S.v. לקביעיה קמא הדר: The *baraita* stands as a תיובתא/rejection of R. Yochanan because his statement is סתמ/without specification, referring to any case, whereas the *baraita* can be explained the other way.

Gemara:

101b-102a: The קשיא/difficulty on Rav Chisda is resolved by assigning the different שיטה/position to a דעת יחיד/lone opinion, namely, Rabbi Yehudah.

Tosafot:

101b, s.v. אלא: Is Rav Chisda against Rav and Shemuel? It looks like he disagrees only with Rav Sheshet. Maybe these דברים הטעונין ברכה/items that require a blessing are only on bread and מיני מזונות/other grains, so there is no dispute between Rav Chisda and Rav and Shemuel, because wine is something that doesn't require a post-ברכה/blessing in the same place.

As one must make another ברכה/blessing over wine, the dispute here is between the interpretation of Tosafot and the interpretation of Rashi and Rashbam.

Another way to explain the Gemara may be to say that in one case, a סעודה/meal is already in progress and so there is no היסח הדעת/diversion of attention for wine. The differing factor here is בני חבורה/members of the social group.

Rif:

- (20a) Explains Rav Chisda as saying that שאין טעונין/"that does not require" refers to fruit and wine and that טעונין refers to bread and מיני דגן/other grains.
- (20b) Rules like Rav Sheshet for *halakha*: everything needs another ברכה/blessing. This is consistent with Rav and Shemuel.

The מחלוקת/dispute between Rashbam and Rif over what things require a ברכה/blessing: for Rashbam, the issue is connected to the ברכה said and the חשיבות/importance of the items; for the Rif, the issue is that upon which people made סעודות/meals.

קב.-: פסחים (בבלי)

תנו רבנן בני חבורה שהיו מסובין וקדש עליהן היום מביאין לו כוס של יין ואומר עליו ברכת המזון דברי רבי יהודה ר' יוסי אומר אוכל והולך עד שתחשך גמרו כוס ראשון מברך עליו ברכת המזון והשני אומר עליו קדושת היום

Pesahim (Bavli) 102a-b

Our Sages taught: If members of a social group are reclining and the sacred day happens upon them, they are brought a cup of wine and one says grace after meals over it: these are the words of Rabbi Yehudah. R. Yosi says: one may keep eating until it gets dark. When they finish, they say grace after meals over the first cup, and Kiddush over the second.

תוספתא ברכות ה:ג-ד

אורחין שהיו מסובין אצל בעל הבית וקדש עליהן היום ועקרו עם חשיכה לבית מדרש חזרו ומזגו להם את הכוס אומרים עליו קדושת היום דברי ר' יהודה ר' יוסה או' והולך עד שעה שתחשך מזגו לו כוס ראשון מברך עליו ברכת מזון מזכיר של שבת בברכת המזון והשני אומר עליו קדושת היום.

Tosefta Berakhot 5:3-4

If guests are reclining at a host's home, and the sacred day happens upon them, and they removed to the Beit Midrash as it became dark, when they return, they mix them a cup and they say Kiddush over it: these are the words of Rabbi Yehudah. R. Yosi says, one may keep eating until the time it becomes dark. When they mix him the first cup, he says grace after meals over it and mentions Shabbat in grace after meals, and over the second, one says Kiddush.

Two different cups are used here, at least in the position of Rabbi Yehuda. There is no חידוש/innovation in Rabbi Yehuda's position, because we know already that he calls for interruption of meal. The Bavli has him calling for both Kiddush and *Birkat Ha-Mazon*, but such a demand is inconsonant with the Tosefta, since they left. Either they left someone behind as in other *baraitot*, or they already said *Birkat ha-Mazon* on their way out.

Essentially, the Bavli's question of two cups goes on Rabbi Yosi, but from the change of נוט/text of the *baraita*, perhaps the question can be asked on Rabbi Yehuda, as well.

102b

Move from ה"יקנ to יקנה"ז because if we're discussing last day, we can still say אין לו/he does not have a second cup.

Two *berakhot* on one cup?   We say, אין עושים מצוות חבילות חבילות/*mitsvot* should not be bundled together, but הבדלה וקידוש חדא מילתא היא/Havdalah and Kiddush are one thing.

Rashi (102b, s.v. קידוש והבדלה חדא מלתא היא): In Havdalah, mention קדושת יו"ט/the sanctity of Yom Tov.

Three explanations for the principle that אין עושים מצוות חבילות חבילות/*Mitsvot* should not be bundled together:

Rashbam, 102b, s.v. חבילות חבילות: Looks like a burden.
Berakhot 49a: חתימות/Closures of berakhot must be on one idea.
Sotah 8a: Don't do two things at once.

The Gemara now discusses Havdalah because this is sometimes the first step of a seder.

קב:-קג.   סדר הבדלת יו"ט שחל אחר שבת

102b-103a   The Order of Havdalah on a Yom Tov that Falls at the End of Shabbat

Tosafot:
102b, s.v. רב:

- Use of בשמים/spices is because of איבוד נשמה יתירה/the loss of the extra soul and on Yom Tov we still have this.
- Another שיטה/position: We didn't have יתירה, but we have שמחה/joy via eating and drinking, which serve same function as בשמים.

(Same bodily sensation is needed for Havdalah to satisfy this נשמה/soul.)

Gemara: There are many positions among the *Amoraim* as to what order to say the blessings of Kiddush and Havdalah when Yom Tov falls at the end of Shabbat.

רב: יקנ"ה

שמואל: ינה"ק

רבה: יהנ"ק

לוי: קני"ה

רבנן: קינ"ה

מר בריה דרבינא: נקי"ה

מרתא משמיה דר' יהושע: ניה"ק

Rav: Wine, Kiddush, Candle, Havdalah

Shemuel: Wine, Candle, Havdalah, Kiddush

Rabbah: Wine, Havdalah, Candle, Kiddush

Levi: Kiddush, Candle, Wine, Havdalah

The Rabbis: Kiddush, Wine, Candle, Havdalah

Mar, son of Ravina: Candle, Kiddush, Wine, Havdalah

Marta in the name of R. Yehoshua: Candle, Wine, Havdalah, Kiddush

Issues:

GR"Sh Lieberman (*Tosefta Kifshuta* Berakhot, p. 96, on 5:30) quoting the Shibbolei HaLeket, in the name of Rabbenu Gershom, says that, contrary to what the Gemara teaches, one should bless over בשמים/spices on Yom Tov that falls at the end of Shabbat, for where there is אור/light, there are בשמים/spices and בשמים precede אור. This is the way the שיטה appears in the Tosefta. Actually, the Yerushalmi flips the שיטות/positions; perhaps the Tosefta was changed to fit the Bavli, or the Bavli was changed because they went according to Beit Shammai.

Rashbatz: The סימן/mnemonic is that the blessings go from lowest sense to highest: mouth, nose, eyes, brain.

מחלוקת רבי מאיר ורבי יהודה בשיטות ב"ש וב"ה והעם נוהג כב"ה אליבא דרבי יהודה.

There is a dispute between Rabbi Meir and Rabbi Yehudah with regard to the positions of Beit Shammai and Beit Hillel, and the widespread practice is according to Beit Hillel as understood by Rabbi Yehudah.

So, if בשמים/spices are subordinate, why are they first? (GR"Sh Lieberman said that אור/light causes בשמים.) Why is the order as it is?

Rashi:

103a, s.v. והלכתא כרבא: Rava's position: Kiddush first, before Havdalah, because if one were to drink first, Shabbat would look like a burden.

s.v. על המזון שהוא בתחלה: *Birkat ha-Mazon* is first because it becomes an immediate חיוב/obligation and אין מעכבין/we should not obstruct it.

Rashbam:

103a, s.v. ק"יהנ אמר ורבה: Havdalah should not be directly juxtaposed with Kiddush, because the former weakens the force of the latter. אין לסמוך הבדלה לקידוש שזה מכחיש כחו של זה. Havdalah emphasizes the קודש קל/lighter sanctity of Yom Tov.

s.v. ה"קני: Levi says that Havdalah must be on wine, since it was established always to be said over wine, while Kiddush can be said over bread, and the wine is placed right before Havdalah, rather than before the spices because otherwise it will look like the wine is for Kiddush and not Havdalah.

s.v. ה"קינ: Rabanan: Normal Havdalah after Kiddush.

s.v. ה"נק: Mar bereh deRavina: Benefit from light first; wine comes first because of תדיר/the principle that more common rituals go first.

s.v. נהי"ק . . . : Havdalah first, wine goes on both.

We understand the משל/parable of R. Yehoshua ben H̲ananya on 103a because Havdalah is first and he says to escort the king away first.

103a: Abaye and Rava on the placement of זמן/the "Sheheh̲eyanu" blessing for Yom Tov

Abaye: יקזנ"ה—Wine, Kiddush, *Zeman*, Candle, Havdalah. Explanation (Rashbam, s.v. ה"ג משל דר' יהושע בן חנניה): Kiddush determines/קידוש גורם.

Rava: יקנה"ז—Wine, Kiddush, Candle, Havdalah, *Zeman*. Explanation for why we rule this way (Rashbam, s.v. והלכתא כרבא: The עיקר/essence of זמן is not on wine; הבדלה is done at the end so that we don't let שבת be like a burden.

When זמן is referred to, that means שהחיינו.

Kiddush may precede Havdalah because it's דאורייתא?

Ran:

20b-21a, in Rif pagination, s.v. רב: Spices are only an issue when moving from complete מנוחה/rest to complete מלאכה/work.

קג.-: ברכות יין

103a-b: Blessings over Wine

By definition, ברכת המזון/grace after meals is היסח הדעת/diversion of attention from the rest of the meal.

Which cup(s) of wine require a blessing?

אמימר   כל כסא וכסא

מר זוטרא   כסא קמא וכסא בתרא

רב אשי   רק כסא קמא

Ameimar: Each and every cup
Mar Zutra: The first cup and the last cup
Rav Ashi: Only the first cup

Rav's students require a new wine ברכה/blessing after ברכת המזון/grace after meals.
Saying נמלכתי/I changed my mind—I wasn't thinking about wine: this is a real היסח הדעת/diversion of attention.

Rashbam
103b, s.v. דרב כתלמידי הלכתא לית: Though *halakha* does not follow Rav's students, it also does not follow Rav Ashi.

קג:-קד.   הבדלה

103b-104a: Havdalah
- The Havdalah torch is a choice *mitzvah*: אבוקה להבדלה מצוה מן המובחר
- Dispute whether the last line before the end of the ברכה/blessing should be similar to the beginning (Pumbeitans) or to the end (Shemuel). מעין חתימה סמוך לחתימתו או מעין פתיחה סמוך לחתימתו

Tosafot
103b, s.v. רב אשי

כל דבר מצוה הטוען כוס א"צ לברך בורא פרי הגפן היכא דלא הוי הפסק.
For any commanded thing that requires a cup, one need not bless "*Borei Peri Ha-Geffen*" if there was no interruption.
In light of this, Tosafot asks why we say בפה"ג/the *berakhah* over wine over the second cup of wine at the seder, at the end of הגדה/the *Maggid* section, and answers that הגדה is actually a הפסק/interruption, and the permission to drink between cups one and two is only until אשר גאלנו/

"... Who redeemed us ... ," which is the הפסק. If another הפסק happened between one and two, we would have to make new ברכות/blessings.

104a, s.v. מאי

In most ברכות, opening and closing are about the same thing. (Here, in Havdalah to Yom Tov, we see different ideas.)

104a, s.v. בעי

The long Havdalah on Yom Tov lists different הבדלות/distinctions.

קד. ברכות הבדלה

104a: The Blessings of Havdalah

Rabbi Elazar said in the name of of Rabbi Oshaya that in Havdalah, one should mention no fewer than three and no more than seven distinctions: רב אלעזר אמר רבי אושעיא: 3 או 7. This teaching is challenged by a *baraita* teaching that even one can suffice as a minimum: מיתיבי — אפשר ברק אחד. The response is תנאי היא/that there was already a *tannaitic* dispute, so we have a מחלוקת/dispute and מיתיבי does not "disprove" Rabbi Elazar's statement in the name of Rabbi Oshaya.

The *baraita* also teaches that there is no Havdalah when transitioning from Yom Tov to Shabbat.

Rabbi Yehoshua ben Levi teaches that one making Havdalah must allude to distinctions mentioned in the Torah. He is getting at: Essentially what is Havdalah?

The חתימה/conclusion: Is this a חידוש/innovation that a חתימה could introduce new information?

The מיתיבי *baraita* mentions the הבדלות/distinctions—God, the Great Divider—that focus on the divisions that God creates; seven subjects mentioned:

	holy and profane קודש לחול	1)
the order of Creation/סדר בראשית	light and dark אור לחושך	2)
Creator Israel and the nations ישראל לעמים		3)
מקדש ישראל	impure and pure טמא לטהור	4)

5)	מים העליונים למים התחתונים/	world with divisions
		upper waters and lower waters
6)	כהנים ללוים	created for Israel
	Priests to Levites	
7)	לויים לישראלים	
	Levites to Israelites	

מעין חתימה: בין יום השביעי לששת ימי המעשה
Akin to the conclusion: Between the seventh day and the six days of doing.

The *baraita* records three views as to the text of the חתימה/conclusion:
1) Who arranges Creation: סדר בראשית
2) Who forms Creation: יוצר בראשית
3) Who sanctifies Israel: מקדש ישראל

קד.-: חתימה מאי?

104a-b: The Conclusion: What is it?
Rav: Who sanctifies Israel: מקדש ישראל — רב
Shemuel: Who distinguishes between holy and profane: המבדיל בין — שמואל
קודש לחול
Like whom does Shmuel hold?

Rashbam:
104a, s.v. ושמואל אמר....: See Ḥullin 26b, where they dispute about Yom
Tov which falls מוצאי שבת/at the end of Shabbat.

Ḥullin 26b: Mishnah reads המבדיל בין קודש לקודש/Who distinguishes
between holy and holy, and the *halakha* is to say at end. Also:
א"ר זירא: יו"ט שחל להיות באמצע שבת, אומר המבדיל בין קודש לחול ובין אור לחושך
ובין ישראל לעמים ובין יום השביעי לששת ימי המעשה. מאי טעמא? <u>סדר הבדלות הוא</u>
<u>מונה</u>.

Rabbi Zeira said: Yom Tov that falls in the middle of the week, one says
". . . Who distinguishes between holy and profane, between light and dark,
between Israel and the nations, and between the seventh day and the six days
of action." What is the reason? <u>One is enumerating the order of distinctions.</u>
Havdalah is essentially about recognizing differences.

Tosafot
104b, s.v. ולית:
The reason why *halakha* does not accord with the view that one says
both מקדש ישראל/Who sanctifies Israel and המבדיל בין קודש לחול/Who

distinguishes between holy and profane is because אין חותמין בשתים/One may not conclude with two themes.

104b

Ulla: "Praised is the One Who distinguishes between holy and profane."
עולא: ברוך המבדיל בין קודש לחול.

104b-105a

הטוב והמטיב > פותח עם ברוך כברכה רביעית של ברכת המזון משום תקנה ולא כמו שאר ברכות.

For the *berakhah Ha-Tov va-ha-Meitiv*—"*Praised are You . . . Who is Good and Who does good,*" one opens with *Barukh*, in the model of the fourth *berakhah* of *Birkat Ha-Mazon*, on account of a special decree, and not like other *berakhot*.

Rashbam:
104b, s.v. ברכת המצות: *Berakhot* for *mitsvot* are short: we do not say many words, and so there is no need for a חתימה/conclusion.
104b, s.v. וברכה אחרונה שבקרית שמע—Third *berakhah* doesn't begin with ברוך because of desire to connect אמת ה', אלקיכם, so that it is said כחדא/ברכה אריכתא/as one long *berakhah*.

קד:-קה.   פתיחות וחתימות בברוך
104b–105a: Opening and Concluding with "*Barukh*"
Rashi:
105a, s.v. היא, חח הודאה הודאה, חח ברכת מצות הודאה/*berakhot* over *mitsvot* being expressions of gratitude: There is no interruption of anything else said as praise or request.

Tosafot
104b, s.v. כל: [The Gemara says that all blessings open with *Barukh* and close with *Barukh*. However, the travelers' prayer (תפילת הדרך) and the morning blessing אלקי נשמה do not open with *Barukh*. The answer is that these are not really blessings/ברכות, but general expressions of praise and mere prayer—שבח ותפילה בעלמא. Blessings/ברכות and prayer/תפילה have different functions.
104b, s.v. וחן: *Berakhot* that depart from this form require explanation. This Tosafot is an essay on topic difference and how some *berakhot*

don't fit the pattern. Normally, a *berakhah* opens and ends with *Barukh* unless it is

1) ברכת מצות/a *berakhah* over a *mitsvah*;
2) over פירות/produce;
3) it is סמוך לברכתה/adjoining another *berakhah*;

    a. The *berakhah* after the Haftarah has no חתימה/conclusion for the first paragraph, nor a פתיחה/opening for the second paragraph: these are one ענין/topic. They then mention that there was a custom for the congregation to say statements of praise between those two paragraphs.

    b. The wedding שבע ברכות/seven blessings: The first three open with *Barukh*.

Tosafot mention that Rashi, on Ketubbot 8a (s.v. שמח תשמח) says that the first of the seven blessings, שהכל ברא לכבודו, was actually established with reference to the gathering of the large community, and should be said by itself. The next two blessings are different creations. The sixth (at the meal)/seventh (at the *ḥuppah*) blessing, אשר ברא, stands alone because it is even said without a new guest present (פנים חדשות). Rabbenu Tam says that the first two blessings, שהכל ברא לכבודו and יוצר האדם have no חתימה because they are short, just like blessings before food and *mitsvot*, so the פתיחה is, itself, the חתימה, and the third blessing, אשר יצר את האדם בצלמו, needs to have a פתיחה because otherwise it would sound like it was a continuation of the previous blessing.

    c. The *berakhah* over Torah study: סמוכה/they are adjoining, i.e., the second part, והערב נא does not open with *Barukh* because the two parts are actually one *berakhah*.

    d. The *berakhah* of Havdalah and מאור/the blessing over the candle, which precedes it: They are not the same issue, but many ideas recognized at once. The *berakhah* of Havdalah opens with *Barukh* even though it adjoins the *berakhah* over the light, so that they do not appear to be one *berakhah*.

    e. ישתבח does not open with *Barukh* because it is סמוכה to ברוך שאמר and the verses in between do not constitute an interruption/הפסק. For the same reason, the blessing after קריאת שמע does not open with *Barukh*, because it is סמוכה to the second blessing before Shema, the verses of Shema not constituting an interruption/הפסק between them.

104b, s.v. הטוב: For the *berakhah* הטוב והמטיב/Who is Good and Who makes good, there is no need for *Barukh*, since the *berakhah* mentions God in many ways.

קה.

כי היכי דקבעה לקידוש כך קבעה להבדלה

105a

Just as Shabbat frames the rules for Kiddush, so does it for Havdalah.

Rashbam

105a, s.v. כשם שקובעת למעשר:

אין אוכלין בשבת אפילו עראי מתבואה שלא נגמרה מלאכתה למעשר אלא אם כן עישר מערב שבת.

On Shabbat, one may not eat even casually from produce that has not been completely fixed with regard to tithing.

Rashi:

105a, s.v. כך קובעת לקידוש and כך: It is forbidden to taste anything without proper Kiddush or Havdalah.

(Perhaps this חידוש/innovation is in opposition to Rabbeinu Hannanel, but what about Yom Tov?)

Why or how does Shabbat establish itself?

Rashbam:

105a, s.v. קובעת לקידוש: Because it is forbidden to taste anything without first doing Kiddush: there is no הפסק/interruption greater than this.[15]

Tosafot, 105a, s.v. והנ"מ

Caution not to eat between Minhah and Ma'ariv on Shabbat. יש לדחות/ This caution should be dismissed in cases where one begins בהיתר/with license.

---

[15] The Rashbam comments that it is prohibited to taste anything Friday night before doing Kiddush, but I don't see anywhere that he says that there is no greater interruption than this.—A.B.

קה.-קו.   מהו שיקדש והולך כל היום כולו

105a-106a: May One Make Kiddush for the rest of Shabbat?
- Continuation of similarity between Kiddush and Havdalah
- How does the first איתיביה work?
- Only one window of opportunity for Havdalah at ideal time, but two specific opportunities for Kiddush.

105b

This second איתיביה/rejection text, namely, ואם איתא לישבקיה עד למחר
ולייעביד בית תרתי, goes on the conclusion of the previous דאי לא קתני.

Rashbam:

105a, s.v. דאי לא קתני: In other words, so what? The fact of the matter is that one should say Kiddush at the correct time.

105a, s.v. כבוד יום כבוד לילה: For which meal should one save the treats?

105b, s.v. חביבה מצוה בשעתה: A *baraita* of Rabbi Shimon who says that the burning of parts of an offering is permitted throughout the night and we don't wait until the end of Shabbat (Pesaḥim 68b).

This is also a defeat of the איתיביה.

Similarly, the difference between the entrance and exit of Shabbat is to bring it in early, but have it depart late.

קו.   קידוש על היין

106a: Kiddush over Wine
Derasha
Tosafot
106a. s.v. זוכרהו:
- Association of זכירה/remembering with wine in Hoshea 14 and Shir Ha-Shirim 1
- Discussion of whether blessing over wine is D'oraita or Derabbanan; they decide that it is Derabbanan.

Regarding קידוש רבה, see She'iltot as to why בורא פרי הגפן is said. During day, one must make Kiddush over a drink. This seems to be an issue in כבוד יום/the honor of the day. There needs to be some היכר/recognition that this is a Shabbat meal. What's with the biblical verses?

Mishna Berura (289:2): These verses are a mistake and one should not say them.

Arukh Ha-Shulḥan (O"Ch 289:3): Wine as היכר: this is the reason of the She'iltot. Saying verses is only an introduction and unnecessary.

קו.   עד כמה בשבת מבדיל?

106a: Until How Late in the Week May One Make Havdalah?

until Wednesday/עד יום רביעי = after Shabbat/בתר שבתא
Division of week

Thursday and onward/חמישי ומעלי = day before Shabbat/יומא קמי שבתא
Definition from Gittin, which comes from a decision needed to answer a question about Tannaim. But, not ברכה על האור/the *berakhah* over light. Why not?

Rashbam
106a, s.v. אבל לא על האור: As taught on 54a, Sat. night is the beginning of Creation, so only then is it fitting to make the blessing over light, and one makes blessings only at specific times.
My thought: This represents a return to מלאכה and the blessing should be made at the time when the return is first permitted.
What about spices?

קו:

106b: Variations on Kiddush
One may not make Kiddush after washing.
Rashi, s.v. נטל ידיו לא יקדש: This would be היסח הדעת/diversion of attention.
Rashbam, s.v. נטל ידיו לא יקדש: One need not wash for Kiddush; this is like washing for fruit, which is considered crass/גסות רוח.

Kiddush over bread:
Rashi (s.v. דחביבא ליה ריפתא) and Rashbam (s.v. דחביבא ליה ריפתא) read this as connected to the previous statement; in a case as this, one need not wash a second time, but can make Kiddush over bread.
From the Gemara and Rashbam, this looks like an issue regarding עונג/ enjoyment: what does he want most?

Rif, 22a in Rif pagination:
Kiddush depends on חביבותא/preference and not on washing.
Ba'al Ha-Ma'or, 21b in Rif pagination:

We are not concerned to follow Rav Beruna, because one can make Kiddush over either wine or bread.

Tosafot,106b, s.v. מקדש:
Rabbeinu Tam: Distinction between הפסק/interruption by bread and by wine.
Issue of wine for Kiddush: could be bread, too; the essence is עונג/enjoyment at the meal.
Regarding Havdalah, wine is needed because of שיר והודאה/song and gratitude.
Rabbeinu Tam holds that one shouldn't make Kiddush on bread and that one shouldn't wash because he holds יש קידוש שלא במקום סעודה/Kiddush can be made in a place other than the site of the meal, and is concerned about people leaving.

קו:-קז.   טעם: מקדש? מבדיל?
106b-107a: One Who Tastes: Does S/he Say Kiddush? Havdalah?
We rule here in accordance with Rava, who says that the one who tastes says both Kiddush and Havdalah.
Over what?
Ameimar fasts when not given wine for Havdalah, because it is forbidden to taste anything before Havdalah. He either holds that wine is needed or is stringent on himself but these are two versions of this story, the second of which is taken for *halakha*. That is that.
Rif, 22a-b, in Rif pagination: חמרא מדינה/a common beverage is suitable
Hagahot Maimoniot (on Mishneh Torah Hil. Shabbat 29:5): Saying Havdalah over wine permits eating, whereas the Havdalah in the Amida permits work.
The reason given for not eating before Havdalah: this is the time when the dead return to Gehinnom.

קז.-קז: סמיכה למנחה
107a-b: The time right before Minhah
1) Gemara's first question: Does this refer to מנחה קטנה או גדולה/The Great Minhah (early afternoon) or The Small Minhah (late afternoon)?
Concerns: למנחה גדולה, ומשום פסח/It refers to the Great Minhah, and is on account of the Pesach sacrifice.
Rashi (107a, s.v. מנחה גדולה and ומשום פסח): Lest he forget to bring the

Pesach sacrifice, which was offered after the תמיד בין הערביים (at 8½ hours on ערב פסח/day before Pesach).

Gemara answers: קטנה למנחה ונשונ נצו/It refers to the Small Minḥah, and is on account of matzah.

Rashbam (107b, s.v. או דילמא סמוך למנחה קטנה): There would be a problem here of consuming the matzah via אכילה גסה/crass eating, for although it is eaten על השובע/on a satisfied appetite, אכילה גסה is not called eating at all, and the Pesach sacrifice may not be eaten גסה, since it is קדשים, and one who eats via אכילה גסה is called a מזיק/damager (see Yoma 80b); nevertheless, this is not as much of a concern with the Pesach sacrifice as with bread either because even a small amount of this kind of eating of bread is considered אכילה גסה, or because matzah applies even now, when the Pesach sacrifice is no longer offered.

קז:-קח.

2) 107b-108a: Appetizers

Baraita: One is allowed to consume things that increase the appetite. There is a זכר/textual hint to this in Yirmiyahu 4:3 נירו לכם ניר ואל תזרעו אל קוצים—Prepare the ground before you plant: Open the digestive organs with a little food before you eat matzah.

תוספתא י:ה

השמש מכביש בבני מעיים ונותנן לפני האורחין אע"פ שאין ראיה לדבר, זכר לדבר: "נירו לכם ניר ואל תזרעו אל קוצים"

Tosefta Pisḥa 10:5

The waiter presses on their bellies, serving the guests. Even though there is no proof for this matter, there is a textual hint to the matter: "Break up the unbroken ground, and do not sow among thorns" (Yir. 4:3).

GR"Sh Lieberman follows the Rashba in his explanation of this passage.
(*Tosefta Kifshuta, Pischa, pp. 649–50*)

The Yerushalmi goes from the issue of הפסקה/interruption straight to the kinds of foods one may eat and not eat, skipping the issues of Kiddush and Havdalah. The sources used in the Bavli from 102b-107a are mostly Amoraic and Babylonian.

In the Bavli, the נקודותיים/colon of 107a may be read either as a return and wrap-up of the issue of הפסקה/interruption and preparation for סעודה/meal or as the beginning of the next issue, which is the preparation for the meal.

Tosafot
107a, s.v. סמוך:
Minḥa is an עת רצון/time of favor: this is when Eliyahu is answered.

107b, s.v. דילמא: Why doesn't the Gemara raise אכילה גסה/crass eating with regard to the Pesach sacrifice? One fulfills the *mitsvah* at זריקת הדם/ the sprinkling of the blood; eating is a separate *mitsvah*. One should eat the Pesach sacrifice in a condition called על השובע/on a satisfied appetite, which means that one should still be somewhat hungry.

Yerushalmi: Rabbi fasts.
Bavli: Rav Sheshet fasts.
Both are said to fast because of being איסתניס/delicate.

From 107a at bottom is a new *sugya* entirely. The new material out of which the first part is built are תוספתות/passages from the Tosefta and מימרות/statements of Amoraim from Berakhot. From סמוך למנחה and on, we are focusing on Pesach.

קח. הסיבה

108a: Reclining
Rav Naḥman's שיטה/position:
Matzah needs הסיבה/reclining, maror does not. But what about wine? Rav Naḥman said that one pair of cups needs it and one does not. The Gemara proposes reasons for both cases and then claims that all four need הסיבה.
The issue is to use this action as further instructor:
> Matzah: to remember the redemption/מצה: זכר לגאולה
> Maror: to remember the slavery/מרור: זכר לעבדות

Tosafot
108a, s.v. מאי:
One could ask about matzah because 1) they eat it after coming out— מאי דהוה/what happened already — plus the Haggadah has already been

said; 2) לחם עוני/"bread of affliction," but this is עיקר סעודה/the essence of the meal, and they already leaned for wine, which is less important, and matzah is also called זכר לחירות/in remembrance of freedom.

קח. מי צריך הסיבה?

108a: Who is Required to Recline?

A תלמיד/student with his rabbi does not lean, because מורא רבו כמורא שמים/"the fear of one's rabbi is like the fear of Heaven" (Mishnah Pirke Avot 4:12). The attack *baraita* concerns a student next to the one who teaches a trade. Then one who teaches a trade is also called רב.

קח.-: ארבע כוסות

108a-b: The Four Cups

נשים חייבות שאף הן היו באותו הנס.

Women are obligated, because they, too, were in the same miracle. What helps this reason?

Ran, 23a in Rif pagination, s.v. שאף: This is like Hanukkah and Megilla, which are דרבנן/*mitsvot* of rabbinic innovation, and it is for this reason that women are חייבות/obligated; otherwise, they would be פטורות/exempt. Holds that every תקנה דרבנן/rabbinic decree is כעין דאורייתא/akin to a biblical law. Just like Tosafot, 108b, s.v. שאף.

Rashi and Rashbam, 108b, s.v. שאף הן היו באותו הנס:
אף הן appears when גאולה/redemption comes about because of women.

Tosafot, 108b, s.v. היו: Rashbam's interpretation is problematic, because אף implies that they are not the essential part of the גאולה/redemption, but are saved "along with everyone else." Moreover, the Yerushalmi's text reads אף הן היו באותו ספק/they, too, were in the same *danger*: would they live or not? As far as why women are exempt from sukkah, even though they were beneficiaries of the miracle of God protecting Israel in sukkot, we say that women are פטורות/exempt from דאורייתא/biblical *mitsvot*, but חייבות/obligated in דרבנן/rabbinic; even though they were in the same נס/miracle, sukkah is a מצות עשה דאורייתא/positive, biblical *mitsvah*.

קח: ארבע כוסות

108b: The Four Cups (cont.)
Statement Rav Yehudah in the name of Shemuel modified by Rava.

	יין/חירות	יין/ארבע כוסות
רשב"ם:	ד' כוסות	שמחת יו"ט
רי"ף:	ד' כוסות	חירות
תוספות:		שמחת יו"ט

	Wine/Freedom	Wine/Four Cups
Rashbam	Four Cups	The Yom Tov celebration
Rif	Four Cups	Freedom
Tosafot		The Yom Tov celebration

Use of Mishle 23: Color of wine causes ogling. This desire to drink goes fulfilled at times and should be pleasurable.

Rambam on הסיבה: Hilkhot Chametz U-Matzah 7:4
- The Gemara says that פרקדן is not considered הסיבה/reclining. The Rambam translates פרקדן to mean leaning on one's face or back.
- One must lean when eating matzah and drinking cups; for the rest of the meal, it is recommended. (Presumably the first two are primary *mitsvot*.)

Why don't women need הסיבה/reclining?
- Because of אימת בעל/the terror of their husbands[16]

The issue of the She'iltot is that נשי אין דרכה למגזי/it is not women's way to mix wine: since women don't drink wine they don't lean, but an "important woman" leans because she drinks wine.

קט:-קי. סכנה בד' כוסות?

109b-110a: Danger in the Four Cups?

ליל משומר ובא מן המזיקין
ראה—שמות יב:יג
ליל שמורים > שדבר רע לא יקרה

---

[16] Matt doesn't say whom he is citing, but I suspect he's seeing it in the Hagahot Maimoniyot's comment to this *halakha* in the Rambam.

The Gemara, noting a tradition warning people not to perform actions in pairs, wonders how the Torah could have commanded drinking four cups of wine, which would seem to be dangerous. Rav Naḥman explains that "a night of vigil" in Shemot 12:42 means "a night protected from damaging spirits." This seems to reflect the content of Shemot 12:13: "And the blood on the houses where you are shall be a sign for you: when I see the blood I will pass over you, so that there will be no plague of destruction on you when I strike the land of Egypt." In this understanding, "a night of vigil"/ליל שמורים means a night when no bad thing will happen.

Therefore, according to the Shulḥan Arukh, in Siman 481, there is no need to say other verses besides קריאת שמע and המפיל/the bedtime blessing at night because this night is one of protection.

Two תירוצים/resolutions to the Gemara's challenge to the requirement of an even number of cups:

1) Rava: One cup goes on ברכת המזון/grace after meals.
2) Ravina: Each cup is itself a *mitsvah* unto itself.
See next *sugya*.

Sara and Elisha Ben Avuyah: Who Is the "Other"?

CELIA DEUTSCH, N.D.S.

We are approaching the twentieth anniversary of Sara's and Matt's deaths in a context of global violence that has only intensified in the past two decades. Recent attacks in Israel and bombings in Beirut on November 12 and in Paris on November 13, 2015, bracket ongoing violence in sub-Saharan Africa, Eastern Europe and Russia, and Central Asia. As paradoxical as it might seem, Sara's and Matt's story provides a way forward without facile answers or bromides.

I knew Sara as her teacher and mentor. In her sophomore year at Barnard College, Sara took my class "Judaism in the Time of Jesus." The students came from a wide variety of religious perspectives and from none at all. Together we engaged in lively discussion of difficult texts. Sara's papers reflected an excepo tional understanding of the primary sources, including material she had never read. Her whimsical sense of humor lightened classroom conversation, especially in those moments when academic analysis challenged previous assumptions. Sara's respect for her colleagues was evident even when they expressed opinions that diverged from her own. I was impressed by her commitment to intergroup relations, revealed to me in conversations outside the classroom.

Sara had entered Barnard as part of the Centennial Scholars' Program, which provided a small group of outstanding students the opportunity for independent research. Students were encouraged to pursue interests beyond their chosen area of concentration. Sara, an aspiring environmental scientist, chose to do a study of rabbinic traditions surrounding the figure of Elishah ben Avuyah,

---

Celia Deutsch is Research Scholar in the Department of Religion at Barnard College, New York. A Catholic nun, she is a member of the Congregation of Our Lady of Sion (in French: Congrégation de Notre-Dame de Sion), abbreviated by its members as N.D.S.

a sage who lived in the land of Israel in the late first and early second centuries, and she asked me to guide her work.

Elisha ben-Avuyah lived much of his life in the period after the war of 66–70 C.E. that came to a climax with the destruction of the Temple. His colleagues included Akiva, Ben Zoma, and Ben Azzai. Among his students was the great R. Meir. Despite recognition of his accomplishments as a sage, Elisha ben-Avuyah was called "*Aher*"—Other—for he was deemed a heretic. Why? We do not know the precise reasons. Stories collected and edited in the rabbinic sources Sara analyzed with such care suggest that even the sages had varying opinions. Had Elisha despaired over the question of innocent suffering? Was he in collusion with the Roman government oppressing his people? Had he become intellectually and spiritually destabilized as a result of mystical speculation? Did Elisha's halakhic transgressions figure into the construal of his status as "Other"?

Such variety leaves a sense of vagueness with gaps to be filled. Sara was drawn to the texts, and to pondering these gaps. When I asked her why she was choosing the Elisha ben-Avuyah traditions as a focus for her research, she said, "I want to know what made him 'Other.' What makes a person 'Other'? How does a person become 'Other'?" Later, in her final project, Sara wrote that this study was part of "a process of religious self-understanding."

Sara proceeded in scholarly fashion. She chose her topic, including the texts to be used and the question that would drive her work. She did her own translations of all the pertinent sources and then analyzed them for herself. She asked broader questions of social and political context, both in relation to what might be known of the historical figure and to the social context of the actual redaction of the sources. She consulted appropriate secondary literature. This consultation took Sara into conversation with others who had analyzed the same texts.

Sara's work was entitled "'Elisha Looked and Cut at the Shoots': Making the Myths of the Other in Ancient Rabbinic Texts." The title itself is evocative. Until this day, there is no settled interpretation of the phrase "Elisha looked and cut at the shoots," or—indeed—why Elisha was deemed "Other." Sara certainly discussed the matter in her work in a thorough analysis of the texts from literary and sociohistorical perspectives. But she looked at these narratives as ways of addressing questions of profound religious and cultural concern, for the rabbis and later readers, including herself.

The unsettled quality of the sources, for all their poignant beauty, suggests that little can be known about "what *really* happened." But, if little can be known of the historical figure Elisha ben Avuyah, the texts suggest ways in which the rabbis were using the narratives to think about their own communities. In Sara's words, the texts serve as "windows" onto the rabbis' world. They provide "a window on the religious, social, and personal landscape of the author or group who wrote it" (Draft, March 28, 1995, p. 1; see p. 174 below).

The stories of Elisha are about otherness, about being Other. They are about belonging and identity. They are about the power and beauty of Torah, the sacredness of Shabbat, and the primary importance of solidarity with one's people, no matter one's privilege, learning, or accomplishment. The narratives are also about repentance, literally "return." Sara notes that the texts suggest that Elisha himself believes that he is beyond the point of return. Sara asks, "Is there a point in a religious system—in thought or deed—which, if crossed, has irreversible consequences?" (p. 189 below).

Sara tells us that she is using her study of the Elisha narratives in her own spiritual journey. She tells us that she is drawn by the question of "otherness." Certainly she was drawn to people who were other: the homeless woman who frequented her college neighborhood, students of ethnic, cultural, gender, and religious identities different from her own. She was genuinely interested in those around her, wanting to learn something of *their* worlds, open to receiving from them. The respect for her colleagues that I witnessed in my classroom, which so many others witnessed, were part of the same mind and heart that could analyze texts about someone who was "other" with such interest, sympathy, and intellectual clarity.

Sara's approach to the study of texts was both academic and intensely personal. She was aware that the question of "otherness" was also one of identity. Ultimately, the question of "otherness" is about the otherness in one's own self. For Sara, there was a question of integration. She was intentional about integrating her life as a woman and a scientist with her religious identity. It was part of her "project" for her year in Israel. She wanted to learn more about how to integrate all the parts of herself, just as she wanted to learn, to make a life with others, and to contribute to healing the world.

Sara was a woman of conversation—conversation with "others," as well as those like herself, whether members of her community or beyond. The violence that took the lives of Sara and Matt and twenty-three other people on the Number 18 bus twenty years ago has steadily increased. We live in a world polarized along many lines: political, religious, racial, ethnic, socioeconomic, gender and sexual preference. Despair is all too easy, but the memory of a woman who chose to probe the stories of one who was called "the Other" challenges us to do the hard work of finding common ground with those who are "other" in our own lives. For all the tragedy of Sara's murder, her memory tells us that the struggle for Justice and the finding of common ground are indeed possible. Twenty years later after the bombing of Number 18, there is no other choice.

"Elisha Looked and Cut at the Shoots": Making the Myths of the Other in Ancient Rabbinic Texts

SARA DUKER

I. Introduction

1. What is this all about?

Elisha ben-Avuyah, a first-century rabbi, is one of the most tantalizingly enigmatic figures of Jewish literature. Known as "Aher," Hebrew for "the Other," he is best known for his apostasy—his denial of something—which the early rabbinic writings describe with both symbolic richness and maddening vagueness. No one knows his precise biography—what he did, what he thought, and how he related to Jewish society during that time—yet (or perhaps therefore) speculation about him has proven to be a rich source for Jewish storytellers in different generations. Questioning religious people hunger to know: What makes a brilliant scholar and religious leader renounce his faith? In what does renunciation consist? When do a person's actions put him definitively outside the folds of acceptable religious behavior, and outside of acceptable society? Who is a Jew, and what does he do, once he is outside? How do regular people deal with the Other? How does God?

My project is another small chapter in the long line of questions, taking apart stories and putting new ones together. My goals began with learning more about Elisha himself, from whatever factual information exists. Without

---

This essay is Sara Duker's Centennial Scholars Project. It was presented to Dr. Celia Deutsch, Department of Religion at Barnard College, on April 26, 1995.

historical records, however, what is more important (and more interesting) is learning how Elisha was represented by his near-contemporaries and by people in succeeding generations. What did people think he did, how did they regard him for it, and how did they express these attitudes? In what contexts did differing representations develop? Often, the story of the Other is used to approach other ideas, providing us a window on the religious, social, and personal landscape of the author or group who wrote it. One goal of this project was to look at early sources for common stories, and examine how they develop in different directions. (This was not a scholarly exercise in text and redaction, but rather a purely literary comparison.) I chose the particular subject of these traditions because it affords the opportunity for asking myself some questions along the way: about what makes a person belong, and what makes him Other? This is part of a process of religious self-understanding. Last, but not least of my goals was to create an occasion to study a selection of aggadic (narrative, as opposed to legal) texts in detail.

2. Approach and methods

The approach to this project has been examination and reexamination of the earliest rabbinic texts regarding Elisha ben-Avuyah. These include the tannaitic[1] works of the Mishnah[2] and Tosefta,[3] and following generations' works that were constructed on them—the Babylonian Talmud (Talmud Bavli)[4] and Palestinian Talmud (Talmud Yerushalmi).[5] I generated my own translations of these sources and compared them with each other for literary and thematic similarities and differences, attempting to reconstruct common seeds of ideas, and

---

[1] From the era of the Tannaim—early rabbis—about 100 B.C.E. to 200 C.E.

[2] The Mishnah is the first written code of the traditional oral law, compiled for several generations, and edited circa 200 C.E. by Rabbi Judah Ha-Nasi (the "prince").

[3] The Tosefta is a compilation of baraitot—tannaitic legal statements, stories, and parables that were not included (or included in terser form) in the Mishnah. Nevertheless, the sources were considered authoritative and were often cited in later legal discussions.

[4] The Babylonian Talmud is the exposition of the Mishnah's legal code (with a large body of narrative and other nonlegal material) by the rabbinic authorities residing in Babylonia, where a large segment of the Jewish population lived during much of the ancient and early medieval period. The compilation was closed ca. 500 C.E. This is considered to be the most authoritative body of Jewish law.

[5] The Palestinian Talmud also is an exposition of the Mishnah, compiled by the rabbis who still resided in Palestine. The compilation was closed ca. 400 C.E. The Palestinian Talmud is shorter and considered less legally authoritative than its Babylonian counterpart.

analyzing their points of divergence. Finally, I have been reading secondary sources for historical context, and other suggestions for reconstruction of the Elisha traditions.

This paper first introduces the landscape of which Elisha is a part. This includes brief background on the history of the period and of the sources. The main body of this essay begins with the literary "window" through which the rabbis of the Mishnah and Tosefta view him—because the context in which he is placed is not necessarily the one a modern reader would consider to be the most obvious. Rather than appearing in a set of stories about heretical philosophies, action, or people, he is part of an exposition on forbidden topics of study that takes on varying degrees of mystical overtone in these and various later works, springing from the mysterious text common to the sources used, "Four went into the *pardes* . . . Elisha looked and cut at the shoots. . . ." An analysis of the Tosefta follows, identifying two possible approaches to this strange piece of text. In examining the amoraic sources—the Talmuds, I have first noted common traditions among them. I then consider their unique perspectives, both as choosing/emphasizing one of the approaches identified in the analysis of the Tosefta, and as generating sets of different questions. I conclude with a glimpse at how some modern storytellers construct Elisha ben-Avuyah based on these texts—what questions are they addressing? How have the windows shifted over time?

II. LANDSCAPE

1. Historical forces at work

Elisha ben-Avuyah the person and the seeds of his story were planted during a time of crisis in the Jewish community of ancient Palestine. In the first century of the Common Era, Jewish internal politics were driven by competing social-religious factions of the Pharisees and Sadducees—the former a popular party known for espousing inherited oral traditions beyond the realm of the written Scriptures, and the latter a more religiously conservative, aristocratic party representing the wealthy ruling class associated with the high priesthood. The early rabbis, practitioners and transmitters of the oral tradition themselves, often harshly criticize the Sadducees in their writings. Other socioreligious divisions also existed, including ascetic and messianic sects; apocalyptic thought was prevalent. In addition, Christianity was in its earliest stages of development. The driving forces for many events were the harsh conditions of Roman rule. Corruption, heavy taxation, and religious repression led to two major revolts in a short period of time. The first, from 66 to 73 C.E., led to the destruction of the Temple in Jerusalem—a calamity of massive political, social, and religious implication—in addition to the upheaval and loss of life characteristic of an extensive time of war. The second rebellion, during the years 132–135 C.E., sprang from renewed repression and unrest, and rising messianic hopes under Bar-Kochba. This war ended more disastrously than the first, with more bloodshed and Roman decrees designed to permanently uproot Jewish life. Hopes for a rebuilt Temple were permanently buried. During this war, many scholars and teachers were martyred, including the venerable Rabbi Akiva. Nevertheless, Jewish life continued its process of reconstruction, the landmark of the age being the compiling of the Mishnah, the first written systemization of the traditional oral law (attributed to Rabbi Judah Ha-Nasi) around the year 200.

2. Life and career of Elisha

Elisha ben-Avuyah was born sometime after the destruction of the Temple in 70 C.E. to a prominent Jerusalem family. He studied with the preeminent scholars of his day, and became one of the leading scholars of his own generation, a contemporary of Rabbi Akiva in both age and ability. Stories in the Talmud associate these two figures also with Simeon ben-Azzai and Simeon ben-Zoma. Elisha was the teacher of Rabbi Meir, who was in turn teacher of Rabbi Judah Ha-Nasi, the editor of the Mishnah. From the company of teachers and disciples in which he was likely to be found, one might guess that Elisha exerted significant influence on Jewish thought of his day. For these same reasons, the effects of his apostasy would have had a profound effect on his generation—probably even greater because of the tumultuous period in which he lived. The texts of the Talmud dub him "Aher," the Other, and his legal opinions are never quoted (except once, indirectly, the tractate Mo'ed Qatan). One aphorism is attributed to him in *Pirkei Avot*:[6]

> When a person studies as a child, to what may he be compared? To ink written on fresh paper. When a person studies when he is old, to what may he be compared? To ink written on blotted paper.[7]

---

[6] Commonly known as "Ethics of the Fathers," *Pirkei Avot* is a collection of moral statements of the rabbis of the generations of the Tannaim. It is generally thought to be a somewhat later addition to the Mishnah.

[7] Jules Harlow, "Pirkei Avot," in Harlow, *Siddur Sim Shalom* (New York: Rabbinical Assembly, United Synagogue of America, 1989), 636–37.

(In *Avot d'Rabbi Natan*, a supplementary text to *Pirkei Avot*, a whole chapter is devoted to Elisha's sayings, predominated by the theme of the necessity of good deeds to make Torah study valuable). In any case, these sparse attributions tell us little about the character of Elisha's scholarship or person.

According to Talmudic sources, after Elisha's apostasy, only his disciple Rabbi Meir stayed in contact with him. These sources offer many suggestions as to the nature of the deeds of the renegade and what caused him to break with tradition. After all, the rabbis contemporary to him, in difficult times, would want to know more than we do—what made this man leave?

3. The sources

The earliest sources about Elisha are tannaitic, were compiled one to four centuries after he lived, and are literary in nature. While the texts that incorporate solely tannaitic material are the Mishnah (which does not explicitly mention Elisha) and the Tosefta, stories from this time period are incorporated into the two Talmuds. Some of these stories do not appear in the earlier texts at all but can be clearly marked by language (Mishnaic Hebrew, as opposed to the dialects of Aramaic in which the main bodies of the Talmuds were written), and by direct parallels between segments found in both books. The Mishnah and Tosefta outline a context in which Elisha makes the briefest appearance, and the Talmuds fill in other, older material in their own "handwriting," and embellish it with original material. The aim of this first part is to examine the framework the older sources create. (These suggestions are based on a superficial literary analysis—again, a full, critical analysis of sources and redactions of the various texts is beyond the scope of this study.) Style, order of arrangement, and variations of detail can offer clues to the composers' intentions and demonstrate the flexibility of the original stories.

III. EARLY RABBINIC WINDOWS

1. The Mishnah and forbidden study

The window through which all of these texts approach the subject of Elisha ben-Avuyah is found in a digression from the main body of subject matter in the tractate Hagigah.[8] The Mishnah strays from its topic to the subject of forbidden or constricted topics of study.

---

[8] Hagigah is a section of the legal codes dealing with special offerings brought by pilgrims to Jerusalem on the festivals.

> One should not expound upon the forbidden sexual relations among three; nor upon Creation [Genesis 1] among two, nor upon the Merkavah[9] with one, unless he is wise and can understand on his own. All those who look at four things are better off not having come into the world: what is above, what is below, what is ahead, and what is behind. And all those who have no remorse for the honor of their creator are better off not having come into the world.

This excerpt from the Mishnah is the point of embellishment of the parallel Tosefta, and a chapter heading for discussion in the Talmuds. This passage is difficult on several counts. Why does the Mishnah, which is full of praise for learning Torah try to sharply limit certain avenues of study? What about these topics singled them out for limitation? What exactly is the Mishnah referring to when it talks about four things that a person is better off not pursuing? (i.e., physical boundaries of the world? time? God?).

The meanings that the original composer(s) and editor(s) intended may be, in the end, lost to us; of all the possibilities, only a few are transmitted to us. Those windows chosen by the Talmuds (particularly the Bavli), through which to filter this information, have become the standard perspective to approach a strange multifaceted text. Generations of teachers, basing their interpretations on those accepted by Talmudic authorities view these topics as potentially misleading to an impressionable student. The laws of forbidden sexual relations demand particular attentiveness between student and teacher, in order that a person not make a mistake in one of the gravest areas of Jewish law. Studying creation as an individual rather than in pairs, is attributed to a biblical verse hinting at such a commandment; however, the body of the discussion in the Bavli suggests a connection between speculation about creation and the mysteries of what is outside it (i.e., what is above, below, etc.). From the text of Genesis itself, one might guess at a potential source of controversy—what if people took literally the verse "Let us make man in our image" and were misled from the path of strict monotheism?

2. The Merkavah

Interestingly, no reason is given for the prohibition of the Merkavah in the Talmudic exposition. One might guess that the anthropomorphic descriptions

---

[9] The prophet Ezekiel's vision of the heavenly chariot (merkavah) (Ezekiel 1; 10).

of God's glory and the "son of man" sitting upon God's throne might have invited some untoward challenges to the doctrines of monotheism as well. Perhaps the reason was well known and taken for granted,[10] as the flow of exposition simply gives conditions under which study may take place and anecdotes about those who study it. In the Yerushalmi, there is a reason offered by Rabbi Akiva: "All agree that this is so one will know to show remorse for the honor of his creator." This "creator," however, seems to refer to a person's instructor in Torah, as it is followed by an exhortation against contradicting one's teachers.

The following anecdotes alternatively demonstrate glory and danger involved with the Merkavah.

> Rabbi [Judah Ha-Nasi] had a distinguished student, and he expounded a chapter of Ma'aseh Merkavah. Rabbi did not agree, and he [the student] was struck with boils. . . . (Yerushalmi, Hagigah 7a)

• • •

> . . . There was an incident of Rabbi Yohanan ben-Zakkai, who was traveling on the road, riding on a donkey, and Rabbi Elazar ben-Arakh was traveling after him. He [R Elazar] said to him: Teach me a chapter of the Merkavah. He [R Yohanan] said: And didn't the sages teach such: "and not the Merkavah, unless he is wise and understands for himself"?
> He said: Rabbi, then allow me to say something before you.
> He said: Speak.
> And when Rabbi Elazar ben-Arakh opened with the Ma'aseh Merkavah, Rabbi Yohanan ben Zakkai got down from the donkey. He said: It is not proper that I should hear the honor of my creator while I am sitting on a donkey. They went and sat under a tree, and a fire came down from the heavens and surrounded them, and the attending angels leaped before them like wedding guests rejoicing before a bridegroom. One of the angels answered from within the fire, "As you say, Elazar ben-Arakh! This is the Ma'aseh Merkavah!" Immediately, all the trees opened their mouths in song, "Then all the trees of the forest will sing" (Psalm 96). When Rabbi Elazar ben-Arakh finished with the Ma'aseh Merkavah, Rabbi Yohanan ben-Zakkai stood and kissed him on the head and said: Blessed are you, God of Abraham, Isaac, and

---

[10] David Halperin notes that the Merkavah chapter was a regular reading in the synagogue liturgy and suggests that a secret, formal exposition of the Merkavah did not really exist (*The Faces of the Chariot: Early Jewish Responses to Ezekiel's Vision* [Tübingen: J. C. B. Mohr, 1988]). Rather, it was representative of a realm of knowledge meant to be exclusive to the rabbis and to bolster their claims to authority.

Jacob, who gave Abraham our father a wise son who can expound on the glory of our father in heaven. There are those who expound becomingly, but do not fulfill becomingly; and there are those who fulfill becomingly, but do not expound becomingly. Rabbi Elazar ben-Arakh expounds becomingly and fulfills becomingly. It is your happiness, Abraham our father that Elazar ben-Arakh came from your loins![11] (Yerushalmi, Hagigah 7a)

• • •

The sages taught: There was an incident of a child who was reading in his teacher's house from the book of Ezekiel, and he understood the *hashmal*,[12] and a fire came out from the *hashmal* and burned him. (Bavli, Hagigah 13b)

This topic is somehow a close encounter with God, even paralleling revelation at Sinai, as both narratives share common symbols (both in the text and the midrash) of fire and the unleashing of the powers of nature, and both narratives were read together in the holiday cycle.

3. The Tosefta (Hagigah 2:3–6)

A. TWO WAYS TO ENTER THE PARDES

Among the various expositions of the Merkavah sections of the Mishnah, Elisha ben-Avuyah is introduced in the following passage, which is contained in similar form in the Tosefta, Bavli, and Yerushalmi. From there, we move to an analysis of the overall Tosefta text.

Four went into the *Pardes*: ben-Azzai, ben-Zoma, Aher, and Rabbi Akiva. One looked and died, one looked and was wounded,[13] one looked and cut at the shoots, and one ascended in peace and descended in peace.[14] Ben-Azzai looked and died; about him scripture says, "Precious in the sight of the Lord is the death of His faithful ones" (Psalm 116:15). Ben-Zoma looked and was wounded; about him scripture says, "If you find honey, eat only what you need," etc. (Proverbs 25:16). Elisha looked and cut at the shoots; about him

---

[11] A similar version can be found in the Bavli, and a shorter, less-detailed one in the Tosefta.

[12] *Hashmal*, a component of the description of the heavenly chariot, has no precise, known definition, and appears nowhere else in Scripture, apart from this chapter of Ezekiel. (In modern Hebrew, the word is used to refer to electricity.)

[13] That is, lost his mind.

[14] Yerushalmi and other manuscripts of Tosefta render, "entered in peace and went out in peace." Bavli, too, makes no reference to ascent and descent.

scripture says, "Do not let your mouth cause your flesh to sin," etc. (Ecclesiastes 5:5). Rabbi Akiva ascended in peace and descended in peace; about him scripture says, "Draw me after you, let us run!" (Song of Songs 1:4).

The first and most obvious question that this narrative provokes is about the *Pardes*. What does it mean literally, and to what does it refer? What exactly did these four people do that was so precarious, that only one came out intact? We can find two answers from a close reading of the Tosefta itself—one is derived from individual parables in isolation, as compared with other *pardes* parables in rabbinic literature; the second from the obvious reading of Merkavah-related speculation in context.

In Hebrew, *pardes* means "orchard." It is a word borrowed between Hebrew, Greek, and Persian, meaning a garden or enclosure. (This is the same root as the modern word "paradise.") Often in rabbinic literature, parables depict an orchard of a king, which is meant to describe a human relationship within the domain of God. Most commonly, they imply entrance into the realm of a "chosen people," such as by Torah study, observance of commandments, prayer, teaching, and the like. Saul Lieberman, in his commentary on the Tosefta on the phrase, "cut at the shoots," simply refers us to a telling parallel in the Midrash Deuteronomy (D'varim) Rabbah.

> Rabbi Simeon ben-Halafta said: Anyone who learned the words of Torah and does not fulfill them—his punishment is more severe than one who did not learn the fundamentals [*kol ikkar*]. To what is this comparable? To a king who had a *pardes*. He brought inside two tenant-workers. One would plant trees and cut them down, and one did not plant even a root [*kol ikkar*] and did not cut them either. With whom is the king angry? With the one who was planting and cutting . . .[15]

This parallel of *pardes* and cutting at the living growth strongly suggests that entering this domain in our text is done by studying Torah and corresponds with its assertion that "cutting the shoots" refers to denial or sin (i.e., "Do not let your mouth cause your flesh to sin"). Such an interpretation is consistent with the little information we know about the characters involved. Rabbi Akiva, who is regarded as one of the greatest teachers of Jewish tradition, died with the words of the Shema on his lips, wholehearted in his faith, and thereby left the enclosure

---

[15] Saul Lieberman, *Tosefta Kifshuta: Biur Aroch L'Tosefta* (10 vols.; Jerusalem: Jewish Theological Seminary of America, 1992–), 5:1289–91.

of learning "in peace."[16] Elisha, on the other hand, according to this *pardes* story, did not remain true to the teachings, and by his discontinuity in Torah, "cut at the shoots."[17] Read on its own, this parable might simply be the tragic story of four of the leading figures in Torah scholarship of this generation. The Tosefta continues with the following parable:

> A parable: to what is this similar? To a *pardes* of a king, and a platform is built above it. What is upon a person—to look, as long as he does not feast his eyes from it.

Lieberman draws this scene as a platform built over an orchard in order to guard it. He further cites sources from other sections of the Mishnah, Tosefta, and Talmuds that look askance at feasting one's eyes on objects that one is guarding, sometimes referring to holy vessels of the Temple, the Temple itself, or the *shekhinah*, the divine presence. (Perhaps it is considered an act of covetousness, of irreverence, of licentiousness). From these references, one might assume that the person to whom this parable is addressed would stand upon the platform, guarding the king's orchard. Taken on their own, these *baraitot* would also simply say that Elisha failed in his task of guarding the precious contents of God's orchard—the laws, the students, the welfare of his people.

The placement of the *pardes* story, however, has a major impact on its meaning,[18] because the parables as we learn them do not have a simple interpretation; the four who enter the *pardes* are in some degree entering an enclosure different from the one Rabbi Simeon ben-Halafta describes in the Midrash Rabbah. The apparently early tradition of placing it in the context of other Merkavah stories causes us to make the obvious association with some aspect of engaging in Merkavah study. *Pardes* is now purely a *mystical* enclosure of the king-God. This association of the *pardes* story with Merkavah speculation puts Elisha in the thick of these mystical endeavors (and turns *pardes* into a potential code word

---

[16] Halperin (*Faces of the Chariot*, 33) derives this from a phrase in Tosefta Ḥullin 2:23, which uses the phrase "went out in peace" to a person who leaves life free of heresy.

[17] I can make an argument for the applicability of this interpretation of the *pardes* for the other characters in the original story; however, a detailed argument for this is outside the scope of this paper (e.g., ben-Azzai died, that is, left no legacy; reputed to be an ascetic, he never married and had no children).

[18] Halperin, *Faces of the Chariot*, 28: "the compiler . . . was a master of creative editing, of the art of gathering and arranging older sources to take on the new meaning he wants them to have."

for mystical trips into the many enclosures of God). The Tosefta's *pardes* of a king, with the platform above it, has a meaning in context: the person who has entered is not in the usual position of being atop the platform guarding, but is beneath it, looking at the king above. Looking at God might be risky indeed. The text brings yet another parable to reinforce the precariousness of the situation—this is no ordinary domain of God.

> And they made further parable to what this is similar[19]—to a public thoroughfare that passes between two paths, one of light and one of snow. One who turns there is burnt by light, one who turns there is burnt by snow. What is upon a person—to walk in the middle as long as he does not turn off to there or to there.

The mystic, in conclusion, must beware of the enclosure, not look inappropriately, and must avoid leaving the well-defined path (whatever this means in practice).

Our reading of Elisha is colored by a sense of a "bad trip"; he becomes part of a polemic warning others away from Merkavah study, and the rabbis and authors who address his story later try to incorporate a mystical sense into his demise. Later, in reading the stories in the Bavli and Yerushalmi, we will see that the two different readings of the *pardes* will play out in the lines of inquiry each one takes.

B. Polemic against mysticism and against Elisha

Particularly for the Tosefta, Elisha's story makes sense as polemic, as the Merkavah and characters associated with it get much shorter shrift here than they do in the Bavli and Yerushalmi, even where the stories are parallel and seemingly identical. The story we read earlier about the miracles that followed Rabbi Yohanan ben-Zakkai and Rabbi Elazar ben-Arakh when they discussed the Merkavah, is found in the Tosefta—but without any of the miracles. Halperin suggests that this is deliberate minimizing of Merkavah (as part of a larger text censorship movement that I do not fully understand), and I would add—perhaps of Elisha ben-Avuyah. Elisha himself is excised in the Tosefta's version of a *baraita* that is connected with this section in the Yerushalmi (and found

---

[19] Yerushalmi contains a similar version of this parable, which begins with "This Torah is similar to two paths . . . ."

elsewhere in the Bavli; Tosefta follows the Bavli's placement). This *baraita* addresses the issue of the suffering of the righteous, concluding that reward and punishment belong to the world to come. The Bavli and Yerushalmi versions present Elisha as an example of a person who held the mistaken belief that the Torah's promises of reward and punishment were literal, and were to be received in this world. Therefore, he apostatized when he witnessed people who suffered while performing commandments with the promise of reward attached to them. (This will be examined further below in the analysis of the Yerushalmi.) The Tosefta, on the other hand, omits this popular attribution and simply states the correct interpretation for an anonymously witnessed event. An argument can be made that this too was deliberate—because the Tosefta version combines some of the wording—for odd details—of both the Bavli and Yerushalmi versions (see Appendix C).

The Tosefta's approach is shaped by a variety of factors. In many ways, it is similar to the Mishnah in format and style. While the editing of this set of *baraitot* is contemporary to the compilation of the Talmuds, its format is much more like the Mishnah. It includes much material that the Mishnah leaves out, but does not add the later material of the Amoraim that forms the bulk of the Talmuds. Having been compiled near the height of the aforementioned text censorship movement, the Tosefta prominently shares the lack of historicism/end-of-historicism, and supernatural speculations characteristic of the Mishnah, but of few other texts of the first centuries of the Common Era. The stories, laws, and parables follow a set, refined, highly edited order, comparable to that of the Mishnah, which was intended for easy memorization. By comparison with either of the Talmuds, the narratives of the Tosefta do not have as strong a sequential narrative connection with each other, but follow each other mnemonically, like the laws. Following is a summary of the *baraitot* of this section of the Tosefta in sequence, to clarify their connection to one another.

> One should not expound upon the forbidden sexual relations among three, but may among two . . . and not upon the *Merkavah* with one, unless he is wise and understands on his own.

> There was an incident of Rabbi Yohanan ben-Zakkai who was riding on a donkey, and Rabbi Elazar ben-Arakh was driving behind him. He [R Elazar] said: teach me a chapter of *Ma'aseh Merkavah* . . . .

> Rabbi Yose ben-Yehuda said: Rabbi Yehoshua discoursed before Rabbi Yohanan ben-Zakkai: Rabbi Akiva discoursed before Rabbi Yehoshua; and Rabbi Hananiah ben-Kinai discoursed before Rabbi Akiva.

Four went into the *pardes*: ben-Azzai, ben-Zoma, Aher, and Rabbi Akiva . . .

A parable: to what is this similar? To a *pardes* of a king . . .

And they made further parable to what is this similar—to a public thorough-fare . . .

There was an incident of Rabbi Yehoshua who was walking on a public thoroughfare and ben-Zoma was coming from the other direction, approached near him, and did not greet him. He said to him: Where from and where to, ben-Zoma? He [ben-Zoma] said: I was contemplating creation, and there is nothing between the waters above and the waters below, even a handbreadth . . .

All who look at four things are better off not having come into the world: what is above, what is below, what is behind, and what is ahead. One might think it was permitted [to look] before creation . . .

This gives us the sense of a purposefully edited book, having chosen its sources and arrangement carefully, rather than a book that haphazardly omitted text. For whatever reason, its editors have chosen to present us with a set of teachings that largely ignore the disruptions of mysticism and apostasy.

4. Common tannaitic themes on Elisha

While the Tosefta is comprised solely of tannaitic material, it is not comprehensive of all tannaitic material. Regarding Elisha ben-Avuyah, there are numerous traditions dating from this period that are found in the two Talmuds but not in the Tosefta. Common themes among them include:

- Attempts to understand why "Aher" may have sinned, including addressing the question of whether he was somehow predestined or predisposed to sin.
- A sense of deliberateness of his sin. And while they do not always conform regarding the nature of the sin, they both contain a story of Aher riding a horse on the Sabbath.
- A sense of his deep knowledge of tradition, still correcting his old student, Rabbi Meir.
- His relationship with Rabbi Meir, who seems to be one of the only (if not the only one of the) rabbis to maintain contact with him, who tries to persuade him to return

- A sense that he is unforgivable—despite the popular and central doctrine that repentance is open to all those who sincerely wish to change.
- That he leaves a powerful legacy, from his burning grave, to Rabbi Yehuda Ha-Nasi, who receives heavenly censure for his reluctance to give alms to Aher's daughter.
- Morals about the power of good contained in the Torah, despite the person who taught it.
- Within this common structure of ideas, each Talmud emphasizes different aspects, in effect, asking and answering different questions about the character of Elisha.

5. *Talmud Bavli*

A. "Aher looked and cut at the shoots": What did he look at?

In response to the common statement "Aher looked and cut at the shoots," there are a number of questions that can be asked by the reader. The Bavli's text first chooses to take up the theme of "what did he look at?" With an eye toward all the mystical potentials of the *pardes,* the Bavli opens its narrative, and includes a unique interpolation in the opening story that significantly changes its tone.

> The sages taught: Four went into the *pardes.* They were: ben-Azzai, ben-Zoma, Aher, and Rabbi Akiva. Rabbi Akiva said to them: When you reach the stones of pure marble, do not say "water water!" because it is written, He who speaks untruth shall not stand before my eyes." (Psalm 101:7).

Rabbi Akiva's warning is meaningful in the context of *Hekhalot* mysticism, in which the pure marble stones that look like water appear in the sixth of seven levels of ascent toward God's throne.[20] Even without understanding a great deal about the characteristics of the ascent through the palaces (*hekhalot*) of God, or knowing definitively what Talmud understood these characters to be doing, we can glean a general meaning of Akiva's warning: that in this realm of the unknown, a person's eyes may deceive him, and that one's verbal response will not be "true." The story of what happens to Aher is written for this context: what he saw, and the falsehood he said as a consequence.

---

[20] Gershom G. Sholem, "Merkabah Mysticism and Jewish Gnosticism," in Scholem, *Major Trends in Jewish Mysticism*, 3rd ed. (New York: Schocken Books, 1972), 52–53.

"Aher cut at the shoots"; about him scripture says, "Do not let your mouth cause your flesh to sin" (Ecclesiastes 5:5). What happened? He saw Metatron,[21] who was given permission [*reshut*] to sit and write the merits of Israel.[22] He said: We learn that above there is no sitting,[23] no contention, no division,[24] and no junction,[25] that maybe, (God forbid) there are two domains [*reshuyot*].[26] They took Metatron and struck him with sixty burning rods. They said to him: When you say to him, why didn't you stand before him? He was given permission [*reshut*] to erase the merits of Aher. A heavenly voice went out and said, "Turn back rebellious children" (Jeremiah 3:22)—except for Aher.

Here Aher saw a deceptive angel who looked as though he was performing God's prerogative, and he arrived at the improper belief that there were two powers. According to this passage, Aher was guilty of believing in Gnostic dualism, with his subsequent actions attributed to this failure of belief.

This is not the only way in which the question of what Aher looked at is addressed. The Bavli does not contain one type of narrative and a single opinion but brings in other sources which have other suggestions.

What was in Aher? Greek song never ceased from his mouth. They said about Aher, that when he would stand up in the house of study, many heretical[27] books would fall from his lap.

From this small passage, we are led to believe that Aher's heretical "looking" was in foreign books and ideologies, rather than into the mysteries of his own faith tradition. The evil effects of the external culture are blamed for his corruption.

Extending the notion of "looking" to other aspects of speculation or ideological failure, we find a serious tension over the issue of repentance—a core of rabbinic doctrine was the belief that all people who sin can mend their ways and

---

[21] Metatron is an archangel. This name appears in some of the Midrashim, but only one other time in the Bavli and not at all in the Yerushalmi.

[22] This was traditionally God's prerogative. Apparently, no one else in the heavenly domain is supposed to sit either, except God.

[23] That is, yeshivah—sitting for deliberation.

[24] According to Jastrow (Marcus Jastrow, *A Dictionary of the Targumim, the Talmud Babli and Yerushalmi, and the Midrashic Literature* [2 vols.; New York: Pardes, 1950], 1059, s.v. '*oref*), Rashi interprets '*oref* as "facing away."

[25] According to Jastrow, Rashi interprets *ipui* as "weariness" (Dictionary, 1073, s.v. '*yp*.

[26] That is, powers.

[27] That is, sectarian.

achieve forgiveness from God. In this text, we are three times confronted with the heavenly voice that says, "Return straying children, except for Aher." However, only one of those times does it emanate from a heavenly source. The other two come from Elisha's own mouth in several exchanges with Rabbi Meir, his former disciple, who is urging his master to return to the faith.

> After he went out to degeneracy, Aher asked Rabbi Meir: What does the verse mean that says. "Gold or glass cannot match its value, nor vessels of fine gold be exchanged for it"? (Job 28: 17).
>
> He replied: These are the words of Torah that are as difficult to acquire as gold vessels and easy to lose as glass vessels.
>
> He said: Rabbi Akiva your teacher did not say that. Rather: Like gold and glass vessels—even if broken, are reparable. So too, even a scholar, even if he has offended, is reparable.
>
> He said to him: Then even you return!
>
> He said: I have already heard the voice behind the partition. "Turn back rebellious children"—except for Aher.
>
> The sages teach of an incident, where Aher was riding a horse on the Sabbath and Rabbi Meir followed him [on foot] to learn Torah from his mouth. He said to him: Meir, turn back. I have already ridden the measure of paces of the Sabbath boundary.
>
> He said: Even you turn back!
>
> He said: Haven't I already told you? I have already heard the voice behind the partition. "Turn back rebellious children"—except for Aher.

This text raises the question: why does it seem that Aher himself is the only one who knows about this heavenly voice? Perhaps this text means to lead us to the conclusion that Elisha is his own barrier to repentance, because he does not believe it is possible. Whether he rejects penitence for himself alone, or for all people who have made serious breaches of their faith, the statement he makes is squarely in opposition to the classic rabbinic ideal.

This interpretation of Aher's attitudes and ability to repent is most certainly not the only one. In fact, arguments could be made precisely to the contrary, that it truly is a divine punishment preventing his return, as can be demonstrated from the heavenly voice's giving the announcement first, and from an exchange with Rabbi Meir that immediately precedes the one we have just read.

> After he went out to degeneracy, Aher asked Rabbi Meir: What does the verse mean which says, "The one no less than the other is God's doing" (Ecclesiastes 7:14)? He replied: For everything that God created, He created its opposite.

He created mountains, He created valleys; He created seas, He created rivers.

He said: Rabbi Akiva your teacher did not teach as such. Rather: He created righteous people. He created wicked people; He created Eden, he created Gehennom [hell]. Every person has two shares—one in Eden, the other in Gehennom. If a righteous person merits, he takes his share and his neighbor's share in Eden; if a wicked man is charged, he takes his own share and his neighbor's share in Gehennom.

The content of the conversation is ominous, with Elisha's last word suggesting that he is twice doomed, earning two shares in Gehennom after he dies. If we understand these passages as meaning that Elisha is certainly beyond hope of repentance, we still are left with questions as to what makes him irredeemable. Is there a point in a religious system—in thought or deed—which, if crossed has irreversible consequences? Has he actually crossed an invisible line that puts him beyond all the bounds of legitimate belief or action? Or, could it be said he has crossed the point of no return simply by denying that there is such a thing as return—in other words, that the repentance may as well not exist for the one who doesn't accept the doctrine and responsibility for acting in accordance with it? (This tension also exists in the Yerushalmi's version of this same story.)

Another set of important questions that is raised in discussing "seeing," understanding, and speaking in regard to the apostate is the point at which thoughts become heresy. Going back to Aher's vision of two powers in heaven, was it his belief in two powers that put him outside? Was it saying so ("maybe there are two domains")? Or was it his acting upon that assumption by committing forbidden acts, such as violating the Sabbath afterward? Similar questions might be asked about studying Greek poetry or sectarian books—was it the studying, the conclusions, or the action that stemmed from them that proved to be most objectionable? As for denying a basic principle of Jewish belief, again, does Aher's assertion that he may not return constitute heresy, or does his transgression of commandments, even as Rabbi Meir tries to give him opportunities to do the right thing?

B. AHER'S ACTIONS: HOW DID HE CUT AT THE SHOOTS?

From here, it makes sense to examine what the text portrays Aher as doing, or "how did he cut at the shoots?" Our first entrance into this realm is in the verse cited to describe Aher's part in the *pardes* incident, "Do not let your mouth cause your flesh to sin." The verse and the misinterpreted vision of Metatron are followed by a description of a sin of the flesh.

> He said: Since this man has been banished from that world, he will go and enjoy this world. Aher went out to degeneracy. He went out and came across a prostitute and propositioned her. She said to him: Aren't you Elisha ben-Avuyah? He tore a radish out of the ground on the Sabbath and gave it to her. She said: He must be another [Aher].

Here, we find a description of hedonism and deliberate violation of the Sabbath as being pivotal sins. More significantly, the Bavli chooses these sins to associate with Elisha's acquiring the nickname "Aher," suggesting that it was not the Metatron vision that made him Other, but his eagerness to transgress the commandments.

Later in the text, we have an additional conception of what Aher did that could be classified as cutting at the shoots in his interaction with young children studying Torah and (perhaps) literally "cutting" the young growth in Torah study. In this scene, Rabbi Meir takes Elisha into houses of prayer to divine his fate from the words of the children who were studying there.

> He grasped him and took him into a house of study. He said to a child: Recite your verse for me![28]
>
> He said: "There is no safety, says the Lord, for the wicked" (Isaiah 48:22).
>
> He brought him up to a different house of prayer. He said to a child: Recite your verse for me!
>
> He said to him: "Though you wash with natron and use much lye, your guilt is ingrained before me" (Jeremiah 2:22).
>
> He went to another house of prayer, and said to a child: Recite your verse for me!
>
> He said to him: "And you who are doomed to ruin, what do you accomplish by wearing crimson, by decking yourself in jewels of gold, by enlarging your eyes with kohl? You beautify yourself in vain . . ." (Jeremiah 4:30).
>
> He went to another house of prayer, until they had gone to thirteen houses of prayer, and all recited verses in like manner. In the final one, he said: Recite your verse for me!
>
> He said: "And to the wicked [rasha'] God said: Who are you to recite my

---

[28] It was thought that truths and predictions could be divined from the chance verse that a given child was studying, as if they were messages from God directed toward the questioner, placed in the mouths of children.

laws, etc." (Psalm 50:16). This child stammered on his words, and it sounded as if he said, "And to Elisha God said . . ." There are those who say that he had a knife in his hand, and he tore him up and sent him to thirteen houses of prayer. Others say: If he had a knife, he would have torn him up.

However, it seems that the compiler of the Bavli was not entirely sure as to the literalness of Elisha's killing young students, tacking on the addendum of "others say." From here, the reader is less inclined to believe that Aher was truly a murderer, but more inclined to speculate that he was full of anger and vengefulness toward the young scholars. It is hard to say why this might be—is he an active agent to destroy the continuity of the tradition, or is he venting frustration at a community who rejects him? (The Yerushalmi, too, contains a narrative about Elisha's killing young scholars, but as will be addressed below, it is of a radically different nature.) In an overall look at Aher's "degeneracy," we do not always have a definite picture of what he does, but rather a sketch that leaves much open to interpretation.

Another issue that the storyteller on Aher addresses is the possible underlying cause of Aher's sins. This is different from stating that he engaged in mystical speculation or read heretical works. Elie Wiesel points out that many people engaged in activities such as Elisha's infamous ones:[29] Rabbi Akiva is also associated with mystical speculation, and many rabbis were known to have been well versed in Greek philosophy and sciences. This reinforces the earlier idea that Aher's distinction comes from action, rather than purely ideological or speculative grounds.

C. WHAT MADE AHER DIFFERENT?

Still, we are left to wonder what was different about Aher that made him fall where others remained whole. The Bavli makes some proposals regarding Aher's predisposition to apostasy, following the anecdotes about his life and deeds. In this exchange between Samuel and Rav Yehuda, we are told of the internal disposition of scholars who go astray.

Samuel found Rav Yehuda leaning against the doorway and crying. He [Samuel] said to him:
Sharp scholar, why are you crying?

---

[29] Elie Wiesel, *Sages and Dreamers: Biblical, Talmudic, and Hasidic Portraits and Legends* (New York: Simon & Schuster, 1991), 258.

He [Rav Yehuda] said to him: Is it a small matter that which is written . . . .
Rabbi Ami said, "Doeg and Ahitofel[30] asked three hundred questions on the
tower fluttering in the air." And the Mishnah teaches, "Three kings and four
commoners have no share in the world to come . . ."[31]
What will become of us?
He [Samuel] said to him: Sharp scholar, there was licentiousness in their
hearts.

What was in Aher? Greek song never ceased from his mouth. They said about
Aher that when he would stand up in the house of study, many heretical books
would fall from his lap.

Nirnos the weaver asked Rabbi Meir: Does all the wool that goes down into
the dye-kettle come out? He said to him: All that was clean from its creation
comes out: all that was not clean from its creation does not come out.

From here, we are to infer that Aher was not "clean" from his creation as a scholar.
Perhaps he was too much affected by the study of secular or sectarian works
before he began his endeavors in Torah study, and this is what made the "dye" of
true teachings not take hold. This could mean anything from an early education
in secular works that gave him a different frame of reference than his colleagues
(teachings not being imprinted on a fresh slate) to suspicion of his motives for
studying Torah to begin with ("licentiousness in his heart"). If he was destined
for a bad end by his own nature, we can explain his failure to excel in areas where
others did. He was too much affected by heretical books by nature, and therefore
couldn't study them to good end. Or, with regard to the mystical trip into the
pardes, he was never wholehearted in his faith, reverence, or some other essential
quality, and therefore was predetermined not to come out in peace.[32]

One telling event that is included in this collection in the Yerushalmi is
omitted here. (It can be found, though, in Qiddushin and Hullin.) The missing
narrative (noted earlier in the Tosefta section) is about Aher's witnessing the

---

[30] Doeg and Ahitofel are biblical characters reputed for cleverness (which to the rabbis
meant wisdom in the law), who used their skills to further bad ends.

[31] Doeg and Ahitofel are among the commoners who have no share in the world to come,
despite their knowledge and skills.

[32] Scholem (*Major Trends*, 52–53) cites a passage from a *hekhalot* text, regarding the vivid
demise of those who are unworthy of seeing the King in his glory. Such people have their senses
confused at the sixth level of ascent, say "water water" when they see tiles of marble, and are taunted
and beaten back by the angels.

suffering of the righteous—those who were promised long life by biblical law, yet died directly as a result of their performance of good deeds. According to this story, his conclusion was that the reward promised in the Torah was false, rather than subscribing to the essential rabbinic belief that reward and punishment belong in the world to come. For whatever reason, the editors of the Talmud did not see fit to attach that incident to others regarding Aher, but included it thematically (twice) with material about the ultimate rewards for good deeds. Aher in Qiddushin and Ḥullin does not exist as a character, as he does here, but as a quick example of ideology gone wrong.

A different, and somewhat more radical, reading of the Metatron text provides yet another interpretation of the underlying cause of Elisha's missteps. One could make a case that Aher's fall may not have been his own fault, or under his control at all. We find that Metatron is physically punished after Aher makes his infamous speculation about two powers in heaven, and the heavenly hosts ask Metatron why he did not stand—presumably, why he committed deliberately misleading behavior. Although Metatron is rebuked for his presumptuous behavior, he is then replaced in the same powerful position in which he was before—this time, to specifically erase all of Aher's merits. Then, the *bat qol* goes out, declaring that all sinners may return, except for Elisha ben-Avuyah. This strange declaration, repeated several times in conversation with Rabbi Meir, haunts the narrative, giving the sense that Elisha is forever dogged by this forbidding voice. We have Elisha living out a strange existence in limbo—doomed forever but still left in the world where good and bad deeds are supposed to be accounted accordingly. The *bat qol* dooms him personally, taking away his purpose for observing the commandments. ("Since this man has been banished from that world, he will enjoy this world.") The unacceptability of his repentance becomes a self-fulfilling prophecy. From this perspective, we have an unfortunate figure who is driven by careless heavenly powers. Even if we do not accept such arbitrariness as characteristic God's realm, this interpretation offers for consideration an Elisha who, not in control of his own fate, is tragic rather than wholly evil.

D. RELATIONSHIP OF THE OTHER TO THE COMMUNITY

An additional aspect of the character of Elisha as the Other that is worth considering is his relationship with Jews who were still inside. The one relationship that is described in detail by the Talmud is that with his formal student, Meir, in the conversations that have been cited previously. These conversations, about points of exegesis, are complex, and also open to a great deal of interpretation.

> After he went out to degeneracy, Aher asked Rabbi Meir: What does the verse mean which says, "The one no less than the other is God's doing" (Ecclesiastes 7:14)? He replied: For everything that God created, He created its opposite. He created mountains, He created valleys; He created seas, He created rivers.
>
> He said: Rabbi Akiva your teacher did not teach as such. Rather: He created righteous people, He created wicked people; He created Eden, he created Gehennom (hell). Every person has two shares—one in Eden, the other in Gehennom. If a righteous person merits, he takes his share and his neighbor's share in Eden; if a wicked man is charged, he takes his own share and his neighbor's share in Gehennom . . .
>
> After he went out to degeneracy, Aher asked Rabbi Meir: What does the verse mean that says. "Gold or glass cannot match its value, nor vessels of fine gold be exchanged for it" (Job 28:17)?
>
> He replied: These are the words of Torah that are as difficult to acquire as gold vessels and easy to lose as glass vessels.
>
> He said: Rabbi Akiva your teacher did not say that. Rather: Like gold and glass vessels—even if broken, are reparable. So too, even a scholar, even if he has offended, is reparable.
>
> He said to him: Then even you return!
>
> He said: I have already heard the voice behind the partition, "Turn back rebellious children"—except for Aher.
>
> The sages teach of an incident where Aher was riding a horse on the Sabbath and Rabbi Meir followed him [on foot] to learn Torah from his mouth. He said to him: Meir, turn back. I have already ridden the measure of paces of the Sabbath boundary.
>
> He said: Even you turn back!
>
> He said: Haven't I already told you, I have already heard the voice behind the partition. "Turn back rebellious children"—except for Aher.

We are told that "after he went out to degeneracy, Aher asked Rabbi Meir, 'what does the verse mean which says . . .'"—that it is Aher who is initiating this talk with Meir. The content of these dialogues is notable because of its similarity to any other dialogue that could have occurred between two scholars. The discussion of proper exegesis of a biblical verse is typical of those recorded in many rabbinic texts. Furthermore, in both rounds of discussion of these verses, it is Aher, the apostate, who gets the last word, quotes Rabbi Akiva, and states the ideologically correct position. On the surface, it seems that although Elisha is, at this point, considered to be outside, his role as a teacher has not greatly changed. Read in this way, this passage might tell us that, while Aher was controversial, out of the mainstream, he was not so terrible as to prevent all association, since we find the greatly respected Rabbi Meir still engaged with him. We could confirm this view from Aher's role in their third exchange, when he is riding his horse on the Sabbath but tells Meir to turn back when they have reached the Sabbath boundary. Aher is simply stating the facts, so that Meir may observe the law properly, even if he himself does not.

These incidents, as recorded in the Bavli, are open to many interpretations that reach below the surface and read a psychological interplay into these stories. One might look at Aher's initiation of conversation with Meir as a challenge to his old pupil, and his use of traditional methods as a weapon to reach the core of Meir's beliefs. The horseback incident is then a taunt—Elisha is effectively asking, "You've followed me to the limit—do you dare to step beyond this line?" This perspective can be reinforced by noting how Aher knows they have reached the boundary—"I have already ridden the measure of paces"—effectively needling, "I have been counting, have you?"

We also might find the tragic portrait of Elisha in these scenes. While he is outside the boundaries of proper belief or action, he has not had all traces of his rabbinic background removed from him. He continues to speak the language of exegesis that is familiar to him, and asks Meir questions because he misses the place he once had as a scholar and teacher. "What does the verse mean which says . . ." is an opening to maintain some semblance of his old relationships.

In any one of these interpretations, the character of Meir is not a passive one. We find Meir pursuing Aher on horseback, "to learn Torah from his mouth." No matter how we read these stories, we consistently find Meir engaged in the attempt to bring Elisha back in repentance, seizing on every mention of reparability and return. Perhaps he even knows the answers to his teacher's questions but gives incorrect or incomplete ones on purpose, to force Elisha himself to cite traditions about the necessity of good deeds and the value of penitence.

(It should be emphasized that aspects of all of these interpretations are possible from these anecdotes, because the Bavli text itself is neutral and does not itself ascribe a particular meaning to these stories. The Yerushalmi, by contrast, lends itself more to particular interpretations by its presentation of these incidents. This will be discussed further below.)

This depiction of the interactions between Elisha and Meir does not clearly delineate the relationship of the heretic to his people. From these texts, Elisha is obviously quite knowledgeable, and Meir might still have something to learn from him. We also find that Meir doesn't see him as beyond hope for return, despite the way Elisha characterizes himself. By the fact that the text places him in a situation with some sort of connection to other Jews, and where he is given some opening for return (however fruitless it turns out to be), one gets the sense that he is not wholly evil. Even the heretic is a Jew at the core. So, what makes a man who is qualified to teach a heretic as well? One might suggest that he is outside, because while he is quite able to quote proper exegesis of verses regarding the potential of scholars who have sinned to be recreated, like new vessels of gold and glass, he does not apply them to himself.

Looking at the anecdote immediately following the conversations between Meir and Elisha about children reciting damning verses in the houses of study, we can also perceive some relationship between Aher and the young students. This story, written in a style and language different from the Meir and Elisha conversations, depicts tension and antagonism between the students and Aher. Thirteen children quote verses about his unforgivability. By the time he reaches the thirteenth, we might see an Aher so antagonized that he hears the child address a condemning verse to him by name, and expresses violent rage. Aher is certainly alienated, yet not so much so that he is indifferent to the verses that the children quote to him.

Elisha, and the apparent contradiction between his knowledge and his heresy, becomes fodder for debate after his death. "How did Rabbi Meir learn Torah from the mouth of Aher?" Can a person truly learn from an apostate? The text alternatively justifies and condemns Rabbi Meir.

> When Rav Dimi came, he said: They say in the west [Israel]: Rabbi Meir ate the early date and threw the skin away.
>
> Rava expounded: What does the scripture mean to say, "I went down to the nut grove to see the budding of the vale" etc. (Song of Songs 6:11)? Why are wise students compared to a nut? To tell you that a nut is just so—even though it gets dirty from mortar and dung, what is inside is not ruined. So a scholar, even though he has degenerated, his Torah is not ruined.
>
> Rabbah bar Sheila found Elijah and said to him: What is the Holy One Blessed be He doing?
>
> He said to him: He is reciting the teachings of all the rabbis, but those of Rabbi Meir he does not recite.
>
> He said to him: Why?
>
> —Because he learned his teachings from the mouth of Aher.
>
> He said: Why? Rabbi Meir found a pomegranate, ate its inside and threw away the peel!

Some state that Meir had extraordinary discretion about what he might learn from Aher. Others prefer to place the power in the study of Torah itself—that true divine knowledge may find itself in an unfit vessel but is never itself contaminated.

Aside from this particular debate, we find that Aher as a scholar, heretic, and contradiction embodied retains a near supernatural power over the scholars of the succeeding generation, as is illustrated by the following exchange between Aher's impoverished daughter and Rabbi Yehuda Ha-Nasi ("Rabbi").

> Aher's daughter came before Rabbi. She said to him: Rabbi, support me!
>   He said: Whose daughter are you?
>   She said to him: I am Aher's daughter.
>   He said to her: There still remains of his seed in the world?! And the scripture says. "He has no seed or breed among his people, no survivor where he once lived" (Job 18:19).
>   She said to him: Remember his Torah and don't remember his deeds.
>   Immediately, a fire descended and singed Rabbi's chair. Rabbi cried and said. "And this to one who makes himself repulsive from it—how much more so for one who is bettered by it!"

In the end, the Bavli chooses to vindicate Elisha's merits, even with heavenly intervention, by emphasizing and reemphasizing the inherent merit of Torah study.

E. Summary of windows

In the Bavli text, we have seen Elisha in many contexts. He is given as a warning against untoward mystical speculation and studying foreign texts. He exists as part of a discourse on the power of penitence and the powerful goodness of Torah study. Not all of these windows, however, are given equal credence by the overall structure of the Bavli text. For example, it should be noted that on the several pages preceding the *pardes* incident warning against engaging in Merkavah study, the rabbis record quite a number of speculations about the nature of the Merkavah and Ezekiel's prophecy. Warning against such mystical speculations, with or without Elisha as an example, is moot for a person who has studied the Bavli's text sequentially until this point. Aher's portrayal as a sinner due to studying foreign texts is also only a small fragment within a much larger discussion. His other transgressions, from relations with a prostitute to Sabbath violations are mentioned but not greatly detailed (unlike they are in the Yerushalmi). We find that the Bavli gives much more attention to two other issues—in the long sequence of dialogues with Rabbi Meir about Aher's potential to repent, and in the later rabbinic argument over the permissibility of learning with the teacher of questionable character. Presumably, what the Bavli's compilers would like their readers to understand through the Aher stories is the centrality of the doctrine of repentance—how important it is for people to possess the power to change—and the pervasive value of Torah. (If Elisha the heretic's Torah is still valuable, then this lends weight to the idea that deeds rather than ideology constitute the essence of heresy.

6. Talmud Yerushalmi (Chapter 2, 7a-8a)

A. "Do not let your mouth cause your flesh to sin." How did he cut at the shoots?

The Yerushalmi, despite being chronologically close to the Tosefta and the Bavli, writes of Elisha with its own distinctive attitude, collecting and arranging some similar and some unique episodes to paint a stark portrait of the apostate. The emphasis of this text is on the actions of a heretic rather than on beliefs or visionary experiences. "Who is *Aher* [the Other]? He is Elisha ben-Avuyah, who would kill all the scholars of Torah."

From these pages of the Yerushalmi, we can compile a list of objectionable deeds attributed to Aher, which, though shorter than the Bavli's, includes items that are much more severe. As above, Elisha is said to have murdered his fellow scholars, as well as undermining the occupation of study among the young students.

> It is said that every student he saw succeeding in Torah, he would kill. And that isn't all. When he would enter the house of study and would see youths sitting before the teacher, he would say: Why are you sitting and working here? This one's trade is a mason, this one's trade is a carpenter, this one's trade is a hunter, this one's trade is a tailor. And when they would hear this, they would abandon him and go off.

He is further denounced as an informer for persecuting Roman authorities, here, by telling them ways to force Jews to violate the Sabbath, in spite of their efforts to use loopholes to avoid the performance of forbidden labor.

> Also, in the time of persecution, they would put loads on them [on the Sabbath]. They would pick them up, and were intending for two to carry [each] one—from there [we learn the law of] two who do one labor. He said: Carry

them singly. They went out and carried them singly, and intended to put them down in a 'Carmelit,'[33] in order not to take them from a private domain to a public domain. He said: Carry them straight through. They went out and carried them straight through.

Elisha himself is also said to have deliberately flouted the law, as the Yerushalmi reports two separate incidents of him riding a horse on the Sabbath, once even passing the Holy of Holies on a Sabbath that coincided with the most sacred Day of Atonement. In comparison with the Bavli's stories of angels, prostitutes, and various possibilities of degeneracy, the Yerushalmi has quickly provided a coherent list of incidents that are shocking indeed.

From this list we ask the question: are these deeds to be taken literally, at face value, or symbolically? Is the reader supposed to interpret that Aher truly went out with a weapon in hand and killed people, or that he did something else that wreaked similar consequences? How does the Yerushalmi understand "Aher looked and cut at the shoots"? Several possibilities exist. One is a literal reading of murder, where he physically cuts down young students. A second, not far from this, is that Elisha's actions led directly to the demise of the scholars. Perhaps, in connection with his alleged activities as a Roman informer, he told where his colleagues and their pupils were studying the Torah, in violation of Roman ordinance, leading to their death at the hands of the government. It is also possible that killing could be taken in a metaphoric sense, as linked to the story of Elisha's causing the children to abandon their teacher. "Aher looked and cut at the shoots ... about him scripture says, 'Do not let your mouth cause your flesh to sin,' since [with his words] he made worthless the works of that man [the teacher]." In this instance, his discouragement alone was enough to make the scholars quit study of their own accord. Or, perhaps his example alone, as a great scholar himself rejecting tradition, was a force so demoralizing that many disillusioned students no longer had the heart to stay involved in Torah study. No matter which one of these possibilities is the most plausible, the Yerushalmi would like us to believe the worst, feeling the full gravity of Aher "cutting at the shoots."

Another aspect of Elisha's apostasy that is highlighted as particularly grave is his deliberate sin, in spite of his intensive knowledge of tradition. The idea that Aher is not just anyone particularly rankles. (See the note above on

---

[33] A Carmelit is an area that is defined neither as a public nor a private domain, such as a courtyard or residential street. Removing something between a private and public domain, or within the public domain, is a forbidden labor on the Sabbath.

Deuteronomy Rabbah: Anyone who learned the words of Torah and does not fulfill them—his punishment is more severe than one who did not learn the fundamentals. . . .) This is brought out by the episode in which Elisha is portrayed as an informer. The Romans would not have known how to make the Jews violate the Sabbath so completely without the contributing knowledge of a Jew. We find Elisha in the paradox of using his extensive scholarship—that which should be a virtue—in the effort to undermine virtue. His awareness of all details of life from the perspective of Jewish law is highlighted in the following conversation with Rabbi Meir, in which Elisha is riding a horse on the Sabbath, and Rabbi Meir is following him on foot.

> He said to him: Enough for you. Meir. Until here is the Sabbath boundary.
>   He [Meir] said to him: How do you know?
>   He [Elisha] said to him: From the steps of my horse which I have been counting—and he has walked two thousand *amah*.
>   He [Meir] said to him: All this wisdom is in you and you do not return?

B. What did Aher see? Ideological differences

The Yerushalmi, however, does not ignore issues of thought and doctrine altogether—in fact, there is explicit mention of heretical doctrine as a cause for Aher's evil deeds. In this case, it is the rejection of the prominent rabbinic tenets of reward and punishment and their ultimate fulfillment in the world to come.

> And where did all this come to him from? Once he was sitting and learning in the Valley of Ginsor, and saw a man go up to the top of a palm tree, take the mother [bird] with the babies, and go down in peace. On the morrow he saw a different man go to the top of the palm tree and send the mother [bird] away, and he went down from there, and a snake bit him so he died. Scripture says, "Send the mother away, and take the babies for yourself, so that there will be good for you, and your days will be prolonged" (Deuteronomy 22:7). Where is the goodness of this one, and the length of days of this one? And he did not know that Rabbi Yaakov interpreted after him, "So that there will be good for you—" in the world to come which is all good; "and your days will be prolonged—"

Alternatively, the text offers a different story, demonstrating a similar response to the suffering of the righteous and clearly explains the significance of Aher's attitude (italics my own).

> Some say that it was due to his seeing Rabbi Yehudah the baker's tongue in the mouth of a dog, dripping with blood. He said: This is the Torah and this

is its reward?! This tongue which had put forth words of Torah as they ought to be, this tongue which labored in Torah all its days—this is the Torah and this is its reward? *As if there is no reward and no resurrection of the dead.*

It should be noted that the Yerushalmi asks a particular question when it presents us with this theory, "And where did all of this come to him from?" This question is not the same as "Who is Aher?" or "How did he cut at the shoots?" What makes Aher destructive and Other for the authors of the Yerushalmi are his evil deeds and deliberate violation of the commandments. These attitudes about reward and punishment may well be controversial, but they are not necessarily what makes the core of apostasy—rather, they provide a possible backdrop for it.

Another doctrinal problem that we encounter—the issue of repentance—is prominent after Elisha becomes an apostate. As in the Bavli, there is some concern over whether he can repent, and as in the Bavli, we have this as a topic of discussion between Elisha and Rabbi Meir. In the passage cited above, Meir uses Elisha's admonishment to go home to urge Elisha to return in repentance. Here, too, Elisha quotes a heavenly voice proclaiming that all may return, except himself. This version, though, has a striking difference from the Bavli's hard-to-pin-down proclamation (italics my own).

> He [Meir] said to him: All this wisdom is in you and you do not return?
> He [Elisha] said to him: I cannot.
> He said to him: Why?
> He said to him: Because once I was passing before the house of the Holy of Holies, riding on my horse on the Day of Atonement that fell on the Sabbath, and I heard a heavenly voice come out of the house of the Holy of Holies, saying, "'Return children—'except for Elisha ben-Avuyah *who knew My power and rebelled against Me.*"

Penitence may be open for the average sinner, but for the one who was closely acquainted with God, yet apostatized, there is no return.

As in the Bavli, we have an inkling that the impossibility of return stems from Elisha's own mind rather than from an outside imposition. When Elisha is on his deathbed, Rabbi Meir once again urges repentance, while Elisha expresses doubt: "And the returners are not accepted!" Again, one might surmise that some of his distance from his people stems from his not sharing a major principle of the faith.

C. Internal nature of the heretic

Still, the Yerushalmi asks the logical question, why did this rabbi take on heretical views, when many other rabbis in similar situations did not? Like the Bavli, the Yerushalmi text searches for a predisposition in Aher to sin. Following the description of his witnessing the suffering of the righteous, the text goes on to cite an incident relating to Aher's mother.

> And some say that when his mother was pregnant with him, she used to pass houses of idol worship and breathe in from that son. And that same smell penetrated her body like a poison of the mind.

Aher also describes himself as being doomed from his beginnings, because his father did not raise him in Torah study for proper motivations. Instead of being concerned with Torah for the sake of good deeds or God's sanctity, his father sees its power as essential.

> As for me—there was an incident of Avuyah my father, who was among the great men of Jerusalem. On the day of my circumcision, he called all of the great men of Jerusalem and brought them into the house. Rabbi Eliezer said to Rabbi Yehoshua in my father's house, ". . . who are eating and drinking, singing, clapping and dancing—" Rabbi Eliezer said to Rabbi Yehoshua, "until they are no longer occupied with it [Torah study]! Let us occupy ourselves with it then." And they sat and involved themselves in the words of Torah, and from the Torah to the Prophets, and from the Prophets to the Writings, and a fire came down from the heavens and surrounded them. Avuyah said to them, "Gentlemen! Why have you come to burn my house on me?" They said to him, "God forbid! We were only sitting, and reviewing the words of Torah, and from the Torah to the prophets, and from the prophets to the Writings, and the words were as happy as when they were given at Sinai, and the fire licked them as it licked them at Sinai. And the essence of their being given from Sinai was but in fire. 'And the mountain was blazing in fire until the heart of the heavens'" (Deuteronomy 4). Avuyah my father said, "Gentlemen, if such is the power of Torah, then if this son will be raised up for me to Torah, then I will dedicate him." Because his intentions were not for the sake of heaven, therefore, it was not raised up in that same man.

The nature of Elisha's internal taint is of a different order from that described in the Bavli. While the Bavli suggests impure motive on Aher's own part, the Yerushalmi places it entirely out of his hands, asserting that he was fated practically by birth, to fail in the enterprise of Torah study. The emphasis on Aher's inherent predisposition to failure from his very beginnings is a running motif in his dialogue with Meir as well. "Better is the end of a thing than its beginning," he says, "only when a thing is good from its beginning." This dialogue will be further considered below.

D. Relationship of the Other and his people.

One final point of analysis of the position of the heretic is his relationship with his people according to the Yerushalmi's tradition. As we have seen in the depictions of Aher's sins, he did not just perform acts that impacted (or severed) his ties with God, but with his people as well. He deliberately caused others to violate the Sabbath. He thwarted the scholarly tradition, by "making worthless" the efforts of the teachers, or even by physically harming the students. As a national figure, he undermined Jewish national authority and religious practice during a time of persecution and conspired with the oppressor. One can imagine that he would have been a despised figure among the Jews of the era.

In this light, how are we to understand the tradition of Rabbi Meir's continuing association with him? As always, there is more than one interpretation for this discussion.

> R. Meir was sitting and expounding in the house of study in Tiberias. Elisha, his teacher passed, riding a horse on the Sabbath. They came in and told him: Your teacher is outside. He interrupted his lesson and went out before him. He said to him: About what was your lesson of the Day of Judgment?
>
> He said: "And God blessed the end," etc. (Job 42).
>
> He said: With what did you open?
>
> He said to him: "And God added on to all that Job had in double."—that he doubled all his possessions.
>
> He said: Alas for the lost and never found! Akiva your teacher did not interpret such! Rather, "And God blessed Job's end more than his beginning,"—by the merit of the commandments and good deeds that were done by his hand in the beginning.
>
> He said to him: What did you expound further?
>
> He said: "Better is the end of a thing than its beginning."
>
> He said: And with what did you open?
>
> He said: [This is said] of a man who begat children in his youth, and they died, and in his old age, they were raised up; so "better is the end of a thing than its beginning."—Of a man who engaged in commerce in his youth and

lost, and in his old age, profited, so "better is the end of a thing than its beginning."—Of a man who learned Torah in his youth and forgot it, and his old
age, revived it, so "better is the end of a thing than its beginning."

He said: Alas for the lost and never found! Rabbi Akiva your teacher did
not interpret such—rather, "better is the end of a thing than its beginning,"
when a thing is good from its beginning. As for me—there was an incident of
Avuyah my father . . .

. . . He [Elisha] said to him: What did you expound further?

He [Meir] said to him: "Gold and glass cannot match its value."

He said to him: With what did you open?

He said to him: The words of Torah are as difficult to acquire as vessels of
gold, and easy to lose as vessels of glass. And just as vessels of gold and glass,
if broken, one can return and remake them into vessels as they were, even a
wise student who has forgotten his learning can return and learn from the
beginning.

He said to him: Enough for you, Meir. Until here is the Sabbath boundary.

If this incident is meant to be yet another extension of Elisha's evil reperd
toire, then one might view this story (as Elie Wiesel does) as a stark contrast
between the loyal and devoted Meir and the flagrantly faithless Elisha. His riding
a horse on the Sabbath in front of the house of study is a deliberately provocative
act toward the faithful, and the person who informs Rabbi Meir of this is doing
so out of shock at the brazen disrespect of his rabbi's old teacher. Rabbi Meir
goes out in order to address this stressful situation, while still showing utmost
respect for his teacher, using every resource at his disposal to reach him. In this
scenario, Elisha's questions to Meir are challenges—what a poor student you are
if you cannot even get such simple exegesis correct! (Wiesel also suggests that
"Rabbi Akiva your teacher did not say that," is meant to be a nasty, jealous barb
at his old colleague.) Meir, it should be noted, knows the full correct exegesis of
the "gold and glass" verse, and unlike in the Bavli, Elisha cannot correct him—
only abruptly tell him to go back. Elisha's reminder to Meir about the Sabbath
boundary, then, is a way to shake off his pesky pupil and demonstrate his flouting
of the law—he can easily inform another on a point of law which he himself
would disregard.

The other reading of this passage is more benign and would produce a story
that contrasts with the dominant attitude of the Yerushalmi (and is probably
more plausible in the Bavli's version). In this one, Rabbi Meir goes out to Elisha
in the middle of his lesson, because he really does feel there is something to be
learned from his old master. He does not view him as wholly evil and genuinely

cares that he be given every opportunity to return. Maybe Elisha reminds him of the Sabbath boundary out of consideration for a man who still believes—while Elisha himself might sin, there is no reason to bring Meir into the same unhappy situation.

No matter which way we read it, though, we must find something in Elisha—maybe his very human tears—that is worthy of the devotion that Meir is prepared to show, from interrupting his lesson, to attending his teacher's deathd bed, to his final act of "espousal," protectively laying his cloak over Elisha's final resting place.

> At that time, Elisha cried, then passed away and died. Rabbi Meir was glad in his heart, and said that it was as if his teacher died in repentance!
>
> When they buried him, a fire came down from the sky and burnt his grave.
>
> They came and told Rabbi Meir: The grave of your teacher is on fire! He went out to the grave and saw that it was on fire. What did he do? He took his cloak and spread it over it.[34] He said: "Lodge here tonight," etc. (Ruth 3:13)—Lodge here, in this world that is like night, and this morning will be the world to come, that is all morning. "If he will redeem you, good—let him redeem you" (Ruth 3:13). —This is the Holy One Blessed be He, who is good, as is written, "God is good to all, and His mercies are on all His works" (Psalm 145:9). "And if he does not desire to redeem you, then I will redeem you, as God lives!" (Ruth 3:13). And the flame was extinguished.

The final lessons that the Yerushalmi offers about Elisha are not about the apostate himself, but the honorable way to regard him.

> They said to Rabbi Meir: In that world, who are you required to distinguish— your father or your teacher? He said to them: I approach my teacher first, and afterwards my father. They said to him: We should listen to you?! He said to them: Don't we teach that we save the casing of a [holy] book with the book, the casing of tefillin with the tefillin? And we save Elisha-Aher with the merit of his Torah.

Overall, we are given a very particular window through which to view Elisha-Aher. The Yerushalmi paints the issues of apostasy as those of national importance. Aher is not merely a sinner but a person who has betrayed his whole

---

[34] This act, like the verse Meir quotes, is a direct parallel to the biblical character of Boaz agreeing to redeem Ruth. According to H. L. Ginsberg's translation of Ruth, the laying of the cloak is a formal act of espousal.

people, and this text (despite a somewhat more conciliatory ending) is unrelenting as it describes the terrible consequences of this highest treason.

IV. SUMMARY OF SOURCES: WHAT ARE WE TO BELIEVE?

From the stories we have read, and from examining their various shades of meaning, we find a lot of possibilities as to who the character of Elisha ben-Avuyah was, and what made him Other. He has been a Sabbath violator, assimilator, lecher, murderer, informer, and provocateur. He has denied fundamental rabbinic doctrines, the unity of God, and perhaps even the very existence of a God who will call him accountable for his deeds. He has seen the throne of God and the suffering of the righteous on earth. Are there any definitive portraits that emerge from these sources?

Elisha's wealth and social stature make it entirely possible that he was in contact with Greek and Roman culture, and perhaps even with the leadership. Maybe his loyalties were too divided for his contemporaries' comfort. Maybe his fate was too entwined with the Roman government's—as a member of the aristocracy, he may have had too much to lose if he did not cooperate with the authorities. Or, perhaps during a time of persecution, he, as a teacher, was more fearful for his life and gave in to government orders to a greater extent than his martyred colleagues.

Louis Ginzberg points to his denial of the common faith in a world to come and resurrection of the dead as a denial of cornerstones of the Pharisaic belief system.[35] Perhaps the aristocratic, hellentistically educated Elisha was a Sadducee, embracing a more conservative religious and social philosophy.[36] If this is true, then our stories may be indicative of an internal political struggle, in which Elisha is used as the subject of Pharisaic-rabbinic polemic against the Sadducees. Even the greatest scholar of the Sadducees, the Yerushalmi then reads, is a murderer of souls and a sellout to the corrupt government.

Perhaps we choose to take the *pardes* episode most seriously and view Aher as on an intellectual quest that leads him astray. We might emphasize his interest

---

[35] Louis Ginzberg, "Elisha ben Abuyah," *Jewish Encyclopedia* (New York: Funk & Wagnalls, 1903), 5:138–39.

[36] This theory, however, does not explain his association with the prominent Pharisees Rabbi Akiva, ben-Zoma, and ben-Azzai, unless his loyalties were said to have changed or evolved over time.

in speculation on esoteric materials and his possession of heretical books. Even within a group of related ideas about this person, a shift in stress changes volumes of meaning. We don't know how clear it was to Elisha's contemporaries that he should have been regarded as a villain. The attitudes of succeeding generations define him in retrospect, according to their own circumstances. It may be only natural for the community writing the Bavli to focus on mystical and ideological aspects of the heretic; they were prosperous, mingled with other cultures, and had broad exposure to the mythological system surrounding them. Their world is populated with angels and demons—why not Metatron as well? The Yerushalmi, by contrast, tends to be more conservative and separate from its surrounding culture,[37] and its community compiled the work during a time of Christian persecution. Elisha ben-Avuyah floats across generational lines, to define heresy for the community who claims him.

V. Modern Windows

In modern times, we continue to do so. Haskalah (Jewish enlightenment) figures, such as Micah Yosef Berdichevsky, romanticize the renegade scholar who left the confines of the house of study to challenge God directly. Elie Wiesel, a Holocaust survivor concerned with the continuity of the Jewish community, condemns a man who, in his challenge to God, was inexcusably destructive and disloyal to his people. Wiesel's Aher, on a selfish personal mission in the *pardes*, could not understand redemption and declared suffering to be purposeless. He rebelled because he needed to satisfy an abstract concept of justice when he saw the righteous suffering and martyred, and he turned the suffering humans into abstractions as well. "Because Elisha placed the law and the idea of man above man himself, his rebellion sprang not out of love for others, but out of conceptual disillusionment."[38] In contrast, Milton Steinberg, another modern writer and an American rabbi, also places Elisha's heresy in terms of a personal quest for justice but views him much more sympathetically. Steinberg's Elisha is a man whose personal life is always tragically unfulfilling, who is repeatedly thwarted in his human desire to express and feel love. Besieged by the sufferings of his closest friends and the oppression of his people, he turns to

---

[37] Louis Ginzberg, "The Palestinian Talmud," in his *On Jewish Law and Lore* (Philadelphia: Jewish Publication Society of America, 1955), 26–29.

[38] Wiesel, *Sages and Dreamers*, 268.

rational, philosophical reasoning to resolve the doubts that have begun to spring up in his faith. Steinberg's *pardes* is the world of Greek philosophy, science, and sectarian works, to which Elisha turns for answers and which also compete for a modern Jew's attentions. The devastating results for the man who proceeds to accomplish a mission without faith to guide him are to be a message for ambitious, secularly educated American Jews who are similarly in danger of forgetting the all important relationships with loved ones and with God in pursuit of their American dreams.

In each portrayal of Elisha ben-Avuyah, we find both the reprehensible and the sympathetic. Each time we are tempted to condemn or praise him altogether, we find some aspect of his personality as transmitted to us from the oldest, extraordinarily rich traditions, both through our own windows and through those of our teachers, that makes us reassess our conceptions of who Elisha was and what made him Other. I still cannot say that I know definitively who Aher was. I am curious, though, as to who he is to my contemporaries, and who he will be to the upcoming generations of scholars and writers.

BIBLIOGRAPHY

Ginzberg, Louis. *On Jewish Law and Lore*. Philadelphia, Jewish Publication Society of America, 1955.

———. "Elisha ben-Abuyah." *The Jewish Encylopedia*. New York: Funk & Wagnalls, 1903. Vol. 5, pp. 138–39.

Halperin, David J. *The Faces of the Chariot: Early Jewish Responses to Ezekiel's Vision*. Texte und Studien zum antiken Judentum 16. Tübingen: J. C. B. Mohr, 1988.

Harlow, Jules. *Siddur Sim Shalom*. New York: Rabbinical Assembly, United Synagogue of America, 1989.

Jastrow, Marcus. *A Dictionary of the Targumim, the Talmud Babli and Yerushalmi, and the Midrashic Literature*. 2 vols. New York: Pardes, 1950. Reprint, New York: Judaica Press, 1992.

Jewish Publication Society. *Tanakh: A New Translation of the Holy Scriptures*. Philadelphia: Jewish Publication Society of America, 1985.

Kehati, Pinhas. *Mishnavot M'vuarot*. 12 vols. Jerusalem: Hemed, 1991.

Lieberman, Saul. *Hellenism in Jewish Palestine: Studies in the Literary Transmission, Beliefs and Manners of Palestine in the I Century B.C.E.–IV Century C.E.*

2nd improved ed. Texts and Studies of the Jewish Theological Seminary of America 18. New York: Jewish Theological Seminary of America, 1962.

——. *Tosefta Kifshuta.* Vol. 5 of *Tosefta.* 10 vols. in 9. Jerusalem: Jewish Theological Seminary of America, 1972–92.

——.*Tosefta Moed.* Vol. 2 of *Tosefta.* 10 vols. in 9. Jerusalem: Jewish Theological Seminary of America, 1972–92.

Margulies, Mordecai. *Midrash VaYikra Rabbah.* 2 vols. Jerusalem: Jewish Theological Seminary of America, 1993.

Midrash Rabbah. Vilna Edition. 2 vols. Jerusalem: H. Vagsal, Inc.1884.

Neusner, Jacob. *Judaism without Christianity: An Introduction to the System of the Mishnah.* Hoboken, NJ: Ktav, 1991.

——. *The Yerushalmi: The Talmud of the Land of Israel: An Introduction.* Northvale, NJ: Jason Aronson, 1993.

Nickelsburg, George W. E., and Michael E. Stone. *Faith and Piety in Early Judaism: Texts and Documents.* 1983. Reprint, Philadelphia: Trinity Press International, 1991.

Safrai, Shmuel. "Elisha. Ben Avuyah." *Encyclopedia Judaica.* New York: Macmillan, 1982. Vol. 6, pp. 668–70.

Scholem, Gershom. *Jewish Gnosticism, Merkabah Mysticism, and Talmudic Tradition.* New York: Jewish Theological Seminary of America, 1965.

——. *Major Trends in Jewish Mysticism.* 3rd rev. ed. New York: Schocken Books, 1954.

Steinberg, Milton. *As a Driven Leaf.* New York: Ktav, 1939.

Steinsaltz, Adin. *Talmud Bavli.* Jerusalem: Israel Institute for Talmudic Publications, 1984.

"Tosefta." *Encyclopedia Judaica.* New York: Macmillan, 1982.

Urbach, E. E. "Mishnah." *Encyclopedia Judaica.* New York: Macmillan, 1982. Vol. 12, pp. 93–109.

Wiesel, Elie. *Sages and Dreamers: Biblical, Talmudic, and Hasidic Portraits and Legends.* New York: Simon & Schuster, 1991.

Appendix A
Structural Comparison of Bavli, Yerushalmi, and Tosefta texts

Talmud Bavli Hagigah 11b-15b	*Tosefta* Hagigah 2:1-6	*Yerushalmi* Hagigah 2:1/77a-b
Forbidden teaching All who look at 4 things...	Forbidden teaching	Forbidden teaching All who look at 4 things...
How to study Merkavah		How to study Merkavah
Incidents of danger		Incidents of danger Parable of 2 paths
R. Yohanan and R. Elazar b. Arakh expound Merkavah... trees sing, fire descends... fire, angels, etc.	R. Yohanan and R. Elazar b. Arakh expound Merkavah... Yohanan: nice job	R. Yohanan and R. Elazar b. Arakh expound Merkavah... fire, angels, etc.
		Incident of R. Yehoshua and ben-Zoma: "I was contemplating Creation, and there is nothing between the waters above..."
Four went into *pardes* (Rabbi Akiva said...) Aher cut at the shoots Rabbi Akiva left in peace.	Four went into *pardes*... Aher cut at the shoots, Rabbi Akiva ascended and descended in peace	Four went into *pardes*... ...Aher looked and cut at the shoots
	Parable of *pardes* of king Parable of 2 paths	
They asked ben-Zoma...		
There was an incident of Rabbi Yehoshua who was standing on the Temple Mount, and ben-Zoma saw him, and did not stand before him... "I was looking	R. Yehoshua met ben-Zoma on the road... "I was contemplating Creation, and there is nothing between them..."	
between the upper waters and the lower waters..."		
(How much space is there between the upper waters and the lower waters?)		
"Aher cut at the shoots" About him scripture says... ...He saw Metatron...		Who is Aher? He is Elisha ben-Avuyah, who would kill

Talmud Bavli	*Tosefta*	*Yerushalmi*
		the scholars of Torah... And that isn't all.... About him scripture says...
		In the time of persecution...
		Rabbi Akiva entered in peace
A heavenly voice went out and said, "Return straying children!"—except Aher.		
"Since this man has been banished from that world, he will enjoy this world..." ...he must be Another.		
Aher asked Rabbi Meir... "The one no less than the other is God's doing."		Rabbi Meir was teaching in the House of Study in Tiberias, Elisha passed riding his horse on the Sabbath... "Better is the end of a thing than its beginning."
		There was an incident of Avuyah my father...
Aher asked Rabbi Meir... "Gold and glass..." Meir: Torah difficult to acquire and easy to lose. Aher: Reparable...		What did you expound further? "Gold and glass..." Meir: Torah difficult to acquire and easy to lose, but scholar is reparable.
Aher was riding a horse on Sabbath, Meir was following... "Turn back, we have reached Sabbath boundary." "Even you turn back!" Voice beyond partition,		Elisha: Turn back, we have reached Sabbath boundary. Meir: How do you know? etc.
		"Even you turn back!" "I was riding my horse on Day of Atonement that fell on Sabbath past Holy of Holies. Voice beyond wall of Holy... "Return straying children, except Elisha ben-Avuyah, who knew My power and rebelled against Me!"
"Return straying children," except for Aher.		

Talmud Bavli	*Tosefta*	*Yerushalmi*
He grasped him and took him into a house of study... Some say he had a knife and tore the child into 13 pieces.		
		Where did all this come from? ...saw man climb tree and send away mother bird... Where is the long life? etc. Saw the tongue of Yehudah the baker... This is Torah and this is its reward?!
		Some say his mother...
When Aher died, they would not judge him... Rabbi Meir said: when I die, I will raise a plume of smoke from his grave.		Elisha got sick, they told Rabbi Meir... "Won't you ...cried and died Rabbi Meir: as if he died in repentance. ...Fire came from heaven and burned his grave... Meir spread his cloak...and the fire was extinguished.
		They asked Rabbi Meir... ...we save Elisha-Aher with the merit of his Torah.
Aher's daughter came before Rabbi, "Support me!" ...a flame came down and singed Rabbi's chair.		Aher's daughters came before Rabbi to receive charity...
How could Rabbi Meir learn Torah from Aher?! Scholars of Torah are like a nut... what is inside is never ruined... Does all the wool that goes into the kettle come out? All that was good from its beginning...		
Rabbi Akiva ascended in peace and descended in peace...		
	All who look at 4 things...	

Appendix B
Comparison of Four versions of *Pardes* Incident

Midrash Songs Rabbah 1 "Hevi'ani" 1	Talmud Yerushalmi Hagigah 2:1/77b	Tosefta Hagigah 2:3	Talmud Bavli Hagigah 14b-15a
"Bring me O King to your chambers." There the sages teach:			The sages teach:
Four went into the *Pardes.*	Four went into the *Pardes*	Four went into the *Pardes*	Four went into the Pardes
ben-Azzai and ben-Zoma, Elisha ben-Avuyah, and Rabbi Akiva		ben-Azzai and ben-Zoma, Aher and Rabbi Akiva.	They were: ben-Azzai and ben-Zoma, Aher, and Rabbi Akiva.
			Rabbi Akiva said to them: When you reach the stones of pure marble, do not say, "Water, water!" because it is written, "he who speaks untruth shall not stand before my eyes."
	I looked and died, I looked and was wounded, I looked and cut at the shoots, I went in in peace and went out in peace.	One looked and died, One looked and was wounded, One looked and cut at the shoots, And one ascended in peace and descended in peace	
Ben-Azzai looked and was wounded and about him it is said, "If you find honey, eat only what you need."	Ben-Azzai looked and was wounded, about him scripture says, "If you find honey, eat only what you need."	Ben-Azzai looked and died. about him scripture says, "Precious in the sight of the Lord is the death of His faithful ones."	Ben-Azzai looked and died about him scripture says, "Precious in the sight of the Lord is the death of His faithful ones."
Ben-Zoma looked and died. About him it is said, "Precious in the sight of the Lord is the death of His faithful ones."	Ben-Zoma looked and died. About him scripture says, "Precious in the sight of the Lord is the death of His faithful ones."	Ben-Zoma looked and was wounded. About him scripture says, "If you find honey, eat only what you need," etc.	Ben-Zoma looked and was wounded. About him scripture says, "If you find honey, eat only what you need, lest surfeiting yourself you throw it up."

Midrash Songs Rabbah	Talmud Yerushalmi	Tosefta	Talmud Bavli
Elisha ben-Avuyah cut at the shoots	Aher looked and cut at the shoots	Elisha looked and cut at the shoots	Aher cut at the shoots
How did he cut at the shoots?	Who is Aher?		
When he would go into houses of worship and study, and see babes succeeding in the Torah, he would say a word over them and silence them.	—Elisha ben-Avuyah, who would kill the teachers of Torah ...and that isn't all...		
About him it is said "Do not let your mouth cause your flesh to sin."	About him scripture says, "Do not let your mouth cause your flesh to sin."	About him scripture says, "Do not let your mouth cause your flesh to sin," etc.	
Rabbi Akiva entered in peace and went out in peace.	Rabbi Akiva entered in peace and went out in peace.	Rabbi Akiva ascended in peace and descended in peace.	Rabbi Akiva went out in peace.
And he said, "Not because I am greater than my companions, rather because so taught the sages in the Mishnah: Your deeds bring you closer and your deeds distance you."			
And about him it is said, "Draw me after you, let us run!"	About him scripture says, "Draw me after you, let us run!"	About him scripture says, "Draw me after you, let us run," etc.	
	Rabbi Meir was teaching... (more incidents of Aher...)	To what is this comparable? The *pardes* of a king...	They asked ben-Zoma...
			(incidents of ben-Zoma, followed by incidents of Aher. "Aher cut at the shoots, about him scripture says...")

Appendix C
Comparsion of Reward and Punishment Texts

Talmud Bavli Hullin 142a	*Tosefta: Hullin* Hullin 10:16	*Talmud Yerushalmi: Hagigah* Hagigah 2:1/77b
...Rabbi Ya'akov says: There is no commandment in the Torah with a reward stated next to it which does not have the resurrection of the dead dependent on it.	Rabbi Ya'akov says: There is no commandment that does not have a reward given next to it and resurrection of the dead is [not] written in it	
In honoring one's parents, it is written, "So that your days will be lengthened, and so that it will be good for you."	As it says, "Send away the mother," etc.	
For sending away [the mother bird] from the nest, it is written, "So that it will be good for you, and you will lengthen your days."		
There was one, whose father said to him, "Go up to the top of those buildings, and bring me the chicks." And he went and sent the mother away, and took the children, and upon his return, fell and died."	"Go up to the top of the tree," and he fell and died; or "to the top of the building," and he fell and died.	Once he [Elisha] was sitting and studying in the Valley of Ginsor, and he saw one man go to the top of a palm tree, and take the mother from on top of the children, and descend in peace. On the morrow, he saw a different man go to the top of the palm tree and send the mother away, and when he descended from there, a snake bit him, so he died.
Where is the length of days for this one, and the good for that?		Where is the good for this one, and where is the length of days for that?
Rather, "So that your days will be lengthened—" —in a world that is all long [eternal]. And "So that it will be good for you—" —in the world which is all good.	We say from here, "So that it will be good for you—" —in the good world. "So that you will lengthen your days—" —in the long [eternal] world.	He did not know that Rabbi Ya'akov expounded after him, "So that it will be good for you—"—in the world to come, which is all good. "So that you will lengthen your days—"— for the future which is all long.

Talmud Bavli: Hullin   *Tosefta: Hullin*   *Talmud Yerushalmi: Hagigah*

Perhaps this didn't happen?

Rabbi Ya'akov saw this
incident...
(Proposals to explain why
this happened.)

...Rabbi Yosef said, "If Aher
had expounded according
to this reading of Rabbi
Ya'akov his grandson, he
wouldn't have sinned."

What did he see?

Some say that he saw this
incident.

Some say that he saw the
tongue of Rabbi Hutzpit the
translator dragging in the
garbage.

He said, "The mouth that
produced jewels should lick
the dirt?!"

He did not know that "So
that it will be good for you—"
"in the world that is all good";
and "So that your days will be
long—" —"in the world that
is long."

Some say that it was because
he saw the tongue of Rabbi
Yehudah the baker placed in
a dog's mouth, dripping blood.
He said, "This is the Torah
and this is its reward?! This
tongue which had put forth
words of Torah as they ought
to be, this tongue which
labored in Torah all its days—
this is the Toah and this is its
reward?! As if there is no
reward and no resurrection of
the dead."

Part Four
Philosophy

Matt at Yeshivat Hamivtar, 1993–1994.
Photograph provided by Eisenfeld family.

Reflection

RABBI SHAI HELD

MORE THAN ANYTHING ELSE, I remember his kindness.

Matthew Eisenfeld was many things—a budding scholar, an aspiring poet, and a promising rabbi. But before any of those things, he was a gentle soul.

Matt and I used to sit at the dining room table of our Rehavia apartment most afternoons, studying for classes and occasionally taking breaks to chat about life and (especially) relationships. One day I found myself sitting alone at the table for hours on end. No sign of Matt. I began to wonder where he could be. When he finally came home, he seemed tired and a bit agitated. I asked him where he had been, and he seemed somewhat reluctant to share. Feeling nosy, I pressed him, and he told me he had been at a toy store.

"For what?" I asked.

"You know that kid I've been tutoring—"

"You went to buy him a present?" I asked.

"No," he answered. "Well, I did buy him a present too, but the reason it took me so long is that I feel like every time I go over to their apartment, his little brother looks at me kind of sadly, as if he wants my attention too. So I went to the store to buy him a present, because I want to make sure he knows that I care about him, too. But I had trouble deciding what he would like because I don't really know him very well."

That was Matt: kind, generous, open-hearted—but never showy about it. Matt was the kind of person who never wanted to be acknowledged for the _ḥesed_ (kindness) he did, because, after all, isn't that what we are supposed to do?

Matt's kindness and generosity were connected to another remarkable quality of his: he was one of the most honest, forthright people I have ever met.

Rabbi Shai Held is Co-Founder, Dean, and Chair in Jewish Thought at Mechon Hadar. His book, *Abraham Joshua Heschel: The Call of Transcendence*, was published by Indiana University Press in 2013.

During our first months in rabbinical school, Matt and I knew each other only minimally. We were in several classes together, but we had never really had any conversations one on one. One day Matt approached me in the library and said, "I hear that you and Matt Berkowitz are planning to live together in Israel next year. I'd really like to live with you guys." I was caught off guard and was puzzled by the request: Why would someone who barely knew me want to live with me? Matt brought the issue up again a couple more times, and each time I hedged—I had been look forward to sharing an apartment with Matt Berkowitz, whom I knew much better and with whom I felt more comfortable. Finally, one day, Matt caught me in the library again, and said, "Look. I know we don't know each other so well yet. But I have a sense that we would have a lot to learn from each other, and I'd like to make that happen." I was struck in that moment by Matt's utter lack of guile. He wanted human connection and he went ahead and asked for it. If it was "uncool" or too forward to be so straightforward about one's motivations, then Matt was more than prepared to be uncool or too forward. I called Matt Berkowitz and we decided that if Matt wanted to live with us so badly, then there was no reason to turn him away.

Two decades later, I remain immensely grateful to Matt for the courage that it took to pose his request, and to pose it so persistently. Because he was right— we became incredibly close friends in the four months we lived together in Jerusalem, and I, for one, learned a lot from him. We'd talk, we'd argue, and then we'd talk some more. We each found ourselves at difficult moments in our relationships, and we spent countless hours talking (and then talking again) about what each of us was struggling with. It still seems odd to say all these years later, but I was close to Matt for four months of my life, and yet he was one of the best friends I ever had. I miss him still and think of him often.

What follows in this book is Matt's undergraduate essay on Martin Buber and Abraham Joshua Heschel. Matt beautifully embodied some of what was most precious to each thinker.

Buber sharply distinguishes between what he calls "experience," on the one hand, and "encounter," on the other. When I experience another person, I am concerned primarily—or even exclusively—with how that person affects me. My interest in them is not in any deep sense about them. When I encounter someone, in contrast, there is a genuine meeting between me and them, and it is with them in all their fullness that I interact. Experience, for Buber, is nonrelational; encounter, in contrast, is truly dialogical; it is about genuine openness to someone else. What matters most in an encounter is not what happens to me but between us. Our humanity is manifested most authentically when there is "a between" (*das Zwischen*) between me and the person I meet. I can't think of a simpler way to describe Matt: he was all about encounter. So much of his life was animated by an intense curiosity about other people and what they thought and felt.

Heschel taught about wonder, which is in large part about acknowledging the "unexpectedness of being as such." The world did not have to be, and human consciousness did not have to be . . . and yet there they are. Heschel taught that we are not observers of the wonder of existence but are instead full-fledged participants in it. "The mystery is not there," he writes, "while we are here. The truth is that we are all steeped in it . . . we are, partly it." To take this to heart is to realize that "the essence of what I am is not mine. I am what is not mine." Wonder can be a delight, but it is not, Heschel emphasizes, an "aesthetic category." Instead, wonder comes with a question attached to it. When I realize how much I've been given, I feel obliged to repay. As Heschel asks, "How shall we ever reciprocate for breathing and thinking, for sight and hearing, for love and achievement?" Matt really knew how to delight in life: I can still see him staring at a page of Talmud, hot cup of coffee in hand—if I may be permitted to say so, delighting equally in both. I can still remember him asking questions of a Shabbat guest, taking in the pleasure of having encountered a new person and made a new friend. And I will never forget the look in his eyes as he would sit with Sara, his great love, relishing so many wonderful moments with her. But Matt was also committed to repaying, in ways both large and small. He wanted to be an *'eved Ha-Shem*, a servant of God, and he was, to his core a *ba'al ḥesed*, a person of great kindness. He understood, to the depths of his being, that worship of God and service to others are inextricably linked—and he modeled that for me, and for countless others.

Matt was not a saint. He could be self-righteous and he could be overly judgmental (who among us can't?). But all of that was secondary—tertiary, really—to who Matt most deeply was—a profoundly good person, a seeker after knowledge and wisdom, a young man who made space for others, and a friend who loved deeply and well.

May Matt's memory continue to be a blessing to all who were privileged to know him.

November 2015

The Phenomenology of the Prophet: Experience and Response

A Comparison of the Religious Philosophies of Martin Buber and Abraham Joshua Heschel

MATTHEW EISENFELD

ALTHOUGH THE INSTITUTION of Israelite prophecy ended over two thousand years ago, the phenomenon of the prophet remains fascinating. Who were these people who were recognized as having experienced the Divine Presence and were the reporters of God's will? How are we to understand their words, and what relevance do they have for Jews today? Abraham Joshua Heschel and Martin Buber consider these questions of religious phenomenology interesting because they regard the prophets as Israel's true religious individuals. Understanding the prophets as role models, they both make the figure of the prophet central to their philosophies of Judaism and religion in general, but they disagree as to how religious people should respond to their message.

While Buber denies that the events recorded in the Bible could have transpired in history as we know it, he does believe that relationships between God and human beings are possible. Divine revelation, then, is a process wherein Man becomes acquainted with God's presence and His desire that man be a partner to Him. The revelation itself is without specific content, but establishing a relationship to God following his I–Thou model, Buber believes that this

Matt submitted this essay to Professor Eliezer Schweid as his "Senior Essay" at Yale, dated April 11, 1993. This was not included in the original Memorial Volume of 1997, and the editor is grateful to the Eisenfeld family for making it available for this edition.

relationship with God confers meaning on existence and affirms this world.[1] When an I meets a Thou, the individual shares in the relationship and is then faced with the responsibility of deciding what actions to take, knowing that all actions will in some way affect the relationship. While an I–Thou relationship is subjective and exclusive, Buber believes relationships with God to be such that though they be exclusive, they not only permit but require the affirmation of all other relationships. True communities form when individuals in relation to God come to the understanding that the relationship to their Thou invariably leads them to one another. The community remains united by its faith, a relationship requiring the participation of the individual's whole being. Buber interests himself in Judaism, as Israel is one such community that claims to exist by virtue of its relationship to God, its Thou.

In studying the Bible, Buber studies the history of Israel's faith relationship to God. Because Israel is a true religious community, its faith is not compartmentalized, and individual Jews bind themselves to the relationship with God in all facets of life. As Buber recognizes, however, I–Thou relationships are uncommon, and most people will never experience this kind of intimacy with God. While faith holds a person in his or her entirety, Buber speaks of "the doubt that is the destiny of Man."[2] While the relationship may be a reality, people are not freed from the impulse to avoid complete participation in this relationship. Reading the Bible, however, Buber learns of the prophetic struggle to preserve the relationship against the impulses of doubt, making trivial, and compartmentalization of God's presence.

Buber writes, "The encounter with God does not come to man in order that he may henceforth attend to God but in order that he may prove its meaning in action in the world. All revelation is a calling and a mission."[3] It is the prophets who succeed in becoming a Thou to God and, by virtue of their individual success, take the responsibility to communicate their knowledge to the rest of the people. Israel must bring the relationship to life by allowing God's presence not only to dominate ritual functions but also to find expression in ordinary, day-to-day interactions.

---

[1] Martin Buber, *I and Thou*, translated by Walter Kaufmann (New York: Charles Scribner's Sons, 1970), 158–59.

[2] Martin Buber, "The Man of Today and the Jewish Bible," in *On the Bible*, ed. Nahum Glatzer (New York: Schocken Books, 1968), 13.

[3] Buber, *I and Thou*, 164.

Unlike Buber, who views revelation as a process without specific content, Heschel accepts the traditional rabbinical position that divine revelation was a concrete historical event. He believes that Moses received the Torah from Sinai and that the prophets were actually addressed by God. In defending the traditional model of Jewish religious belief, Heschel asks how Jews should understand God's presence. His inquiries lead him to focus on the correct response, which he argues consists of Torah study and fulfillment of Jewish law. Heschel, too, believes in a God who enters into relationships with human beings and communicates His pathos to humankind. Somehow, God suffers when man sins and rejoices when man conforms to the moral order that is His will. Heschel writes that "the phenomenon of prophecy is predicated upon the assumption that man is both in need of and entitled to divine guidance."[4] As God knows the moral order, cares for human beings, and desires that man turn to Him, God turns to man in His revealing of the Torah and addressing the prophets in order that man may succeed in improving the human condition. Heschel writes that "the Bible is itself a *midrash,*" or a report about God's overtures to people and human flight from God.[5] Man can return to God guided by faith with the prophets, adhering to Jewish law, and yet always trying to increase understanding as to the meaning of the laws.

In evaluating the prophetic experience, Buber and Heschel explore the question of what it means to "hear" the voice of God and how human beings should respond. While they agree that God desires personal relationships, they disagree as to what form this relationship should take. Buber endorses personal choice and stresses the responsibility of each individual to make decisions, shunning the possibility that a law code could deny choice to an individual or, worse, reduce the reality of God to a set of rules. Buber's model of religiosity need not apply to Jews only, yet Israel is his quintessential faith community. Heschel argues that the rabbinical model upholds the faith community and was originally designed so as to avoid the danger of becoming a mere set of rules. He stresses that the individual retains a great deal of responsibility in seeking God. Perhaps individual responsibility even increases as the individual is challenged to go beyond the mere fulfillment of law in order to come close to God. All should constantly seek to broaden their understanding as to why Jews accept particular laws. As advocates of completely different models of religiosity, these

---

[4] Abraham Joshua Heschel, *The Prophets,* vol. 1 (New York: Harper & Row, 1962), 202.
[5] Abraham Joshua Heschel, *God in Search of Man: A Philosophy of Judaism* (New York: Farrar, Straus & Cudahy, 1955), 185.

two thinkers force us to choose between two attractive but in the end irreconcilable modes of religiosity.

I. Buber

1. The Meaning of Relationships

The concept of the I–Thou relationship permeates Buber's religious philosophy as he claims that we find meaning from our relationships to both people and objects. To be alive is to interact with the world. It is with this understanding that Buber begins his work *I and Thou,* where he writes, "The world is twofold for man in accordance with his twofold attitude. The attitude of man is twofold in accordance with the two basic words he can speak."[6] These two basic expressions, I–Thou and I–It, express the two modes of the individual's interaction.

I–It relationships are experiential, bound by time and space. They are predictable and subject to measure. Through the I–It mode, men establish relationships of utility which are necessary for survival. Examples of this type of relationship would include my use of a pen to write a letter or my hiring a painter to paint my house. In both cases, I do not participate with my "whole being"[7] because the interaction does not entail recognition of anything beyond that which I need immediately. I interact with the pen only insofar as it IS an object by which I might write a letter and the painter only insofar as I need him to paint my house. As these relationships are necessary, there is nothing inherently wrong with the I–It, and Buber does not argue that all I–It relationships should ideally become I–Thou. I can treat the painter with respect and understand that while I use him to paint my house, he simultaneously uses me in order to earn money. However, Buber writes, "All actual life IS encounter,"[8] meaning that people become who they are and find meaning in their lives only through relationships in which they participate with their full being. This kind of relationship can only be I–Thou.

The I–Thou IS an exclusive relationship of one individual to another. Such an encounter does not take place between the souls of two participants; if that were possible, the relationship would be incomplete, as it would be an interaction that did not require the participation of one's whole being. The relationship

---

[6] Buber, *I and Thou,* 5.

[7] Ibid., 54.

[8] Ibid., 62.

cannot be assigned a time or place, as this also would set limits to the interaction, nor can it be described as an object of experience.

The I–Thou relationship is possible between people and the natural world, people and other people, and people and spiritual beings. Necessarily, the relationships express themselves in different manners. One cannot speak to a tree or a painting the way one speaks to a fellow human being. When one interacts with God, one is not spoken to, at least not in the manner normally identified as speaking. Rather, we participate in this type of relationship in "creating, thinking, acting: with our being we speak the basic word, unable to say You with our mouth."[9] Nevertheless, though they differ as to form, all three variations of the I–Thou are possible. Buber illustrates this type of interaction in the case of a tree:

> . . . as I contemplate the tree I am drawn into relation, and the tree ceases to be an It. The power of exclusiveness has seized me.
>
> This does not require me to forgo any of the modes of contemplation. There is nothing I must not see in order to see and there is no knowledge I must forget.
>
> . . . it confronts me bodily and has to deal with me as I deal with it—only differently.
>
> One should not try to dilute the meaning of the relation: relation is reciprocity.
>
> Does the tree then have a consciousness, similar to our own? I have no experience of that. But thinking that you have brought this off in your case, must you again divide the indivisible? What I encounter is neither the soul of a tree nor a dryad, but the tree itself.[10]

Once one begins to describe the tree, however, one moves away from the relationship and has moved into the It world, as one is reduced to discussing the tree insofar as it is tall, has green leaves, is an oak tree, and so on. Were I to say, "I look at the tree because it makes me happy," I would be describing yet another I–It relationship, as I would be describing an experience insofar as it affects me in a specific manner. Relationships to other people or to spiritual beings are no different in this respect.

The recognition that participation in an I–Thou relationship requires the inclusion of one's whole being raises the question as to how one of these

---

[9] Ibid., 57. Kaufmann took issue with Ronald Gregor Smith's translation of *Du* as "Thou." He translates the word as "You." See "I and You," his prologue, 14–15. In this essay, I have chosen to use "Thou," as is standard, but will be faithful to Kaufmann in quoting his work.

[10] Ibid., 58–59.

relationships begins. To this question, Buber answers only, "The You encounters me by grace—it cannot be found by seeking."[11] The encounter simply is, and cannot be mediated by any other due to its exclusive nature. Buber postulates that the human condition is such that it is simply our nature to form such relationships. From these I–Thou relationships, we become who we are because it is the interaction that lends any meaning to existence. I–It relationships can be assessed in terms of value because when asking about value, we in truth consider our possibilities of interaction. In an I–Thou relationship, value is not a question because there is only the encounter.

When people encounter God, they always encounter God as a Thou. Buber writes, "Through every single You the basic word addresses the eternal You. The mediatorship of the You of all beings accounts for the fullness of our relationships to them—and for the lack of fulfillment."[12] In relation to God, however, all other relationships are potentially fulfilled, contingent upon the decisions made by him who stands in the relationship. While the relationship between the individual and God is as exclusive as any other I–Thou, Buber argues, "In the relationship to God, unconditional exclusiveness and unconditional inclusiveness are one."[13] Paradoxically, the ultimate subjectivity of a relationship is that which leads the participant into all other relationships.

Buber addresses the paradox by asserting that we form a relationship with God in the same manner that we form relationships with others. He posits that "the concept of personhood is of course, utterly incapable of describing the nature of God; but it is permitted and necessary to say that God is *also* a person."[14] Persons, as learned earlier, interact with the world. In fact, Buber calls God the "Absolute Person" who relates to all others, yet who is unchanged by relationships to others, remaining God always. As God engages Himself in relationship to all of existence, interactions with God therefore involve the rest of human experience. By virtue of God's presence within these relationships, all relationships acquire meaning.

When God enters into a relationship with a human being, what is received "is not a 'content' but a presence, a presence as strength."[15] In this relationship, man is made aware of the reciprocal nature of the relationship to God. Clearly,

[11] Ibid., 62.

[12] Ibid., 123.

[13] Ibid., 127.

[14] Ibid., Afterword, 181.

[15] Ibid., 158.

God relates to man differently than man to God, analogous to the case of the tree. Buber admits ignorance as to how the tree relates to man, but the reciprocity nevertheless exists. Everything in the world is then confirmed as meaningful, as the relation to God is expressed through "creating, thinking, and acting," as mentioned above. The meaning conferred is this-worldly, "and it wants to be demonstrated by us in this life and this world."[16] In other words, the encounter with God is, in effect, an affirmation of the world. As this conferred meaning demands action, what it is actually demanded is a reevaluation of the other relationships. If the world really is twofold, and all life is actually made up of relationships between individuals, then action is merely the expression of some relationship. The revelation of new meaning entails that our actions will henceforth be different.

Buber proposes that God enters into relationships with man because God needs man. For this reason, Buber calls revelation a "calling and mission." The challenge is for man to be a Thou to God. Buber writes:

> That you need God more than anything, you know at all times in your heart. But don't you know also that God needs you—in the fullness of his eternity, you? How would man exist if God did not need him, and how would you exist? You need God in order to be, and God needs you—for that is the meaning of your life. . . . The world is not divine play, it is divine fate. That there is the world, man, the human person, you and I, has divine meaning.[17]

Because God enters into relationship with the entirety of the world, the divine fate then is the fact of innumerable reciprocal relationships. As the divine fate is in the relationship, God is constantly revealing Himself to individuals, challenging them to hear and to decide. Revelation, therefore, cannot be a historical event, but a constant process by which God makes Himself known.

Man is led to turn to God just as God turns to man, and it is in this turning that the community forms. While the relationship to God affirms and lends meaning to the other relationships, Buber writes "that man, however he may include the world in his encounter, can still go forth only as a person to encounter God—all this does not satisfy man's thirst for continuity. He thirsts for something spread out in space, for the representation in which the community of the faithful is united with its God. Thus God becomes a cult object."[18] The

---

[16] Ibid., 159.
[17] Ibid., 130.
[18] Ibid., 162.

community forms as a response to the encounter with God, because, while relationships in which one participates with one's whole being are not confined by space and time, people's lives are.

In seeking to live the relationship, the community formalizes its "You-saying" through ritual and symbol, which point beyond the actions themselves to the relationship. Buber compares the members of these "genuine" communities to "radii that lead from all I-points to the center,"[19] where all members of the community affirm each other by virtue of their relationship to their Thou. These are the communities that can be called religious.

Though according to Buber all religious communities form in this way, they may not continue. While ritual and symbol point to the relationship and represent one mode by which man turns to God, subsequent generations run the risk of trivializing the relationship by overemphasizing the importance of form. The danger inherent is that the faith relationship, which Buber identifies as "a relationship of my entire being,"[20] is compartmentalized to the ritual function. When this happens, the relationship is no longer total, and "[i]nstead of a union, a false relationship obtains between the spirit and everyday life."[21] Thus, even the relationship with God can be reduced to I–It. The challenge of the religious community, then, is to retain its faith relationship against the forces that seek to tear it apart. These forces include inertia, or desire simply to accept the answers to questions proposed by earlier generations, institutionalized fear of mistakes, or simply refusing to hear the call. Buber argues that this is what happens to most communities because "religion was always real only when it was free of fear, when it shouldered the load of concreteness instead of rejecting it as something belonging to another realm, when it made the spirit incarnate, and sanctified everyday life."[22] However, even the community that sinks to this level has the potential to return. Those who remain a Thou to God and who exhort the community to return are called prophets by Buber.

The prophets are figures freed from fear in that they are full participants in the relationship with God. They offer rebuke to the communities they love in order to encourage the community to stop divorcing the "spiritual" life from everyday living and to reactualize the relationship. Buber studies the Hebrew

---

[19] Ibid., 163.

[20] Martin Buber, *Two Types of Faith,* trans. Norman P. Goldhawk (New York: Macmillan, 1951), 8.

[21] Martin Buber, "The Man of Today and the Jewish Bible," in Glatzer, *On the Bible,* 2.

[22] Ibid., 3.

Bible as a faith history of early Israel, which he believes to have been the quintessential community, which turned to God, faltered, and then continued to develop as prophets grew out of Israel's midst. In Israel's prophets, Buber sees individuals who preserved the faith community and landmarked the faith's essential developments.[23]

2. Israel and Its Faith History

Israel's prophets grow out of the faith community as chronicled in the Bible. In the opening to his book *Moses*, Buber writes, "In order to learn first hand who Moses was and the kind of life that was his, it is obviously necessary to study the Biblical narrative. There are no other sources worthy of serious consideration."[24] The same consideration is true regarding the other prophets. As a record of the faith relationship between the people Israel and God, Buber identifies the Bible's function as to "bear witness to the spirit's will to perfection and to the command to serve the spirit in its search for union with life."[25] Yet the Bible is not divine revelation in the sense that has been traditionally understood; Buber does not believe that the Torah was handed to Moses at Sinai. Instead, Buber evaluates the Bible as a saga because "[t]he happenings recorded there can never have come about in the historical world as we know it, after the fashion in which they are described." Because a saga "is generally assumed to be incapable of producing within us any conception of a factual sequence,"[26] were Buber to treat the Bible as objective history, it would involve sacrifice of intellectual honesty, which would in turn prevent him from participating in a faith relationship with his entire being.

The saga does not record historical fact as such, but the human experience of the event. If, for example, the Bible records the experience of the Israelites standing at Sinai as the mountain burned with fire while God spoke, what is important to the faith historian is that the people "comprehended the words of their leader Moses as a message from their God, a message that simultaneously established a covenant between them and a covenant between Him and their

---

[23] Martin Buber, *The Prophetic Faith*, trans. Carlyle Witton-Davies (New York: Macmillan, 1949), 2.

[24] Martin Buber, *Moses: The Revelation and the Covenant* (New York: Harper & Row, 1958), 13.

[25] Buber, "Man of Today and the Jewish Bible," 4.

[26] Buber, *Moses*, 13.

community."[27] That Israel received a divine revelation from Sinai may not be a historical truth, but it is accepted as a cultural truth. The understanding of that recorded experience has shaped the Jewish faith throughout history.

Buber accordingly begins his historical investigation with what he believes to be the earliest narrative that captures the essence of the relationship between Israel and its God. He finds this expression in the Song of Deborah. In this celebration of a military victory, Buber locates what he believes to be the four major points of early Israel's faith. He writes that these points are the following:

> (a) YHVH is "the God of Israel." Israel is "YHVH's people." ... (b) If Israel acts and accomplishes itself as Israel, YHVH is to be "blessed" for "the righteous acts to His peasants in Israel." (c) YHVH leads Israel and He Himself goes at the head of the companies of the people, as it is put in the prose version where Deborah says to Barak ([Judges] 4:14) "Has not YHVH gone out before thee?" And they must "willingly" follow Him, "come to his aid." (d) The important point is to "love" YHVH.[28]

Israel recognizes itself and its fate as intimately connected to this God who chooses the path for His people to follow, leads them in battle, and is glorified when Israel acts in accordance with the reality of the relationship. In other words, the Song of Deborah is written by an author who views Israel's relationship to God as its reason for nationhood. Were it not for this relationship, there would be no need for the tribes to have united and the author would have no cause to criticize those tribes who did not come to battle. However, precisely because God allows Himself to be connected to Israel, failure to act well sullies God's name as it detracts from the relationship. The failure to "act well" in this case is understood to mean that the participants are not participating fully in the relationship.

New historical realities bring changes that challenge old ideas and force the relationship between God and the nation to adapt. While God may be eternal, Israel's situation is subject to constant flux. The people often do fail to participate in the relationship with God as a Thou and are thereby continually addressed by the prophets, who call to them to examine their deeds. Buber traces the relationship through the Bible, from the time of Deborah through the judges, to the kings, and on through the Babylonian exile. In every era there exists a new challenge.

---

[27] Ibid., 16–17.
[28] Buber, *Prophetic Faith,* 10.

As the land is conquered and secured, for example, Israel no longer lives as a nomadic community but settles to an agricultural lifestyle. In this "new status of life . . . [t]his is the central sphere in the existence of the primitive peasant: the secret of the fertility of the ground, the astonishing phenomenon, from the discovery of which agriculture springs."[29] The people are tempted to worship the *ba'alim* or local Canaanite fertility gods, along with child sacrifice, cult prostitution, and all the rites of Canaanite custom. Even if the people did not go this far, the people and later their kings would "baalize" YHVH. While still recognizing their God as unique and addressing their prayers and sacrifices to the God of Israel, they would attempt to interact with Him as with one of the Canaanite deities. Buber exemplifies the baalization process with the story of King Ahaz, who performs such a Canaanite practice to incur divine favor while attempting to gain foreign aid from Assyria:

> The young king Ahaz decided to summon the help of . . . Assyria. But at the sight of increasing danger, he also did . . . what West Semitic kings used to do in such circumstances, . . . he "makes his son to pass through the fire"—a deed which may be understood as a real offering of the first born, or as a substitution for it by a symbolic act . . . at all events there is a transformation of YHVH the *melekh* into "Moloch."[30]

The danger inherent in acts such as these is the loss of the special relationship between God and Israel because in an act such as this not only does YHVH lose His individuality, but Ahaz attempts to force His hand. In this example, God becomes an object of use, to be invoked at the whims of men. He ceases to be a Thou to Israel and is treated instead like a good-luck charm.

Ancient Israel need not go as far as human sacrifice in order to reduce the I–Thou relationship to I–It. As Moses stands before the burning bush, he asks for God's name and is told *'Ehyeh 'asher 'ehyeh,* which is usually translated, "I am that I am." Buber reads this phrase to imply a promise, "I shall be present that I shall be present."[31] In these words, God conceals from Moses His true name, not allowing even His greatest prophet superfluous knowledge; superfluous because

---

[29] Ibid., 71.

[30] Ibid., 134. *Melekh* means "king." As YHVH was seen as the people's leader, He was to be recognized as Israel's true king. For this reason Gideon refuses the throne (Judges 8:23) and Samuel opposes Saul's ascension (1 Samuel 8:11-19). Moloch was a Canaanite deity whose worship consisted of child sacrifice.

[31] Buber, *Moses,* 52.

God's desires for Israel are always communicated anyway. The concealment of such knowledge is an act of love preventing Israel from ever thinking itself in position to "use" God for means other than God's own. Buber interprets this statement, 'Ehyeh 'asher 'ehyeh to mean, "I would have you know that I indeed befriend you ... if the first part of the statement ['ehyeh] states: 'I do not need to be conjured for I am always with you,' the second ['asher 'ehyeh] adds: 'but it is impossible to conjure me.'"[32] However, when living a reality similar to that of another culture in which people conjure their gods to aid, Israel attempts to do the same. This is the mistake of King Ahaz, which earns him Isaiah's rebuke.

The use of God for ends not receiving divine sanction can be connected to the mechanization of ritual such that people who perform the rituals mistakenly think themselves to have thereby discharged their "obligations" as partners in the relationship. At this point, ritual is replaced by magic or manipulation of elements to produce a desired result requiring no input from faith.[33] So too rituals and laws, which ideally acquire their form through "a mixture of You and It,"[34] do not require faith in order to be done. This problem of mechanization confronts Israel especially at the time when the Temple is built, when sacrifice has become the accepted medium for Israelite worship, and when the priests take on a highly specialized yet entirely ritualistic role. Worship is thus reduced from true expression of a sacred relationship to mere obligation. Buber argues that such obligatory worship is problematic since "obligations one has only toward the stranger";[35] God cannot be a stranger to a faith relationship. Amos, Hosea, and Micah protest against the degeneration of the moral values as the cult centralizes and grows because Israel must participate in the relationship to God with its entirety. If the poor are oppressed while rams and bullocks are led to the altar, God is not glorified. Israel cannot say Thou to God only insofar as animals continue to be slaughtered in the Temple.

Protesting against this misuse of ritual and the attempt to use God for improper means, the prophets direct Israel toward recommitment to God but do not offer any specific formulas of action. When Amos says in God's name,

---

[32] Ibid., 52-53.

[33] This is one of the reasons why Paul opposed Torah law. See Buber, *Two Types of Faith,* chapter 4.

[34] Buber, *I and Thou,* 167.

[35] Ibid., 157.

> I hate, I despise your feasts, and I will not smell the sacrifices of your solemn
> assemblies. Though you offer me burnt offerings and your meal offerings, I
> will not accept them; neither will I regard the peace offerings of your fat
> beasts. Take away from me the noise of your songs; for I will not hear the
> melody of your lutes. But let justice well up like waters, and righteousness as
> a mighty stream. (Amos 5:21–24)

he plainly tells the people what will not improve the relationship, but his instruc-
tions do not include any specific commands as to what the people should do.
"Let justice well up like waters and righteousness as a mighty stream," is a powerful command, yet it does not say how this should be done. If Amos were to
specify what Israel should do, however, Buber believes that this would further
harm Israel in that he would deprive Israel of the important step of taking responsibility for one's actions. Israel must do something, yet the decision of what to
do must come freely from Israel's initiative. It is like the Hasid in *The Way of Man*
who asks his Rebbe for advice on how to serve God. When the Rebbe instructs
the man to decide for himself, Buber learns that the "great and holy deeds done
by others are examples for us, since they show, in a concrete manner, what greatness and holiness is, but they are not models which we should copy."[36] Here, too,
the people need somehow to learn to recapture the original feeling of closeness
to God, and this will be done through moral perfection rather than through
punctilious observance of ritual. That the people's return will not take the same
form as their ancestors is of crucial importance. Circumstances have changed, as
have the people who now interact with the God of Israel. The nation no longer
wanders in the desert but lives a settled life with a centralized cult. Nevertheless
God "desires no religion. He desires a human people, men living together, the
makers of decision vindicating their right to those thirsting for justice, the strong
having pity on the weak, men associating with men."[37] Though the relationship
may change, this search must remain constant.

The relationship evolves even as Israel experiences moments of crushing
defeat. Jeremiah suffers for the people, warning them in vain of approaching
disaster while clinging to the hope that the people might turn to God. He is a
prophet called upon to pronounce a message of doom and is persecuted by
those whose authority he challenges. Buber places him "among the martyrs of
the ancient world, whose afflictions are not only told us, but who himself opens

---

[36] Martin Buber, *The Way of Man* (New York: Carol, 1966), 15.
[37] Buber, *Prophetic Faith,* 172.

for us the door to share in them by occasionally committing to writing an expression of his sufferings with the same directness as he whispers or cries them to his God."[38] As he watches Israel near its horrific fate, he aches for the people whom he loves, but is powerless to save them. God does not even allow Jeremiah to pray for the people (Buber refers to 7:16). The nation will fall, swallowed by a mightier power. Concurrently, Jeremiah's life teaches that "the way of martyrdom leads to an ever purer and deeper fellowship with YHVH. Between God and suffering a mysterious connection is opened. In every generation, God's emissaries not only worked and fought by his order, but they also bore suffering in the course of their work and fighting."[39] In the face of disaster, the relationship was to adjust again.

This "way of suffering" finds further expression during the Babylonian exile in the writings of Deutero-Isaiah.[40] How could Israel's faith relationship, as celebrated in the Song of Deborah survive? Then, YHVH was the God who had connected Himself to Israel. That Israel was YHVH's people was their reason to exist. God had led Israel and demanded that Israel love Him. Now, "He 'leaves His house (Jerusalem),' He withdraws to heaven, now only He becomes wholly God of heaven, God of the world, God of all; He wants to be recognized as 'God from afar,' filling heaven and earth (23, 23f), perceiving all and yet remaining above all."[41] Yet Deutero-Isaiah maintains that God retains special care for Israel, who is to be a "light unto the nations" (Isaiah 42:6). He prophesies salvation; Israel will be redeemed in days to come. Israel's collective suffering is but a stage in the divine drama.

Buber writes that, at this time, Deutero-Isaiah is unique in that his "task to prophesy salvation is blended with the fact that his prophecy is in Israel the first prophecy according to the accepted sense, that is to say, he has to foretell things fixed and unchangeable."[42] Earlier prophets, such as Amos, had preached their message of doom as a possibility. Yet, like Moses (Exodus 32:11–14) before him, his prayers had temporarily moved God to withhold punishment from Israel. Now, however, the prophet speaks of a time to come which human action can

---

[38] Ibid., 180.

[39] Ibid., 183.

[40] According to Buber and most Bible scholars, Deutero-Isaiah is author of chapters 40–55 of the book of Isaiah. Buber writes that his work is called "Isaiah" because he saw himself as a student of the First Isaiah.

[41] Buber, *Prophetic Faith,* 182. The quotation is from Jeremiah.

[42] Buber, *Prophetic Faith,* 210.

delay but not avert. Deutero-Isaiah speaks of the "Suffering Servant," whom Buber identifies as a personal figure, "not to be comprehended in the life span of a single man. [Such prophets] are the way of one servant, passing through all different likenesses and life cycles."[43] Through the work of these individuals, the relationship between God and Israel will be redeemed.

In success or failure, rulership or exile, God remains connected to Israel throughout the Bible. Situations change and the prophets speak different messages, yet they consistently call upon Israel to be a Thou to God. The relationship takes on different forms and requires differing actions, yet the encounter between God and man is eternal.

II. HESCHEL

While agreeing with Buber that God shares the pathos of the human situation and that God enters into personal relationships with people that require one's whole being, Abraham Joshua Heschel believes in divine revelation in the traditional sense and endorses normative Jewish law as the correct religious response for Jews. His religious philosophy can be summarized by his statement in *God in Search of Man:* "There is no substitute for faith, no alternative for prophecy, no surrogate for tradition."[44] Whereas Buber's inquiry as to the nature and function of prophecy stems from his theory about relationships or modes of interaction within the world and leads him to read the Bible as the saga of Israel's faith relationship to God, Heschel begins his philosophy of religion discussing wonder. He believes that not only is it wonder that keeps life interesting, but that it is wonder that leads one to ask ultimate questions about the meaning of life and to seek answers.

Prophecy interests Heschel in that he considers the prophetic message to be "a divine understanding of the human situation. Prophecy, then, may be described as an *exegesis of existence from a divine perspective.*"[45] In other words, the prophets' words teach us how God views humanity and what God expects. As God communicates His understanding to humanity, people are given the beginnings of an answer to their ultimate questions and are called upon to respond. God's understanding of men is superior to their own. However, because

---

[43] Ibid., 230.
[44] Heschel, *God in Search of Man,* 152.
[45] Heschel, *Prophets,* 1:xiv.

God connects Himself to human beings and shares in their situation, God is caused suffering by human failure. As God has entered into a special covenantal relationship with the people Israel, God is especially grieved by Israel's failures and communicates His pathos to His messengers, turning to man in an attempt to improve the human situation. These messengers, the prophets, are important "not only in what they said, but also in what they were,"[46] because they respond to God's pathos with sympathy and fulfill their mission to prophesy, even when they are assured from the outset that their success will not be in their lifetime.[47]

In outlining his methodology, Heschel writes, "Philosophy is reflective thinking, and philosophy of religion may be defined as religion's reflection on its basic insights and basic attitudes, as *radical self understanding of religion in terms of its own spirit.*"[48] He further explains that this means that one must clarify those insights and then in some way examine the plausibility of the claims made. In studying prophecy, Heschel evaluates the message, questions the possible explanations for prophetic inspiration, and then concentrates on designing the correct religious response. He concludes that Judaism successfully answers humankind's ultimate questions and that Jews should dedicate themselves to living the prophetic message.

1. Faith

Heschel devotes the first section of his work *God in Search of Man* to a discussion of the wonder that leads people to question the meaning of existence. One may marvel at the regularity with which nature works or at rare events such as thunderstorms or tornadoes. One may also marvel at things taken for granted—that we are alive and breathing, for example. Through the human experience, we become aware of powers greater than us and we are forced to confront our imminent mortality. That we are placed in such a world for a limited amount of time can be ignored or can lead an individual to ask questions. Perhaps there exists some meaning in all of existence. Perhaps the lone human being, small as he or she may be compared to the vast expanses of the universe, has some special role to play in the world. Can this possibly be true?

Heschel admits that ultimate questions cannot be answered positively or

---

[46] Ibid., 1:ix.

[47] See, for example, Isaiah 6:11–13 and Jeremiah 1. These prophets are given missions in which they cannot "succeed." God lets them know that the people will not repent.

[48] Heschel, *God in Search of Man,* 8 (italics original).

negatively, but that in confronting these questions, we are drawn to a working understanding of how the world works and to find our place within the cosmos. This is where Heschel chooses his first leaps of faith, affirming that the world does have purpose and is ruled by a God who cares for humankind. He does not try to prove this assertion but argues that "this IS indeed the greatness of man: to be able to have faith. For faith IS an act of freedom, of independence of our own limited faculties, whether of reason or sense-perception."[49] Holding onto faith that there are answers enables man to hear them if in fact they are actually offered. Wonder, then, "is *a form of thinking*. It is not the beginning of knowledge but an act that goes beyond knowledge; it does not come to an end when knowledge is acquired; it is an attitude that never ceases," and furthermore, that "the beginning of our happiness lies in the understanding that life without wonder is not worth living."[50] Heschel believes life to be a continual process of asking questions, and religion to be an answer. To discover answers to the questions is to decipher God's desires and to take steps to improve one's own life in the faith relationship.

2. The Bible

Were God to withhold knowledge of His will from humankind, He could not be considered good. Jews accept the Bible as God's revelation to humankind. According to Heschel, the Bible is a record of God's turning to man, and man's flight from God.[51] Biblical heroes recognize that they have special roles to play in their lives that go beyond themselves. They spur their communities and later generations to action, pursuing peace through morality. Heschel accepts traditional claims of the Bible's origin, writing that it "is an answer to the question: how to sanctify life."[52] As the events recorded in the Bible tell tales of people inspired by wonder who use their understanding to pursue newly learned meaning in life, Heschel feels justified in taking this next leap of faith.

Accepting that God cares for the world, Heschel learns of God's suffering for the world through the words of the Bible itself. If God does indeed suffer alongside humanity, then to allow people to stumble unguided would increase God's own suffering. Heschel writes:

---

[49] Ibid., 118.

[50] Ibid., 46.

[51] Ibid., 185.

[52] Ibid., 237.

This notion that God can be intimately affected, that He possesses not merely intelligence and will, but also pathos, basically defines the prophetic consciousness of God. . . . Pathos denotes, not an idea of goodness, but a loving care; not an immutable example, but an ongoing challenge, a dynamic relation between God and man; not mere feeling or passive affection, but an act or attitude composed of various spiritual elements; no mere contemplative survey of the world, but a passionate summons.[53]

God has a need to make people aware of their failures and communicates this extreme disappointment and remorse through the mouths of the prophets.

Revelation, then, is not a process by which God and man become acquainted, nor is God's will made known to man gradually. God addressed man, revealing His will at Sinai. Because people continue to flee from the obligations of a relationship with God, God sends prophets to Israel who seek to remind the people of the difference between right and wrong, calling upon them to return to Him. The prophet is a model of human excellence, as Heschel writes, "The soul of a prophet is a mirror to God."[54] Religious individuals find themselves in the position of responding to prophecy, because they are the role models of those who live in sympathy to the divine pathos.

God's turning to man is an event in the life of the prophet initiated by God to which the prophet must respond. When called, the prophet is overwhelmed by God's pathos and sympathetically accepts the divine task. In fulfilling the mission, the prophet retains self-consciousness and often suffers greatly. All prophets speak out of love for Israel and love for God. As the bearers of harsh messages, prophets are tortured in their loyalty to two loves, God and Israel. Though they fulfill their tasks, it is not always in joy. Many plead with God to forgive the crimes of the people; some like Amos, with success (7:2–6), and some like Jeremiah, failing. Some prophets, like Jeremiah and Jonah, even protest their lot in being called to prophesy—Jonah because he understands God's mercy and desires not to see Nineveh, the capitol of Israel's enemy, Assyria, saved from destruction; Jeremiah because he knows his warnings will go unheeded.

Regardless of how the prophet may respond to the divine calling, the significance of the prophetic experience "lies not in those who perceive it, as happens in mystical experience, but in those to whom the word is to be conveyed."[55]

---

[53] Heschel, *Prophets,* 2:4.

[54] Ibid., 2:249.

[55] Ibid., 2:225.

The Bible does not speak of prophets who keep to themselves, but rather of those who address all of Israel. Heschel writes, "To the prophet no subject is as worthy of consideration as the plight of man. Indeed, God Himself is described as reflecting over the plight of man rather than contemplating eternal ideas,"[56] because the plight of man intimately affects God. Amos, for example, is a shepherd from Tekoa who leaves his flock to prophesy to the kingdom of Israel. He decries the zeal of the people to offer sacrifice while they lethargically pursue righteousness. Such an experience is telling with regard to what God desires because Amos is a prophet from the kingdom of Judah, often at war with Israel.[57] Here he stands, away from his livelihood, warning not his own country but Israel about coming destruction. He even goes so far as to pray for Israel. Readers of the Bible encounter in Amos a messenger whose actions are surprising. Amos is warning Israel against destruction out of sympathy for God and because it is right, even if such an action does not appear politically expedient for a resident of the southern kingdom. The ancient resident of the northern kingdom would thereby observe Amos pursuing righteousness with zeal, living the message he preaches.

Heschel writes that "the prophets know that religion could distort what the Lord demanded of man"[58] because when a cult is formalized, one may erroneously believe one's responsibilities to be fulfilled. The prophets act so as to prevent this distortion. What God does demand is that people recognize that they are greater than they take themselves to be, and that they thereby rise above the image they currently espouse of themselves. The prophet himself "is human, yet he employs notes one octave too high for our ears. He experiences moments that defy our understanding. He is neither 'a singing saint' nor a 'moralizing poet,' but an assaulter of the mind."[59] Consider the case of Jeremiah, who enters the Temple, prophesying that it will be destroyed, or standing before the nobles of Judah wearing a yoke to symbolize the yoke of Babylon. Acts such as these are incomprehensible to the observer who would have believed the false prophet Hananiah that all was well. Yet Jeremiah tries to bring those notes to the common people's level because the message is intended for them. His desire is that the people elevate themselves by turning back to God. Our ideal self is with God, greater than our own conception.

---

[56] Ibid., 1:5.

[57] Ibid., 1:27. Heschel writes that Israel expanded "southward at the expense of Judah."

[58] Ibid., 1:11.

[59] Ibid., 1:10.

Aside from the actual prophets themselves, Heschel also evaluates recurring themes in the prophetic message. When he discusses divine chastisement of Israel, for example, he notes that "the prophets themselves seemed to have questioned the efficacy of punishment. In the Bible, punishment has three aims: retributive, deterrent, and reformatory."[60] In the case of God's punishing Israel, we expect God's anger to serve the latter two ends. But how can punishment serve these ends? Heschel might argue that punishment for the failure to uphold an agreement allows the participants to take the idea of a covenant seriously. If obligations are to hold sway over the human psyche, then there must be some consequence for negligence. Otherwise, the law, or the "will of God" is reduced to a mere suggestion as to the good life. Somehow, partners in a covenant must be allowed to suffer, to feel the consequences of their actions in order to learn to take responsibility for actions. Israel must experience a measure of the divine pathos so that it too will respond to God sympathetically. Yet "the prophets, however, discovered that suffering does not necessarily bring about purification, nor is punishment effective as a deterrent."[61] Human beings continue to commit acts of iniquity and God suffers. God can punish man for sin, but man still does not listen.

3. The Plausibility of Heschel's Claims

Heschel's approach acknowledges the traditional model of divine revelation. He knows that he is without the means to prove that this is what actually happened and does not make this attempt. In order for him to remain consistent with his own principles and come to the religious understanding he adopts, Heschel must somehow show that revelation as we read could have happened.

Sensitive to this criticism, Heschel devotes much of *God in Search of Man* and volume 2 of *The Prophets* to the process of demonstrating that God could have actually spoken to humankind and revealed a will. As explained earlier, Heschel can hypothesize God's existence from his wonder about the world and reasonable leap of faith. He mentions the argument from design[62] as a possible

---

[60] Ibid., 1:187.

[61] Ibid., 1:188.

[62] David Hume rightly pointed out in *Dialogue Concerning Natural Religion* that the argument from design cannot prove that there is one and only one God; however, that there may be problems with the argument from design is beyond the scope of this paper. Heschel's purpose is only to affirm the possibility that his leaps of faith are reasonable.

proof of God's existence and adds that the idea takes the observer, the observed, and the very process of observation for granted. He notes that this is all an "incomprehensible fact."[63]

In volume 2 of *The Prophets*, Heschel turns to the problem of prophetic inspiration itself. Were the prophets ecstatics? Poets? Rhetoricians? Or were they simply deluded? Heschel addresses these questions in turn. For example, he considers ecstasy in the classical sense, in which individuals would seek union with the deity, and concludes that the prophets could not have been ecstatics. Because the prophet himself was as important as the message he conveyed, and because the prophet did not lose his personality in receiving the divine word, the prophet cannot be classified as an ecstatic. Furthermore, most ecstatics seek ecstasy whereas the prophets claim to be called. Jeremiah, for example, tries to withhold the prophecies that cause him such suffering (20:9) and curses the day he was born (20:14–15).

Perhaps, Heschel suggests, prophets were recognized as such not because they were actually divinely inspired, but because during that time period, "prophecy" was simply an accepted institutionalized religious role. While there may have actually been many "prophets" in ancient Israel, Heschel asks, "Why did the 'spirit of the age' produce no prophets in Assyria and Babylonia, among the Phoenicians or Canaanites?"[64] Furthermore, Heschel argues that men inspired by "the spirit of the age" would not be outraged when Israelite kings offered their children as burnt offerings as did their neighbors. If the prophets were not genuine, but rhetoricians, then they were not truthful. Heschel finds it unbelievable that those "who condemned the lie as a fundamental evil should have lived by the lie."[65] For all such questions, Heschel is unable to find a convincing confutation of the traditional model.

Concerning the message God sends to the prophets, Heschel asks:

What did the prophet mean by the phrase "God spoke"? To understand the statements of the prophet about his experience we must keep in mind the following principles about the nature of these statements: (1) things and words have many meanings. (2) the prophet's statements are understatements. (3) the language of the prophet is the language of grandeur and

---

[63] Heschel, *God in Search of Man,* 109.

[64] Heschel, *Prophets,* 2:193.

[65] Ibid., 2:197.

mystery. (4) there is a distinction between descriptive and indicative words. (5) the statements of the prophet must be taken responsively.[66]

Heschel argues that this means that (1) Not all words of the Bible should be read literally. (2) Prophetic statements convey a "*minimum of meaning*" in order to be understandable to those to whom the message is addressed. (3) The prophets employ language so as to lead the audience to recapture the feeling of wonder with the universe. (4) Some words are descriptive, meaning that they "stand in fixed relation to conventional and definite meanings, such as concrete nouns," and some words are indicative, "which stand in a fluid relation to ineffable meanings. Their meanings can be intuited if not fully comprehended. (5) The correct way to understand the prophet is by responding to the prophet.[67] Heschel thereby feels entitled to read the message as a call to communal action requiring Jews to return to God through *halakha*.

4. Response

Ideally, the prophets would see Israel turn back to God. The correct Jewish response clothes spiritual understanding in action, as Heschel writes that, in Judaism, "spirituality is the goal, not the way of man."[68] The divine presence requires a response not only in feeling but in deeds between people and God, and between people and other people. Jews are required to move from what Heschel calls "faith in the prophets," meaning believing that their words are in fact a message from God, to "faith with the prophets," or living the message. He writes that "to share the faith of a prophet means more than perceiving what other people fail to perceive; it means being what common people fail to be: a mirror to God. To share the faith of a prophet means rising toward the level of his existence."[69] In a footnote to this statement, Heschel explains that this statement refers to fulfilling Jewish law, which combines intention to serve God with an action.

---

[66] Ibid., 2:178.

[67] Ibid., 2:178-83.

[68] Heschel, *God in Search of Man*, 297.

[69] Ibid., 249. Heschel footnotes this statement with a quotation from *Mekhilta* on 14:31: "He who accepts even one single *mitsvah* with true faith is worthy that the Holy Spirit should rest upon him."

While revelation may have already happened and institutionalized prophecy no longer exists, Jews continue to respond to God's presence through study of the Bible, rabbinic literature, and through *halakha,* Jewish law. Revelation itself is accepted as finished, but just as wonder is an attitude that never ceases, so too does the response to the greatest wonder imaginable never end. Heschel defends Jewish law as the attempt of a community to rise to God in which each individual plays a role and is faced with the responsibility to choose the *halakhic* path. Where Buber fears that normative action can become mechanical because many people simply respond to what the community expects instead of struggling to decipher the requirements of a personal encounter with God, Heschel believes that because any relationship with God must involve all facets of existence, the community should have a way of cooperating in their endeavor to serve God. The individual does not mold his personality in a vacuum, but allows his environment to influence him. His growth is invariably tied to that of his community, and communal religiosity should take a recognizable form so as to accommodate for the participation of many. Heschel emphasizes the importance of studying *agada,* or rabbinic lore, as well as the law, because he agrees that actions without the spirit are less meaningful. Even if, as some Jews[70] would argue, the laws are in essence God's laws explicable only to Him, and not merely our working response to Sinai, Heschel would still stress the importance of Jews serving God further by coming to an understanding as to why specific laws are important in daily living.

III. EVALUATION

Because Heschel endorses the *halakhic* system as the superior religious path for Jews to follow while Buber stresses personal choice, their two philosophies are in principle irreconcilable. While in truth Buber would encourage someone who claimed to encounter God through observance of the law, he does not promote the system as does Heschel because he believes that "as soon as the relationship has run its course or is permeated by a *means,* the You becomes an object among objects, possibly the noblest one and yet one of them, assigned its measure and boundary."[71] Their differing approaches lead them to explain the formation of

---

[70] This is a more traditional position, which Heschel would not ignore. The argument holds that every act a Jew performs carries metaphysical significance of which we can have no knowledge.

[71] Buber, *I and Thou,* 68.

true religious life differently. They critique one another in three primary areas regarding how their ideas can come to fruition. First, they espouse different conceptions of the status of the community in the individual's religious life. Next, they differ as to how they conceive of the effect of law on the individual's responsibility. Does God's presence require an independent reformation of the relationship by each individual, or is this process more of a communal endeavor? By what criterion can we judge whether the individual has more or less responsibility when a member of a community? Finally, they both strive for intellectual honesty and should be evaluated as to how honest they actually remain.

1. Community

Both Buber and Heschel argue that the true religious community exists only by virtue of its relationship to God. This lesson which Buber learns from the Song of Deborah is the same lesson that Heschel learns in accepting the Torah and prophets as divine revelation. Both would agree that the importance of the faith community cannot be overestimated, but disagree as to the best way to preserve this community over time.

Heschel argues that law and lore bind the community together. While the danger of compartmentalization exists constantly, Heschel believes that continual study and self-evaluation serve as safeguards against this danger. In asking why Israel's relationship is so sacred, Heschel writes:

> Jewish existence is not only the adherence to particular doctrines and observances, but primarily the living *in* the spiritual order of the Jewish people, the living *in* the Jews of the past and *with* the Jews of the present. It is not only a certain quality in the souls of the individuals, but primarily the existence of the community of Israel. It is neither an experience nor a creed, neither the possession of psychic traits nor the acceptance of a theological doctrine, but the living in a holy dimension, in a spiritual order. Our share in holiness we acquire by living in the Jewish community. What we do as individuals is a trivial episode, what we attain as Israel causes us to grow into the infinite.[72]

As we wonder at the world and question the meaning of our existence, we individuals are humbled. The earth existed long before us and will continue to exist after our deaths. As group members, however, we are drawn immediately into

---

[72] Heschel, *God in Search of Man,* 423.

relationships with other people, experiencing our need of them and their need
of us. It is in the community where people's attachments and responsibilities are
most pressing.

The communal focus of *halakha* assures that Jews of the present benefit
from the experience of Jews past. When Heschel writes that Jews of today "live
in Jews of the past," he means that, because they asked the same kinds of questions (if not the same questions themselves), we have before us their answers.
Today's generation relives the struggles of the ancestors and adds new perspectives to old questions. Heschel recognizes the danger, writing, "Teachers of religion have always attempted to raise their insights to the level of utterance,
dogma, creed. Yet such utterances must be taken as indications, as attempts to
convey what cannot be adequately expressed, if they are not to stand in the way
of authentic faith."[73] In other words, they say, "This lesson is important. You owe
it to yourself to consider what I have to say." Later generations as the heirs of the
former must understand that their ancestors had insights from which they may
benefit while at the same validating their own achievements.

Buber would not disagree that those who live today benefit from the insights
of those past and present. However, while he argues that any relationship to God
turns one to validate all other relationships, he rejects law as a means of accomplishing this community affirmation because the relationship that is mediated
by definition cannot be a true encounter. Instead, the encounter is replaced by a
substitute. Buber does not endorse any specific set of actions in order to build
the community but rather promotes the strengthening of the relationship
between God and the individual itself. The more the individuals participate in
their I–Thou relationships with God, the stronger the community becomes by
virtue of their commitment. The situation is analogous to a community that
espouses an ideal as its raison d'être. When the community loses touch with the
ideal, the community itself begins to suffer and the power of laws to keep the
society running smoothly are limited.

Heschel, on the other hand, considers it a proper expression of the relationship to God to dedicate oneself to the study of what is perceived as God's
will in order to contribute to the growth and flourishing of the community.
Traditionally, Jews learn Torah in pairs. A relationship between two members
of a community forms while they study. As this endeavor ideally happens on a
large scale, the community promotes at least thought about God and discussion

---

[73] Ibid., 103.

of ideals believed to be communicated from God. In this turning away from the individual and focusing on the community, Heschel is able to strengthen relationships between individuals and keep the community directed toward the relationship. If, as Buber argues, we catch glimpses of the eternal Thou in all other I–Thou relationships, then Heschel's emphasis on the preservation of the community with law may accomplish this task more easily. He would agree with Buber that the individuals continually turn to God in order that the law not divorce itself from life, but he maintains his belief that "spirituality is the goal, not the way of man." While the relationship itself is of primary importance, it is structure that builds a community and not a common spiritual bond.

2. Personal Responsibility

In opposing a law code, Buber fears that God will be reduced to a set of rules. As in the case of Amos's protest against the northern kingdom of Israel's so-called religiosity, it becomes too easy to think of the relationship as an obligation requiring ritual fulfillment. One can easily consider this obligation fulfilled once the ritual is complete and forget the reality of the ever-presence of God. However, in failing to take responsibility for oneself and simply following a code, Buber argues that one distances oneself further from the relationship than one who decides against God. If the encounter with God forces upon the individual a decision, then relationships form when he or she acts upon whatever decision is made without reservation. Buber argues:

> Only he that funnels all the force of the other into the doing of the one, absorbing into the actualization of what was chosen the undiminished passion of what was not chosen, only he that "serves God with the evil impulse," decides—and decides what happens. Once one has understood this, one also knows that precisely this deserves to be called righteous: that which is set right, toward which a man directs himself and for which he decides; and if there were a devil he would not be the one who decided against God but he that in all eternity did not decide.[74]

Furthermore, when an individual comes to choose, he should not imitate others, but seek his own method of serving God. Conceivably, this individual could correctly choose for himself a way common to other people, but the usual urge

---

[74] Buber, *I and Thou*, 101.

of the individual is to conform rather than to struggle. Not only is this the sense in which chapter 2 of *The Way of Man* was previously cited, but it is the message Buber learns from the prophets themselves.

Heschel could accuse Buber of misreading both the story of the Seer of Lublin and the prophetic message. In the former case, the Seer of Lublin would not have encouraged his disciple to leave the *halakhic* system in seeking his particular way of serving God. Rather, Rabbi Baer is encouraged to experiment within the freedom that the system opens to him.[75] Concerning prophecy, Heschel believes that the prophets address a nation to make specific lifestyle changes. When Amos commands in God's name, "Let justice well up like waters and righteousness like a mighty stream" (5:23–24), Heschel and Buber would agree that he is advocating a national undertaking to achieve righteousness as a nation. Yet Heschel would note that this righteousness somehow requires formalization, and Amos receives his inspiration from the same God who revealed the Torah at Sinai. Thus, the prophet's audience had an idea as to what he meant in specific. Though no two individuals would attempt to fulfill his words in exactly the same manner, those who listened would do so through Torah principles.

Heschel would argue that, as the Seer of Lublin challenges Rabbi Baer to find his own particular way in serving God, he advises his disciple to rise above the letter of Jewish law. When discussing how one should serve God, the Torah commands, "With all your heart, with all your soul, and with all your might" (Deuteronomy 6:5); fulfillment of the *halakhic* requirements represents the bare minimum of divine service. The law itself requires understanding so as not to become a mechanical process of deadening ritual. Study of law and lore, however, is necessary as a tool to fine tune relationships within the community, yet the law itself should be seen only as the starting point. While one acts consistently according to a set of principles agreed upon by the faith community, one should seek out his or her particular way in which to further actualize the relationship with God.

Nevertheless, the danger remains that most individuals will not come to this understanding of law as only a small part of the response to God's presence. Heschel would argue that because not all will succeed does not imply that law itself is a process that deadens the relationship between God and humankind. Rather, the relationship is alive and constant. Torah study only serves to enhance the relationship as the individual is forced to evaluate himself against Torah and rabbinic

---

[75] Freedom in the sense that Rabbi Baer will not have to worry that his particular way will dissolve the community or his attachment to the community. That the community is kept together by *halakha* ensures against this danger.

norms. It is only in considering the alternatives posed by those before that the individual can rise to a level where the decision can be approached responsibly.

3. *Intellectual Honesty*

Neither Buber nor Heschel can prove God's existence or demonstrate that God does in fact enter into relationships with human beings. In Buber's philosophy, relationships are simply taken as given, and his purpose is to describe these different modes of human interaction. Heschel evaluates the working response of the faith community but needs somehow to demonstrate the plausibility of his claims to truth.

In his article "Modern Man and the Jewish Bible," Buber writes that he cannot accept many of the biblical events recorded as actually having happened without sacrificing intellectual honesty and thereby losing the faith relationship in which his whole being participates. This is why he reads the Bible as a saga. Once Buber has accepted this model, he learns about the faith history of early Israel and can use this knowledge to increase his own religious understanding and improve his relationship with God.

Heschel, as seen above, understands that he must justify his leaps of faith and demonstrate that, given his assumptions, divine revelation as we are told is not impossible. We have seen how, taking wonder seriously, he is led to posit God's existence and how divine revelation should follow in some form. After discounting a few of the possible objections to the theory that prophets were not divinely inspired, he has grounds to claim justification, yet remains without proof.

Buber could still respond that because Heschel's whole philosophy finds its support from leaps of faith, it cannot be considered if one wishes to retain the highest standard of intellectual honesty. Given that words have different meanings and that not everything is to be read literally, where does one draw the line between reading literally the account of the Red Sea splitting or Sinai burning, and the statement "And God called to Moses . . ."? Heschel could counter that there has been for the last few thousand years a tradition as to how to read the Bible. One may be guided by such a tradition, and this represents one way in which the individual benefits from the *halakhic* community. While Heschel would acknowledge that his philosophy is anchored in leaps of faith, he would respond that his leaps of faith are not any less reasonable than communities commonly take. As he posits that "faith is *sensitivity, understanding, engagement,* and *attachment . . .* not something achieved once and for all, but an attitude one may gain and lose,"[76] what is important to him is not so much the objective truth of our accepted propositions but the continuing response to those propositions we have adopted. He believes that because his ideas are not impossible, he is allowed to construct his system without sacrificing intellectual honesty. Nevertheless, Buber could still claim to be more intellectually honest in that he does not build a system from leaps of faith but from actual encounter.

Heschel might ask Buber how he justifies his ideas concerning how I–Thou relationships form at all, for Buber has produced no evidence to suggest that we interact as he claims. Can there really be a contentless interaction? Heschel would agree that God interacts with people, yet God does not change His revealed will. Any interactions between God and man are beyond the level of law. Perhaps this is the sense in which Heschel would read the Seer of Lublin's advice to Rabbi Baer.

IV. CONCLUSIONS

In investigating the prophetic experience, Buber and Heschel represent different outlooks concerning the nature of faith. Both agree that faith is a relationship of totality and is not easily maintained. They raise the question, What is the best way to serve God? Does one serve God through accepting certain premises as true because they may be reasonable, or through asking the "forbidden" question in hope of coming to a distinctively individualistic understanding? Both seem to advocate a dialectic between the two possibilities, but their approaches lead them to emphasize different aspects of consideration in that dialectic.

Buber represents the path of the individual who learns to recognize holiness but understands the impossibility of imitating the ways of others. Relationships between human beings are entirely subjective, as are relationships between people and objects, given that no two people are the same. All bring different histories to the encounter. If the actualization of the relationship with God changes over time as learned from *The Prophetic Faith,* then the relationship between God and the individual is different for each person. If we assume this to be true, then no mediation can substitute for what Buber calls "stepping before the countenance," and experiencing God as a Thou. Form and artifice cannot help but will eventually intrude, if not from the outset.

Heschel can be read as representing the path of the community but would

---

[76] Heschel, *God in Search of Man,* 154.

reject this label, as he sees the community to be integral to the formation of the individual. His mode of inquiry, too, is individualistic, as he discusses ultimate questions asked by both people and groups, the answers to which he believes are given by the prophets. Yet these answers are in actuality only the beginnings of answers. The correct Jewish response is to study and act, to carve one's niche in life, arriving at a working understanding of God's will. This is a continual process, as human wonder never ceases.

The question of intellectual honesty remains, but the faith relationship seems to be such that it somehow incorporates doubt and requires untestable assertions of truth to some degree. This seems to be the sense behind Buber's continual assertion that individuals in relationships carry the responsibility to make free decisions, and it is nonsensical to speak of free decisions wherein one is robbed of doubt concerning the consequences. Were there to be any certainty, moreover, it would be nonsensical for Heschel to discuss ultimate questions.

In choosing to take a leap of faith, then, we are drawn to evaluate the reasons that lead one to take such a step. Heschel seems to present a program wherein Jews are led into the kinds of relationships spoken of by Buber. However, Buber argues that "the You encounters me by grace," so one cannot be led into these types of relationships. In Buber's terms, Heschel is reduced to saying, then, that he endorses the idea of revelation and the *halakhic* system because it seems to him that it is in this kind of community that he encounters God and believes that the community leads others to encounter God as well. But Heschel does not accept Buber's terms; he comes to his own answers as the answers he would accept in response to his ultimate questions. Buber would say that this is "as if a man went his way and merely wished for it to be *the* way."[77] Heschel, given his inability to prove that his assumptions are true, is forced to agree. Nevertheless, he will walk in the path he desires to be true. Whether or not he is actually correct, he has faith that he will learn this from the road signs.

BIBLIOGRAPHY

Buber, Martin. *I and Thou.* Translated by Walter Kaufmann. New York: Charles Scribner's Sons, 1970.

———. "The Man of Today and the Jewish Bible." In *On the Bible: Eighteen Studies*, edited by Nahum Glatzer. New York: Schocken Books, 1968.

---

[77] Buber, *I and Thou,* 128.

————. *Moses: The Revelation and the Covenant.* New York: Harper & Row, 1958.

————. *The Prophetic Faith.* Translated by Carlyle Witton-Davies. New York: Macmillan, 1949.

————. *Two Types of Faith.* Translated by Norman P. Goldhawk. New York: Macmillan, 1951.

————. *The Way of Man: According to the Teachings of Hasidism.* New York: Carol, 1966.

Heschel, Abraham Joshua. *God in Search of Man: A Philosophy of Judaism.* New York: Farrar, Straus, & Cudahy, 1955.

————. *The Prophets.* 2 volumes. New York: Harper & Row, 1962.

Part Five

Additional Essays

Matt made a *siyum* on Massekhet Qiddushin on February 3, 1996, in his apartment in Jerusalem. See Matt's statement of education goals on p. 25. (Photo by Edward Bernstein)

Food for Thought on Shabbat and Festivals

MATTHEW EISENFELD

THE EATING AND DRINKING of a *se'udat mitsvah* have significance beyond the immediate effect of satisfying one's hunger and providing an occasion for friends to spend time together. Aside from the pleasantry of the meal itself, the food and drink act as *parshanut* (commentary) to create realities to which verses of the Tanakh, or sayings of the rabbis aspire. Not only do these *mitsvot* seek to create realities; they also create attitudes. The quintessential *se'udat mitsvah* in which edible *parshanut* is most readily understood is the Seder. One reads the verse "And they embittered their lives" and seeks to understand how our ancestors' lives were made difficult by the Egyptians. We may discuss the various forms of labor our enslaved ancestors were forced to endure, or we can eat *maror*. As in every generation we are required to see ourselves as having personally been brought out of Egypt; the night seeks somehow to return us to the moment of redemption. In fact, we do not remember leaving Egypt and so are presented with considerable difficulty as we attempt to tell the tale in a convincing and instructive manner. The *mitsvot* of the evening, then, serve to direct us through whatever channels may be available.

If we can understand the *se'udat mitsvah* to serve an educational purpose, we then have a perspective from which to evaluate the first eight pages of the tenth chapter of Masekhet Pesaḥim in the Bavli. The issues chosen for discussion, interruption of a meal, Havdalah, and Kiddush, seem to be chosen because of their relationship to the Seder. The first *maḥloqet* of the chapter, for example, concerns the time when one should refrain from eating on the day before Shabbat or Yom Tov, but is resolved in the case of Erev Pesaḥ (according to the opinion of Rav Huna) because everybody agrees that eating in the afternoon may prevent one from eating matzah that night. Similarly, the Gemara bothers itself with issues of Kiddush and Havdalah, as they may be the first *mitsvot* fulfilled during the Seder. However, that Kiddush and Havdalah appear in the Seder seems not to be the only reason the Bavli chooses to discuss them here. Rather, as the Seder is the archetypal *se'udat mitsvah* which serves an educational function, so too Kiddush and Havdalah, which are components of a *se'udah* serve educational functions.

For an example of how Kiddush may be seen as an attitude-creating *mitsvah,* consider the opinion of Shmuel, who says, "*'Ayn qiddush 'ela be-maqom se'udah,*" or, "One should not make Kiddush except in the place where one eats" (100b–101a). According to Rashbam, this opinion seeks to bring to life Isaiah 58:13, which reads, "If you refrain from trampling the Sabbath / from pursuing your affairs on My holy day; / If you call the sabbath 'delight,' / The Lord's holy day 'honored' / And if you honor it and go not your ways / Nor look to affairs, nor strike bargains [nor speaking of vain matters]." The *derash* (traditional interpretation) of this verse says, "In the place where you declare (call) *shabbat*, there you should have delight." Kiddush should be made in the place where one will eat, because the immediate action following this declaration that tonight begins Shabbat is to experience *'oneg*, delight. Thus, the verse comes to life, as one can truly call Shabbat a delight.

From this verse, we actually learn two concepts related directly to *se'udot* (festive meals). The first concept is that of saying Kiddush in the place where one eats. The second concept is that of *kavod Shabbat,* or "honoring" Shabbat. The relationship between *kavod* and food fuels the question at which meal one should consume a glass of wine for Kiddush if only one glass is available (105a-b). On one hand, one should perform a *mitsvah* in its proper time, to the best of one's ability. On the other hand, one is required to "honor" Shabbat with fine food, in order to distinguish Shabbat from the rest of the week.

As the laws of Kiddush seek to concretize the issues of *'oneg* and *kavod,* so too Havdalah teaches beyond itself. A key line to understand Havdalah is found on 102b, which reads "Havdalah and Kiddush are the same," insofar as both recognize God as the Great Divider, who made Shabbat or Yom Tov special. On one level, Havdalah is ideally made over wine, just as Kiddush is ideally made over wine, functioning as a bookend (I heard this explanation from Sara Duker). On another level, Havdalah provides us with an opportunity to recognize another aspect of God with the departure of Shabbat. As mentioned above, this is God's role as Divider, as we learn from its formula (103b–104b). We recognize aspects of God by making *berakhot,* careful to say them only at times and events when particular aspects of God are apparent. In this sense, Havdalah presents us with a small but comforting message as we leave Shabbat and begin the week. Even though we return to our labor, we do so as a function of God's acting in the world.

In summary, we see that the consumption of food, like the saying of *berakhot* or recitation of the Haggadah catapults us into a reality where we understand better the messages the *mitsvot* communicate. Kiddush over wine helps us to understand what is meant by *'oneg,* and special foods teach us about what it is to show *kavod.* Once Shabbat has been honored and enjoyed, the prohibition of work takes on a new character—just as we honored Shabbat with food, so now we must refrain from work. Shabbat ends as it began, with the wine of Havdalah, signifying that, although the Sabbath departs, our devotion to God continues, only under a different rubric for the next six days. We think about God as the Creator of the world as we return to our own creative endeavors. The wine, spices, and light all reinforce us. As the Psalmist writes, "Taste and see that the Lord is good," because taste is internal. Sometimes, when *mitsvot* seek to create attitudes and change the actor more than the surrounding world, sight and action alone are simply not enough.

Reflections on Israel

SARA DUKER

"ISRAEL PUT THE KIPPAH back on our heads," declared our Ramah director during the summer of 1991, in an effort to demonstrate the impact the founding of the Jewish State had on young American Jews of his generation. Jews, once reluctant to acknowledge their Jewish identity, began to come out of the woodwork in response to astonishing underdog military victories, pressing national needs and the realization of two-thousand-year-old hopes. Today, on Jewishly active college campuses, similar ideals are invoked in order to bolster Zionist pride and activism. Zionism is considered one among many outlets for Jewish expression, a source of national and cultural heritage, including among those who do not consider themselves ritually religious. However, changes in the State—both the development expected of a modern country and problems unique to Israel and its society—have uncovered an erosion of Jews' automatic support for Israel and our ability to use Zionism as a quick ticket to Jewish pride. Thirty years ago, [Rabbi Abraham Joshua] Heschel foresaw the potential crisis in Jewish nation building and personal identity in his book *Israel: An Echo of Eternity*, in which he emphasizes the need for continued Jewish vision, "realizing that," even in 1995, with advanced technology, a booming economy and prospects for peace, "the economic, political, and spiritual development is still in a stage of beginning."

Is Israel unique? Does it set an international standard of care for its citizens and hold a moral banner even higher than most democracies? Are those Jews who founded and live in the State stronger and more Jewish? The answers seem easy to a Jewishly active college student, until she is confronted with "ISRAEL: THE HIJACK STATE" emblazoned on a pamphlet being distributed in the student center by a socialist group. A young man with great visions of social

Winner, Israel Aliyah Center Essay Contest, 1995.

justice claims that Israel is nothing more than a capitalist, imperialist arm of the most corrupt elements of the Western world. It has greedily expropriated the land of the natives, and continues to exploit the laboring class, he says. Other students find their assumptions about the sacredness of their nation challenged by mainstream political correctness—the best liberals have taken up the cause of Palestinian rights, and Zionism is dismissed as a glorified racism. Even students who tend to be removed from the campus political arena (with the hyperbole it often engenders), can't help but be aware of the newspapers, which tell us that Israel is far from perfect. Political parties experience corruption there, too. Extremism characterizes political debate, with deep [divisions] between the religious and secular Jews. And, no matter what our national and religious beliefs are regarding the West Bank and Gaza, there are few Jews who do not experience at least some discomfort with Israeli politics toward the Palestinian Arabs. The temptation arises to distance oneself from such a contentious state—to deny one's Jewish connections (or apologize for them), or to claim an American Jewish ideology separate from Israeli dilemmas. It often seems tempting for us Americans to pursue Judaism as we think best, and to leave difficult ideological decisions of defending the Jewish State to Israelis.

How are our Israeli peers faring? A young Israeli man in New York, recently released from his three-year tour of duty in the [Israeli] army, used to tell anyone who asked him that he did not believe in God. He believed in his people and the horrors that have happened to them. He went to the army, he said, so that a Holocaust, which decimated his parents' generation, would not do the same to his. An American 'olah [immigrant to Israel], a tour guide in Yad Vashem, related incidents during her presentation of the required tour to Israeli soldiers being inducted to the army. She says that she hears frequent grumbles from her mostly secular groups when they are addressed with the Holocaust. "This doesn't affect us," they say. "When are we going to get over it and move on?" If this group—at the forefront of Israel's material progress and already uninterested in the religious nature of its country—finds that even national tragedies are losing their power to motivate and unify, what then will inspire the next generation of Israeli Jews to continue to fulfill the heavy demands of their people?

Until now, we have taken for granted that Israel would "put the kippah on our heads," that Israel would do much of the work of shaping Jewish identity. As Israel continually struggles with its own identity, it is important to be reminded of the essence of Heschel's statement: "The State of Israel is a spiritual revolution, not a one time event, but an ongoing revolution." The key ideas are "spiritual" and "ongoing." A spiritual revolution goes beyond the national security and material support Israel was built to provide to Jews, to look at a larger raison d'etre. We pour forth catch phrases about history, martyrdom, God's land and community, but how often do we think carefully about what each of these really means? Why is Jewish community so important in our time? Is our history unique? Do we believe that we are God's chosen people and Israel is a chosen land? What implications does this have for our behavior—not just on a large political scale but for the everyday life of a Jew? How does this inform our treatment of one another? If we do not believe in God as a presence in Jewish history, then what other ideologies do we have to guide us? What is the role of Diaspora Jewry? What can we contribute beyond our yearly checks to UJA? This is not to suggest that we can automatically provide deep and meaningful answers. Each reconsideration of old questions constitutes a revolution, by re-creating and renewing our visions of Israel.

This process, of course, must be ongoing. We face a startling sense of inadequacy when our notions, unchallenged, become irrelevant in the face of new situations. The effort of building a physical home and the cooperation it required, was a communal, spiritual process for the pioneers, but we, lacking that same urgent sense of need, soon find that the tangible construction is not enough to answer the spiritual questions of this generation. We have not come into full national self-awareness. And, as with any other process of development, disuse of spiritual sense causes it to erode. In the end, Israel will not guarantee our Judaism until we give the labor of our hands as well as our hearts and minds to guaranteeing Israel's Judaism.

From Irkutsk to Jerusalem

SARA DUKER

THOSE OF YOU WHO HAVE BEEN in touch with me have been asking me to tell you more about my exciting adventurous life in Israel. My life here, despite not being at a U.S. address, is not that exciting.... My little bits of news include things like making my very own pot of borscht, winning a fare war with an Israeli taxi driver, and giving an oral presentation in Hebrew class about Buryat roadside rituals. Besides, I have been looking forward to having an opportunity to reminisce with you all about Siberia. As a compromise, I'll tell you one strange story of Jewish geography that stretches the lengths of two oceans.

At the end of our week in Irkutsk, the day before the saddest fast day of the Jewish calendar, I was anxious to visit a synagogue. While I am a regular atendee at home, the unique locations we were in throughout the summer made gathering with community impossible. With a chance to spend some spiritual time with my "family," people both the same and different, fully on the other side of the globe from where I grew up, I began making inquiries. It turned out that Debra's host, Irina, knew where the one functioning synagogue was located, and although she had never been there herself, she offered to be my guide for the morning.

Neither of us knew what we were getting ourselves into. We arrived an hour early for services, to a building that looked once stately, now wearing thin at the seams, with ominously peeling blue paint on the walls and a forbidding padlock on the wooden doors. With a lot of time on our hands, we strolled the neighborhood nearby and worked on getting to know each other a little. We spoke Russian, and there were times when I wanted to stop struggling with language and just look around, imagine what life here must be like, let the lines

The Tahoe-Baikal Institute Newsletter (January 1996).

blur between this place and other places I have lived for short periods of time. Still, I learned that the Jewish community in Irkutsk had been recently decimated by waves of emigration to Israel. Irina, while not planning to leave in the near future, was proud of her daughter, who was recently accepted to an Israeli medical school.

We entered the synagogue a few minutes before the start of the service. Several people were gathered at the front of the room, one of whom I quickly identified as a fellow American. I happily greeted a man shaped like Yogi Bear, wearing thick glasses, pants pulled up a little too high, with a loud, jovial manner—who proceeded to play "Jewish Geography" with me. This entails finding out where the other person is from, and how many people they know in common. (I don't know too many Baltimore Jews, but he knows a rabbi who's a friend's father back in Teaneck, New Jersey.) He then proceeded to explain to the Russians standing around, in Russian markedly worse than mine, with a comically exaggerated American accent, where I was from and what I was doing in Irkutsk. I then spoke to a man who seemed to be in charge of the morning's proceedings—a short, dark man in an aqua polo shirt and brown plaid hat. He was agitated at the state of affairs in the synagogue, and in five minutes asked me to help get donations from abroad for repairs and new Torah scrolls (two of their old ones had been stolen and sold), and for a visit to America. What made his requests all the more strange was the presence of his high-school-aged children, who were home for the summer, after spending the past two school years in Israel. They intended to go back to Israel in September—for good. Irina looked on from the side without saying anything. The remainder of the worshipers that morning were few, not nearly enough to fill more than a couple of rows of the spacious room.

The service was led alternately by the American man and by an elderly congregant with precise Hebrew reading. The elderly man read slowly enough to give me a chance to look around. The floors of the sanctuary were an unevenly surfaced chocolate brown, and the various sections were separated by simple, decorative woodwork painted in white with pale blue trim. Around the ark and the platform from which services were led burned bright electric-bulbed "candles." I fell in love with the strange misty-cloudy-pastel ceiling that had Jewish stars scattered around it. On each wall hung a prayer in Hebrew and Russian for the government of the USSR. Something about the patchwork quality of the decor reminded me of the small eastern synagogues in Israel, a comparison that is laughable when I think about it in retrospect.

While more people drifted in to the service as it progressed, the grand total of persons present was probably somewhere in the range of thirty. Most did not know the prayers at all, excepting the man in the plaid hat, the elderly leader, the Americans, and the several kids who had been in Israel. The man in charge polled the men present as to whether they knew how to "read Kaddish," the mourners' prayer. Four did, and each recited in turn. One boy of about sixteen was showing his neighbors the place in the prayer books, while the plaid-hatted man's kids were silent, occasionally snickering in the background. Meanwhile, the two-plus-hour service was surely more than Irina had bargained for—although she refused to consider letting me find my own way home or rushing me out early.

At the Kiddush—wine and light refreshments after the service—I learned from Ilya (now Eli, in Hebrew) and the American traveler what had brought Jews to Irkutsk. Some had been in the army and had settled here with their old institutions, while others had been exiled by Stalin in the 1930s—an exile what saved their lives, as the Nazis liquidated Jewish settlements in Ukraine and the west. Ilya's English was excellent, and he would give me funny looks every time I attempted to say anything in Russian. Meanwhile, the plaid-hatted man's daughter asked me questions in Hebrew. I was excited—this is a foreign language I'm fluent in. Frustratingly, all my words tumbled out as Russian, and those I didn't know in Russian I just forgot altogether. She laughed at me and told me I could speak Russian if I wanted. In this surreal experience, in this community unsure whether it was awakening or dying, losing language, feeling like a new immigrant, twice a foreigner, I was half sure, as Irina led me back to Akademgorodok, that the old buildings, the women in summer dresses, the fruit sellers on the streets, the unfamiliar mixed with the surprisingly familiar—might suddenly transform into the Jerusalem city center if I closed my eyes for too long.

I arrived in the actual city of Jerusalem three months ago, according to my passport. Being here, in many ways, is not the paradise I descirbed to myself and others in the isolation of Siberia. Here, I am at "home" among my people, but also deeply disenchanted and disaffected. I am enjoying buying sweet melons, fresh pitas, bright tomatoes in abundance all winter, enjoying that winter here is never below freezing, enjoying being with friends. But in this city, where the winds are gentle and sweet, and the views of the hills inspiringly beautiful, the air is getting harder to breathe. In two years, I can sense the difference, and scientists say that the pollution here will be as bad as L.A. or Mexico City in fifteen years. The extraordinary geography and history of this country are being ploughed under at an alarming rate by more and more roads, malls, housing developments. . . . Where do you put an expanding population that needs to be separated from another expanding population? Religiously, there is a great deal of beauty—the songs, prayers, national recognition of holidays—but also a lot of ugliness. So much intolerance between religious and secular, almost as much as between religious people of different sects. The escalation of political rhetoric to violence—the shocking results—now go without saying. Personally, I find being here a difficult adjustment culturally, because one has to be a truly aggressive person to survive here. (I'm getting better—"What do you mean, 20 shekels?! I'm not riding for more than 12!!!") There is a myth that Israelis are prickly on the outside, sweet inside—but it often seems that only the first half is true. Where does a person find a home when there seems to be no room in the place that is supposed to be home?

Family has been one thing keeping me relaxed and sane here. I have American cousins in Jerusalem, a sister at the university in Beer Sheva to the south, and Russian cousins in Kiryat Gat, a town not far from Beer Sheva. ("In America/ Russia, we are Jews; in Israel we are Americans/Russians.") I visited my Russian cousins for the first time on this stay in Israel, just as my first wave of Russia-homesickness and missing TBI friends hit.

Kiryat Gat, a sort of haphazardly expanding town, is nothing like Dzherginsky Zapovednik, let it be said, but my cousins have helped relieve the sadness of leaving. These cousins are distantly related—third cousin for me and my sister and our closer cousins who live here. Yet they have taken us in like family—as if we were the ones who were new to Israel and unfamiliar with the language. The grandmother of the family cooks up a storm of homey Russian foods—wonderful borscht, zucchini pancakes, cheese and apple varieties of blini, ubiquitous "chai" that you can't get from tea-bags. More than food, it is the smiles, hugs, and kisses that these are served with that make me feel happy and alive like I did this summer.

On this particular visit, some Siberian neighbors popped in. Upon hearing that I had been in Irkutsk, they began asking me in Russian about the people I knew there. Jewish Geography. But who would I know in less than a week? First name—no match. Second name, "Arkady Kalikhman." For some reason, the last name sounds familiar. Why? I venture a guess—"I don't know an Arkady Kalikhman, but I may have met an Irina Kalikhman. . . ."

"That's his daughter!!" they exclaim. Maybe a different Kalikhman? A coincidence? There are zillions of Irinas floating around, so why wouldn't Arkady have a daughter named Irina?

"Is she a professor at the university?" I ask.

"Yes, yes," they reply.

"And she lives in Akademgorodok?"—of course . . . I tell them that she was the one who brought me to the synagogue in Irkutsk.

My cousins are thrilled, and laugh and talk excitedly among themselves. I translated the encounter for my sister into English, and we find ourselves smiling in three languages, speaking Hebrew nouns, Russian verbs, English colloquialisms—and while none of us have more than half a language in common, everything makes sense and is understood. I can't wait to go back and tell everyone what has happened, when I go back to Irkutsk—

—Next year in Irkutsk? Next year in Jerusalem?

Be in touch, everyone.

Love,

Sara

Every Yid a Prince: An Interview with Rabbi Shlomo Carlebach

MATTHEW EISENFELD

"ONE DOES NOT HAVE TO PLAY WELL, just play." This was the advice that Rabbi Shlomo Carlebach received as he began his musical career in the 1950s. Since then, Rabbi Carlebach has achieved fame as a singer, songwriter, and Hasidic storyteller. On September 20, Rabbi Carlebach visited the Yale–New Haven Jewish community to share his talent, inspiring a packed room in Linsly-Chittenden Hall with his love of being Jewish. After the concert, I enjoyed an open interview with the Rabbi. I asked him only two questions, from which the entire interview flowed.

Rabbi Carlebach was born into an Orthodox German-Jewish family. His grandfather was one of the Izbitzer Rebbe's followers, a small group whose members were required to memorize the entire Torah and Talmud. Rabbi Carlebach describes his family as prince-like. Though they lacked the wealth of royalty, the Rabbi remembers that his father always taught, "'Every Yid is a prince. You have to be a prince, have to be.' I remember the time in 1935, my brother came home crying because somebody had called him a 'Dirty Jew.' 'What am I supposed to do, call them back, Dirty Goy?' Father says to him, 'Only a slave answers back when insulted. A prince doesn't react. And *yiden* are princes.'" When his family moved to America, the Rabbi entered yeshiva, where he grew close to the present Lubavitcher Rebbe. It was the Rebbe who, in 1951, told him to use his talent to inspire others. When Rabbi Carlebach expressed concerns to the Lubavitcher Rebbe regarding the continuation of his learning, he was told to think less about himself.

From *Urim v'Tumim: A Student Quarterly of Yale's Jewish Community* 7, no. 1 (fall 1992): 10–11. Matt Eisenfeld is a senior in Saybrook College and is majoring in Religious Studies.

According to Rabbi Carlebach, Lubavitcher Hasidism was significantly different then. Today it resembles a corporation, receiving money from Jews everywhere, but back then the group owed thousands of dollars. Rabbi Carlebach worked without pay, simply because there was no money. He told us that Lubavitcher Hasidim often slept in cars. "When I didn't have money for a hotel, I'd find a car whose door was open and go to sleep. When the owner would come the next day and say, 'It's my car!' I'd say, 'Really? My car's just like it!'"

Rabbi Carlebach left the Lubavitchers in 1955, deciding that it was time to start out on his own. He wandered for several years; "I was *mamash* [really] like a homeless person." He finally took a job as a rabbi in a small New Jersey town, where his salary was five dollars a week. It was at this time that he began to succeed as a singer, composing songs on the synagogue piano. He then met a guitar player who taught him to play and gave him encouraging advice. According to the Rabbi, "After the Second World War, there was no one left. All of the composers of Hasidic music didn't make it. So everything I made was instantly a best seller."

I asked the Rabbi about one of the major problems concerning world Jewry: while many Jews seem to be searching for some meaning in their Judaism, they often turn away in frustration, claiming that Judaism appears to be devoid of spirituality. Rabbi Carlebach is involved in the movement to bring dissatisfied Jews back to their roots.

The Rabbi's primary concern rests with young Jews. He is critical of those who turn away from Judaism because he feels that they haven't given Judaism a fair chance. "Ask eighty percent of Jewish kids; they know more about every guru in the world than they know about the Rebbes." He related the story of a girl from Haifa who had joined one of the yogis. "Having grown up in Haifa, in the Holy Land, I asked her, 'did you need to come to Phoenix to find God?' She said to me, 'In Haifa, nobody believes in God.' I said, 'You can only tell me that your parents don't believe in God! What do you mean, nobody believes in God? There are 250 synagogues in Haifa—it's outrageous, right?' But she didn't even bother looking for her own."

He told a similar story of a man from Brooklyn who had turned away from Judaism. At every Passover Seder, this man's uncle would read all the dirty jokes he'd collected over the year instead of the Haggadah. Again, the Rabbi responded that the uncle was not representative of all of Judaism. "You see what it is? Sad, all the so-called 'spiritual' people looking for God have absolutely no respect for their own. And sad enough, it's not their fault. The way their parents taught them about *yiddishkeit* was so obnoxious and disgusting." Yet Rabbi Carlebach remarks that one must recognize that no search for God can be one hundred percent effective; those seeking spiritual fulfillment must look upon such a quest with a realistic aim.

Many young Jews simply have not been exposed to the experiences which the Rabbi believes are necessary to establish a lasting commitment to traditional Judaism. He states, "On one hand, we can be angry with the kids for not giving us a chance, but on the other, I wouldn't be here had I not had such a gevalt upbringing myself and let the rebbes encourage me."

Unfortunately, he says, for a long time various religious establishments, including the Federation and other traditional Jewish institutions, had no interest in creating Jewish opportunities for these disaffected young people. Although Rabbi Carlebach's House of Love and Prayer has been highly successful in bringing people back, it has occasionally run into problems. The Rabbi reports that the organization used to host over four hundred kids every Friday night for Shabbat dinner and was successful in preventing and reforming juvenile drug addicts. However, the Jewish Federation in San Francisco cut off his funding because, "Sunday morning the garbage was ten feet high. The president of the Federation walked by, saw all the garbage, and decided that he didn't want to fund the House anymore."

The *frum* (traditional religious) community was not helpful back then, and according to the Rabbi, often still fails to share itself and its experiences with returning or non-religious Jews. They called Rabbi Carlebach "a dope addict, because all those dope addicts come to me. They say the House of Love and Prayer is a house of prostitution and dope addicts." The religious community did not support Rabbi Carlebach, but "they remembered me when their kids got lost. Only in the last few years did God open their hearts, and they permitted me to live in peace."

Throughout his work, Rabbi Carlebach has been happy and privileged to witness the return of thousands of young people to *yiddishkeit*. However, even today he feels that while the Jewish community is right to encourage *ba'ale teshuvah* (newly observant Jews), it is often done inappropriately. Too often, religious Jews will treat less observant or non-observant Jews without the respect they deserve. He disdains one rabbi's apathy for the non-religious. According to this rabbi, non-religious Jews have no reason to come to the Western Wall; they take up space and cause the religious to worry about whether or not they dress modestly or wear *kippot*. Rabbi Carlebach reacted with disbelief. "We lost six million *yiden*, and every *yid* is precious, and the Holy Wall waits for every *yid* to come. The other rabbi says, 'Who needs another non-religious?'" Jews such as this rabbi erect and strengthen the walls between us.

Rabbi Carlebach quoted Rav Abraham Isaac Kook, who said that the body of *Eretz Yisrael* is built by non-religious people while the soul is built by the religious Jews. The Rabbi agrees, but argues, "When it comes to the Torah of *Eretz Yisrael*, the *frum* community builds the body, the *halakha*; the *neshama* [soul] will be rebuilt by the non-religious people." Rabbi Carlebach calls for patience. Jews are returning to *yiddishkeit*, he claims, and urges religious Jews should welcome them back with open arms, serving as role models, not "tailors" prepared to shape these *ba'ale teshuvah* to their own image of the good Jew.

The Rabbi also spoke of the religious tension in Israel. He dispelled the myth that Israelis are not religious, exclaiming, "How can anybody say of a soldier who's ready to die a thousand times over that he's not religious? The *Yidele* who wakes up, drinks his coffee, prays, and goes to work—he's religious, but the soldier out there on guard is not? So why is the soldier not learning about Shabbas with this *Yidele*? Because the soldier is not interested in his Shabbas. He's interested in Shabbas, but not *his* Shabbas." Rabbi Carlebach recommended that if religious Jews really want to teach more non-religious Jews about Shabbat, they ought to see to it that "every Friday night, all the coffee shops are open, but they are paid for. Nobody has to pay. I will sit there and tell *Hasidishe* stories. *Mamash*, all of Dizengoff [a street in Tel Aviv] will be observing Shabbas."

The interview ended when the Rabbi remarked that he was so tired that he would not last unless the messiah were to come at that instant. Rabbi Carlebach advised that religious Jews who care deeply about Shabbat and holidays should invite their non-religious friends home to share the delight which they have been privileged to enjoy. *Yiddishkeit* is open to all Jews, not just those who have Torah and *mitsvot*. Therefore, we are all obligated to open our hearts and minds.

Leaps of Faith:
Uncertainty's Role in Religion

MATTHEW EISENFELD

IN HER ARTICLE "Without God: My Life as a Jew" (Winter 1991), Valerie Maltz describes the hypocrisy she feels when participating in Jewish activities. She identifies with the cultural bonds of the Jewish community, but feels she must falsely accept a theistic belief imposed on her by the Jewish community. I do not believe Maltz is a hypocrite. While I do not profess an ability to answer the questions she rightfully asks, I offer my reflections and pose a few questions of my own.

Maltz's feelings of hypocrisy are based on the notion that she does not believe in God. But what is the role of belief? Can anybody believe that God exists with certainty? The concept of belief, by its very nature, cannot entail certainty. Mere faith is the weakest source of knowledge compared to empirical concepts such as sensory experience, reason, and authority. Yet, we must accept that all knowledge is ultimately based on faith—faith that our methods of perception, on which empirical knowledge is based, are correct. We believe things, or accept certain assumptions as true, either because we are convinced of their truth or because we place some kind of value on the implications of the desired truth of an assumption.

Belief in God is perhaps the most tenuous of all beliefs, because we cannot perceive God directly. Since nobody can know for certain whether or not God exists, we are reduced to believing or disbelieving. Denying God's existence and professing atheism, however, implies as strong a statement of faith as affirming

Matt Eisenfeld, "Leaps of Faith: Uncertainty's Role in Religion," *Urim v'Tumim: A Student Quarterly of Yale's Jewish Community* 6, no. 3 (spring 1992): 24–25. Matt Eisenfeld is a junior in Saybrook College and is majoring in Religious Studies.

271

unequivocally that God does exist. No one can prove either assertion without making leaps of faith in which we leave logical and empirical certainty behind. Our uncertainty forces us all, believers and non-believers alike, to be doubtful at heart. I doubt that anybody can truly be an atheist as much as I doubt that anyone can unquestioningly know that God exists.

Doubt plays a central role in any religion. Some people will even assert that doubts or uncertainties—uncertainty about death, the world around us, or the meaning of life—cause religion in the first place. These critics may be correct, but religion serves other functions as well. It can teach people how to appreciate the world, or offer ways to make the world worthy of appreciation. Maltz mentions that Judaism gives her a sense of cultural identity which she values although she does not know why. Agreeing that religion does have some purpose, let us now consider the tenets of Judaism on which we base our beliefs and actions.

Our religion regulates our lives based on the assumptions that God exists, that we are the chosen people to whom God has revealed his will, and that we are correct in our interpretation of God's will. We know that these fundamental assumptions are not unique to Judaism. While it would seem helpful to know with certainty whether or not we are correct, these claims must be doubted precisely because we cannot know for sure. In fact, doubt is actually better than certainty.

Our doubt gives meaning to our actions, making them precious. After all, in our religion we believe that not only has God promised us blessings for fulfilling the *mitsvot,* but that punishment awaits us should we transgress the *mitsvot* or fail to fulfill them. We are free to choose either the blessing or the curse, as the rabbis claim (believe) that we have free will. However, if God holds over us a blessing and a curse, then are we truly free to choose? This is equivalent to being held at gunpoint and being told to do something with the promise that we will be praised for succumbing to the gunman's will. If our predicament entails choosing between reward or denial of our share in the world to come, then we cannot be praised for our "worthy" actions, because our motivations may not be praiseworthy. Are we motivated by love of God, or by self-interest? Here I address the *mitsvot* that mediate between God and people. Among these *mitsvot,* I would include prayer, observance of Shabbat, *kashrut,* the *mezzuza,* and other laws of ritual. These *mitsvot* can and do affect relations between people, but on the surface and in form, they primarily concern people and God.

This seems to be the area where Maltz is least comfortable. If we knew for certain that God existed, then fulfilling these seemingly trivial inconveniences, as we perceive them, could not be praiseworthy. On the contrary, we would be doing so only to satisfy God. Who, after all, always honestly enjoys fixed prayer or other obligations? I pray every morning and aspire to fulfill my obligation to pray in the afternoon and at night as well, yet I do not feel equally motivated every time. I do not enjoy keeping kosher when it causes problems for me to eat with non-Jews or fellow Jews for whom this observance has little meaning. If we knew that God existed, then performance of all these acts would be assuredly within my self-interest and I would have virtually no choice in the matter, since I would want to avoid divine punishment and wrath.

Furthermore, the commandment to love God poses greater dilemmas. Is it really possible to love when forced to do so out of compulsion? In order to love God, we must be given an honest opportunity to not love God. I am happier facing the uncertainty of God's existence, because it allows me to fulfill a *mitsvah* with the understanding that there may be no divine judge who watches me, holding me accountable for whether or not I say the right words when I recite the *Amida* prayer.

These effects do not constitute some kind of other-worldly changes, but happen right here in our daily lives. Judaism has always been extremely concerned with this world and our responsibility to imbue it with holiness. We search for beauty in this world and try to embellish it. We also recognize that which is not beautiful in the world, and attempt to change it to the extent that we can. Judaism does not teach us that this life is an illusion. Rather, our experiences are real and meaningful to us. And if we can doubt God, then there exists a possibility that this world is important on its own merits and not contingent upon some inexplicable supreme being.

I cannot adequately explain why I desire to fulfill religious obligations, other than that I see many purposes for my participation in these "Jewish activities." For example, I genuinely feel a need to take time out of my daily schedule to thank God for the blessings I have received. Maltz names a few good reasons to do so herself: her mother and the rest of her family, for example. Moreover, she wants to retain a Jewish identity, despite her disbelief in God. Because she connects her sense of belonging (or not belonging) to the Jewish community with both culture and belief in God, she feels guilty of irrationality. The paradox intimidates her.

We should not, however, label these worries as irrational, because she still feels a strong connection that is meaningful to her. Regarding Judaism as a culture distinct from secular American culture seems valid to me, since human beings do not grow up in isolation. Our "personal culture" is made up of the values we are taught from an early age, the experiences we share with those near to us, and many other factors particular to our situation. Our past is meaningful to us precisely because it is *our* past. Similarly, our religion, culture, and identity are meaningful to us because they are ours.

Entering a synagogue should not provoke an unnerving sense of hypocrisy. Though we are all Jews, our motivations are clearly not always the same. I deny that Maltz's reason for attending synagogue—to be with her mother (as opposed to doing it from the love of God)—is wrong. Perhaps by loving her mother enough to inconvenience herself, Maltz fulfills the commandment to love God better than the rest of us do. Internal questions as to why we should attend synagogue at all should not plague people with guilt, because most other people in the synagogue ask themselves similar questions. A wiser outlook would be to continue questioning, in the belief that these inquiries yield important answers.

Furthermore, it is wrong to think that one must do everything tradition dictates in order to avoid the label of "hypocrite." Tradition is certainly a path to God which merits attention because it has succeeded for thousands of years, but tradition is not God itself. When I take my leap of faith, I learn that only God is God.

Maltz has just as much a right to live as a Jew as any one else, and I think she realizes that. People who make her feel unwelcome are insecure themselves and perceive her questions as threatening. But it is precisely her continual need to grapple with these issues of religion and identity that is fundamental to Judaism and is appropriately incorporated into our own religious struggles.

Hannah's Prayer

MATTHEW EISENFELD

According to rabbinic tradition, three childless women were "remembered" by God on Rosh Ha-Shanah. They became pregnant and gave birth to extraordinary sons the following year. According to tradition, these three women were Sarah, Rachel, and Hannah. Today we read about Sarah in the Torah reading and about Hannah in the Haftarah. We will hear about Rachel in tomorrow's Haftarah reading. I hope to discuss the Torah readings with many of you at the first class that I offer Thursday night. The classes will be run according to the model by which Jews have studied texts for centuries. This format is called _hevruta_ study—also known as study with partners. The time will be divided into private work time, to be followed by a group discussion. I hope that the D'var Torah I will say today will be a taste of what is to come through our study.

For today, I would like to discuss the story we find in our Haftarah reading of the day—that is, the story of Hannah. From a historical point of view, as represented in our Tanakh (Jewish Bible), Hannah is a woman whose efforts redeem the people of Israel. She accomplishes this almost single-handedly.

Like many stories of the Tanakh, Hannah's story begins long before her birth. In fact, her story begins after the Jewish people cross into the Promised Land, conquer it, divide it among the tribes and families, and then settle the Land. This time becomes known as the period of the judges. It was a time before Israel had a king and a time when the people were subjected to entirely different living conditions than they had known previously. No longer nomadic, but settled, Israel was lured by the lifestyle of the Canaanites and other neighbors who

---

D'var Torah—First Day of Rosh Ha-Shanah. Delivered September 25, 1995, Sons of Jacob Congregation, North Bay, Ontario.

worshiped other gods. Thus, the settlement and success of Israel created a new problem: Could Israel maintain its national identity in a constructive fashion?

Verses 11–19 of the second chapter of the book of Judges summarize Israel's situation. They read:

> And the Israelites did what was offensive to the Lord. They worshiped the Baalim and forsook the Lord, the God of their fathers, who had brought them out of Egypt. They followed other gods, from among the gods of the peoples around them, and bowed down to them; they provoked the Lord. They forsook the Lord and worshiped Baal and the Ashtaroth. Then the Lord was incensed at Israel, and He handed them over to their foes who plundered them. He surrendered them to their enemies on all sides, and they could no longer hold their own against their enemies. In all their campaigns, the hand of the Lord was against them to their undoing, as the Lord had declared and as the Lord had sworn to them; and they were in great distress. Then the Lord raised up judges who delivered them from those that plundered them. But they did not heed their judges either; they went astray after other gods and bowed down to them. They were quick to turn aside from the way their fathers had followed in obedience to the commandments of the Lord; they did not do right. When the Lord raised up judges for them, the Lord would be with their judge and would save them from their enemies during the judge's lifetime; for the Lord would be moved to pity by their moanings because of those who oppressed and crushed them. But when the judge died, they would again act basely, even more than the preceding generation, following other gods, worshiping them, and bowing down to them; they omitted none of their practices and stubborn ways.

And so the book of Judges reads like a downward spiral. Israel finds itself in a pattern of backsliding, saved periodically by charismatic leaders supported directly by God. The leaders themselves are blemished, and the blemishes become more and more severe with time. The "flaw" of Ehud, an early judge, is that he is left-handed and must perform a stealthy assassination before leading an outright battle. Later judges were more deeply flawed. Gideon has difficulty in trusting God. Jephthah is first introduced as the son of a prostitute, and later gains infamy as he sacrifices his own daughter to fulfill a vow—an exact reversal of the story we will read tomorrow.[1] The last of the judges is Samson, a man

---

[1] The reference is to Genesis 22, traditionally read in synagogue on the second day of Rosh Ha-Shanah.

whom even his fellow Israelites willingly hand over to the Philistines. Yet understanding Samson's birth may be our key for understanding Hannah.

My teacher, Rabbi Menachem Schrader, describes Samson as God's attempt to create a judge from the womb, as his generation lacks any person capable of leadership. The story begins when an angel appears to another childless woman, who remains nameless but is referred to as the wife of Manoach and informs her that she will give birth to a son who will begin to redeem Israel. This child is to have a special status so that all those who look at him will know that he is chosen by God—he is to be a *Nazir*. Though we do not practice *Nezirut* today, in ancient Israel, individuals could choose for themselves a special rigorous path to serve God. The *Nazir* would not cut his or her hair, would abstain from wine and from contact with the dead. Samson is even given an extra kick—his mother is instructed not only to allow his hair to grow but to abstain from drinking wine or eating anything ritually impure herself. His *Nezirut* is to begin even before he is born. Yet this attempt fails, and Samson does not become the judge desired.

The book of Judges ends with the story of a terrible civil war, in which the tribes unite to fight against the tribe of Benjamin. When the dust settles, the nation is weeping in the shock of what has just happened. A tribe has almost been eliminated from Israel. The only unity with which the people could act leads to divisiveness and destruction.

In the wake of all this chaos begins the story of Hannah, a childless woman harassed by her rival, Peninah, and ineffectively comforted by her husband Elkanah. Hannah brings her frustration to the Mishkan at Shiloh and prays for a son. Her request will be granted, and she will give birth to a son who, unlike Samson, really will begin to redeem Israel. We can say that Hannah reverses Jewish history because her story and that of her son, Samuel, heal the wound opened by the story of the wife of Manoach and her son, Samson. Both Samson and Samuel are sworn to divine service, yet the first by God, and the second, by his mother. Hannah's taking of initiative makes all the difference in her story and in the story of Israel. Not only is she an important historical figure, but the rabbis of the Talmud learn the laws of prayer from Hannah.

This history lesson leads us to ask a question: Who is Hannah, and what does she do that we should learn from her example? In truth, she is a character to whom we are introduced in the Haftarah we will soon read, and from whom we will not hear again in the Tanakh. She appears, we hear a part of her life story, and then she fades into the great narrative of Israel. Careful attention to the verses of Haftarah reading give us some information as to her situation in life.

We know that she is married to a pious man, who every year makes pilgrimages to the Mishkan to worship and to sacrifice. We know that she is not the only wife of this man but has a rival, whose name is Peninah. Like Leah and Rachel, the childless woman is the preferred wife, yet, unlike Leah, Peninah wages a campaign to humiliate Hannah. Every year, the man Elkanah gives portions from the sacrificial meal to the members of his family, allotting to Hannah a double portion every year. Peninah upsets Hannah to the point where she is unable to eat. Accordingly, Elkanah tries to comfort Hannah every time. This pattern repeats every year, and we don't know for how long this ordeal continues. Was it three years? Five years? Ten? Fifteen? Hannah must have dreaded this annual pilgrimage to Shiloh! Furthermore, if going to worship and partake of sacrificial meals as a household was so stressful, a time when people are expected to put on their best behavior, just imagine what life was like the rest of the year! So for years, Hannah wallows in her loneliness and feelings of inadequacy as she cannot give birth. Yet this year, she takes the initiative to stand before God in prayer. Perhaps she has some hope after all. But why has she not done this before? Alternatively, even if she has prayed for a child before, why have her prayers not been answered favorably until now?

In attempting to answer this question, I'd like to offer one disclaimer. Hannah is not the only childless woman to have prayed with desperation for a child. Throughout world history, families have suffered from childlessness. Hannah's prayer is to be answered exactly as she asks, even according to the rabbis, to the point of shortening Samuel's life span to tailor her inadvertent request. Most people in the world are not answered with such dramatic affirmation. I wish that prayer alone could solve all of our problems, but we see that this is not the way in which the world works. Even Moses, the greatest master of prayer ever known, was denied when he pleaded with God to be allowed to enter Eretz Yisrael. While this talk may be a lesson in how to pray, motivated by the inordinate amount of praying we Jews do together at this time of year, the efficacy of prayer is often beyond our immediate recognition. Prayers are often answered in ways different from our immediate intention. Sometimes prayers take generations to be answered. Nevertheless, a Jew has an obligation to pray, and we learn from Hannah how to properly fulfill this obligation.

In the Talmud, the rabbis discuss the laws of prayer that we learn from Hannah in tractate Berakhot 31a-b. Follow if you will, in the text. Look at verse 13 as I paraphrase Rav Hamnuna: "Now Hannah was praying in her heart." From here we learn that the one who prays must direct the heart. "Only her lips moved."

From here we learn that the lips must move, actually saying the words. "But her voice could not be heard." From here we learn that it is forbidden to raise one's voice in prayer. "So Eli thought she was drunk." From here we learn that it is forbidden to pray while drunk. These laws are guidelines that we follow with certain exceptions. One is permitted to raise one's voice, for example, if it helps to direct the heart. However, one must not be so loud as to disturb others within the congregation. On Rosh Ha-Shanah and Yom Kippur, it is even recommended that one pray loudly as the clamor builds and carries all of our voices up to heaven together. Yet the Talmud continues to identify ways in which we learn from Hannah, both by reading the words of the story and by adding additional insight into what Hannah actually did. Let us follow their lead in understanding why Hannah is so effective.

Hannah's prayer is effective not only because of what she says, but because of how she says it. She prays in tears, understanding the wretchedness of her situation. Hannah's needs are heartfelt as she states clearly that she would like to give birth to a male child. She is unambiguous and understands that she is asking for a miracle. In our own prayers, we need not ask for miracles in order to be sincere. A story is told of Rabbi Nosson, the greatest disciple of the Hasidic master Rabbi Nachman of Bratzlav. The student was missing a button from his coat. The master instructed his disciple to pray that even this need would be fulfilled. Rabbi Nosson, thinking this instruction outlandish, gave his master a strange look, to which Rabbi Nachman responded, "Is it beneath your dignity to make such a request?" In other words, prayer gives us an opportunity to regard our needs as sent by God, in order that we may better our relationship to God through recognizing that we are limited and that we constantly need divine assistance.

Alternatively, the story can be told from the other side. A king's young son once wandered away from his caretakers and was lost. A band of gypsies found the boy, adopted him, and trained him to dance. The boy became a spectacle, and crowds would throw money as he danced, that the gypsies prospered on his account. Years later, the caravan arrived in the city where the king ruled and saw a sign that the king had posted describing his lost son, offering a handsome reward to anybody who could return the boy to him. The gypsies promptly delivered the boy to the palace, were rewarded, and left. As the boy sat dazed and confused in the surroundings of the palace, the king sought to warm his son to him. He took the boy to the treasury, showed him amounts of wealth the likes of which he had never seen, and asked the son to choose a gift for himself. The boy stood there blinking, and asked for a new pair of dancing shoes. This boy could have had anything he wanted, and he asked for something inappropriate to his situation because he was shy. So too we, when we stand before God, the King of the Kings of Kings, we have the opportunity to make requests appropriate to who we are, affecting us, Israel, and all people everywhere, and we often settle for a new pair of shoes. To avoid this mistake, the sages recorded basic prayers for us to say daily, and especially on the holidays.

Hannah's prayer is aided by her imaginative capacity. Though she is unambiguous and knows for what she asks, the rabbis scramble to make sense out of her words. In the Talmud, the rabbis debate the meaning of her words, "if You will grant your maidservant *zera' 'anashim*." In English, we translate these words, *zera' 'anashim*, as "male child," but the rabbis read more into Hannah's request. They read Hannah as imagining the specific characteristics she desires of her son as they ask:

What is *zera' 'anashim*? Said Rav, "A great man among men." Shmuel said, "A man who would anoint two men as kings. And who were they? Saul and David." Rabbi Yohanan said, "Offspring that would be equal to two men, and who were they? Moses and Aaron, as it is written, 'Moses and Aaron were among your Kohanim, and Samuel among those who called upon your name.' The rabbis said, "Offspring that will blend into the rest of mankind." When Rav Dimi came, he explained that this meant, "not overly tall nor short, neither weak nor strong, not too ugly nor too good-looking, not overly intelligent nor stupid" (Babylonian Talmud Berakhot 31b).

Hannah's request had to conform to at least one, if not all, of these ideas, because this is what Samuel became. The more specific Hannah is, the more honest her prayer and the more she empowers herself to do whatever becomes necessary to fulfill the request.

The rabbis who read Hannah as asking God to allow her to give birth to a future leader must read her as imagining a self far beyond where she is now. It would be so easy for Hannah not to dream, to remain that harassed woman who is mistaken for a drunkard accomplishing little, but she dares to dream. The vision of these rabbis in describing Hannah is articulated beautifully by Nietzsche. In one of his earlier works entitled "Schopenhauer as educator," Nietzsche describes self-image. He writes:

But how can we find ourselves again? How can man know himself? He is a thing dark and veiled; and if the hare has seven skins, man can slough off seventy times seven and still not be able to say: "this is really you, this is no longer outer shell." Moreover, it is a painful and dangerous undertaking thus to tunnel into oneself and to force one's way down into the shaft of one's being by the nearest path. A man who does it can easily hurt himself so that no physician can cure him. And moreover again, what need should there be for enmities, our glance and the clasp of our hand, our memory and that which we do not remember, our books, and our handwriting. This, however, is the means by which an inquiry into the most important aspect can be initiated. Let the youthful soul look back on life with the question: what have you truly loved up to now, what has drawn your soul aloft, what has mastered it and at the same time blessed it? Set up these revered objects before you and perhaps their nature and their sequence will give you a law, the fundamental law of your own true self. Compare these objects with one another, see how one completes, expands, surpasses, transfigures another, how they constitute a stepladder upon which you have clambered up to yourself as you are now; for your true nature lies, not concealed deep within you, but immeasurably high above you, or at least that which you usually take yourself to be.[2]

According to this interpretation of Hannah's request, her prayer experience has somehow led her to a much greater understanding of who she is and what she is capable of doing. Not only is she empowered to ask for a miraculous childbirth, but yet another miracle, that this son will become one of Israel's greatest leaders.

The other interpretation of the words *zera' 'anashim* suggests that Hannah's request is more modest, and that she desires only a son who will survive and succeed among humankind. Yet again, here she is specific as well, as she will not omit any detail that would enable her son to survive. According to this understanding,

---

[2] Matt seems to simplify the language somewhat. Compare this text to http://en.m .wikisource.org/wiki/Schopenhauer_as_Educator: "But how can we 'find ourselves' again, and how can man 'know himself'? He is a thing obscure and veiled: if the hare have seven skins, man can cast from him seventy times seven, and yet will not be able to say 'Here art thou in very truth; this is outer shell no more.' Also this digging into one's self, this straight, violent descent into the pit of one's being, is a troublesome and dangerous business to start. A man may easily take such hurt, that no physician can heal him. And again, what were the use, since everything bears witness to our essence,—our friendships and enmities, our looks and greetings, our memories and forgetfulnesses, our books and our writing! This is the most effective way: to let the youthful soul look back on life with the question, 'What hast thou up to now truly loved, what has drawn thy soul upward, mastered it and blessed it too?' Set up these things that thou hast honoured before thee, and, maybe, they will show thee, in their being and their order, a law which is the fundamental law of thine own self. Compare these objects, consider how one completes and broadens and transcends and explains another, how they form a ladder on which thou hast all the time been climbing to thy self: for thy true being lies not deeply hidden in thee, but an infinite height above thee, or at least above that which thou dost commonly take to be thyself."

Hannah's request mirrors that of William Butler Yeats, who in his poem "A Prayer for My Daughter" nervously paces the room in which his baby daughter sleeps as a wild storm rages outside. Wondering what characteristics will aid his child best, he writes the following lines:

> May she be granted beauty and yet not
> Beauty to make a stranger's eye distraught,
> Or hers before a looking-glass, for such,
> Being made beautiful overmuch,
> Consider beauty a sufficient end,
> Lose natural kindness and maybe
> The heart-revealing intimacy
> That chooses right, and never find a friend.

A few stanzas later he adds the following thought:

> An intellectual hatred is the worst,
> So let her think that opinions are accursed.
> Have I not seen the loveliest woman born
> Out of the mouth of Plenty's horn,
> Because of her opinionated mind
> Barter that horn and every good
> By quiet natures understood
> For an old bellows full of angry wind?

These words, of course, are from a poet and politician who lived by the exchange of intellectual ideas and opinions. Like Hannah, he wishes for his child true happiness, which is brought about by honest companionship and modest being.

Hannah's prayer is a transformative experience. Her imagination leads her to picture her request in terms so concrete that she does not hesitate to act even while voicing her request. Our tradition of cantillation emphasizes the words *va-tidor neder*, "and she made a vow," as we read the Haftarah portion to highlight Hannah's readiness to obligate herself in bringing her prayer to fruition. This prayer is no mere utterance of the lips accompanied by direction of the heart. Hannah's prayer is so powerful that her entire orientation to the world is changed at this moment. We would expect a would-be mother to ask for a child, as this is the expectation of every parent. Hannah wants a child for herself, yet she vows to dedicate this child to God's service, to be raised by Eli the High Priest. Somehow Hannah has come to understand that if she is to give birth, then a miracle will have been performed so great that her role cannot be as expected, and she will never be a normal parent. If she is to give birth, then, like Sarah and Rebekah, and Rachel before her, God is using her for a role greater than she can immediately understand. So Hannah swears a vow, that she will dedicate her son to the service of God. She returns to her tent happy, and finally eats from the portion given to her by her husband.

Hannah conceives, gives birth to a son, and names him Samuel. When her husband prepares for his annual pilgrimage, Hannah refuses to go, requesting that she be allowed to keep her son until he is weaned. We can sense that, though Hannah is prepared to fulfill her vow, she retains the anxiety of a parent who does not desire to give away her son. "Just a little longer!" we can almost hear her saying quietly as she nurses her infant, the boy who will grow into one of Israel's greatest leaders ever. But when the time comes, she brings Samuel to Shiloh and passes him to the charge of Eli the High Priest. Echoing the story of Abraham, she does not withhold her son, her only son. Her story ends with a thankful prayer of victory. She praises God who has granted her request, God who controls life and death and who is responsible for success and failure in both individuals and nations. Hannah should know, because she is living proof that it is God, and nothing else that controls the world.

Today is Rosh Ha-Shanah, and we are here to learn and to pray. Our prayers are as effective as our ability to make observations about our own state of affairs and to identify our needs. Our job is to ask God for the necessities to fulfill our function. On Rosh Ha-Shanah, like all holidays, we say daring things about God because we are so specific. For example, starting last night, and for all of the Days of Awe, we close the first blessing of the Amidah with the words *ha-Melekh ha-qadosh* which mean "the Holy King" instead of *ha-El ha-qadosh* , which means, "the Holy God" because "king" is a more specific and concrete image than "God." During these days, when we think about our desire to better ourselves and to rise as a community to a higher standard, we are better able to recognize God as King, and are therefore obligated to say it in our prayers. If we accidentally pray as normal, then we have not fulfilled our obligation on this day.

Today we view the world as created anew, bursting with new possibilities. God is King, and we are the servants who will bring these new possibilities into action. We celebrate our continued effort to better ourselves, our community, and the world, and we rejoice while simultaneously recognizing that our tasks remain incomplete. As Hannah's paradigms through which she viewed the world were changed in her prayers, may the worship of today allow us to open our own minds and hearts. Let us search ourselves for both good and evil over these next ten days and challenge ourselves to leave each service or study session we attend with at least one new thought, or better understanding of one new prayer, that our efforts to improve this community be done cheerfully and effectively. May we be an inspiration to one another.

The Essence of the Shofar

MATTHEW EISENFELD

I LIKE TO THINK that the *mitsvot*, or laws and customs that we Jews observe, exist in order to teach us lessons about the world, about our place and responsibilities, and about God. *Mitsvot* present us with concrete ideas about these issues and act to effect the world around us. They do not remain as passive thoughts whose purpose is intellectual entertainment only. Some *mitsvot* are relatively easy to understand because they regulate interpersonal relations and create a standard of morality to which we are challenged to adhere. In studying these laws, we strive to perfect our ethical behavior because we believe that this is what God requires of us—we believe that acting ethically is to imitate God, were that possible. On the other hand, the Torah also presents us with numerous laws that we usually associate with ritual, and they are not as easy to understand. The rabbis often refer to the ethical laws as *mishpatim*. In his commentary to the Torah, Rashi, the most widely known commentator of them all, explains that these are the laws that we feel we understand—that even if the Torah did not command them, we would be expected to adhere to them. These laws include ordinances such as not to steal, not to murder, and not to commit adultery.

The ritual laws are referred to as *ḥuqim*, and concerning these laws, Rashi writes, "these are the laws of which evil inclination and the nations of the world make sport," because the ultimate reasons for such *mitsvot* are unavailable to us. *Mitsvot* of this category would include keeping kosher, observing Shabbat according to all of its restrictions, and many of the rituals specific to our holidays, as we will see.

On the other hand, Rashi makes another, seemingly contradictory comment further on, when he says that our laws are the mark by which the nations

Sermon for Rosh HaShanah—Day Two. Delivered September 26, 1995, Sons of Jacob Congregation, North Bay, Ontario.

of the world praise us. When the nations of the world see the way in which we Jews fulfill the laws of the Torah, they exclaim, "What a wise and discerning people this is!" They might for example, watch us keep kosher and exclaim how wisely we act in relation to the food we eat. "Wow! They deny themselves pork and lobster! What a holy people they must be that they have such discipline!" However, Rashi is quick to qualify this praise that we can expect to receive. The nations of the world praise us only when our observance is accompanied by study, because "otherwise, they will think you are crazy." In that case they exclaim, "What idiots! They don't eat pork or lobster! What's the matter, don't you claim your God created these animals, too?" The challenge before us, then, is to try to understand the *ḥuqim,* or these ritual laws that seemingly are without ultimate reason. This challenge brings me to the issue I would like to discuss today, which is the significance of the shofar. Almost every one of our holidays has a theme as well as special *mitsvot* particular to the day. On Passover, for example, we eat matzah. On Sukkot, we sit in the sukkah and wave a lulav. On Rosh Ha-Shanah, we listen to the blowing of the shofar. Presumably, study of the *mitsvot* pertaining to the day will increase our understanding of the day's theme. I have to admit that, as a child, I was always disappointed by the shofar. Each year in religious school, we would study about this event, and then the sound was never as dramatic as I would imagine. Now that your community has asked me to blow shofar, I've had to rethink the meaning of this *mitsvah* and would now like to share some recent thoughts.

In examining the meaning of the shofar, I would like to first note that the shofar is a *kli qodesh,* or holy utensil, that we use. It is a symbol that presents us with ideas we need to consider. On the deepest level, the shofar is a metaphor for ourselves. I would like to focus on two primary functions that the shofar seems to serve, those of prayer, which is directed from us toward God, and of a wake-up call to improve ourselves, directed from God toward us. Since yesterday's discussion was about prayer, let's begin today's discussion about prayer as well.

Our first indication of how the shofar acts as an aid to prayer is its shape. In Tractate Rosh Ha-Shanah, the rabbis debate the question of whether a shofar should be straight or crooked. Although they decide that the shofar should ideally be crooked, one fulfills one's obligation to hear the shofar if blown from a straight horn. The shape tells us something about our mood. If the shofar is straight, then we think about our trust in God, and about how the holidays serve to improve our relationship to God and to the Jewish community. Today is a joyful occasion as we gather with families and celebrate our community's continued existence, and the blowing of the shofar should reflect that happiness.

On the other hand, if the Shofar is crooked, then our primary motivation is one of humility in standing before God. The Shofar is bent, just as we are bent over in prayer, full of reflection over the past year and full of new hopes for the future. As we know, prayer is not easy, and requires one to transform oneself. Accordingly our utensil resembles our posture, and this is the ideal that the rabbis choose.

Yet perhaps we can understand how the shofar is meant to aid us in prayer in another way. If we think about Hannah, we can remember that the rabbis believed her prayers to be effective because she was able to use her imaginative capacity as she prayed. One of the clearest explanations of this idea is that of Rabbi Abraham Isaac Kook, the first Chief Rabbi of Israel [1921–1935, during the British Mandate]. Rabbi Kook's comments can be found in explanation of a line in Tractate Berakhot where another rabbi, Rabbi Elazar, says, "From the day when the Temple in Jerusalem was destroyed, the gates of prayer have been locked, but even though the gates of prayer have been locked, the gates of tears remain open." Rabbi Kook explains that the Temple in Jerusalem was a place in which the imagination of all Jews could be sparked. Imagine the scene: A Jew brings his sacrifice to the Temple. Perhaps it is a sacrifice to help atone for a ritual transgression. Perhaps it is an offering to give thanksgiving upon a wonderful event. He removes his shoes before entering. As he enters the courtyard, he is surrounded by people who have come for the same reasons he is there. The sweet smell of incense fills the air. His ears are filled with the songs of the Levites, and Kohanim dressed in extraordinary garments greet him to perform the sacrificial duties on his behalf. From an elevated altar, this Jew sees sacrificial smoke rising from the altar, ascending skyward. If it is the first day of the month, then this smoke is accompanied by the blast of silver trumpets. The prayers this man offers are more graphic and detailed, as the atmosphere in which he participates helps him to dream.

Now that the Temple has been destroyed, our prayers are without such explicit drama. Through study of the Torah, however, we can recapture an understanding of much of the symbolism that greeted our ancestors. We take cues from the world around us and from the people around us to again spark a deeper sense of self-understanding, until we long to achieve those goals that we know are within our reach. These tears, to which Rabbi Elazar said that the gates of heaven are open, are not tears of sadness but tears of longing, motivated by self-discovery. Hannah cried as she prayed, perhaps because she could visualize a desire that seemed so close to her.

Imagination alone, however, does not change fantasy to reality. To make things happen, says Rabbi Kook, imagination needs to intersect with intellect. The development of our imaginative capacity must mirror the development of our intellectual powers, that we imagine things we can actually achieve. When I was young, for example, I loved to play Dungeons & Dragons with my friends. Creating adventures wrought with danger, fantastical creatures, treasures, and faraway lands was a great pleasure, and I would spend hours of my free time drawing maps and thinking up adventure scenarios my friends would enjoy. But none of the worlds I would imagine were real, nor would they be desirable. The activity was one of fantasy, appropriate for a child.

Unfortunately, our imaginative capacity is often arrested in childhood, as we are encouraged to develop our intellect throughout our education. The story is told of a college professor who on the first day of class made a small mark on the blackboard with chalk. "What is this?" he asked the students. For a few minutes, the room was silent, until one student raised a hand and shyly answered, "it's a chalk-mark." The professor shook his head and remarked that were he to ask the same question to a class of kindergartners, the responses would be much more interesting. "It's a squashed bug!" they might say, or "A mouse's footprint!" Actually, in eighth grade, I was privileged to have a history teacher whose name was Ms. Leahy. Ms. Leahy was an unusual person, whose first assignment was to make a collage about doors. None of us understood the assignment or what possible historical significance was held by a door. About a month later, we were asked to somehow illustrate the song, "America the Beautiful." When we protested, we were told that since we seemed to understand, she looked forward to seeing our projects as our example would help teach the class. It was only years later, and after Ms. Leahy had passed away, that I really understood and appreciated what she had done, encouraging us to think differently about what history was all about and why. I had been so "scripted" in memorizing names and dates!

When we blow the shofar today, we may be reminded of the worship of our ancestors. The sound, unusual in a synagogue, should help us to rebuild our imaginative capacity and draw us into the effort of renewal. Hopefully the sound will help our prayers to be said better.

This idea leads us to the second major function of the shofar. While prayer is directed toward God, perhaps we may think of the shofar as directed toward us. In *Hilkhot Teshuvah*, the Laws of Repentance, Rabbi Moses Maimonides writes, "Even though the blowing of the Shofar is a scriptural ordinance (without explicit reason), there is a hint to its meaning, which is to say 'Awaken you sleepers from your sleep, and slumberers, rise from your slumber! Investigate your deeds, return in repentance, and remember your Creator!' The Shofar is like an alarm clock which gets you out of bed in the morning. We pay attention to alarm clocks because our livelihood depends on our arrival in the places where we are supposed to be, whether work, school, or just an appointment with a friend. On Rosh Ha-Shanah, we blow the shofar to alert us to the nature of our deeds. Where are we in the scheme of our lives? What goals do we entertain?

Accordingly, there are two distinct voices to the shofar. The fundamental blast is the Teru'ah—sometimes modified with what we call Shevarim. This blast is supposed to resemble a person weeping bitterly. One of my teachers once asked, "How many times do our actions resemble that of the Teru'ah or Shevarim? We start and stop, start and stop. Where is the commitment?" On the other hand, the Teru'ah must be accompanied by simple blasts, before and after—the voice we call Teki'ah. Perhaps this Teki'ah stands to remind us that in fact we are capable of completing our tasks and becoming the kinds of people we long to be. It is no accident, then, that the shofar blasts of the Musaf prayers will end with a Teki'ah Gedolah—the longest blast of the day. It is no mistake that Yom Kippur will end also with the blast of Teki'ah Gedolah.

At this point, I must reiterate the challenge with which we are faced: What can we do to improve our communities even more? This is a challenge faced not only by North Bay, Ontario, but by every Jewish community across the world. It is a challenge I will face as I travel to Jerusalem where I will continue my studies with my classmates, and it is a challenge faced by the leaders of governments worldwide. We should think about these specific issues:

- Improving communal prayer
- Raising awareness of social problems and responding with activism
- Study of Jewish texts
- Environmental awareness
- Improving relations among members of the congregation

Furthermore, [we ask] what talents and abilities does each of us offer as the individuals who make up the community? Do we dare make a sincere effort to cooperate with one another? Can we spare any time and energy in the process of self-improvement?

Such questioning brings us to another function of the shofar. Jewish communities worldwide are accustomed to blowing a shofar made from a ram's horn. In Tractate Rosh Ha-Shanah, Rabbi Abahu states that we blow on a ram's horn in order that God remember the binding of Isaac, which is the subject of today's Torah reading. In other words, when we blow the shofar, we invoke a concept known as *Zekhut 'Avot,* or the Merit of the Fathers, Abraham, Isaac, and Jacob. *Zekhut 'Avot,* like other ideas, is at least double-edged. On one hand, the merits of our ancestors provide us with role models of righteousness to which we too may aspire. Perhaps we can all recall members of our families whom we have admired, and of whom stories continue to be told. Recognition of the achievements of these individuals makes us understand that it is in fact possible to be a decent individual and to live well. Correspondingly, careful study of the book of Genesis, which is all about the deeds of our national ancestors, provides us with ultimate models of who we can become. As long as we can hold onto our models of righteousness, we have hope. On the other hand, the recognition of the Merits of the Ancestors provides us with the knowledge that they did not complete everything they set out to accomplish in their lives. Much of what they began remains in our hands either to complete or to further develop. Accordingly, we too will begin tasks that will not be completed in our lifetimes, which our progeny will hopefully find important enough to continue.

I know of two stories that describe this idea well. The first is a Chinese story about an Old Man who every day leaves his hut and crosses a mountain to go to a village on the other side. As the man grows older, he begins to tire of each day's journey, and so one day, he leaves his hut with a shovel and begins to dig. When villagers pass by, they ask him what he is doing. "I'm tired of this mountain," he says, "and so I'm removing it." The villagers explode in laughter, "Foolish old man!" they exclaim, "you'll never complete such a task!" For days and days this cycle continues, and people begin to make sport of the Old Man. One day, however, the Old Man stops digging, and faces his tormentors. "No, I won't finish this task," he says. "But I have a son, and he will continue my work. And then my son will have a son who will continue after him. And then that son's son will continue after him, and so on and so forth until the mountain is removed!" When the mountain heard the words of the Old Man, it became so frightened, that it picked itself up, and moved elsewhere.

A second story concerns our father Isaac and is found in Tractate Shabbat 89b. In the future, says the Talmud, we will be redeemed because of the merit of Isaac. At that time, God will appear before Abraham and say, "Your children have sinned against me." Abraham answers, "Master of the Universe, destroy them for the holiness of Your Name." In shock, God says, "I will go to Jacob, because he had problems raising children. Maybe he will plead on their behalf." God goes to Jacob and says, "Your children have sinned against me." Jacob answers, "Master of the Universe, destroy them for the holiness of Your Name." Unwilling to take this advice, God goes to Isaac and says, "Your children have sinned against me." Isaac answers, "My children and not Your children, You say? At Mount Sinai, when Israel promised to do the commandments even before understanding them, you said, 'My child, my first-born.' Now You say My children and not your children?" Like his father Abraham concerning the fate of Sodom and Gomorah, Isaac then launches a campaign to show God that Israel's sins really are not so terrible, and that God should be able to endure. If not, Isaac says, "then associate their sins with me, because I was bound as a sacrifice!"

While Abraham and Jacob are frustrated in this story with Israel's failure and with the embarrassment caused to the ideals for which we are supposed to live, they ask God to remove the source of embarrassment and redeem the world in another way. Isaac's argument, however, invokes the deeds both of Israel and of himself. When the Israelites accepted the Torah, they were accepting a special mission to live as examples of righteousness to show the world. This is not a task accomplished by one generation. Furthermore, if that were not enough, then God should remember that he, Isaac, was bound as his father carried out a command to bind him. The effort to raise the whole world to a level of holiness, to the level achieved by himself and by Abraham, continues, and God should be patient. If the people slip and stumble along the way, they should not be destroyed but should be encouraged to return to the task that was begun long ago. Isaac himself was perhaps one of the most patient of the heroes of the Tanakh. He could love even Esau. When we blow the shofar, this is the man whom we remember, our father Isaac, who was bound as a sacrifice.

And so today, we've learned about three functions served by the shofar: (1) The shofar aids us in prayer by sparking our imagination; (2) it serves as an alarm to awaken us to turn to God; (3) it invokes the memory of the binding of Isaac. So now, we would think, we can blow the shofar with pomp and fanfare, and nobody will leave disappointed. But we need to remember what Rashi said about *ḥuqim,* or ritual law: these are the laws of which the evil inclination and the nations of the world make sport because their ultimate significance is unavailable to us. After all is said, and after all our speculation, Rashi is right. *Ḥuqim* may have wonderful effects, but are these the real reasons? Has everything possible been said about the shofar, or matzah, or the lulav? In the end, something will always remain incomplete, and this is where we personally are given an opportunity to reflect. Remember that the shofar, after all, is just an object, a ritual object of which we make use. It has a shape and can withstand certain kinds of blemishes and still be used. When we ask what the shofar means, we need to ask ourselves: What kind of vessels are we? What ideas, dreams, and ambitions do we represent? How much perversion of these ideals can we tolerate? The shofar's incompleteness, like our own incompleteness, may become our opportunity. What can we add to this day? What can we add to our experience of this *mitsvah*?

A Reflection on the Marriage
of Two Friends

MATTHEW EISENFELD

FROM THE OUTSET, I wanted to note that in this week's *parsha* (Torah portion), *Parshat Tsav*, we arrive at the midpoint of verses in the Torah. This midpoint appears between verses 7 and 8 of chapter 8, verse 8 reading, "And he put the breastplate upon him, and he put in the bracelet the *'Urim ve-Tumim.'* So you see Josh, you marry a Yale woman, and KERPOW! You're catapulted to the middle of the Torah!

The wedding ceremony is in many ways reminiscent of Yom Kippur. The fasting, wearing of white, *miqveh*, forgiving of sins, are all symbols shared between the ḥupah and the holiest day of the year. As Yom Kippur is the most joyful day of the year for the Jewish community, so too the day of the ḥupah is touted as the happiest day in the lives of two individuals. Perhaps some of the most suggestive symbolic connections between Yom Kippur and marriage,

---

Matt wrote this D'var Torah in March 1995 on the occasion of the wedding of two friends, Tal Brudnoy, a friend from Yale (and also a high school classmate of Sara) and Josh Weinberger. It was to be delivered at a *Sheva Brachot* dinner, which, due to a conflict, Matt was unable to attend. Nonetheless, we have the written text of the D'var Torah he was to give. Traditionally, the spirit of a wedding continues for an entire week, and the bride and groom are hosted at feasts throughout. The seven nuptial blessings that are recited at the wedding ceremony are recited after each meal in the presence of the newlyweds during the festive week following the wedding.

Matt is addressing an audience of knowledgeable and observant Jews. The original text is frequently peppered with Hebrew phrases from the Bible and Talmud without any translation. He also uses the Hebrew names for Biblical characters. This edition includes translations of Hebrew phrases in parentheses. For the Biblical characters Eve and King Solomon and Yeho'ash, king of Judah, I have used their English names, rather than "Hava," "HaMelekh Shlomo," and "Yeho'ash, Melekh Yehudah," respectively, as originally written.

though, can be understood through an examination of the laws pertaining to the *miqdash* itself, which was once the center of all the action.

The *miqdash* represents a model of *qedushah* that is foreign to us now, as we live in an era without the *ḥiyyuv* (obligation) let alone ability to bring *qorbanot* (sacrifices). Understandably, a *ḥiyyuv* to offer a *qorban ḥata't* in order to gain atonement from *'averot* (sins) makes sin ridiculously expensive, as the *ḥatan* (bridegroom) and I once discussed two summers ago. Yet somehow, this form of worship was irresistible to our ancestors. Take the example of Yeho'ash, king of Judah, whose praise is qualified in 2 Kings 12:3–4, "And Yeho'ash did that which was right in the sight of the Lord all his days as Yehoyada the priest instructed him. But the high places were not taken away: the people still sacrificed and burned incense in the high places." Perhaps *qorbanot* were so popular because they represent a tangible means by which an individual can turn to God. Just as, explains the Ramban, prophecy is sealed by symbolic action, so too individuals are comforted by visual signals of their success when they do *teshuvah* (repentance). This whole idea fits another need. We are commanded to become a *mamlekhet kohanim ve'goi qadosh* (a kingdom of priests and a holy nation; see Exodus 19:6). Clearly, *mamlekhet kohanim* is a metaphor, and we Jews have always done our best to preserve our metaphors that we may learn from them.

Such a symbol motivates King Solomon in his construction of the *Bet Ha-Miqdash* (Holy Temple). He opens his prayer of dedication of the *miqdash* entreating God to keep constant vigilance over the House completed. The verses (1 Kings 8:28–30) read:

> Turn to the prayer of your servant and to his supplication, O Lord, my God, to hearken to the cry and to the prayer, which your servant prays before You today. That your eyes may be open towards this House night and day, towards the place of which You have said, "My Name will be there," that You may hearken to the supplication of your servant, and of your people Israel, when they shall pray towards this place, hear in Heaven your dwelling place and forgive!

When the people have a model of *qedushah* toward which they can turn, their prayers are somehow bettered. Perhaps they become more honest, or more thought through, or are simply more passionate. Though Shlomo knows that God's creation does not contain God, we worshipers need to build in order to concentrate our energy here below.

Now let's return to Yom Kippur, the day of love between God and the

Jewish people. . . . Yom Kippur is the day on which we cleanse the *miqdash* from the *tum'ah* (impurity) of *'averot* committed over the past year. How did *tum'ah* come to be associated with *'averot*? Such a question goes back to the Garden of Eden, where Adam and Eve traded life for knowledge (see Genesis 2). We were supposed to live forever, differing from God only in that God would know good from evil, and we would remain in ignorance. Adam and Eve were warned concerning the *'Ets da'at tov ve-ra'* (the Tree of Knowledge between Good and Evil) but not the *'Etz Hayyim* (Tree of Life). After they disobeyed God's command, they were thrown out lest they eat from the tree of life and live forever.

At *Ma'amad Har Sinai* (Revelation at Sinai; see Exodus 19) God agreed to dwell in the midst of the Jewish people, and we were made responsible to introduce to the world a model of the holiness of God. In order to accomplish our task, we needed to act to preserve the distinction between God and us—to preserve this distinction between mortals who die and God, who will live forever. The primary sources of *tum'ah* include dead bodies, scale disease, and life-giving/supporting fluid from a genital organ. And then there's the metaphoric *tum'ah*, that of *'averot*. They remind us of that first sin, which passed a death sentence over all of us.

On Yom Kippur, the *Kohen Gadol* (High Priest; see Leviticus 16) brings a bullock as a *ḥata't* (sin offering) as well as a ram for an *'olah* (burnt offering). His *qorbanot* resemble those of the *kohanim* we read about in the Torah portion of your wedding, *Parshat Tsav*. His seven days of preparation prior to the day mirror their seven days of preparation. During this time, they bring a bullock as a *ḥata't* and a ram as an *'olah*. These offerings are accompanied by the application of blood to the right ear, thumb, and big toe. Perhaps this sprinkling resembles that of Mount Sinai, when Moshe sprinkled the entire nation.

So we see that Yom Kippur is a rededication in the most basic sense. On Yom Kippur, the *miqdash*, which has attached to itself all the *'averot* of Israel, is cleansed, as good as new if not better. Once again the *miqdash* may be dedicated as the focal point with the same fervor with which Shlomo spoke on the day of its first dedication. But the original dedication of such a structure took place in the wilderness, as we read in *Parshat Tsav*, and this is the *parsha* during which you were married.

And now we install you. It will take these next few days while we place you on a pedestal and honor you. This ceremony is for us, perhaps more so than for you, because on these days, you are our model of *qedushah*. You, Josh and Tal, care so deeply about each other, and your commitment to *halakha*, and to each other's commitment to *halakha*. We need to make a fuss over you because we need you. It's really that simple. We want you to know how special the two of you are, and the level of your responsibility. And this is one reason why we do *Sheva Brakhot* (the seven blessings).

I close with a pair of *drashot* from one of my teachers, Rabbi Morris Shapiro.[1] He asks, concerning the creation of woman, why does the verse read, *'E'eseh 'ezer kenegdo*, "I will make a helper against him?" (Genesis 2:18). The traditional answer says, "If he merits, she will be his helper. If he does not merit, she will be against him." Rabbi Shapiro says that this *drasha* is not satisfying, and he offers two new readings. The first reads, "When is she his helper? When she is against him! Because then he learns how to become better than he was before." No problem here. Tal, I'm sure Josh will enter *'Olam ha-ba'* (the World to Come) as a veritable *tsadiq* (righteous person). Maybe even a *Lomed-Vov tsadiq*.[2] The second *drasha* goes like this: "*Kenegdo* refers to the *yetser ha-ra'* (evil inclination). If he merits, she is his helper. If he does not merit, then she too will stand with him against the *yetser ha-ra'*." Again, no problem here.

> May your marriage be happy, and may many be brought close to the Torah through you.

---

[1] Rabbi Morris Shapiro received rabbinic ordination from Yeshivat Ḥokhmei Lublin. After surviving the Holocaust, he immigrated to America and became a pulpit rabbi in the Conservative Movement, serving most notably for many years at the South Huntington Jewish Center. Upon his retirement from the pulpit, he served for many years at JTS as the rabbi of the Beit Midrash who guided students through their preparations for Talmud classes. He was renowned not only for his photographic memory of Talmud and related commentaries but also for regaling students with Hasidic stories and other recollections from his youth in Poland. While Rabbi Shapiro was always popular among students, Matt was very much influenced by him during the 1994–1995 academic year. Matt, in turn, was influential in helping other students experience Rabbi Shapiro's special charisma and old-world charm. Matt helped to organize Shabbat dinners and Hasidic *tisch* celebrations featuring Rabbi Shapiro.

[2] This is a reference to mystical lore that asserts that the world is sustained based on the existence of thirty-six truly righteous individuals.

Reflection

DR. TAL WEINBERGER

Dear Matt and Sara,

I feel humbled by the responsibility of being asked to honor your memory, and in many ways, it is an impossible task to perform adequately. It is now twenty years since we lost you; in some ways it still feels like yesterday, and in others, it feels like forever. My oldest daughters are the same ages now as we were when we were friends.

I don't want to spend a lot of time reflecting on your death, because on a personal level, that is the least important part of your lives. But you should know that I think about you every time I say "*sheheheyanu*."[1] To me, that has been one enduring lesson of your loss—how fragile life is, how every day we are alive is truly a *brakha* (blessing). In the medical profession we put an infinite amount of time, effort, and mental energy into maintaining life and quality of life—and then it can be gone in a second, like how we lost you.

Sara, I remember how one day in high school, you came in wearing a ring you had just bought. It quickly became one of your favorites, and you wore it every day after that. It fit you in a way that is hard to describe—it is silver, in the shape of two hands that circle around to the front of the ring, holding a purple stone. It is sweet and quirky just like you were and is somehow delicate and strong at the same time. After you died, your mom let me choose some of your jewelry that she thought would be meaningful to me. I took the ring and have worn it every day since, as a constant reminder of you.

---

[1] Tal Brudnoy Weinberger, M.D., is a specialist in psychiatry and human behavior at Jefferson University Hospital in Philadelphia. She attended high school with Sara at the Frisch School and college with Matt at Yale.

My oldest daughter, who was born less than a year after you died, is named after you—her middle name "Sarit," for "Sara." Over the years, I have had the opportunity to meet multiple children named for both of you, by friends who were struggling for a meaningful way to perpetuate your memory. Now, in 2015, they are just a few years younger than you were, and they are all over the world. I currently live in a suburb of Philadelphia, and one of my friends here who had gone to rabbinical school with Matt gave her oldest son the middle name "Moshe," after Matt. My friend and I found out by accident, a few years ago, that both of our children are named for you.

I remember spending hours with both of you independently, discussing and debating multiple existential issues, especially about the role of women in Judaism. I remember many long walks with you, Matt, in both Yerushalayim and New Haven, trying so hard to understand the un-understandable, and to understand each other. I was so happy when the two of you became a couple—you shared an unusual drive to understand and connect both with truths about life as well as with other peoples' needs and feelings, in a way that somehow didn't clash—people and ideas were always both essential. Over the years, I have periodically thought about the different paths our lives may have taken if you had both lived into your forties. Despite this, I believe all three of us would have continued to learn and grow from each other. It is truly an irreplaceable loss that I no longer can share my own ideas and struggles with both of you.

I remember during my first pregnancy, there was a day where it suddenly occurred to me that my children would never know what your voices sounded like, and this seemed unspeakably tragic to me. Twenty years later, there are prominent memories of you throughout my house—the widely publicized picture of the two of you sitting on the *mirpeset* (porch) in Yerushalayim, a large picture of you, Sara, as a bridesmaid at my wedding, multiple old letters, the Dr. Seuss book you got me for our high school graduation, and many others.

My husband, Josh, and I kept the bottle of wine you brought when you both came to us for Shabbat after we got married, right before you left for Israel, which was the last time we saw you. This dust-covered bottle has moved with us from apartment to apartment, from house to house. It was Shabbat Nahamu, and I vividly remember Matt singing the Reb Shlomo Carlebach nigun *"Nahamu, Nahamu Ami,"*[2] with true intention and deep concentration, as if it were yesterday.

---

[2] "Comfort, comfort my people," from Isaiah 40:1.

I spoke about you, Sara, at my oldest daughter's bat mitzvah six years ago, about how I hoped the strength, courage, and idealism of her namesake could be an example to her even though you had never met. One of my other daughters, who is sixteen, inhaled Mike Kelly's book about you as soon as we had it in the house. I spent a lot of time talking with her after this, answering all her questions about you, about our friendship, and about the unique people you were.

You are a powerful part of our lives, not in the way I would have wanted or imagined at age twenty-two, but you truly are, both as dear friends and as amazing, inspiring people. You remain irreplaceable. But please know that you do live on, in big and small ways, in our homes, in our children, and in how we live our lives.

Love,

Tal

Application for Dorot Fellowship in Israel

SARA DUKER

ESSAY #2

I HEARD THE FOLLOWING STORY when I slipped into a discussion group at a Shabbaton that was designed to promote Jewish pride and activism on campus.

Jewish Identity, the protagonist, is being threatened by the evil Assimilation on college campuses, helped inadvertently by the bumbling Disorganized Hillel and Self-Righteous FFB's.[1] How can we save Jewish Identity from the attacks of Apathy, Ignorance, Embarrassment, and Cultural Relativism, before it gets overrun by vampish Inter Sisters, Dating and Marriage? What is faster than an anti-Semitic slur? Able to leap tall prejudices in a single bound? Israeli Folk Dancing? Havurah prayer groups. Zionism? No!! It's Jewish Education, our hero who has come to save the day . . .

Do I dare disagree with such an assessment? Of course I recognize that American Jews are wringing their hands over the quiet crisis that has befallen more than half of our number. And of course education is the only real long-term solution to Identity's problem. But I had to ask the earnest people sitting in the circle, "Who cares?" What made Jewish Identity such a big shot in a world full

---

Sara applied to the Dorot Foundation (www.dorot.org) for a fellowship for the 1995–1996 academic year in Israel. Each year, Dorot provides funding for several young Jewish adults from North America to study for a year in Israel with the expectation that fellows return to North America to develop as lay leaders of the North American Jewish community. This is one of several essays that Sara wrote as part of her application. While she did not receive the fellowship, this essay captures Sara's passion for fostering Jewish identity.

[1] "*Frum* From Birth"; *frum* is a Yiddish word that connotes religious observance. FFB is someone who grew up steeped in tradition and the cultural norms of a religious community as opposed to those from more secular backgrounds who either remain secular or come to religious observance later in life.

of numerous other endangered species? Why are we discussing him, instead of minding our own business?

An uncomfortable lull followed. A new convert to Identity's cause reiterated his point. Someone else mentioned the Future and the difficulty facing Jewish Survival without their needed sidekick. They repeated themselves for emphasis. "You're missing the point," I asserted, when I got the floor back. "I'm asking you, why does Survival matter? Why can't the world just do without him?" Then, they got annoyed, thought I was being deliberately difficult, and went back to long-windedly agreeing about the insidiousness of Assimilation.

I really did want to hear their answers. I would have liked to hear fifteen reasons why Judaism is important, one from each member of the circle. But in all our discussion, we mentioned a bit of history, a bit of *halakha,* and nothing at all about God.

This, to me, is one of the most critical problems we face in the Jewish community. We can mourn the demise of the community from apathy, intermarriage, assimilation, anti-Semitism, internal dissent, and a host of other factors, but I don't believe we can do anything about it until we begin talking to each other about why it matters. How can we tell an intermarried couple to take synagogue classes and raise their children Jewish, tell a teenager to keep Shabbat against the wishes of his parents, tell our friends to go to Israel, if we don't have any reason why these things are compelling? We have an even bigger crisis than we imagine if those of us who are securely involved cannot figure out why we bother (beyond pure dogma, of course).

I use God as a starting point because it seems like the most obvious place to begin. What would our Torah be without God? A hall mate of mine speculated in like manner about his molecular biology textbook. That's good—we're going somewhere. What kind of God is this? Do we emphasize God's power, and interpret Judaism as a path to reward and punishment? Do we prefer to focus on God's compassion, and view Judaism as a guide to creating a charitable and just society? Or do we stress the aspect of God as our lover and partner, to whom we must relate as a responsible equal? I want people to talk about this, argue, get confused, change their minds, and stand firm, as they explain what it is that drives them personally to (or away from) belief, ritual observance, and community affiliation. Let people give credit to God unforgivingly for the Holocaust.

Let's forget, for the time being, all of the old haggles over God's demands vis-à-vis electricity on Shabbat and the reliability of the *hekhsher* on Newman's Own salad dressings. Can we ask God to help us out on burning questions, such as whether I ought to give money to the panhandlers who beg every day outside the supermarket, and what's the proper way to treat gay Jews? God should remind me to visit my grandparents more often, and to be more compassionate with my troubled friends. The more we stay up late into the night wrestling with these, the more successful we are—we know then that people are concerned with what they are doing.

One might think that this theological focus would alienate many Jews who are atheists, agnostics, or have otherwise deconstructed God. Ironically, I would say that the opposite is true. I propose God, and they can dispute God, and instead tell me a hundred things that are compelling about a Godless Judaism. They have now stated their case—and all of Judaism's case—one hundred times better.

As a Jewish leader (and that role still makes me nervous, as many times as I assume it), I hope to be in a position to ask these questions in many guises and be taken seriously. The greatest teachers do not tell us answers, but ask a tremendous amount. Then, perhaps, we have some tools with which to vanquish Apathy, shore up Education, and keep Jewish Identity afloat.

Part Six

Remembering Matt and Sara

BOMBINGS IN ISRAEL: VICTIMS; 2 Students Found Faith, Love and Death

JOHN SULLIVAN

They were in love with their faith and with each other, and they died together as the victims of hate.

Two American students, Matthew Eisenfeld, 25, of West Hartford, Conn., and Sarah Duker, 23, of Teaneck, N.J., were traveling from Jerusalem to Jordan yesterday when a bomb ripped through a packed city bus. Twenty-five people, including the students, were killed.

Friends shocked by the loss spoke repeatedly yesterday of how bright they were, how dedicated, and of the utter senselessness of their deaths.

"Such wonderful young people, who could have been great leaders, great people, are lost," Rabbi Benjamin Segal, the president of the seminary where Mr.

This story from the *New York Times,* February 26, 1996, is reprinted by permission.

Eisenfeld was spending a year, said in a telephone interview from Israel. "It is an old story. The best of our youth has always been on the front lines."

From their home in West Hartford, the Eisenfeld family said yesterday in a statement that they hoped steps toward peace in the Middle East would continue and succeed "so that what happened to Matt never happens to anyone else in the future." They said that Mr. Eisenfeld was someone who always believed he could make a difference.

His uncle, Larry Port, said: "He was a scholar in every sense of the word. He lived for his family and he lived to learn, and that's what he was doing when he was killed."

Mr. Eisenfeld, a Talmudic scholar, hoped to become a rabbi and one day open his own school, friends said. He was studying in Israel as part of the program at the Jewish Theological Seminary in Manhattan, where classmates said he was an outstanding scholar and a leader in his class.

When Prime Minister Yitzhak Rabin was assassinated in November, Mr. Eisenfeld was chosen to speak about his death. Mr. Eisenfeld's roommate, Shai Held, said in an interview in Manhattan yesterday that he spoke about the value and importance of peace.

"He was sympathetic to the peace process," Mr. Held said. "But I hope his death does not become political fodder. I know that he would have had no sympathy for those who would exploit it."

Mr. Held said that Mr. Eisenfeld loved music and poetry, and the pair would often sing Jewish folk songs late into the night. He said Mr. Eisenfeld was working on a poem about Ms. Duker shortly before his death.

"He loved books, but he always remembered to love people more," Mr. Held said.

David Lerner, a friend of Ms. Duker and Mr. Eisenfeld, said that he had recently traveled to Jordan, and had recommended such a trip to them. He said they were on their way to the border on the morning they were killed.

"They were just two of the most special people that I ever knew," Mr. Lerner said, his voice breaking in a telephone interview from a friend's home in Manhattan.

Aryeh Bernstein, 20, said his older brother Edward Bernstein was roommates with Mr. Eisenfeld at the seminary in 1994–95.

During what was their first year at the seminary, they lived in an apartment near the campus where Mr. Bernstein said his older brother, Mr. Eisenfeld and Ms. Duker would invite friends over for Sabbath dinners. He described them as very spiritual gatherings, during which they worked hard to make traditions meaningful for their friends.

Mr. Lerner said Mr. Eisenfeld and Ms. Duker met while he was an undergraduate at Yale and she at Barnard.

At Yale, Mr. Eisenfeld helped begin a singing group which focused on Jewish music. "I am realizing now how much the group was shaped by him, how much enthusiasm he brought to it." said Judah Cohen, 22, a fellow graduate.

The singing group attended an annual theater and music festival at the seminary yesterday and dedicated songs to Mr. Eisenfeld. Last night, 300 people attended a two-hour memorial service at the seminary.

Dorothy Denberg, dean of Barnard College, remembered Ms. Duker as "someone who always had a twinkle in her eye."

Ms. Duker, who was elected to Phi Beta Kappa, was a member of a special program for gifted scholars and studied environmental science. She was studying science at Hebrew University in Jerusalem.

"Originally, she was talking about settling in Israel, but then she became very interested in environmental issues," said Ms. Denberg, who served as Ms. Duker's faculty adviser. "She was also an outstanding writer. She really could have done anything."

Ms. Denberg said that one of Ms. Duker's constant interests was the struggle for peace.

"For a terrorist to kill her just kills me," Ms. Denberg said. "She was such a quiet person and a gentle person. She was very committed to peace in the Mideast."

Rabbi Kenneth Berger, the rabbi for the Duker family's congregation, said that Ms. Duker was one of three children, and that her sister is also studying in Israel. He said Ms. Duker and Mr. Eisenfeld had planned to marry, but had not set a date.

At the Jewish Theologial Seminary yesterday, students who gathered for a concert spoke of Mr. Eisenfeld's death and pledged to honor him with psalms throughout the night. Prof. Raymond P. Scheindlin remembered Mr. Eisenfeld as an extremely religious and bright student.

"He was a thinking person, he wanted to be intellectually challenged," Mr. Scheindlin said. "He was one of those students who really made an impression."

Rabbi William Lebeau, vice chancellor and dean of the Jewish Theologial Seminary, said Mr. Eisenfeld's family and teachers all had great hopes for him. "What could be the meaning of violence like this, the utter waste of his life and the lives of all who were killed?" Rabbi Lebeau said. "What could be the value of destroying such a life?"

Ms. Duker was the second person from New Jersey killed by Islamic militants in less than a year.

Alisa Flatow, 20, of West Orange, was killed in April when a suicide bomber drove his explosives-laden car into a bus in which she was riding in the Gaza Strip. The Associated Press said Ms. Flatow and Ms. Duker both went to Frisch Yeshiva High School in Paramus.

From Jewish Advocate

This photo is from the ceremony at Ben Gurion Airport in Tel Aviv, February 26, 1996, where the caskets of Matt and Sara were placed on an El Al plane to New York in advance of their burial in West Hartford, CT. Rabbi Edward Bernstein is seen in the front row, second from left. Other identifiable persons include: Rabbi Joshua Heller (JTS classmate of Matt; front, left); Tracie Bernstein (Pardes classmate of Sara, wife of Rabbi Michael Bernstein, JTS classmate of Matt; near center, to right of Israel Defense Forces Cantor); Rivkah Duker Fishman (Sara's cousin; front, far right); Martin Indyk, then U.S. Ambassador to Israel, spoke at ceremony; his head is partially visible over Edward Bernstein's right shoulder.

Eulogy for Matt Eisenfeld and Sara Duker

Moshe Melekh ben Yehudah U'Zehavah

Sarah Rachel bat Ben Zion V'Ora

RABBI WILLIAM LEBEAU

12 Adar 5756 (March 3, 1996)

Beit Midrash, Yerushalayim

On the fifth of Adar, 5756, two gentle, precious souls entered *Taḥat Kanfay Ha-Shekhinah*—into God's sheltering presence. These two souls were in love on earth—in love with God Who created them and in love with each other.

For a very brief number of years these souls were contained in lovely bodies. Our recollections of their eyes, their hair, their voices, provide us with a way of remembering their physical presence with us. It was the way they used their physical attributes that made God's Image so clearly visible in their smiles, their radiance, and their actions.

Their bodies were shattered by an act of inhumanity, but their souls escaped the carnage without scar or blemish. The beauty and purity of the souls of Moshe Melekh ben Yehudah V'Zahavah and Sara Rachel bat Ben Zion V'Ora have been preserved for their journey together in Eternity.

Rabbi William Lebeau is the Senior Consultant for Rabbinic and Institutional Leadership for the Rabbinical Assembly, the international association of Conservative rabbis. Previously, he served the Jewish Theological Seminary as Vice Chancellor for Rabbinic Development and as Dean of the JTS Rabbinical School. He offered Matt admission to the Rabbinical School in December, 1994. In his role as Rabbi of the JTS synagogue, Rabbi Lebeau hired Sara to serve as gabbai (sexton) for High Holiday services. This eulogy was delivered at the Schechter Institute in Jerusalem at a memorial service one week after Matt's and Sara's deaths. Rabbi Lebeau had attended their burial in Connecticut a few days earlier then flew to Israel to attend this service and support Matt's bereaved classmates.

Violence was the antithesis of their lives. Still, their bodies lying together in a small path of God's earth are testimony that human beings have the power to destroy God's physical creations. But our faith and perseverance and our sanctification of memory give greater testimony that the souls of our loved ones and the collective soul of our people cannot be destroyed by any act of human terror or intimidation.

The deaths of Matt and Sara captured the world's attention. Violence always captures attention, but people were drawn to this tragedy sensing something special in their deaths. They saw two people in love, two religious people in love and a love denied fulfillment. The romantic ideal of the world was shattered once again in this explosion of violence.

We who are a part of Matt and Sara's worlds were drawn together by our love and now our sorrow for them. How thankful we must be that we are Jews. Even in the chaos that overtook our lives just a few days ago we had direction—a mandate for action. Jewish tradition demanded that we respond immediately to assure *K'vod Ha-Met*—proper honor for the bodies of our dead. Fellow students, teachers, and friends in Israel escorted their bodies to the airport for their return to their families. They were surrounded by *Tehilim* (Psalms) and words of love and praise. Two classmates flew with them to New York, where they were met by other friends and teachers. They were never left alone until they reached their final resting place.

Immediately upon the completion of burial, we turned our efforts to our commanded responsibility to be *M'nahem Aveilim*, comforters for the mourning families and for each other. Essential to the process of comforting is the need to talk about the lives of Matt and Sara and the experiences we shared with them. Our recollections have been painful, but the endurance of that pain is necessary for us to better comprehend the meaningfulness of their lives. The more we speak and remember, the more we guarantee that the tragedy will not overwhelm our sense of their vitality and their accomplishments that we so cherish.

And so, throughout these long, intense days and nights, at every opportunity for discussion and eventually in public eulogy, we have spoken of their lives. At the same time, out of our need to express our outrage, we also spoke of the violent, sudden, irrevocable end to their dreams and our expectations for them. We all expressed our affection with the certainty that even the most expansive praise was not exaggeration.

What emerged was a story of two people whose lives had such a profound impact on everyone who encountered them. It is critical that we understand why we were so attracted to them. If we better understand their essence—that which motivated them to live as they did—then we will be more inclined to emulate them.

They have been called *tsadiqim*, pious, spiritual, kind, giving, respectful of parents, family, teachers, and more. Why do we believe they deserved these designations of praise so highly valued in our tradition? I believe an insight of Abraham Joshua Heschel helps explain our response to them. He wrote, "Judaism is averse to generalities; averse to looking for meaning in life detached from doing, as if meaning were a separate entity. It is by enacting the holy on the stage of concrete living that we perceive our kinship with the Divine. What a person does with his/her concrete, physical existence is directly relevant to the Divine. In this world music is played on physical instruments. To the Jew, the *mitsvot* are the instruments on which the holy is carried out. The individual's insight alone is unable to cope without the guidance of tradition on which we must rely."

I believe we were all so inspired to love and respect Matt and Sara because they enacted the holy on the stage of concrete living. In their lives we discerned their connection to the Divine. Their need to search out deeper understanding of God's Will, rather than to trust only their instincts, and their profound commitment to Jewish tradition moved us all.

Almost everyone has commented on Sara's and Matt's commitment to prayer. At the Seminary Matt davened in the nonegalitarian *minyan*. Sara was a leader of the egalitarian *minyan*. Both prayed each weekday with *tallit* and *tefillin*. Their discussions on prayer provided each of them the opportunity to consider, more intensely, the views of *halakha* on matters of worship and religiosity for men and women in Judaism. Their steady presence in those *minyanim* and their prayer while in Yerushalayim so impressed us that we called them pious and spiritual.

They befriended a homeless person, channeling her ability to crochet into a business of *kipah* making—of allowing her to provide beautiful head coverings for men and women. They did this not only because they were by nature kind and concerned but because they truly felt obligated by God's expectations that human beings must perform *G'milut Hasadim*. By providing the woman a way to be productive and earn money for subsistence, they allowed her to have financial resources in ways other than seeking charity. They gave her dignity. For this and so many other acts of kindness, we called them righteous *Tsadiqim*.

They heeded the admonition we all know so well of *Talmud Torah Keneged Kulam*—that the study of Torah stands as the most important of God's commandments. They demonstrated unwavering devotion to study. They studied not only to gain knowledge, but they learned Torah in order to teach it. They learned in order to know how to act so they could better carry out God's *mitsvot* with a full and understanding heart. For this, we called them scholars and our teachers.

And so it was that in just a few short years they concretized Jewish living in their lives. The redemption of the world depends on human beings making the decision to create harmony with God's instruments by responding to the rhythms of God's order of time and observance in the days, weeks, months, and years of their lives. They blended the cadences of God's rituals with the nuances of God's commandments so that they have left us with a model of how we should act with kindness toward one another. Matt Eisenfeld and Sara Duker were learning to play so beautifully on God's instruments and for that we honor them.

They have taught us the power of each day by earning our collective esteem in such a brief number of days. Imagine what the world might be like if we adopted their sense of urgency and intensity. For this reason we must emulate them.

Amar Rabbi Abin HaLevi, Ha-niftar meḥavero, 'al yomar lo lekh be-shalom 'eleh lekh le-shalom—Rabbi Abin HaLevi said, "When a person separates from a friend don't say to that person go with peace, but rather go toward peace." Embrace the Torah and help move yourselves and the world toward peace. Don't be discouraged. As Matt and Sara left us, I am certain they were calling insistently to us *"Lekh le-shalom."*

Ha-niftar min ha-met, 'al yomar lo lekh le-shalom 'eleh lekh be-shalom— "When a person separates from the dead, do not say go toward peace but rather go with peace; go with a sense of completeness." And so we say to Sara and Matt, *"Lekh be-shalom."* Go with peace and satisfaction for you have achieved so much. You have brought us closer to God and to each other. May God see in your lives the very best of what human beings can become. *"Lekh le-shalom."*

Reflection on the First Anniversary
of the Death of Matt and Sara

AMY EISENFELD

WHILE MATT WAS THE BEST BROTHER and role model a sister could ever have, we were not always friends or study partners in a formal sense. A sibling bond changes over a lifetime, and many times the years between us felt like decades. Our relationship was built through a shared childhood. Our family moved a few times to new cities, forcing Matt and me to look to each other for support and companionship. There were also a dozen summers at overnight camp, where, depending on the year, we either spent a lot of time together or pretended that we didn't know each other's names. And of course there were countless family vacations and going through the day-to-day events, like flipping a coin to see who would walk the dog and citing homework as an excuse not to do the dishes.

Until Matt went to college, we shared many experiences since we lived in the same house and were united by our parents. Many times I wondered how we both came from the same place. But despite our differences, the bond between us remained strong because we were always able to find a way to communicate.

The last letter I received from Matt was written on his twenty-fifth birthday, three weeks before he died. The letter was a good one and is typical of our relationship. He wrote,

---

Amy Eisenfeld Genser is Matt's younger sister. She delivered these remarks at the dedication of the Matthew Eisenfeld and Sara Duker Beit Midrash at JTS held on the occasion of the first anniversary of their death, February 11, 1997. She was single at the time and has since married. She and her family live in West Hartford, CT, where she works as an artist.

REFLECTION BY AMY EISENFELD

Dear Amy,

As usual, it is great to hear from you and your letter this time just made me laugh and laugh. For the most part, things have gone well, but I miss you and wish you could come. I think we could have a good time in Israel. We don't have to go look at ruins. We could hang out in Me'ah She'arim and race to see who can touch 100 fur hats first. If that got boring, we could go feed all the cats in the city. Anyway, I live on a beautiful street named after a famous rabbi from Spain, "Alfasi Street." I know, it sounds like a character from the muppets, but he really was an important person. We call him "Rif." It makes him sound more musical.

I'm 25 today. Can you believe that? I'm smack dab in the middle of my 20s. A friend asked me if I felt different and was joking, but I answered that I did feel different. I'm expecting my beard to change color any minute now. Why do I have a beard? I got so damn sick of my shaver which never does a good job that I said "to hell with it" and let it grow.

When Matt thought about me coming to visit, and enticed me by describing events that I would enjoy, he made an effort to communicate on my terms. But we both knew that our being together would be enough. I was lucky to have had the chance to let him know in my last letter to him, in my own words, how I felt about him and what he was doing. I wrote,

> I wish you would come home already. I am trying to make my life plan around where my favorite people are going to be living. So where are you going to live when you grow up? Wherever it is, I am moving next door and you are going to be my rabbi. My children will love you because you will let them sleep outside on Sukkot and they will be allowed on the bimah and able to talk into the microphone when no one is looking.

This past year my family has been engulfed by the loss of Matt. I have experienced waves of emotion that I never knew existed. One day when I was feeling particularly sad, my mom reminded me about Matt's attitude toward the horrible and compelling tragedies that have befallen our people. While he was insistent that events such as the Holocaust and Rabin's death need to be respected and remembered, we should never forget that Judaism is about a rich and joyous legacy, and a community that is nourished and sustained by learning and living Torah. He also loved singing and sharing celebrations. Matt believed that this should be the essence and focus of our lives. This comforts me and reminds me to remember the twenty-five amazing years of his life, and not dwell on the horror of his death. The truth is that I am blessed to have shared my first twenty-two years with him, and my parents, twenty-five. I wish many of you could have known him longer, although you know how special he was.

I'd like to read you another passage from Matt's letter that told me how his studies were going. He wrote,

> In other news, I finished Tractate Kiddushim, which is a section of the Talmud dealing with marriage. I invited my whole class, and about 30 to 40 people came, along with two of my teachers. Rabbi Schraeder also came from Brovender's. It was a thrill to see him, even after all that's gone on between the yeshiva and me. In any case, I gave a lesson to the class which lasted about an hour on issues within the tractate. Now the other people are all wanting to finish tractates! So you can be proud of your ole brother.

Of course I was proud.

Finally, I'd like to tell you one more thing. When Matt and I were children, we used to knock on the wall between our bedrooms at night. It was our way of saying goodnight, answering to each other that we were there. In a way I feel like I am knocking again and being answered by you. The *beit midrash* is the echo. This is where Matt's heart and soul would have been.

Sisterly Love

TAMARA DUKER FREUMAN

I WAS TWENTY when my older sister Sara was killed, so the twentieth anniversary of her death marks a particularly sad milestone for me: I've lived on this earth without my sister for as many years as I have lived here alongside her.

My childhood was spent largely in Sara's shadow, and this fact was marked by her exceptional intellectual talents and academic achievements. As is often the case with younger siblings, much of my own self-identity was defined in comparison to my big sister. She was the ruler against which I measured my own growth and evaluated my future trajectory.

When Sara died, the reality set in that I would eventually come to surpass my older sister, my benchmark. I'd eventually learn more than she had, achieve more than she did, think more sophisticated thoughts, see more of the world. In other words, I would one day soon step out from my older sister's shadow, frozen as it was in time at age twenty-two. It was a disorienting prospect, and the thought of it somehow made her loss that much more tangible to me.

Reflecting on Sara's writings compiled throughout this volume, however, I realize with both humility and awe what folly it was to worry that I'd one day leave a youthful Sara behind on my path to full-fledged adulthood. The deep personal reflections, intellectual enquiries and passionate beliefs about spirituality and the importance of family that Sara so eloquently and painstakingly recorded as a young twenty-something are more thoughtful, profound, and complex than those I have managed to muster as her now forty-year-old "younger" sister. I see little evidence of the trite or clichéd musings one might expect when looking back on the writings of a clever—but still twenty-two-year-old—idealistic recent

Tamara Duker Freuman is a registered dietician and author of a blog at www.tamaraduker.com. She and her family live in the New York area.

college grad. As I consider her words all these years later, I continue to recognize in them my first mentor, the wearer of those still-too-big (purple) shoes I continue to strive to fill.

Indeed, twenty years later, I have only just recently begun to internalize and embrace many of the values that were so core to Sara's existence as a very young adult: the critical importance of environmental stewardship, the priority of cultivating strong family connections, and the importance of keeping our relationship with God and those with our fellow human beings at front and center as we define and express our Jewish identities. In other words, it has taken me the past twenty years to figure out what Sara knew instinctively as a twenty-two-year-old.

An Israeli Family Member Recalls
Sara and Matt

DR. RIVKAH DUKER FISHMAN

I remember Sara and Matt, but since Sara was my cousin (her father Ben Zion, z"l, was my first cousin), I remember her more, so I will devote my brief statement to four things that Sara loved—her greatest love of course was Matt z"l.

Family: Sara loved our extended family. She knew the Duker-Gorodinsky family tree, lore and stories about her grandfather Sam, one of my father's younger brothers. In Israel, she became friends with my two older children, several years younger than she was. (They were teenagers at the time she was murdered.) Sara knew Russian and formed a close relationship with our Russian cousins, new immigrants in Kiryat Gat. She could really talk to them and visited them. It was through Sara that our immediate family came to know them. Sara, often with Matt, but also on her visit in 1994, often graced our Shabbat and holiday table. She would bring vegetarian delicacies that she prepared. She enjoyed the family connection and was a *bat bayit*, a member of our household.

Nature: Sara loved nature. When she was in Eilat on a scholarship to do research on the preservation of marine plants and animals, my older children visited her. My daughter returned, proudly announcing: "Sara is not afraid of animals or bugs." She enjoyed field trips and loved sleeping in the sukkah during Sukkot because she sensed that it made her closer to nature and to God's creation. She knew the names of trees, plants, flowers, and animals and about them. She loved rainy weather too. I think it was part of the environmentalism that she

---

Dr. Rivkah Duker Fishman is lecturer in Jewish history at the Rothberg International School of the Hebrew University of Jerusalem.

espoused. But for her it was genuine, not simply mouthing slogans about "saving the planet." She had an innate feeling for nature that I appreciate because it is largely missing from my life. She taught me about it.

Judaism: Sara loved Judaism—praying, learning, observing, experiencing Shabbat and holidays, and delving deeply into traditions and texts. She was curious, inquisitive, and occasionally critical. But her criticism came from love, not from spite. She sincerely wanted to make our religion more inclusive of women and the unfortunate. Once she asked me: "Why don't you wear a *tallit* and *tefillin* (the required prayer shawl and phylacteries for men during the daily morning prayer)?" I simply replied: "That is for your generation." But Sara did not just attend women's prayer groups or non-Orthodox synagogues. While in Jerusalem, she went to different ethnic *shuls*, small Sephardic structures, and mainstream modern Orthodox synagogues. Again, she did so out of love and curiosity and a desire to be part of what I call "Jewish" Israel—the variegated and rich experience of Jewish life in all its facets in the Jewish state. It does not exist anywhere else. It is here for those who seek it with an open mind and loving heart.

When I taught the Second Temple and Talmudic periods of our history, I often would begin with Sara's memorable lines from her article on Elisha ben Avuyah, *Aher*, the heretic of the late first–early second century c.e., as follows: "I love working with the texts of my tradition, and these in particular, because they have a story to tell if one is patient enough to listen to them. They are challenging, both in terms of their content, and because they are part of a sacred canon. From where does a modern woman approach them? . . . Part of my challenge has been to understand the people behind the texts as well as their sacredness—to try to maintain an intensive dialogue with my ancestors."[1] There is no nastiness here, no anger, no meanness—only a desire to communicate with the past and make it relevant and embrace it—but not like a robot. That was Sara's positive approach to difficult problems of our tradition.

Israel: Both Sara and Matt loved Israel. They traveled throughout the country and became acquainted with its people. Of course, Sara criticized certain policies and aspects of life here, but it was a criticism out of love, not meanness. For Sara, Israel was the Jewish homeland. It had historic meaning and religious significance. She even accompanied me on tours of ruins from the Roman period in the summer of 1994. She simply felt very much at home here and enjoyed

---

[1] "Elisha Looked and Cut at the Shoots: Making the Myths of the Other in Ancient Rabbinic Texts," in: *Iggrot ha'Ari: The Lion's Letters. Columbia University Student Journal of Jewish Scholarship*, 1 (Spring, 1997): 9–35.

learning about Jewish history, the land, the Bible—the way one can learn it only in Israel. She had a sense of its historic and present importance.

Unfortunately, today too many young people in the Diaspora (even rabbinical students) pride themselves on finding fault with Israel. (We do have faults; it is true that no one is perfect.) They do so because of some personal feeling they harbor against the Jewish state. They lack the *neshamah* (soul), real empathy and attachment that Jews traditionally have had for *Eretz he-'Avot* (the Land of Our Fathers). Since it is Sara, I shall say *Eretz he-'Avot ve-ha-'Imahot* (Land of Our Fathers and Mothers). Sara did not seek the company or approval of Israel's enemies and critics. She truly loved this country and loved Jerusalem.

May the memory of Sara and Matt z'l be blessed forever and may God grant us comfort among the mourners of Zion and Jerusalem.

November 18, 2015
6 Kislev 5776

Were Matt and Sara Planning to Marry?

RABBI MICHAEL AND TRACIE BERNSTEIN

EACH YEAR WHEN WE THINK about our friends, countless images come to mind, many of them involving their incredible commitment to a life lived with purpose and bettering the world. Tracie had known Sara since college, and Michael met Sara during our year together at Pardes. Sara was a graduate of Barnard, passionate about science and the environment, as well as struggling with the questions at the heart of the Jewish tradition. Matt was Michael's classmate and study partner in rabbinical school. He combined a formidable capacity for discipline and intellectual rigor, profound humility, and a palpable joy in engaging in the practices of being Jewish. Sara and Matt were both suffused with great compassion for others and a talent for putting their dreams into action. And, somehow more than anything else, they loved each other.

Many of the official reports described Matt and Sara as engaged, but if they were it wasn't known to their friends. What we do know is that only weeks before the day they were killed, they asked if they could come over for dinner to our Jerusalem apartment to discuss something important. We were happy to oblige. Sara was a vegetarian even though Matt decidedly was not, so we made a dairy meal. They brought over a side dish—steamed zucchini with ripe avocado and fresh lemon. To this day, each time we make that dish we think of them.

We also often think about the question they had in mind to discuss: What is great about being married? The question did not reveal a skepticism about marriage, but instead showed how Matt and Sara approached their relationship with the same depth and thoughtfulness that attended all of their most important pursuits and passions. For us, as newlyweds, it was not only an honor to be

The authors attended Pardes Institute in Jerusalem with Sara, and Michael entered JTS Rabbinical School with Matt in Fall 1994. Rabbi Bernstein is the spiritual leader of Congregation Gesher L'Torah in Alpharetta, Georgia, and Tracie is sales director for the Development Corporation of Israel, Atlanta office.

among those they looked to for such wisdom, but a reminder to keep asking ourselves this very question, despite that neither of us felt equipped to give much of an answer at that time.

Both of us felt a combination of being humbled in the face of the earnest request and a little pressured to say something profound. Between the two of us we came up with something along the lines of "marriage makes official the choice that you have made to trust in and wake up next to another person every day from here on in. That they'll be there for you and you for them no matter what for the long term." It didn't feel so wise and it wasn't all that original. However, if Matt and Sara were left less than inspired by our responses they did not show it. In retrospect, the most profound element of the conversation, apart from the delicious zucchini, was in the way it was engaged with an openness to love unalloyed with any cynicism or fear of cliche.

However, as significant a connection as we feel about the deepest and loftiest aspects of Matt and Sara's love for each other, our thoughts about the two of them never are far from how romantic, lighthearted, even silly they were together and as individuals. Matt had been Michael's roommate the first year of rabbinical school. The night we got engaged, Michael needed Matt to buy time while he made sure everything was in place for the big moment. Matt decided to stall Tracie by pretending to have just written a poem for Sara. Tracie politely smiled, listening to this quickly cobbled together bunch of rhyming lines. While Matt had written many more elegant verses expressing what was in his heart, it is those verses that will always stand out for us as the ultimate love poetry. Similarly, those who knew both Sara and Matt will always remember them for silly hats, spontaneous songs, and hilarious Purim costumes just as much as for academic excellence, tremendous kindness, true friendship, and profound love.

This is what is meant by the searing words of the biblical section known as the Song of Songs: "Place me as a seal upon your heart for love is fiercer than death." Not only do we find that our bond with those we love survives even being bereft of them. We also realize that the absurdity that is the love between two people can somehow be more certain, more powerful, more transformative even than death itself.

To delight in another person is not frivolous, it is a gateway into what gives the world meaning. It's what makes it possible to commit a lifetime to being together with one other person and what makes the two of us think so fondly about a small Jerusalem kitchen, a dish of zucchini, avocado, and lemon, and the profound love we were so privileged to share with such good friends.

"Friends of Matt and Sara"

ELLI SACKS

THE IMMEDIATE POST-COLLEGE YEARS are by their nature itinerant—at age twenty-three, at age twenty-five, few of us have even begun to put down the roots that will tie us to a particular place or community. We may move several times within the space of a few years in search of professional training or professional advancement, across the country and sometimes even across the globe. This presents a unique challenge for youthful friendships, especially those forged out of the deep soul-searching of late-night talks and of shared formative experiences—those special, intense friendships that spring up from within the intimacy of a close circle of friends. And then suddenly, with those friends thrust out into the world, the geometry of that circle begins to change. It becomes oblong, lumpy, until eventually it assumes the shape of an indefinable blob. The proximity that once held this circle together is gone. With its members dispersed, far removed from that special time and place, a new means of communication must be found to keep those friendships alive and vibrant.

Matt Eisenfeld and Sara Duker, who were loved so dearly by so many, were killed at such a time. Many of their friends had recently begun venturing out into the wider world or were on the cusp of making moves to new venues that would eventually become their homes. And for this reason, a community of young friends that found so much joy and fulfillment in their day-in, day-out interactions with Matt and Sara during their lifetime would find it physically much more difficult to come together as a community of mourners, year-in, year-out, to remember them and pay homage to their memory.

Elli Sacks attended Yale University and lives in Modi'in, Israel, where he works as a commercial real estate analyst and as an academic and literary translator. He created the "Friends of Matt and Sara" Facebook Group.

It was for this reason that in 2007 we started a group on Facebook called "Friends of Matt and Sara," https://www.facebook.com/groups/35089781487. One could say it was for selfish reasons. We missed them terribly. We missed the warmth of their personalities, their quirky humor, the intensity of their ideas, and the passion of their commitments. We craved their company and the company of other friends who shared in this special bond. Moreover, we missed the conversations, the sharing of our intimate thoughts that through the spoken word became somehow transformed and solidified into important realizations about who we were and what we wanted of and for ourselves. The Facebook group provided us with an outlet to share our memories of Matt and Sara, and in some way to continue on those conversations.

Today the group has 370 members. Each year it becomes especially active around the time of their *yahrtzeit* with memories, poems, reflections, photos, and the like, but members also post throughout the year about important events in their lives that they would have wanted to share with Matt and Sara. We see wedding announcements and pictures of babies growing up who bear the names, in one form or another, of Moshe Melech and Sara Rachel. We take solace in the realization that, though Matt and Sara were robbed of the opportunity to create their own family and set down those deep communal roots, the seeds of their friendship have been carried to the four corners of the earth, where miraculously they still somehow manage to form a community of memory and a community of life. May their memories and their continuing conversations be a blessing for us, always.

Modi'in, Israel
5775 (2015)

Two Shining Lights

RABBI DAVID LERNER

I WILL NEVER FORGET that most horrific morning, when everything was turned upside down. I was visiting some friends in Manhattan on semester break during our year in Israel when I got a call from my parents. They had to speak to me urgently and in person. This was not normal; this was not good.

A few minutes later, they had driven in from Teaneck, New Jersey, to tell me the devastating news that Matthew Eisenfeld and Sara Duker had been killed on the #18 bus by a suicide bomber that morning.

Everything came to a stop.

Images filled my mind. Not only images of loss, but of beauty, of hope, of light.

I had the unique gift of studying, of learning Torah, with both Matt and Sara.

I grew up with Sara in Teaneck, New Jersey. We *davened* in the same *shul* when we first moved to town. We both attended the Solomon Schechter Day School of Bergen County. I remember the tragedy of her father Ben-Zion's death when she was just a child. May his memory be for a blessing.

Sara was smart, very smart, and had a soul that liked to skip gently from place to place. We overlapped at college, but I had a real opportunity to get to know her better when we were both students at Pardes in the early 1990s. We learned together and those *hevruta*/study-partner sessions were unlike those with my other study partners. Sara had a unique ability to make connections between different texts and different genres. When we were looking at Talmud, it would remind her of an English poem. When we were looking at the weekly Torah portion, she would find a connection to something she had experienced on a hike. Like the Kabbalists, Sara saw the universe as one. Where others would

Rabbi David Lerner is Spiritual Leader of Temple Emunah, Lexington, Massachusetts.

see division and strife, she would see the unity, the underlying oneness of all things. She could see God in a way that most could not.

No matter what the setting—praying, eating, or walking along the beach—or what the topic—the peace process, the Talmud, the environment, or egalitarianism—for Sara, they were all part of the same continuum. They were all manifestations of the same oneness.

While our friendship moved on, I was so happy that Sara found a soulmate in Matt.

Matt and I did not share as long a history, but were rabbinical school classmates at JTS and spent a lot of time together during 1995–1996 as _hevruta_ (study partners) in our main Talmud class. We didn't start out that way. Somehow, after much shuffling of study partners, both Matt and I found ourselves without a _hevruta_. He came up and asked me to learn in the sincere and matter-of-fact style that animated much of our time together.

Even among a large group of serious and accomplished students in our Jewish Theological Seminary rabbinical school class and among the twelve of us in the accelerated rabbinic track, Matt stood out for his methodical and deliberate approach to his learning.

Matt wrote down his vision for what he wanted to learn and accomplish during the year explicitly and then further broke this down into smaller goals. He approached our learning in the same manner.

Each and every morning that year, he showed up after _minyan_ with his _tallit/tefillin_, his Talmud and a cup of coffee. After placing his _tallit/tefillin_ down on the next table, he would open his Gemara to wherever we stopped and take a long sip of coffee. We would begin by checking in with each other. He asked me about my relationship with Sharon, who would become my wife, who was living in New York at the time. And I would ask him about Sara and how things were between the two of them.

After we spent time nurturing our _qesher_, our connection, we would turn to our learning. Our professor, Shamma Friedman, was teaching us the esoteric skill of mastering different _girsa'ot_, different versions of the Talmud. It was painstaking work, and at times I felt that I did not have the discipline to master it. Matt was patient with me, making sure that we went slowly and that I understood each step in the process.

When I got frustrated with the relevance of this type of learning, Matt smiled gently and simply reengaged me in the task; he would not take the bait of a diversion! For Matt, all Torah learning was a reflection of God, and that discipline and dedication would have taken him wherever he wanted to go in his learning.

At the end of the first semester, my father came to visit my sister, who was also studying in Israel for the year, and me. Since Israel had just signed a peace agreement with Jordan, we decided to take a three-day trip to Jordan. When we returned, Matt and I spent several days together reviewing the entire semester of Talmud. Again, it was tedious work, but Matt had the intellectual strength and the perseverance necessary to complete it.

At the end of our learning, I shared with Matt the details about how to go on a similar trip to Jordan. He was so excited to go with Sara on such a journey. He and Sara were on the #18 bus that morning, on their way to the Jerusalem Central Bus Station, setting out for Jordan, where Matt was to propose to Sara. . . .

Over the last twenty years, not a week has gone by when I have not thought about Matt and Sara. While their lives were tragically cut short by hate, their love and their light continue to shine.

Countless times over the last two decades when I have needed an extra measure of dedication, I have thought of Matt—his sincerity, his honesty, and his sense of commitment—helping me accomplish my goals. When I have taught something about the environment or nature, I have thought of Sara and her *derekh*/path in the world.

Rereading some and reading for the first time other parts of their writings now in this exquisite collection that Rabbi Eddie Bernstein has lovingly collected for us, a sense of joy and pain comes over me.

There is great sadness: so much was taken from us, so much was taken from the world. Who knows what great insights and wonderful Torah Matt and Sara would have been able to share with us?

And yet, we can hold onto this collection and smile, between the tears. Matt and Sara's Torah, Matt and Sara's light continues to shine.

May we all merit to receive it.

Stop This Day and Night

DR. DEVORAH SCHOENFELD

APRIL 1994

I'm sitting with Sara on the *Tayelet* overlooking Jerusalem and she's telling me that Matt told her that he wanted to be with her by sending her these lines from a Walt Whitman poem:

> Stop this day and night with me and you shall possess the origin of all
>   poems,
> You shall possess the good of the earth and sun, (there are millions of suns
>   left,)
> You shall no longer take things at second or third hand, nor look through
>   the eyes of the dead, nor feed on the specters in books,
> You shall not look through my eyes either, nor take things from me,
> You shall listen to all sides and filter them from your self.

Sara tells me about the book *Like Water for Chocolate* and how the protagonist eats matches until she bursts into flame.

SEPTEMBER 1994

I'm in New York for a visit and Matt and I are learning furiously in the JTS *beit midrash*. One night during Sukkot we lead a study session together and then decide that we're going to stay up all night learning in the Sukkah. We fall asleep eventually. Sometime in the night the Sukkah is covered over and in the morning

---

Dr. Devorah Schoenfeld is Associate Professor of Jewish Theology at Loyola University of Chicago. She studied with Sara at Machon Pardes in Jerusalem, 1993–1994, during which she came to know Matt as well.

331

Matt wakes me up and tells me that we've been sleeping in a *pasul* (legally unfit) Sukkah. Oops.

NOVEMBER 1994

Matt and I visit UTJ and talk about maybe going there. I wrote in my diary that it struck me as a group of idealistic people committed to Torah and an honest relationship with God. They had some problem with mixed-gender *ḥevrutot*[1] but we told them that we wanted to learn together and they said maybe they could figure it out.

OCTOBER 1995

Sara comes with me and my roommate Avigayl[2] to the small Kurdish congregation across the street from my apartment in Jerusalem. Morning prayer is at 4:30 in the morning, and Sara and Avigayl are wearing *tefillin*. They explain that their rabbi, who heads a large yeshiva in New York, told them that wearing *tefillin* is the right thing for them to do. The rabbi of the Kurdish synagogue isn't impressed with Sara's stories about her rabbi but he's impressed with her, and he says if she's willing to come to pray at 4:30 on a weekday he sees no problem with her wearing *tefillin*.

NOVEMBER 1995

Matt and I are in deep in conversation about the possibility of a post-denominational yeshiva. I really believed that we could change the world. Matt wrote in his diary, "Rather than read poems, I could live a poem. Do I dare?"

FEBRUARY 1996

We're at the *Kotel* and Sara is crying in my arms because she's afraid she doesn't know how to love. She's afraid she can't love Matt, she's afraid she can't

---

[1] Plural of *ḥevruta,* study pair discussing classical Jewish texts.
[2] In 1995–1996, Devorah shared an apartment with Avigayl Young, a classmate of Matt and close friend of Sara. Avigayl received rabbinic ordination from JTS in 1999 and lives in Houston, Texas.

love anyone. She's not sure she could be a mother because she's not sure she could love a child. And of course she can love, I've seen it, but I also see her pain. I hold her and believe that she loves better than she knows.

February 1996

After their death I sit *shiva*, which I know is arrogant, like I have any right, but I can't think of any reason I should care if I am arrogant or not. People bring me food and I don't eat it. "Matt was my *ḥevruta*," I say. "Sara was my closest friend." Eating food feels disgusting, because it's something that people do when they are alive, and being alive means that I'm not with them. And there's something about things being that completely not-okay, you never know if things will ever be okay, not in any sense, not ever again.

October 2015

I am teaching Judaism to Catholics, which is the work that I now do and love. I show my students how Jewish textual interpretation always finds multiple meanings in every verse, in every line. And I think about Matt and Sara, because I can't not.

What was it that we were fighting for all those years ago? *Halakhic* Judaism[3] with a space for women in leadership roles. Breaking down the denominational walls that we saw as dividing the Jewish community. I look around the Jewish world and things have changed since 1996: there are thriving post-denominational communities, rabbinical schools that ordain Orthodox women, exciting and vibrant new Jewish worlds. The people doing the work to make these things happen are wise scholars that I respect, and Matt and Sara are not among them. The world is changing, the world has changed, and it just goes on changing without them, and there is still a hole in the heart of the world where their voices were. We will never know what the Jewish world—what the world—would have been today if they had continued to take part in shaping it.

Or maybe we were just fighting for a little bit of space to figure out who we were. If only we just had more time.

---

[3] Judaism as governed by *halakha*, classical Jewish law.

Photo of Matt and Sara, by Edward Bernstein.
January 6, 1996

Appendix

1. P. 336. Photocopy of *New York Times,* February 26, 1996, story of deaths of Matt and Sara. See also p. 307 in this volume for a transcription of the article.
2. P. 337. Photocopy of Matt's interview with Rabbi Shlomo Carlebach. From *Urim v'Tumim: A Student Quarterly of Yale's Jewish Community* 7, no. 1 (fall 1992): 10–11. See also p. 266 in this volume for a transcription of the article.
3. P. 339. Photocopy of Matt's article "Leaps of Faith: Uncertainty's Role in Religion." From *Urim v'Tumim: A Student Quarterly of Yale's Jewish Community* 6, no. 3 (spring 1992): 24–25. See also p. 271 in this volume for a transcription of the article.

BOMBINGS IN ISRAEL: A Day of Ghastly Revenge

VICTIMS

2 U.S. Students Together In Faith, Love and Death

By JOHN SULLIVAN

They were in love with their faith and with each other, and they died together as the victims of hate.

Two American students, Matthew Eisenfeld, 25, of West Hartford, Conn., and Sarah Duker, 23, of Teaneck, N.J., were traveling from Jerusalem to Jordan yesterday when a bomb ripped through a packed city bus. Twenty-five people, including the students, were killed.

Friends shocked by the loss spoke repeatedly yesterday of how bright they were, how dedicated, and of the utter senselessness of their deaths.

"Such wonderful young people, who could have been great leaders, great people, are lost," Rabbi Benjamin Segal, the president of the seminary where Mr. Eisenfeld was spending a year, said in a telephone interview from Israel. "It is an old story. The best of our youth has always been on the front lines."

From their home in West Hartford, the Eisenfeld family said yesterday in a statement that they hoped steps toward peace in the Middle East would continue and succeed "so that what happened to Matt never happens to anyone else in the future." They said that Mr. Eisenfeld was someone who always believed he could make a difference.

His uncle, Larry Port, said: "He was a scholar in every sense of the word. He lived for his family and he lived to learn, and that's what he was doing when he was killed."

Mr. Eisenfeld, a Talmudic scholar, hoped to become a rabbi and one day open his own school, friends said. He was studying in Israel as part of the program at the Jewish Theological Seminary in Manhattan, where classmates said he was an outstanding scholar and a leader in his class.

When Prime Minister Yitzhak Rabin was assassinated in November, Mr. Eisenfeld was chosen to speak about his death. Mr. Eisenfeld's roommate, Shai Held, said in an interview in Manhattan yesterday that he spoke about the value and importance of peace.

"He was sympathetic to the peace process," Mr. Held said. "But I hope his death does not become political fodder. I know that he would have had no sympathy for those who would exploit it."

Mr. Held said that Mr. Eisenfeld loved music and poetry, and the pair would often sing Jewish folk songs late into the night. He said Mr. Eisenfeld was working on a poem about Ms. Duker shortly before his death.

"He loved books, but he always remembered to love people more," Mr. Held said.

David Lerner, a friend of Ms. Duker and Mr. Eisenfeld, said that he had recently traveled to Jordan, and had recommended such a trip to them. He said they were on their way to the border on the morning they were killed.

"They were just two of the most special people that I ever knew," Mr. Lerner said, his voice breaking in a telephone interview from a friend's home in Manhattan.

Aryeh Bernstein, 20, said his older brother Edward Bernstein was roommates with Mr. Eisenfeld at the seminary in 1994-95.

'The best of our youth has always been on the front lines.'

During what was their first year at the seminary, they lived in an apartment near the campus where Mr. Bernstein said his older brother, Mr. Eisenfeld and Ms. Duker would invite friends over for Sabbath dinners. He described them as very spiritual gatherings, during which they worked hard to make traditions meaningful for their friends.

Mr. Lerner said Mr. Eisenfeld and Ms. Duker met while he was an undergraduate at Yale and she at Barnard.

At Yale, Mr. Eisenfeld helped begin a singing group which focused on

Photographs by The Associated Press

Matthew Eisenfeld, 25, of West Hartford, Conn., and Sarah Duker, 23, of Teaneck, N.J., who were killed in the bombing of a bus in Jerusalem.

Jewish music. "I am realizing now how much the group was shaped by him, how much enthusiasm he brought to it," said Judah Cohen, 22, a fellow graduate.

The singing group attended an annual theater and music festival at the seminary yesterday and dedicated songs to Mr. Eisenfeld. Last night, 300 people attended a two-hour memorial service at the seminary.

Dorothy Denberg, dean of Barnard College, remembered Ms. Duker as "someone who always had a twinkle in her eye."

Ms. Duker, who was elected to Phi Beta Kappa, was a member of a special program for gifted scholars and studied environmental science. She was studying science at Hebrew University in Jerusalem.

"Originally, she was talking about settling in Israel, but then she became very interested in environmental issues," said Ms. Denberg, who served as Ms. Duker's faculty adviser. "She was also an outstanding writer. She really could have done anything."

Ms. Denberg said that one of Ms. Duker's constant interests was the struggle for peace.

"For a terrorist to kill her just kills me," Ms. Denberg said. "She was such a quiet person and a gentle person. She was very committed to peace in the Mideast."

Rabbi Kenneth Berger, the rabbi for the Duker family's congregation, said that Ms. Duker was one of three children, and that her sister is also studying in Israel. He said Ms. Duker and Mr. Eisenfeld had planned to marry, but had not set a date.

At the Jewish Theological Seminary yesterday, students who gathered for a concert spoke of Mr. Eisenfeld's death and pledged to honor him with psalms throughout the night. Prof. Raymond P. Scheindlin remembered Mr. Eisenfeld as an extremely religious and bright student.

"He was a thinking person, he wanted to be intellectually challenged," Mr. Scheindlin said. "He was one of those students who really made an impression."

Rabbi William LeBeau, vice chancellor and dean of the Jewish Theological Seminary, said Mr. Eisenfeld's family and teachers all had great hopes for him. "What could be the meaning of violence like this, the utter waste of his life and the lives of all who were killed?" Rabbi LeBeau said. "What could be the value of destroying such a life?"

Ms. Duker was the second person from New Jersey killed by Islamic militants in less than a year.

Alisa Flatow, 20, of West Orange, was killed in April when a suicide bomber drove his explosives-laden car into a bus in which she was riding in the Gaza Strip. The Associated Press said Ms. Flatow and Ms. Duker both went to Frisch Yeshiva High School in Paramus.

INTERVIEW

Every Yid a Prince: An Interview with Rabbi Shlomo Carlebach

by Matt Eisenfeld

"One does not have to play well, just play." This was the advice that Rabbi Shlomo Carlebach received as he began his musical career in the 1950s. Since then, Rabbi Carlebach has achieved fame as a singer, songwriter, and Hasidic storyteller. On September 20, Rabbi Carlebach visited the Yale-New Haven Jewish community to share his talent, inspiring a packed room in Linsly-Chittenden Hall with his love of being Jewish. After the concert, I enjoyed an open interview with the Rabbi. I asked him only two questions, from which the entire interview flowed.

Rabbi Carlebach was born into an Orthodox German-Jewish family. His grandfather was one of the Izbitzer Rebbe's followers, a small group whose members were required to memorize the entire Torah and Talmud. Rabbi Carlebach describes his family as prince-like. Though they lacked the wealth of royalty, the Rabbi remembers that his father always taught, "'Every Yid is a prince. You have to be a prince, have to be.' I remember the time in 1935, my brother came home crying because somebody had called him a 'Dirty Jew.' 'What am I supposed to do, call them back, Dirty Goy?' Father says to him, 'Only a slave answers back when insulted. A prince doesn't react. And *yiden* are princes.'"

When his family moved to America, the Rabbi entered yeshiva, where he grew close to the present Lubavitcher Rebbe. It was the Rebbe who, in 1951, told him to use his talent to inspire others. When Rabbi Carlebach expressed concerns to the Lubavitcher Rebbe regarding the continuation of his learning, he was told to think less about himself.

According to Rabbi Carlebach, Lubavitcher Hasidism was significantly different then. Today it resembles a corporation, receiving money from Jews everywhere, but back then the group owed thousands of dollars. Rabbi Carlebach worked without pay, simply because there was no money. He told us that Lubavitcher Hasidim often slept in cars. "When I didn't have money for a hotel, I'd find a car whose door was open and go to sleep. When the owner would come the next day and say, 'It's my car!' I'd say, 'Really? My car's just like it!'"

Rabbi Carlebach left the Lubavitchers in 1955, deciding that it was time to start out on his own. He wandered for several years; "I was *mamash* [really] like a homeless person." He finally took a job as a rabbi in a small New Jersey town, where his salary was five dollars a week. It was at this time that he began to succeed as a singer, composing songs on the synagogue piano. He then met a guitar player who taught him to play and gave him encouraging advice. According to the Rabbi, "After the Second World War, there was no one left. All of the composers of Hasidic music didn't make it. So everything I made was instantly a best seller."

I asked the Rabbi about one of the major problems concerning world Jewry: while many Jews seem to be searching for some meaning in their Judaism, they often turn away in frustration, claiming that Judaism appears to be devoid of spirituality. Rabbi Carlebach is involved in the movement to bring dissatisfied Jews back to their roots.

The Rabbi's primary concern rests with young Jews. He is critical of those who turn away from Judaism

10

because he feels that they haven't given Judaism a fair chance. "Ask eighty percent of Jewish kids; they know more about every guru in the world than they know about the Rebbes." He related the story of a girl from Haifa who had joined one of the yogis. "'Having grown up in Haifa, in the Holy Land,' I asked her, 'did you need to come to Phoenix to find God?' She said to me, 'In Haifa, nobody believes in God.' I said, 'You can only tell me that your parents don't believe in God! What do you mean, nobody believes in God? There are 250 synagogues in Haifa—it's outrageous, right?' But she didn't even bother looking for her own."

He told a similar story of a man from Brooklyn who had turned away from Judaism. At every Passover Seder, this man's uncle would read all the dirty jokes he'd collected over the year instead of the Haggadah. Again, the Rabbi responded that the uncle was not representative of all of Judaism. "You see what it is? Sad, all the so-called 'spiritual' people looking for God have absolutely no respect for their own. And sad enough, it's not their fault. The way their parents taught them about yiddishkeit was so obnoxious and disgusting." Yet Rabbi Carlebach remarks that one must recognize that no search for God can be one hundred percent effective; those seeking spiritual fulfillment must look upon such a quest with a realistic aim.

Many young Jews simply have not been exposed to the experiences which the Rabbi believes are necessary to establish a lasting commitment to traditional Judaism. He states, "On one hand, we can be angry with the kids for not giving us a chance, but on the other, I wouldn't be here had I not had such a gevalt upbringing myself and let the rebbes encourage me."

Unfortunately, he says, for a long time various religious establishments, including the Federation and other traditional Jewish institutions, had no interest in creating Jewish opportunities for these disaffected young people. Although Rabbi Carlebach's House of Love and Prayer has been highly successful in bringing people back, it has occasionally run into problems. The Rabbi reports that the organization used to host over four hundred kids every Friday night for Shabbat dinner and was successful in preventing and reforming juvenile drug addicts. However, the Jewish Federation in San Francisco cut off his funding because, "Sunday morning the garbage was ten feet high. The president of the Federation walked by, saw all the garbage, and decided that he didn't want to fund the House anymore."

The frum (traditional religious) community was not helpful back then, and according to the Rabbi, often still fails to share itself and its experiences with returning or non-religious Jews. They called Rabbi Carlebach "a dope addict, because all those dope addicts come to me. They say the House of Love and Prayer is a house of prostitution and dope addicts." The religious community did not support Rabbi Carlebach, but "they remembered me when their kids got lost. Only in the last few years did God open

their hearts, and they permitted me to live in peace."

Throughout his work, Rabbi Carlebach has been happy and privileged to witness the return of thousands of young people to yiddishkeit. However, even today he feels that while the Jewish community is right to encourage ba'ale teshuvah (newly observant Jews), it is often done inappropriately. Too often, religious Jews will treat less observant or non-observant Jews without the respect they deserve. He disdains one rabbi's apathy for the non-religious. According to this rabbi, non-religious Jews have no reason to come to the Western Wall; they take up space and cause the religious to worry about whether or not they dress modestly or wear kippot. Rabbi Carlebach reacted with disbelief. "We lost six million yiden, and every yid is precious, and the Holy Wall waits for every yid to come. The other rabbi says, 'Who needs another non-religious?'" Jews such as this rabbi erect and strengthen the walls between us.

Rabbi Carlebach quoted Rav Abraham Isaac Kook, who said that the body of Eretz Yisrael is built by non-religious people while the soul is built by the religious Jews. The Rabbi agrees, but argues, "When it comes to the Torah of Eretz Yisrael, the frum community builds the body, the halakha; the neshama [soul] will be rebuilt by the non-religious people." Rabbi Carlebach calls for patience. Jews are returning to yiddishkeit, he claims, and urges religious Jews should welcome them back with open arms, serving as role models, not "tailors" prepared to shape these ba'ale teshuvah to their own image of the good Jew.

The Rabbi also spoke of the religious tension in Israel. He dispelled the myth that Israelis are not religious, exclaiming, "How can anybody say of a soldier who's ready to die a thousand times over that he's not religious? The Yidele who wakes up, drinks his coffee, prays, and goes to work—he's religious, but the soldier out there on guard is not? So why is the soldier not learning about Shabbas with this Yidele? Because the soldier is not interested in his Shabbas. He's interested in Shabbas, but not his Shabbas." Rabbi Carlebach recommended that if religious Jews really want to teach more non-religious Jews about Shabbat, they ought to see to it that "every Friday night, all the coffee shops are open, but they are paid for. Nobody has to pay. I will sit there and tell Hasidishe stories. Mamash, all of Dizengoff [a street in Tel Aviv] will be observing Shabbas."

The interview ended when the Rabbi remarked that he was so tired that he would not last unless the messiah were to come at that instant. Rabbi Carlebach advised that religious Jews who care deeply about Shabbat and holidays should invite their non-religious friends home to share the delight which they have been privileged to enjoy. Yiddishkeit is open to all Jews, not just those who have Torah and mitzvot. Therefore, we are all obligated to open our hearts and minds.

Matt Eisenfeld is a senior in Saybrook College and is majoring in Religious Studies.

338

RESPONSE

Leaps of Faith:
Uncertainty's Role in Religion

by Matt Eisenfeld

In her article "Without God: My Life as a Jew" (Winter 1991), Valerie Maltz describes the hypocrisy she feels when participating in Jewish activities. She identifies with the cultural bonds of the Jewish community, but feels she must falsely accept a theistic belief imposed on her by the Jewish community. I do not believe Maltz is a hypocrite. While I do not profess an ability to answer the questions she rightfully asks, I offer my reflections and pose a few questions of my own.

Maltz's feelings of hypocrisy are based on the notion that she does not believe in God. But what is the role of belief? Can anybody believe that God exists with certainty? The concept of belief, by its very nature, cannot entail certainty. Mere faith is the weakest source of knowledge compared to empirical concepts such as sensory experience, reason, and authority. Yet, we must accept that all knowledge is ultimately based on faith—faith that our methods of perception, on which empirical knowledge is based, are correct. We believe things, or accept certain assumptions as true, either because we are convinced of their truth or because we place some kind of value on the implications of the desired truth of an assumption.

Belief in God is perhaps the most tenuous of all beliefs, because we cannot perceive God directly. Since nobody can know for certain whether or not God exists, we are reduced to believing or disbelieving. Denying God's existence and professing atheism, however, implies as strong a statement of faith as affirming unequivocally that God does exist. No one can prove either assertion without making leaps of faith in which we leave logical and empirical certainty behind. Our uncertainty forces us all, believers and non-believers alike, to be doubtful at heart. I doubt that anybody can truly be an atheist as much as I doubt that anyone can unquestioningly know that God exists.

Doubt plays a central role in any religion. Some people will even assert that doubts or uncertainties—uncertainty about death, the world around us, or the meaning of life—cause religion in the first place. These critics may be correct, but religion serves other functions as well. It can teach people how to appreciate the world, or offer ways to make the world worthy of appreciation. Maltz mentions that Judaism gives her a sense of cultural identity which she values although she does not know why. Agreeing that religion does have some purpose, let us now consider the tenets of Judaism on which we base our beliefs and actions.

Our religion regulates our lives based on the assumptions that God exists, that we are the chosen people to whom God has revealed his will, and that we are correct in our interpretation of God's will. We know that these fundamental assumptions are not unique to Judaism. While it would seem helpful to know with certainty whether or not we are correct, these claims must be doubted precisely because we cannot know for sure. In fact, doubt is actually better than certainty.

Our doubt gives meaning to our actions, making them precious. After all, in our religion we believe that not only has God promised us blessings for fulfilling the *mitzvot*, but that punishment awaits us should we transgress the *mitzvot* or fail to fulfill them. We are free to choose either the blessing or the curse, as the rabbis claim (believe) that we have free will. However, if God holds over us a blessing and a curse, then are we truly free to choose? This is equivalent to being held at gunpoint and being told to do something with the promise that we will be praised for succumbing to the gunman's will. If our predicament entails choosing between reward or denial of our share in the world to come, then we cannot be praised for our "worthy" actions, because our motivations may not be praiseworthy. Are we motivated by love of God, or by self-interest? Here I address the *mitzvot* that mediate between God and people. Among these *mitzvot*, I would include prayer, observance of Shabbat, *kashrut*, the *mezzuza*, and other laws of ritual. These *mitzvot* can and do affect relations between people, but on the surface and in form, they primarily concern people and God.

This seems to be the area where Maltz is least comfortable. If we knew for certain that God existed, then fulfilling these seemingly trivial inconveniences, as we perceive them, could not be praiseworthy. On the contrary, we would be doing so only to satisfy God. Who, after all, always honestly enjoys fixed prayer or other obligations? I pray every morning and aspire to fulfill my obligation to pray in the afternoon and at night as well, yet I do not feel equally motivated every time. I do not enjoy keeping kosher when it causes problems for me to eat with non-Jews or fellow Jews for whom this observance has little meaning. If we knew that God existed, then performance of all these acts would be assuredly within my self-interest and I would have virtually no choice in the matter, since I would want to avoid divine punishment and wrath.

Furthermore, the commandment to love God poses greater dilemmas. Is it really possible to love when forced to do so out of compulsion? In order to love God, we must be given an honest opportunity to not love God. I am happier facing the uncertainty of God's existence, because it allows me to fulfill a *mitzva* with the understanding that there may be no divine judge who watches me, holding me accountable for whether or not I say the right words when I recite the *Amida* prayer.

These effects do not constitute some kind of other-worldly changes, but happen right here in our daily lives. Judaism has always been extremely concerned with this world and our responsibility to imbue it with holiness. We search for beauty in this world and try to embellish it. We also recognize that which is not beautiful in the world, and attempt to change it to the extent that we can. Judaism does not teach us that this life is an illusion. Rather, our experiences are real and meaningful to us. And if we can doubt God, then there exists a possibility that this world is important on its own merits and not contingent upon some inexplicable supreme being.

I cannot adequately explain why I desire to fulfill religious obligations, other than that I see many purposes for my participation in these "Jewish activities." For example, I genuinely feel a need to take time out of my daily schedule to thank God for the blessings I have received. Maltz names a few good reasons to do so herself: her mother and the rest of her family, for example. Moreover, she wants to retain a Jewish identity, despite her disbelief in God. Because she connects her sense of belonging (or not belonging) to the Jewish community with both culture and belief in God, she feels guilty of irrationality. The paradox intimidates her.

We should not, however, label these worries as irrational, because she still feels a strong connection that is meaningful to her. Regarding Judaism as a culture distinct from secular American culture seems valid to me, since human beings do not grow up in isolation. Our "personal culture" is made up of the values we are taught from an early age, the experiences we share with those near to us, and many other factors particular to our situation. Our past is meaningful to us precisely because it is *our* past. Similarly, our religion, culture, and identity are meaningful to us because they are ours.

Entering a synagogue should not provoke an unnerving sense of hypocrisy. Though we are all Jews, our motivations are clearly not always the same. I deny that Maltz's reason for attending synagogue—to be with her mother (as opposed to doing it from the love of God)—is wrong. Perhaps by loving her mother enough to inconvenience herself, Maltz fulfills the commandment to love God better than the rest of us do. Internal questions as to why we should attend synagogue at all should not plague people with guilt, because most other people in the synagogue ask themselves similar questions. A wiser outlook would be to continue questioning, in the belief that these inquiries yield important answers. Furthermore, it is wrong to think that one must do everything tradition dictates in order to avoid the label of "hypocrite." Tradition is certainly a path to God which merits its attention because it has succeeded for thousands of years, but tradition is not God itself. When I take my leap of faith, I learn that only God is God.

Maltz has just as much a right to live as a Jew as anyone else, and I think she realizes that. People who make her feel unwelcome are insecure themselves and perceive her questions as threatening. But it is precisely her continual need to grapple with these issues of religion and identity that is fundamental to Judaism and is appropriately incorporated into our own religious struggles.

Matt Eisenfeld is a junior in Saybrook College and is majoring in Religious Studies.